Edible Gender, Mother-in-Law Style,
and Other Grammatical Wonders

Edible Gender,
Mother-in-Law Style,
and Other
Grammatical Wonders

Studies in Dyirbal, Yidiñ, and Warrgamay

R. M. W. DIXON

Language and Culture Research Centre
James Cook University

OXFORD
UNIVERSITY PRESS

OXFORD
UNIVERSITY PRESS

Great Clarendon Street, Oxford, OX2 6DP,
United Kingdom

Oxford University Press is a department of the University of Oxford.
It furthers the University's objective of excellence in research, scholarship,
and education by publishing worldwide. Oxford is a registered trade mark of
Oxford University Press in the UK and in certain other countries

First Edition published in 2015
Impression: 1

Published in the United States of America by Oxford University Press
198 Madison Avenue, New York, NY 10016, United States of America

British Library Cataloguing in Publication Data

Data available

Library of Congress Control Number: 2014954264

ISBN 978-0-19-870290-0

Printed and bound by
CPI Group (UK) Ltd, Croydon, CR0 4YY

In loving memory of
Chloe Grant (1903–1974)
dear friend and teacher
keen of intellect
resolute in character

Contents

List of tables, diagrams, and map

Tables

Diagrams

Map

List of abbreviations

Dialects of Dyirbal (section 1.3.1)

A	Gambil-barra Jirrbal	N	Ngajan
G	Girramay	P	'Mourilyan' Mamu
J	Jabun-barra Jirrbal (Jirrbal)	U	Gulngay
L	Walmal	W	Wari-barra Mamu (Wari)
M	Dulgu-barra Mamu (Mamu)	Y	Jirru

Dialects of Yidiñ (section 1.3.3)

c	coastal Yidiñ	t	tableland Yidiñ
g	Gunggay	w	Wanyurru/Majay

Language styles

Ev	everyday language style	Ja	Jalnguy avoidance language style

Kin terms (chapter 4)

M, mother; F, father; B, brother; Z, sister; S, son; D, daughter; W, wife; H, husband; Sib, sibling; Ch, child; Sp, spouse; e, elder; y, younger; ♀, female ego; ♂, male ego.

Other abbreviations

/	intonation break	ALL	allative case
#	word boundary	APASS	antipassive
I – IV	genders in Dyirbal (see chapter 2)	APPLIC	applicative
		AVERS	aversive
1	1st person	C	consonant
2	2nd person	CAUS	causative
3	3rd person	CONTIN	continuous
A	transitive subject	DAT	dative case
ABL	ablative case	DELOC	delocutive
ABS	absolutive case	du	dual
ACC	accusative case	ERG	ergative case

FUT	future tense	PERF	perfect
GEN	genitive marking	POS.IMP	positive imperative
IMP	imperative	PURP	purposive
INCH	inchoative	RC	relative clause
INST	instrumental case	REDUP	reduplication
LINK	linking element	REFL	reflexive
LOC	locative case	REL	relative clause marking
NEG.IMP	negative imperative	S	intransitive subject
NOM	nominative case	sg	singular
NP	noun phrase	SVC	serial verb construction
O	transitive object	UNM	unmarked
pl	plural	V	vowel

1

Background

A language is a social phenomenon. Some books concerning language seem to consider each word as an isolated item, each sentence as being complete in itself. Little insight is gained in this way. The meaning and function of a word should be considered with respect to the meanings and functions of related forms—how they interrelate and contrast. A sentence only has significance within a context of utterance; one needs to know who said it, to whom, in what circumstances. It is relevant to be aware of the social relationships between the participants in this act of communication. And also what is assumed, what is implied, and what is hoped to be achieved.

A critical factor, which is relevant to understanding, concerns the situation within which something is said. A certain utterance (for example, *The scheme looks as if it were meant to fail*) will have diverse implications depending on whether it is said in deliberate fashion during a formal meeting or as a whispered aside. And whether it is said with a harsh biting intonation or more tentatively, as a kind of gentle enquiry.

One can only fully comprehend the interwoven underpinnings and implications of a language through having some familiarity with the shared cultural heritage of its speakers. To be an effective member of the English language speech community, it is useful to have some acquaintanceship with nursery rhymes, parts of the Bible, and some of the works of Shakespeare. In similar fashion, in order to achieve a decent understanding of the language used by a community of Aboriginal Australians, it is of great help to be acquainted with some of their legends and beliefs.

Beginning in 1963, I worked—in the rainforest of north-east Australia—with communities speaking the Dyirbal, Yidiñ, and Warrgamay languages. *The Dyirbal language of North Queensland*, which is an ethnologically-informed grammar, was published in 1972. I have a collection of seventy-eight Dyirbal texts and a comprehensive thesaurus/dictionary, which are currently being prepared for publication. *A grammar of Yidiɲ*, in 1977, was followed in 1991 by *Words of our country: stories, place names and vocabulary in Yidiñ*. Materials on Warrgamay were published in 1981, within volume 2 of the *Handbook of Australian languages*.

In all my writings I have tried to let a language speak for itself, illustrating its cultural milieu. Elicitation was kept to a minimum. Instead, I relied on what speakers volunteered spontaneously, and on texts of all kinds—legendary tales, historical accounts, autobiographies, instruction on how to perform daily tasks, the manufacture of implements, techniques for dealing with ailments, and so on.

Putting to one side the many laudatory reviews, the comments I treasure most are in a 1973 letter from renowned anthropologist Ashley Montague:

I have been reading your *The Dyirbal language of North Queensland* with enthusiasm and excitement. I have always believed that the only genuine way to understand the way another people thinks and feels is to study their language, and your book has, of course, confirmed me in that belief... Having studied linguistics with Boas and read it for 40 years, I have not found any work on an aboriginal language anywhere nearly as good as yours.

The present volume extends and expands on information presented in the grammars. There is discussion of how the world is categorised, through a system of four genders in Dyirbal and a set of around twenty classifiers in Yidiñ— chapters 2 and 3. As in other Australian languages, social interaction is mediated through the highly-articulated kinship system—chapter 4. When in the presence of a relative of a particular 'avoidance' class, it was obligatory to employ the special Jalnguy speech style (dubbed 'mother-in-law language' by bilingual speakers)— chapters 5 and 6.

Yidiñ and Dyirbal employ contrasting narrative techniques. A story is generally told in 1st person for Yidiñ but in 3rd person for Dyirbal. This has led to different syntactic principles for clause linking in the two languages—chapter 7. In Dyirbal, two verbs can be combined to form one predicate, a 'serial verb construction'—chapter 8. It was at first surprising to me that Dyirbal has no complement clause construction (similar to *Mary saw [that John killed the kangaroo]*COMPLEMENT.CLAUSE in English). Close investigation reveals that it has, instead, a number of what can be called 'complementation strategies'—chapter 9.

In most Australian languages (including Dyirbal and Yidiñ) verbs fall into two syntactic classes, intransitive and transitive, and into two or more phonologically-defined classes, or conjugations. There is generally some association—but not identity—between these sets of classes; for example, most (but not all) intransitive verbs are in a certain conjugation. One dialect of Warrgamay has changed in a way that rationalises this, so that syntactic classes and conjugation classes now exactly coincide—chapter 10.

Information was obtained on two dialects of Warrgamay, and four of Yidiñ; these are fully documented in Dixon (1981a) and Dixon (1977a, 1991a) respectively. The 1972 grammar of Dyirbal was confined to description of just three—of the original ten or so—dialects. Further work has expanded this corpus; surveys of cross-dialectal grammatical and lexical variation are provided in chapters 11 and 12.

Intermarriage and social contact between tribal groups has led to the development of areal linguistic traits. Phonologically contrastive vowel length evolved in Yidiñ and in the adjoining dialects of Dyirbal. In the most northerly Dyirbal dialect, this phonological gain was counter-balanced by loss of the contrast between two rhotic consonants—chapter 13. In chapter 14 there is investigation of how Yidiñ, Dyirbal, and Warrgamay have influenced each other in various grammatical and phonological respects, with the likely directions of diffusion for each being examined.

The effects of European invasion—from the 1860s in this region—have been devastating. Many Aborigines were murdered with others being transported to missions or government settlements, where children were separated from their parents in order to arrest transmission of culture and language. For the remainder, situations where traditional language would be used gradually contracted. When I began fieldwork, fifty years ago, there were half-a-dozen old people with a good command of Warrgamay and the same for Yidiñ; all are now gone. There were in 1963 several score fluent speakers of Dyirbal; the last of them died in March 2011, leaving only a handful of semi-speakers.

As a language fades away, it may change in interesting ways. Traditional Yidiñ had an underlying form for each noun and adjective, from which surface forms were created by application of certain rules. In chapter 15 there is an account of how the last semi-speakers of Yidiñ re-analysed the system, now deriving all other surface case forms from the absolutive. Chapter 16 chronicles the gradual decline of Dyirbal, over a half-century, as the fluent speakers—dialect by dialect—gradually died. The two most vibrant dialects merged, but are today only represented by semi-speakers; their talk shows simplification of paradigms, loss of gender contrasts, and further grammatical levelling.

When *The Dyirbal Language* was published, in December 1972, it attracted immediate attention, mainly due to the explicit descriptions of morphological and syntactic ergativity. There were a considerable number of papers (of variable quality) which attempted to reanalyse the system. *A grammar of Yidiɲ*, in 1977, attracted attention for the intricacy of its phonological rules, and also spawned a number of re-statements. I have chosen not to survey these here (only a couple of them provided useful further explanation).

The overarching theme of studies in the present volume is how the patterns in a grammar are explainable by factors outside it. For example, chapter 2 shows that the allocation of nouns to the four genders in Dyirbal can only be understood in terms of cultural ideas concerning physical association, eating habits, and harmfulness, together with knowledge of legends and beliefs. As a further example, chapter 7 describes how the contrasting story-telling techniques employed by speakers of Dyirbal and Yidiñ explain the differing syntactic orientations of these two languages.

NOTE. Most of the chapters in this book are revisions of earlier publications; details are provided at the end of each chapter. Only this chapter and chapter 11 are completely new.

1.1 Culture

Speakers of Dyirbal, Yidiñ, and Warrgamay lived in well-watered mountainous country—predominantly rainforest—with many short rivers, waterfalls, and swamps. There were numerous animals to hunt, fish to catch, and fruits and vegetables to gather (some requiring lengthy preparation). Indeed, one of the four gender classes in Dyirbal is 'edible', referring just to non-flesh food; around 200 plants have been identified as belonging to it.

A tribe consisted of a number of 'local groups'. Each would be based in a particular location, but would move around the whole tribal territory according to the availability of foodstuffs. For example, the coastal groups of Yidiñ-speakers would be likely to ascend to the tablelands—to eat yellow walnut (*gaŋgi*) and lawyer-vines (*mudi* and *yabulam*)—in the wet season, when the coastal flats were particularly hot, humid, and insect-ridden. And the tablelands groups would come down to the coast—for black walnut (*digil*) and quandong (*murrgan*)—in the winter, thus avoiding some of the worst of the mountain frosts and mists.

There was cannibalism, of a mild variety; people were never killed simply in order to be eaten. The grave of a recently deceased person from a neighbouring tribe was sometimes raided and the body consumed. Or a local person judged by the group to be guilty of a serious crime (for example, a man misbehaving with someone else's wife, who was in a tabooed relationship to him) could be killed. The flesh was eaten and the blood given to young men to drink.

The people had a goodly array of artefacts—finely honed boomerangs, spears, woomera, and shields, intricately woven baskets, and traps. A special weapon in this area was the hardwood duelling sword, a metre and a half in length. This was slung in single alternating strokes from over the head against the opponent, who would attempt to defend himself with a shield.

The stock of oral literature explained how the landscape came into being, the ways in which places were named, the origin of everything now considered mundane. A number of birds and animals were people in legendary times and have a special significance today. Songs would mimic events in the world, or convey a message of love. The volume *Dyirbal song poetry* (1996a)—which I compiled together with musicologist Grace Koch—documents the words and music of 174 Dyirbal songs across five distinct styles of performance, each with its own metrical pattern and linguistic and musical characteristics.

Some legends appear to have historical authenticity. Creator beings were able to walk to what are now off-shore islands, which was possible before sea levels rose ten millennia ago. One story tells of a volcanic eruption and how at the time there was just open forest at that place, not the thick jungle one finds there today. Scientists have found that, indeed, the jungle is only about 7,000 years old. (For further details, see Dixon 1972: 29, 1977a: 14–15.)

Young men were initiated at puberty, scars being cut across the chest. The highest grade of Dyirbal elder was a *Gubi*, someone who was a proven hunter, had a deep knowledge of customs, legends, and songs and—sine qua non—who had drunk human blood.

Inter-tribal corroborees were regular events. Grievances would be settled, generally by single combat (leading just to minor wounding). News was exchanged, new songs learnt, and marriages arranged, amidst a great deal of dancing and jollity.

The overarching feature of all Australian Aboriginal societies is the classificatory kinship system. By applying a series of principles, each person is in a relationship to every other person. Mother's sisters' and father's brothers' children ('parallel cousins') are regarded as equivalent to one's own siblings. In contrast, 'cross-cousins', the children of father's sisters and mother's brothers, have a quite different status. They must never be directly addressed and, if talking in their presence, a special speech style called Jalnguy has to be employed. *Waymin* and *ñubi* are the labels for daughters and sons of father's elder sisters and mother's elder brothers. They are potential mother-in-law and father-in-law. That is, one should marry the child of a classificatory *waymin* or *ñubi*. (More on this in chapter 4.)

Kinship links determine not only who one may marry, but also every kind of social responsibility. They indicate who may be joked with, and who is not available for friendly interaction. Who has the obligation to organise a boy's initiation, or a certain relative's funeral. When a brace of wallabies was brought home, these would be carefully butchered and portions shared out among all the people in the camp, according to their relationship to the hunter.

Marriages were arranged a long time in advance, generally between a young boy and a baby girl. There is a verb in Dyirbal, *ŋilbi-l* 'look longingly on a promised spouse'. As the potential wife advanced in years, she watched and admired her husband-to-be gaining in prowess and status. In turn, he delighted in watching the girl blossom into an attractive woman. Of course, they could not marry until the girl reached puberty. And until the boy had proved himself to be a good provider. When he brought home a carcass, the choicest portion would be ostentatiously presented to *waymin*, the potential mother-in-law, as a hint that she might soon consider him to be ready for the marriage.

Vagueness was held to be a severe fault, a mark of stupidity. In the everyday language style, each type of plant and animal had a specific name, which should be used. About twenty species of frog were recognised and named in Dyirbal. There was no generic term 'frog' since it is always possible to identify a frog—by size, colour, behaviour, and call. There was a generic term *wadam* 'snake', but this would only be used when a snake could not be identified, perhaps if just the tip of its tail were seen. (And *wadam* did not quite cover all the snakes; it excluded those considered edible—the 'carpet snakes' or pythons—which were in any case easily identifiable from their size and colouring. See chapter 2.)

1.2 Jalnguy, the 'mother-in-law' style

Each tribe in this region had two speech styles. When in the presence of certain relatives with whom contact should be avoided (classificatory mother-in-law, father-in-law, son-in-law, or daughter-in-law), the Jalnguy [jalŋuy] style had to be employed. In all other circumstances the everyday language style was used.

My first great Dyirbal teacher, Chloe Grant, described Jalnguy as 'mother-in-law language'. However, it is not really a distinct language, rather a different language style. The everyday style and Jalnguy have identical phonology (and phonetics) and grammar. All grammatical suffixes—case and tense endings and the like—are the same, as are fully grammatical words such as pronouns, demonstratives, the negator *gulu* 'not', and so on. But all lexemes—members of open word classes noun, adjective, and verb—differ. (With just one exception: the four terms for grandparents are the same.)

Many Australian languages have a set of special lexemes to be used in the presence of 'avoidance kin'. But it is generally a smallish set, a couple of dozen items (see Dixon 2002a: 92–6). Languages in north-east Queensland are unique in that every lexeme is different between everyday and avoidance styles.

However, there are fewer lexemes in Jalnguy than in the everyday style. What we get is a many-to-one relation between the everyday style and Jalnguy vocabularies. This can be illustrated with an example from each major word class—noun, adjective, and verb.

(1) As mentioned just before, there are in the everyday style, about twenty names for species of frog. For example *baŋguy* 'green tree frog' (*Litoria caerulea*), *daŋgu* 'northern barred frog' (*Mixophyes schevilli*), *yudi* 'water frog with a sharp nose' (*Rana daemeili*), and so on. There is in Jalnguy a single lexeme, *guwaga* 'frog', corresponding to each of the score of names in the everyday style.

(2) The everyday style has adjective *jamar* 'bitter taste (said to be like quinine or lemon)' and *muymur* 'sour, salty'. There is just one Jalnguy adjective corresponding to both of these, *ŋumuy*.

(3) Consider the following verbs in the everyday style:

- *baga-l*, pierce with a sharp-pointed implement, including: dig with a pointed yamstick, sew, row a boat (the action of the oars on the water), squeeze a boil, sting (as a bee does), and spear something, throwing the spear by means of a spear-thrower or woomera
- *jinba-l*, spear something, throwing the spear from the hand, without use of a woomera
- *jurrga-y*, spear something which can be seen, holding onto the spear
- *waga-y*, 'blind spearing', using the spear held in the hand to try to impale something which cannot be seen, e.g. spearing among underwater tree roots in case

an eel is hiding there, or jabbing a spear into long grass where movement has been seen

- *jiñju-l*, poke a stick into a hollow log to see if there is an animal in it.

There is just one Jalnguy verb corresponding to these five (and a couple more) verbs from the everyday style—*ñirrinda-l*.

It can be seen that, whereas one should be as precise as possible in the everyday style, the Jalnguy style is deliberately generic. It is appropriate to be vague in the presence of an avoidance relative.

One can be more specific by adding modification to the Jalnguy word. For example, describing the nature and habits of a frog species, saying that a *ŋumuy* taste is 'like a lemon', or adding *jugari-ga*, the Jalnguy for 'in a hollow log' to *ñirrinda-l* for a more specific correspondent of *jiñju-l*. In essence, it appears that Jalnguy has the minimum number of lexemes compatible with it being possible to say in Jalnguy everything which can be said in the everyday style.

There is mention of Jalnguy in chapter 2, on genders in Dyirbal. Then chapter 5 provides a detailed discussion of the use, nature, and semantic organisation of the Jalnguy style in Dyirbal, and chapter 6 contrasts the forms of Jalnguy lexemes between Dyirbal and Yidiñ.

Note that forms quoted in the discussion above are from the Jirrbal dialect of Dyirbal.

1.3 Tribes, languages, and dialects

Each tribe was identified by the name for its mode of speaking. In some—but not all—cases the label for the tribe itself, and the territory it occupied, involved an addition to this. For example, the tribe speaking Yidiñ was called the Yidiñ-ji, and it lived in Yidiñ-ji territory. Derivational suffix -*ji* means 'with' in Yidiñ. The Girramay-gan people spoke Girramay and the Warrgamay-gan spoke Warrgamay; in contrast to -*ji* in Yidiñ, the ending -*gan* does not occur outside these names.

Speakers of Jirrbal occupied a considerable territory. The group which lived in the mildly hilly country at the foot of the mountains (not far from the coast), was called Jirrbal-ŋan (-*ŋan* is not found outside this name) while the group which lived up on the tablelands was called Jirrbal-ji. I was told that the criterion for being a tribe was that its members were 'all blooded'; that is, that they were related to each other. Generally one married someone from the same tribe, preferably from another local group within the tribe. Ida Henry told me that her mother was Jirrbal-ŋan, from near the coast. She married a Jirrbal-ji man and went to live with him on the tablelands. Then Ida herself married Spider Henry, from the Jirrbal-ŋan, and went back downhill to live.

There was a limited amount of marriage between tribes, this being specially arranged and generally reciprocal—what is called 'sister exchange'. When a Ngajan-ji

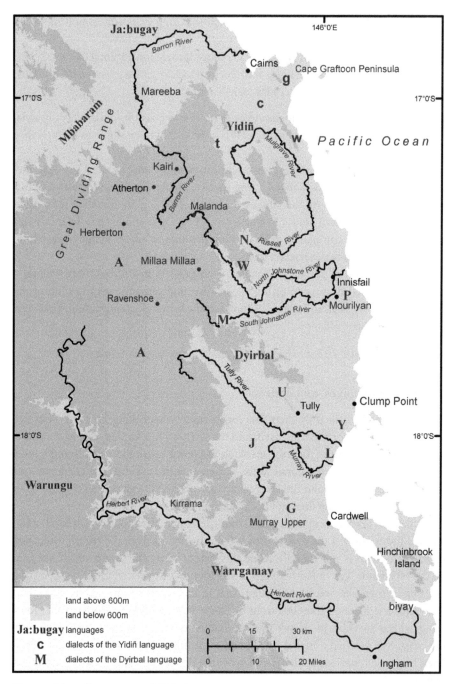

MAP 1.1 Map of languages and dialects

man married a Yidiñ-ji woman, it was expected that the brother of the Yidiñ-ji woman should marry the sister of the Ngajan-ji man.

If two modes of speaking are mutually intelligible, they are regarded as dialects of a single language. Typically, a number of contiguous tribes can be grouped together as speaking dialects of one language. Each could understand the others. They were aware of (and, often, proud of) the minor differences between them, but these did not impair intelligibility. We can now list the dialects on which material has been collected for the languages dealt with in this volume. Each is assigned a code letter, for ease of reference and for location on the map.

1.3.1 The Dyirbal language

(Note that this name is an alternative spelling of the name of a central dialect, Jirrbal.)

N   The Ngajan dialect, spoken by the Ngajan-ji tribe, living around the Russell River and across to the headwaters of the Barron River.

W   The variety of Mamu spoken by the Wari-barra group, living around the deep gorges (*wari*) of the North Johnstone River. (Suffix *-barra*, found in Dyirbal, Yidiñ, and Warrgamay, means 'belonging to'.)

M   The variety of Mamu spoken by the Dulgu-barra group, living in the thick jungle (*dulgu*) around the South Johnstone River.

P   Only known from 137 words of 'the Mourilyan language' in an 1884 letter from 'Christy Palmerston, explorer' to anthropologist A. W. Howitt. Probably from the Jirri-barra group of Mamu speakers.

A   Gambil-barra Jirrbal, spoken by the Jirrbal-ji groups on the tablelands (*gambil*), around the headwaters of the Tully River and the Herbert River.

J   Jabun-barra Jirrbal, spoken by the Jirrbal-ŋan people, in country at the base of the mountains towards the coast (*jabun*), on the north side of the Murray River.

U   Gulngay [gulŋay], spoken by the Malan-barra people, living around the lower Tully River. (In Gulngay, *malan* is 'sandbank', which are plentiful on the lower Tully.)

Y   Jirru, spoken by the Jirrubagala (I have no etymology for this), around Clump Point along the coast.

G   Girramay, spoken by the Girramay-gan people, living just inland from the coast, south from the Murray River almost as far as Cardwell, and westwards up the range to Kirrama Station (which is an attempt to write Girramay/Kirramay).

L   Walmal, known only from a manuscript list of 175 words, taken down by W. E. Roth in 1900 and labelled 'coast line from Tully to Murray'.

Commencing in 1963, and extending over 40 years, I was able to gather materials on eight of the dialects just listed (all but P and L). A goodly collection of texts, detailed grammatical information, and a substantial vocabulary were obtained for each of M,

J, and G. Also for N, except that here it was not possible to record texts. Materials in Jalnguy, the 'mother-in-law style', were gathered for N, M, and J. A fair amount of lexical and grammatical information could be obtained for W, some for A, rather less for Y and U. I also made use of short word lists which earlier investigators had compiled (commencing in 1900) on the various dialects; see Dixon (1972: 365–7).

It is likely that, in pre-invasion days, there were additional dialects which disappeared before they could be recorded. Speakers told me that there were further dialects between P and Y on the coast, and inland from Y. There were probably several dialects of N, of W, and possibly also of G; the evidence available suggests that these would have differed in only very minor ways. Gambil-barra Jirrbal (A) covered a considerable area and there is here definite evidence for several sub-varieties. The manuscript vocabularies gathered by W. E. Roth at Atherton and Herberton around 1900 differ in a few items from the data I obtained in the Ravenshoe area (this agrees fairly well with Tindale's manuscript word list from 1938). I visited Herberton in 1979 and could only gather a few score forms but these did contain a number of critical items agreeing with Roth, and supporting his work.

It is interesting that tribal names Jirrbal-ji and Ngajan-ji are like Yidiñ-ji in including -ji. This is a suffix in Yidiñ but not in Dyirbal, suggesting that the technique of naming a tribe by adding -ji to the dialect name diffused from Yidiñ into these two neighbouring dialects of Dyirbal.

1.3.2 The Warrgamay language

There is evidence for the following varieties of this language:

- The dialect called Warrgamay, spoken by the Warrgamay-gan people along the lower Herbert River.
- Dialects called Biyay, spoken by the Biyay-girri people. *Biyay* is 'no' in these dialects ('no' is *maya* in the Warrgamay dialect) and *-girri* is, in all dialects, a derivational suffix 'with' (probably cognate with *-ji* in Yidiñ).

There appear to have been two varieties of Biyay: (a) spoken by people on the mainland, around the mouth of the Herbert River; and (b) spoken by people on Hinchinbrook Island and the adjacent mainland, south from the present town of Cardwell.

There was more intensive colonisation in Warrgamay lands than in some parts of Dyirbal territory. As a consequence, the language moved towards extinction at a faster rate. I was able to gather some grammatical and lexical data from the last two speakers of the Warrgamay dialect (one of them also provided five short texts) and from the last speaker of Biyay dialect (a). There were also a few early word lists (see Dixon 1981a: 9–13). Biyay dialect (b) is known only from nineteenth-century materials, mainly the word list which Houzé and Jacques (1884) took down in Brussels from Aborigines who had been captured by an American showman and exhibited (like animals) all over the USA and Europe.

1.3.3 The Yidiñ language

There were three tribes speaking dialects of this language:

- The Gunggay [guŋgay] dialect, spoken by the Guŋgañji [guŋgañji] people, living on Cape Grafton Peninsula; shown as 'g' on Map 1.1.
- Majay (spoken by the Majañji) and Wanyurr(u) [wañurr(u)] (no tribal name known), which may have been distinct dialects or else alternative names for one variety. These were spoken around the mouths of the Mulgrave and Russell Rivers; shown as 'w' on the map.

Gunggay and Wañurr(u) are known only from old vocabularies, from 1896 to 1953; full details are in Dixon (1977a: 508–12). Nothing was recorded on Majay. All had passed into extinction by the time I began fieldwork.

- The Yidiñ dialects, of the Yidiñ-ji tribe. These were spoken over a wide area, from low-lying country west of the Murray Prior Range, up over the tablelands as far as the present-day town of Kairi. My material relates to two major varieties (with their map codes):
  c Coastal Yidiñ, spoken from the city of Cairns and along the lower Mulgrave River (not quite to its mouth).
  t Tableland Yidiñ, spoken up the Mulgrave River and as far as the headwaters of the Barron River.

There were half-a-dozen local groups within the tablelands territory (see Dixon 1977a: 3–4), presumably showing some dialect differences, but these are likely to have been rather minor.

There was more intensive European intrusion into Yidiñ-ji territory than into the lands of people speaking dialects of Dyirbal. As a consequence, the material I was able to record was less rich than that for Dyirbal (but more copious than that for Warrgamay). This comprised 20 texts, around 2,000 lexemes in the everyday language style, and about 200 in the Jalnguy style (all are in Dixon 1991a).

To the north of Yidiñ there was Ja:bugay, spoken by the Ja:bugañji tribe (there is good documentation in Patz 1991). It is a near genetic relative of Yidiñ—the two languages are about as similar as Spanish and Italian. Dyirbal shows no close genetic connection with Yidiñ, to the north, or with Warrgamay, to the south. Nor is there any genetic link between Warrgamay and its southerly neighbour Nyawaygi (documented in Dixon 1983).

Languages to the inland are also unrelated. To the west of Yidiñ there was Mbabaram (the last fragments of this are in Dixon 1991b), and to the west of Dyirbal and Warrgamay there was Warungu (a poorish account of this is in Tsunoda 2012).

1.4 Phonology

There are many similarities, and also important differences, between the phonological systems of Dyirbal, Yidiñ, and Warrgamay.

1.4.1 Word structure

A word typically consists of two syllables with the following structure:

$$CVC_{1-3}V(C)$$

That is, there is an obligatory consonant at the beginning, an optional consonant at the end, and one, two, or three consonants between vowels. There are no sequences of vowels. A longer word repeats the middle portion: $CV[C_{1-3}V]^n(C)$.

There are no monosyllabic words in Yidiñ. Dyirbal has six: the interjections *ŋa* 'yes' and *ŋu* 'alright', plus reduced versions *ban, bam, ŋan,* and *ŋam* of noun markers *balan, balam, ŋalan,* and *ŋalam* (see chapter 2).

Warrgamay does have a small set (in the corpus collected) of about a dozen mono-syllabic words. These all have a long vowel, with structure CV:(C); for example *ma:l* 'man', *ji:n* 'eyebrow', *wi:* 'sun', *ŋa:* 'not'.

1.4.2 Consonants

There is a basic system of 13 consonants, set out in table 1.1.

The stops have voiced and voiceless allophones; they could, alternatively, have been written as 't, c, k, p'.

The apico-alveolar rhotic, *rr*, is in all languages a trill or tap. The apico-postalveolar (semi-retroflex) rhotic, *r*, is generally a continuant but can be realised as a trill articulated at the back of the alveolar ridge (further back than *rr*).

TABLE 1.1. **Basic system of consonants**

	apico-alveolar	apico-postalveolar	lamino-palatal	dorso-velar	bilabial
stop	d		j	g	b
nasal	n		ñ	ŋ	m
lateral	l				
rhotic	rr	r			
semi-vowel			y		w

The one deviation from the standard system is in the Ngajan dialect of Dyirbal where an historical change has neutralised the rhotic contrast (see chapter 13). Ngajan has a single rhotic phoneme, written as *R* to distinguish it from *rr* and *r* elsewhere. It is generally pronounced as an alveolar tap.

In earlier publications—notably the three grammars, Dixon (1972, 1977a, 1981a)—some phonetic symbols were used. These have now been replaced by the 'practical alphabet' set out in table 1.1.

- the apico-alveolar rhotic was originally written as *r*, now as *rr*
- the apico-postalveolar rhotic was originally written as *ɼ*, now as *r*
- the lamino-palatal stop was originally written as *ɖ*, now as *j*
- the lamino-palatal nasal was originally written as *ɲ*, then as *ny*, now as *ñ*

So that the names of tribes, dialects, and languages should only use letters of the roman alphabet, 'ŋ' is here written as 'ng'. Thus Ngajan for [ŋajan], Gulngay for [gulŋay] and Gunggay for [guŋgay].

1.4.3 Vowels

All three languages have a system of three vowels: close front *i*, close back *u*, and open vowel *a*. There is a contrast between short vowels *(i, u, a)* and long vowels (*i:, u:, a:*) in Warrgamay, in the two northerly dialects (N and W) of Dyirbal, and in Yidiñ. The nature and development of this contrast are dealt with in chapters 13 and 14.

These languages have the smallest phoneme systems found in Australia. For an overview of phonological systems across the continent, see Dixon (2002a: 547–658).

1.4.4 Phonotactics

The three short vowels can occur in any syllable for all three languages. The same applies for long vowels in the N and W dialects of Dyirbal. In Warrgamay long vowels are only found in the initial syllable of a word, and in Yidiñ they are restricted to non-initial syllables.

In word-initial position, all three languages have the four stops, the four nasals, and the two semi-vowels. The lateral, *l*, does not occur word-initially—save in one word in Yidiñ and in one word in the Girramay dialect of Dyirbal.

In Warrgamay both rhotics may commence a word. In Yidiñ and the adjacent N and W dialects there are no initial rhotics (except in recent loans from English). The remaining dialects of Dyirbal have a few score words commencing with *r*, none with *rr*. There is discussion of initial rhotics in section 14.5.

Word-finally, we find *y*, *l*, *n*, *ñ*, and *m* in all languages, never a stop or *w*. Dyirbal and Warrgamay have no final *ŋ*. In Yidiñ a root may not end in *ŋ*, but a suffix can (presumably due to historical changes of reduction). A word may end in either rhotic in Yidiñ and Dyirbal (in the single rhotic in the N dialect) but only in *rr*, not *r*, in Warrgamay.

Between vowels we get, in outline (i) a lateral, rhotic, or y, followed by (ii) a nasal, followed by (iii) a stop. Or just (i) plus (ii), or just (i) plus (iii), or just (ii) plus (iii). Or any single consonant (this is the only position where all consonants contrast). The full details differ a little from language to language—see Dixon (1972: 272–4, 1977a: 35–7, 1981a: 21–2).

1.4.5 Stress

Rules for which syllables in a word are stressed (shown by an acute accent on the vowel) vary between languages.

In Dyirbal the basic principle is that the first and every alternate syllable of a word should be stressed, except that a final syllable never bears stress. This applies irrespective of whether a vowel is long or short. For instance, 'spear' is *báŋgay* in most dialects but *báŋga:* in Ngajan, with the initial short vowel stressed and the final long vowel unstressed. In addition, the first syllable of an affix may be stressed (conditions for this are set out in Dixon 1972: 274–5).

If the first syllable of a word in Warrgamay has a long vowel, this receives primary stress. If there is no long vowel, stress goes on the first syllable of a word with two or four syllables, and on the second syllable of a word with three or five syllables. Secondary stress then goes onto every second syllable after the one with primary stress excepting that, as in Dyirbal, a final syllable cannot be stressed. (See Dixon 1981a: 20–1.)

Turning now to Yidiñ, stress is assigned to the first syllable with a long vowel. If there is no long vowel, it is assigned to the first syllable of the word. Further stresses are then allocated to alternate syllables forwards and backwards from this. Note that long vowels always occur in a stressed syllable; in keeping with this, two long vowels are always separated by an odd number of syllables. (Full details are in Dixon 1977a: 39–42.)

Note that it is neither possible nor profitable to distinguish between two degrees of stress in Dyirbal and Yidiñ, as was done for Warrgamay.

1.5 Typological characteristics

These languages have a basically agglutinative structure, with many suffixes but no prefixes. There are four main open word classes:

noun
⎫
⎬ nominal
⎭
adjective

verb
⎫
⎬ verbal
⎭
adverbal

Nouns and adjectives take the same set of cases and share other morphological properties. A main criterion for distinguishing them in Dyirbal is that generally a noun can occur with the marker of only one gender, while an adjective may be associated with several genders. There is a similar criterion in Yidiñ with respect to classifiers. See chapters 2 and 3.

Verbs and adverbals show the same morphological possibilities. Just as an adjective typically modifies a noun, so an adverbal typically modifies a verb. Examples are *gija-n* 'do quickly' in Yidiñ, *gulma-l* 'do something that shouldn't be done' in Dyirbal, and *ga:ma-l* 'do like this' in Warrgamay. The nature and function of adverbals (in Dyirbal) are discussed in chapters 8 and 9.

In each language verbals are grouped into two or three conjugations, according to their allomorphic choices for suffixes. These are shown by a hyphenated letter after the root; for example *bura-l* 'see, look at' in Dyirbal belongs to the '-l' conjugation. There is also a division into intransitive and transitive. In Dyirbal and Yidiñ, transitivity correlates—but does not coincide—with conjugation membership. Dyirbal has two conjugations; the -y class is predominantly intransitive while the -l class is predominantly transitive. The two major conjugations in Yidiñ, -n and -l, correspond to -y and -l classes in Dyirbal. Yidiñ also has a small -r conjugation, mostly transitive. Warrgamay has undergone a fascinating change whereby transitivity now does coincide with conjugation—see chapter 10.

Dyirbal and Yidiñ each has a system of verbal inflections which includes tense, purposive, apprehensive, positive and negative imperatives, and subordinate clause markings. There are generally two tenses: these are future/non-future in southern dialects of Dyirbal, and past/non-past in northern dialects of Dyirbal and in Yidiñ. In Ja:bugay—Yidiñ's northerly neighbour and close genetic relative—there are three tenses: past, present, and future. Warrgamay is distinctive in having no tenses at all, but instead a number of aspectual-type distinctions; see chapter 10.

Each language also has classes of time words, locational words, particles (including 'not'), interjections, demonstrative(s), and, of course, pronouns.

As in many Australian languages, 1st and 2nd person pronouns and nominals have different ways of showing core syntactic functions. The most complex situation is found in Warrgamay and in Girramay, the contiguous dialect of Dyirbal, as illustrated in table 1.2.

In Warrgamay and Girramay, 1st and 2nd person singular pronouns have distinct forms for A, S, and O (what is called 'tripartite marking'). Non-singular 1st and 2nd person pronouns have one form (nominative) for both S and A and another form (accusative) for O. In Yidiñ, and in other dialects of Dyirbal, all 1st and 2nd person pronouns are on a nominative/accusative basis. In all three languages nominals have an ergative case for A function and are in absolutive form, with zero case marking, for both S and O. (This is known as 'split-ergative' morphological marking.)

The ways in which syntactic functions A, S, and O are grouped together for clause linking is also a matter of interest. In some circumstances S and O are linked; this is

TABLE 1.2. Marking of core syntactic functions in the Girramay dialect of Dyirbal

	1st and 2nd person non-singular pronouns, e.g. 1dual	1st and 2nd person singular pronouns, e.g. 1sg	nominals (nouns and adjectives) e.g. 'man'
transitive subject (A)	ŋali NOMINATIVE FORM	ŋaja	yara-ŋgu ERGATIVE CASE
intransitive subject (S)		ŋayba	yara ABSOLUTIVE FORM
transitive object (O)	ŋali-ña ACCUSATIVE CASE	ŋaña	

called 'ergative syntax'. In others S and A are linked: 'accusative syntax'. These circumstances are described and explained in chapter 7.

Pronouns in Warrgamay and Dyirbal have three number forms: singular, dual, and plural. Just in northern dialects of Dyirbal, there are two 1st person dual pronouns, depending on the relationship between the people referred to. For example, *ŋali* is used for 'me and a sibling or grandparent' and *ŋanaymba* for 'me and a parent or child'; see section 4.3. Basically, Yidiñ just has a singular/non-singular distinction plus the 1st person dual form *ŋali* which is probably a recent borrowing from Dyirbal; see section 14.4.

Only in Warrgamay do we find a full set of 3rd person pronouns. These occur in singular, dual, and plural, each having separate forms for A, S, and O functions (like 1st and 2nd person singular). In Yidiñ, demonstratives fill some of the roles associated with 3rd person pronouns in other languages. And in Dyirbal 'noun markers' (which show gender) fill some of the roles of a 3rd person singular pronoun; these are discussed in chapter 2. Dyirbal does have dual and plural 3rd person pronouns, the forms varying between dialects; see chapter 11.

Looking now at demonstratives, Warrgamay has a two-way contrast, 'this' versus 'that'. In the other two languages there is a three-term system. The meanings are 'here and visible', 'there and visible' and 'not visible' all through Dyirbal (see Dixon 2014) and in the adjacent tablelands dialect of Yidiñ, but 'here', 'there, mid-distance', and 'there, far' in the coastal dialect of Yidiñ. There is discussion of this in section 14.2.

Each of the three languages has two possessive constrictions. If the 'possessed' item is a part, it is simply apposed to the 'possessor'. A Dyirbal example is *yara jina* 'man's foot'. If the 'possessed' is a kin term or some object, then the genitive suffix is added to the 'possessor', as in *yara-ŋu yabu* 'man's mother' and *yara-ŋu waŋal* 'man's boomerang'.

We can now in chapter 2, consider the workings and semantic basis of the gender system in Dyirbal, with its unusual member 'edible gender'.

A prefatory note is needed. The reader must excuse me for using the word 'sex' in its traditional meaning, for the biological difference between women and men, rather than 'gender', which is properly a grammatical label. I can then say 'female sex is marked by feminine gender', which is clear, whereas 'female gender is marked by feminine gender' sounds distinctly obtuse.

Part I

Genders and Classifiers

Dyirbal has a system of four genders (including one which refers just to edible plants) while Yidiñ exhibits a class of about twenty noun classifiers. These are phenomena of quite different grammatical natures which, nevertheless, achieve a similar result. The next two chapters deal, in turn, with the two mechanisms. At the end of chapter 3 there is comparison of their semantic roles.

Gender constitutes an obligatory grammatical system. It involves:

- a grouping of all the nouns of a language into a smallish number of genders so that each noun relates to one gender;
- an obligatory indication of the gender of a noun in any clause in which it occurs, an indication which cannot be entirely within the form of the noun itself.

There is no absolute limit on the number of terms in a gender system but it is generally between two and ten (only occasionally more). There are sometimes a small number of nouns which can relate to two genders; these typically involve a male/female distinction, as in Dyirbal where we find both *bayi jaja* 'male infant' and *balan jaja* 'female infant'.

Gender is sometimes shown through a prefix or suffix to the noun itself, as in Swahili where noun *-kombe* 'cup' takes the inanimate gender prefix (in singular number) *ki-*, giving *ki-kombe*. Whether or not gender is marked on the noun, it must be shown somewhere outside the noun. In Swahili, the *ki-* will recur on any adjective or number word modifying the noun, and on a verb for which the noun is subject argument.

The marking of gender is generally by a bound morpheme, typically fused with some other grammatical specification. Such specifications include number in Swahili, definiteness for articles in French, and—as will soon be described—distance/visibility and case in Dyirbal.

An 'edible' gender is found only in Australian languages. Of the 45 or so languages of Australia which have a fully-fledged system of genders, about one half of them have a gender whose primary reference is to plant foods; see Dixon (2002a: 463–512) and especially table 10.5 there, which provides information on the semantics of 'edible' genders in twenty-one languages. Dyirbal may be the only language with a gender which deals exclusively with plant foods.

Cross-linguistically, a set of **noun classifiers** usually has a fair number of members, most often between ten and a few score (although there can be fewer, or a lot more). A classifier is a free form, which occurs in a noun phrase with the noun it classifies, in syntactic construction with it. Not every noun in a language relates to a classifier, and some nouns may relate to several. For example, in Yidiñ *digil* 'black walnut tree (*Endiandra palmerstonii*)' is used with classifier *jugi* 'tree' when referring to its timber, and with *mayi* 'edible plant food' when referring to the fruit.

Perhaps the best-known variety of classifiers is 'numeral classifiers', obligatorily used with lexical number words. For counting—or any quantification—a classifier must be included to indicate what type of thing is being counted. Yidiñ had no counting, and its classifiers fulfil a number of varied syntactic roles, described in chapter 3. Their meanings are not unlike those associated with numeral classifiers in other languages— relating to inherent nature, to function, and to use.

The term 'gender' was traditionally used, in the grammars of European languages, for a smallish system which included 'masculine' and 'feminine'. When linguists began to study languages from other areas, such as Africa, they preferred the label 'noun classes' for larger systems whose terms did not necessarily include a male/female contrast. I originally talked of 'noun classes' in Dyirbal (Dixon 1968b, 1972, 1982a) but now embrace the revived employment of 'gender'.

There are further types of classifiers besides those just mentioned—'verbal classifiers', 'locative and deictic classifiers', and more. Aikhenvald (2000) has a full account, and also discussion of 'noun classes' and 'genders'. Earlier, and shorter, general accounts are in Dixon (1968b; 1982a: 159–77, 211–33; 1986). Corbett (1991) provides an accessible general introduction to gender.

There had been a fair number of accounts of noun classifiers which are used with lexical number words (so called 'numeral classifiers') but my account of Yidiñ (1977a) appears to have been the first comprehensive analytical study of noun classifiers unrelated to number words. This phenomenon has since been described for Meso-American, South American, and Austronesian languages (see Craig 1986, Aikhenvald 2000: 97).

Note that neither a gender system nor a set of classifiers occurs in Warrgamay.

2

Edible and the other genders in Dyirbal

This chapter will explain the principles determining which of the four genders a given noun is assigned to. The explanations require reference to legends and beliefs, perceived physical associations, and the indication of special properties such as eating habits and harmfulness. They interrelate with the scope of generic terms, and with correspondences in Jalnguy, the 'mother-in-law style'.

Before embarking on the semantic examination, we describe the markers for genders, and how these fit into the grammar.

2.1 Grammatical properties

The head of a noun phrase (NP) can be a pronoun, a proper noun (the name of a person or of a place), or a common noun. The head may be modified by one or more adjectives. An NP with a noun as head generally includes a 'noun marker', which shows the gender of the noun. Note that this is the only indication of its gender.

Basic forms of noun markers for the four genders are (in absolute case, with unmarked locational reference):

I, bayi   II, balan *or* ban   III, balam *or* bam   IV, bala

Their use can be illustrated in short sentences from texts (with noun markers underlined):

(1) [<u>bayi</u>   jigubina]$_S$ yugan-da-rru   warri-ñu
     THERE.ABS.I shooting.star(I) sky-LOC-ACROSS fly-PAST
     The shooting star was flying across the sky

(2) [yabu   <u>bala-n</u>]$_S$ yalaba-ñu
     mother(II) THERE.ABS-II do.like.this-PAST
     Mother (spoke) like this: <direct speech follows>

(3) [jubula   bala-m]$_O$ bilmbabaga-ja-ñu
     black.pine(III) THERE.ABS-III bury.in.hole-ALL-PAST
     All the black pine nuts (*Prumnopitys amarus*) were buried in a hole
       (being stored for use in times when fresh food was scarce)

(4) [yugu   bala]$_O$ bana-n
     stick(IV) THERE.ABS.IV break-PAST
     A (long) stick was broken off (a tree, to tie a noose to it, in order to catch
       a black goanna up a tree)

It can be seen that *jigubina* 'shooting star' takes gender class I marker *bayi*, *yabu* 'mother' takes class II marker *balan*, *jubula* 'black pine nuts' takes class III marker *balam*, while *yugu* 'tree, stick, wood' takes class IV marker *bala*. Word order is remarkably free in Dyirbal, so that noun and noun marker may occur in either order. The noun marker most often comes first, as in (1), but does often follow, as in (2–4). (Agreement in case indicates that a number of words, which may be scattered through a sentence, constitute one NP.)

These basic forms of noun markers are used in intransitive subject function (S), as in (1–2), and transitive object function (O), as in (3–4). In keeping with the ergative character of the language, a transitive clause may just involve an O NP, without a transitive subject NP (A function) being explicitly stated, as in (3–4).

If an NP has a noun as head, all of its member words agree in case. This is absolutive (with zero marking), for S and O functions, ergative (with basic form -*ŋgu*) for A and instrumental functions, dative (basic form -*gu*) for indirect object function, and so on. The four noun markers have forms for all these functions:

(5)

Gender	ABSolutive (S and O functions)	ERGative (A function) and INSTrumental	DATive	GENitive
I	bayi	ba-ŋgu-l	ba-gu-l	ba-ɲu-l
II	bala-n ~ ba-n	ba-ŋgu-n	ba-gu-n	ba-ɲu-n
III	bala-m ~ ba-m	ba-ŋgu-m	ba-gu-m	—
IV	bala	ba-ŋgu	ba-gu	ba-ɲu

Hyphens in (5) indicate morphological analysis. The final element is -*l* for gender I, -*n* for II, -*m* for III (and zero for IV). This is preceded by case markers -*ŋgu*- for ergative/instrumental, and -*gu*- for dative, plus -*ɲu*- for genitive. The absolutive gender I form *bayi* is irregular; it would be expected to be *bala-l*. For genders II and III absolutive, long and short forms *bala-n* and *ba-n* and *bala-m* and *ba-m* bear no semantic difference and are in free variation. There is no genitive form for gender III because a fruit or vegetable cannot be an alienable possessor. (The genitive suffix is used only to mark alienable possessor.)

A further textual example illustrates these forms:

(6) [ba-ŋgu-l   gurrijala-gu]ₐ   [ba-n   muɲarra]ₒ
     THERE-ERG-I eaglehawk(I)-ERG THERE.ABS-II scrub.turkey(II)
     yalama-n   [ba-gu-n=girra]   budil-ŋay-gu/
     do.like.this-PAST THERE-DAT-II=MAYBE carry-APASS-PURP
     The scrub turkey [*Alectura lathami*] was asked (lit. done like this) by the
     eagle-hawk [*Aquila audax*], to perhaps carry it (that is, fetch the only
     fire (II) in the world from the clutches of the rainbow serpent)

As mentioned in the last chapter, the language has no 3rd person singular pronouns (or dedicated anaphoric elements), but noun markers help to fill this role.
An NP can consist just of a noun marker, where the identity of the understood
head noun is clear from the textual context. The full dative NP for (6) would be
ba-gu-n buni-gu (*buni* 'fire' is gender II). The *buni-gu* has been omitted, but its gender, II, is shown by noun marker *bagun*. (It is followed by clitic *=girra* which indicates an element of doubt as to whether the scrub-turkey will succeed; in fact she
fails.)

Dyirbal has a great deal of ellipsis. Any word in an NP can be omitted. For example,
the O NP in (6) could be *ban muɲarra*, or just *ban*, or just *muɲarra*. In an NP with
head noun and adjective, the head noun may be omitted. Consider NPs including
adjective *midi* 'small':

(7) FULL NP: CAN BE REDUCED TO:
     bayi gurrijala midi 'small eaglehawk'   bayi midi
     balan buni midi 'small fire'   balan midi
     balam jubula midi 'small black pine nuts'   balam midi
     bala yugu midi 'small stick'   bala midi

It was mentioned in the previous chapter that nouns and adjectives show the same
case inflections and share other morphological properties. One criterion for distinguishing the two word classes is that most nouns can occur with only one gender
marker (a few take two) while, as in (7), an adjective can occur in an elliptical NP with
all four. (Such an NP can be understood as referring to something mentioned earlier
in the discourse, or else evident from the context.)

The first element in a noun marker indicates distance and visibility:

(8) ya(la)- here and visible
     ba(la)- there and visible
     ŋa(la)- not visible (audible, or remembered from the past)

The *ba(la)-* forms are by far the most frequent. They have a default function, being used when distance and visibility are not relevant.

The paradigm for noun markers commencing with 'non-visible' *ŋa-* is identical to that for *ba-* in (5), with *ŋa-* replacing initial *ba-*. Example (9) comes from the story of a man in a fight. He holds up his shield and *buum* represents the sounds of spears hitting it. *Bigin* 'shield' is of gender II and thus class II noun marker *ŋala-n* is used.

(9) jumba-n   ba-ŋgu-l$_A$ bigin$_O$;   *buum*;
    hold.up-PAST THERE-ERG-I shield(II) onomatopoeia
    ŋala-n$_S$ banda-ñu
    NON.VISIBLE.ABS-II be.impacted.on-PAST
    He held up his shield, *buum*, it (the shield) was heard being hit

Here the pivot argument, linking the two clauses, is made up of class II noun *bigin* 'shield' and class II noun marker *ŋalan*. This is in O function for transitive verb *jumba-l* 'hold up', and in S function for intransitive verb *banda-y* 'be impacted on'. Note that the NP is split, with *bigin* being included in the first clause and *ŋalan* in the second one.

The paradigm for 'here and visible' *ya-* is basically the same as (5), with *ya-* replacing initial *ba-*. For example:

(10) bala$_O$ ya-ŋgu-l$_A$ galga-n,
     THERE.ABS.IV HERE-ERG-I leave-PAST
     [bala   yirrgun]$_O$ wanda-n
     THERE.ABS.IV jawbone.of eel(IV) hang.up-PAST
     The man here (lit, gender I, here) left it, hung up the jawbone of an eel

Here the pivot NP linking the two transitive clauses is *bala yirrgun*, 'jawbone of an eel', in O function in each. It is represented by just the noun marker in the first clause, and by both words in the second. The NP in A function in the first clause consists just of a class I noun marker *yaŋgul*. It is understood to refer to the ancestral being Girugarr, the subject of the story from which this sentence is taken.

In fact, absolutive forms commencing with *ya-* 'here' (*yayi, yalan, yalam,* and *yala*) are used only in complex combinations. The absolutive forms used in their place are the demonstratives (which exist only in absolutive, for S and O functions):

(11) giyi   'this gender I'   giña-m 'this gender III'
     giña-n 'this gender II'   giña   'this gender IV'

As before, suffixes -*n*, -*m*, and zero are used for genders II, III, and IV, with the gender I form, *giyi*, being irregular. The gender III demonstrative *giñam* is illustrated in the verbless clause (VC):

(12) [giña-m   buñjan]_{VC.SUBJECT}   buga_{VC.COMPLEMENT}
      THIS.ABS-III soaked.walnut(III) stinking
      This soaked walnut is stinking

An important point of Dyirbal grammar is that the *ya-* noun markers mean 'here' but are *not* demonstratives. That is, they do not have a deictic function of pointing. Since the demonstratives, in (11), are only used in S and O function, in order to make a demonstrative out of an argument in underlying A function, it must be put into derived S function through applying an antipassive derivation. (See chapter 7.)

There is one further set of noun markers, with interrogative locational meaning 'where'. (They can also have an indefinite sense, 'somewhere'.) The paradigm is similar to that in (5), with the gender I absolute form again being irregular: *wuñjiñ* where **wuñja-l* would be expected:

(13)	Gender	ABSolutive (S and O functions)	ERGative (A function) and INSTrumental	DATive	GENitive
	I	wuñjiñ	wuñja-ŋgu-l	wuñja-gu-l	wuñja-ŋu-l
	II	wuñja-n	wuñja-ŋgu-n	wuñja-gu-n	wuñja-ŋu-n
	III	wuñja-m	wuñja-ŋgu-m	wuñja-gu-m	—
	IV	wuñja	wuñja-ŋgu	wuñja-gu	wuñja-ŋu

A textual example is:

(14) (a) [bayi   ñalŋga-ñalŋga]_S ŋanda-ñu: ŋagi   wuñjiñ
           THERE.ABS.I REDUP-child   call.out-PAST grandfather WHERE.ABS.I
           Male children cried out: 'Where is grandfather (mother's father) (I)?'
      (b) ŋaliji-na_O galga-n   wuñja-ŋgu-l_A
           1dual-ACC leave-PAST WHERE-ERG-I
           'Where is he who left us two?'

Alongside noun markers, which accompany a noun, there is a set of verb markers which modify a verb and indicate 'at a place', 'to a place', 'in a direction', and 'from a place'. The initial elements are, again, *ba(la)-* 'there', *ya(la)-* 'here', *ŋa(la)-* 'not visible', and *wuñja-* 'where/somewhere'. Unlike noun markers, verb markers do not show gender. Their paradigm is:

(15)

	THERE	HERE	NOT VISIBLE	WHERE/SOMEWHERE
'at'	bala-y	yala-y	ŋala-y	wuñja-y
'to place'	ba-lu	ya-lu	ŋa-lu	wuñja-rru
'to direction'	ba-li	ya-li	—	wuñja-rri
'from'	ba-ŋum	ya-ŋum	ŋa-ŋum	wuñja-ŋum

In keeping with its location, in mountainous and well-watered country, Dyirbal has two sets of bound forms which can be attached to a noun marker or a verb marker, indicating the location of the referent of the noun. The first set is:

(16)
-bayj-i	'short distance downhill'	-day-i	'short distance uphill'
-bayj-a	'medium distance downhill'	-day-a	'medium distance uphill'
-bayj-u	'long distance downhill'	-day-u	'long distance uphill'

-balb-ala	'medium distance downriver'	-daw-ala	'medium distance upriver'
-balb-ulu	'long distance downriver'	-daw-ulu	'long distance upriver'
	-guya 'across the river'		

-bawal 'long way (in any direction)'

Whereas the *-balb-* and *-daw-* forms only relate to river, those commencing in *-bayj-* and *-day-* essentially refer to anything other than a river; that is, up or down a hill, or a cliff, or a tree, etc. In just the N, W, and M dialects, there is a thirteenth term, *-ŋarru* 'behind'. A textual example with *-bayji* is:

(17) <u>bala-m</u>-bayj-i$_O$ ŋaja$_A$
    THERE.ABS-III-DOWNHILL-SHORT.WAY 1sg.NOM
      muyur$_O$ budi-ŋu
      soaked.black.pine.nuts(III) carry-RELATIVE
      I had carried some soaked black pine nuts a short distance downhill

Note that, as is quite frequent, the NP in O function is discontinuous; its two words, *balam-bayji* and *muyur*, occur either side of the NP in A function, ŋaja 'I'.

The second set of bound forms which can follow a noun marker or a verb marker is:

(18) -gala 'up (vertically)'
    -gali 'down (vertically)'
    -galu 'out in front'

A textual example of this comes from the same legend as (6):

(19) [bayi-n-gala   bayi yamani]_S bungil-gani-ñu

     THERE.ABS.I-LINKER-UP   rainbow(I) lie-CONTINUE-PAST

     The rainbow (serpent) continued to lie up there (on top of a mountain,
     with the fire)

It is not unusual to find two occurrences of a noun marker in one NP, as here. This is
just a matter of narrative style. (We also find combinations of *ba-* form plus demonstrative, e.g. *bayi giyi*.)

    In the Mamu dialect, a noun marker or a verb marker may be followed by either a
form from set (16) or one from set (18). However, in the Jirrbal and Girramay dialects
both may be included, one from (16) followed by one from (18). In one legend, a boy
dies and his mother cuts off his head as a remembrance (before burying the body):

(20) bala-day-i-gala_O   [ba-ngu-n   yabu-ngu]_A

     THERE.ABS.IV-UP.SHORT.WAY-UP   THERE-ERG-II mother(II)-ERG

     wanda-n   dingal_O

     hang.up-PAST head(IV)

     Mother had hung the head high up

When a body part is in situ, it is treated as an inalienable possession, and is in apposition with the noun referring to the whole, which determines the gender of the NP; for
example *balan yabu* (II) *dingal* 'mother's head' and *bayi numa* (I) *dingal* 'father's head'.
But when a body part is detached from its body, as in (20), it takes class IV marker,
bala. Note that (20) includes another instance of a discontinuous NP: *bala-dayi-gala
. . . dingal*.

Fuller grammatical detail will be found in Dixon (1972): NP structure on pages 60–4, and noun markers
and verb markers on pages 44–7, 56–8, and 254–64. Dixon (2014) discusses 'non-visible' noun markers and
verb markers, commencing with *na-*.

The bound forms in (16) have an important role in Jalnguy, the 'mother-in-law style'; this is discussed in
section 5.7.

2.2 Outline of semantics

While working on the grammar of Dyirbal I did, of course, assemble a vocabulary,
enquiring for each noun which gender marker it occurs with.

    An outline of the members of the four genders is in table 2.1.

    The lists in the columns of this table seemed so heterogeneous that at first I won-
dered whether there was any principled basis for gender assignment. General statements such as 'fishes are *bayi*, birds are *balan*' showed so many exceptions as to be of

TABLE 2.1. Outline of members of the four genders in Dyirbal

I. *bayi*	II. *balan*	III. *balam*	IV. *bala*
proper names of male humans	proper names of female humans		proper names of places
men and boys	women and girls		almost all body and other parts
most animals	bandicoots, platypus, echidna, dog		
some bats	some bats		
most snakes	some snakes		
frogs, lizards	turtles		
some birds	most birds		
most fishes	some fishes		
shellfish	prawns, crabs		
most insects	some insects		
	fire		
	stars		
moon	sun		
rainbow, thunder, lightning, rain			wind, cyclone, cloud, dew
boomerang	shield		sword
woomera	most spears		axe, knife, clubs
fishing line, hook	firestick		gun
	spouting, bottle		bags, baskets
	fighting ground, waterfall		camp, hut, hill, cave, stone, clay, mud
			language, noises
	drinkable liquids		flesh food (meat/fish)
	some non-edible plants	edible plants	most non-edible plants
		honey	bees

little value. Remembering Bloomfield's (1933: 280) pessimistic view that 'there seems to be no practical criterion by which the gender of a noun in German, French, or Latin could be determined', I wondered if the same might apply for Dyirbal.

But then I paused. It seemed that speakers did not have to learn the gender of each noun on an individual basis, but did instead operate in terms of some general principles. As a further clue, loan words were immediately assigned, by different speakers, to the same gender. Then I realised that I had been looking at things the wrong way round.

The world hosts a multiplicity of objects, properties, states, actions, concepts, ideas. In contrast, every grammar has a compact format, with a limited number of categories, parameters, and construction types. As a consequence, one typically finds that several real-world distinctions are mapped onto a single grammatical contrast. This means that the set of words with a particular grammatical profile is likely to be heterogeneous.

By trying to discern something in common to the words in each column of table 2.1— a 'grammar-prior' approach—I had adopted a method which was unlikely to bring results. A better way was to start with the semantics, study which real-world contrasts are regarded as significant by speakers of Dyirbal, and see how these are mapped onto the grammar. As the work proceeded, it became apparent that the tribes' repertoire of legends and beliefs, and their general perception of the world, could also help to explain the composition of the columns in table 2.1.

Gender membership in Dyirbal may largely be explained in terms of (i) certain basic concepts associated with the various genders, and (ii) general principles for assigning or transferring genders.

THE BASIC CONCEPTS ARE:

I, *bayi*—male humans; non-human animates
II, *balan*—female humans; fire; drinkable liquids; fighting
III, *balam*—edible plant food
IV, *bala* is then a residue gender, dealing with everything else (including body and other parts, place names, and flesh food (meat and fish))

THE GENERAL PRINCIPLES ARE:

A. If some noun has characteristic X (on the basis of which its gender would be expected to be decided) but is—**through belief or legend**—associated with characteristic Y, then it will be assigned gender on the basis of Y.

B. If the referent of some noun X is perceived to have a **physical association** with the referent of a noun Y, then the gender assignment for X may reflect this. The association can be of several types: there may be a physical similarity, the referent of X may be used to make or catch the referent of Y, or there may be a complementary relationship between the referents of X and of Y.

C. If a set of nouns belongs to a certain gender, and referents of just a subset of this set have a particular **important property**, then this subset may be assigned to a different gender. The important properties are: (a) that referents of the subset may be eaten, (b) what they eat, and (c) the fact that they are harmful to humans.

We should also make two observations. The first relates just to Dyirbal:

D. **All nouns with animate reference are in the *bayi* and *balan* genders,** excepting only bees which are *bala* (the reason for this will be explained). In contrast, nouns with inanimate reference may be in any of the four genders.

The second observation applies across the languages of Australia:

E. A single term may be used for something which has the **potential** for being X, and for something which is an **actual** X. For example, Dyirbal noun *balan jiman* is used for a fire-making implement (a 'firestick') and also for the tree from which it is made, the tetra beech (*Tetrasynandra laxiflora*). Another example is verb *bungi-l* which is used for both the actual activity of going to sleep, and also for just lying down (which carries the potential of going to sleep).

One important point should be made: this concerns the inadvisability of providing genders with glib labels. The *balam* class can appropriately be called 'edible plant food' since this is all it deals with (hence the title of this chapter, and book). But it would be misleading in the extreme to label the *bayi* and *balan* genders as 'masculine' and 'feminine' respectively. This could lead to statements such as 'fire belongs to the feminine gender' or (looking ahead) 'stinging trees and harmful fishes are classed as feminine'.

What we must say is that feminine (female humans), anything to do with fire or with fighting, and drinkable liquids all *belong to the same gender*. The older speakers who instructed me in the language emphasised that no connection is implied between, for instance, fire and women. They just happen both to take *balan*. There are many things in the world but the language has only four genders; hence, several phenomena are necessarily placed in the same gender without there being any implication of connection between them. When I noticed that most fishes are (as non-human animates) classed as *bayi* but that a handful of harmful fishes are set off by being *balan* (principle C), I casually remarked that they were 'like women', only to be firmly reprimanded. Harmful fishes are in no way 'like women'; they just happen to be placed in the same gender as women.

Section 2.3 discusses the basic concepts assisted with the four genders, and then in section 2.4 there is exemplification of the principles for assigning and transferring genders.

Linguistic research has moved on since Bloomfield's time, and his statement has indeed been shown to be overly pessimistic. See, for instance, Zubin and Kopcke (1984, 1986) on the semantic basis of gender assignment in German.

For the actual/potential link in Australian language, see O'Grady (1960) and Dixon (1980: 102–3, 481).

2.3 Basic concepts

(a) **Male and female**. Proper names of people are generally accompanied by a noun marker—*balan* with the name of a woman, and *bayi* with the name of a man. A story about Girugarr—an ancestral male hero who travelled up the coast, naming places on the way—begins:

(21) [bayi   Girugarr]ₛ mulu-ŋunu bani-ñu
      THERE.ABS.I Girugarr   end-FROM   come-PAST
      Girrugar came from the end (of the earth)

Turning now to common nouns, most kinship terms are sex-specific: *balan yabu* 'mother', *bayi ŋuma* 'father' and so on. Just a few cover both sexes with the inclusion of *bayi* or *balan* providing full specification; for example *bayi bimu* 'father's elder brother' and *balan bimu* 'father's elder sister'. A full list is in table 4.1 of chapter 4.

Designations for types of people are generally sex-specific. They include *bayi gubi* 'wise man', *bayi dilŋarran* 'man with more than one wife', and *balan balgari* 'woman (of any age) who has never had a child'. There are sex-differentiated labels for every stage in life after the age of ten or twelve. From *balan gajiya* 'girl who has just reached puberty' and *bayi marrgara* 'boy who has just reached puberty', on up to *balan jambiba* 'old woman' and *bayi bugiba* 'old man'. For young children, sex is not inherent in the noun but is provided by a gender marker; for example *balan/bayi malay* 'new-born baby', *balan/bayi jaja* 'child up to the age of three or so', *balan/bayi ñalŋga* 'child from about three until the onset of puberty'.

'Spirit of a dead child' is *balan* or *bayi murña*, depending on the sex of the deceased. But when an adult dies there are different nouns: *balan guyŋgan* 'spirit of a dead woman' and *bayi guwuy* 'spirit of a dead man'. The names of legendary spirits, and characters from creation times, are generally sex-specific.

Gender markers can be manipulated, to describe unusual phenomena. I heard *balan* used of a man who had significant female characteristics, the feminine gender marker drawing attention to his hermaphrodite nature.

Most terms for infirmities (headache, chest cold, fever, sores, diarrhoea, and so on) are *bala*, like body parts and bodily fluids. However, two ailments are believed to be due to grubs biting inside the body. These are accorded the regular non-human animate gender marker *bayi*, giving *bayi rirrarr* 'rheumatism (grub)' and *bayi ŋamay* 'toothache (grub)'.

Each species of animal, bird, fish, and insect is assigned either to the *bayi* or to the *balan* gender; for example *bayi barrgan* 'sand wallaby (*Macropus agilis*)' and *balan gujila* 'short-nose forest bandicoot (*Isoodon macrourus*)'. But it is possible to employ a non-standard gender marker in order to draw attention to the sex of a particular animal: *balan barrgan* for a female wallaby, and *bayi gujila* for a male bandicoot.

(b) **Fire.** Anything to do with fire, if it is hot, takes gender marker *balan*. Terms include *balan buni* 'fire', *balan ñara* 'flame', *balan yiŋgiñ* 'flying spark', and also words for bush fire, hot coals, flaming torch, plus loan words *balan marrji* 'match' and *balan lambi* 'lamp'. 'Smoke' and 'ashes' are not hot and are in gender IV: *bala bumba* and *bala garran*, respectively.

The generic term for 'star'—and specific terms for 'morning star' and 'evening star'—are *balan*, since stars are like flying sparks in the sky (albeit that their heat cannot be felt). The milky way is looked upon as something apart and is described in various ways, always with *bala*. In the Ngajan dialect it is called *bala ŋulban*, literally 'cloud', in Mamu it is *bala yalgay*, 'road', while in Jirrbal and Girramay it is *bala bumba* 'ashes, dust'.

(c) **Drinkable liquids.** Gender II marker *balan* is used for almost everything to do with water, and for any liquid considered drinkable. *Balan bana* is prototypically 'fresh water' but can also be used as a generic term for any kind of water (including the sea) and for some other liquids.

Most nouns referring to things which consist of water take *balan*. Thus *balan yuramu* 'river', *balan garray* 'current in river', *balan bugun* 'spring', and also terms for headwaters, whirlpool, lake, swamp, flood, spray, and steam. However, we get gender IV marker in *bala jarra* 'foam on fresh water' and *bala jirñjir* 'bubbles of water (typically caused by a fish or animal below the surface)'. I was told that a gully should be described as *balan jarrga* when water is flowing in it, and as *bala jarrga* when it is dry.

Bala is used for *bala jurbu* 'dew on the ground in the morning' and *bala malga* 'water lying on twigs or branches after rain', perhaps because this source of water was not used for drinking. We also find *bala* in *bala balbay* 'hailstone, hailstorm', which is water in solid form. However, *balan* is used for 'saltwater, sea', *balan waraŋan*, because it is a mass of water, even though not drinkable. *Balan* is also employed with nouns for wave and ripple (which are found on freshwater lakes as well as on the sea).

In accord with the actual/potential principle, E, *balan ŋamun* is used for both breastmilk and the female breast itself. Similarly, cow's milk receives the loan word *balan milgi*. However, *bala* is used for all other bodily fluids: *bala dagal* 'saliva', *bala jujar* 'urine', and also spittle, phlegm, vomit, and semen.

Alcoholic drinks, such as wine and beer, are *balam gurugu* (a loan from English *grog*) since they are made from edible plants, which are *balam*.

There are a number of nouns describing particularly useful kinds of sap, which is a kind of liquid. All take *bala*; for example *bala julŋun* 'sap from milky pine, pink bloodwood, and a number of other trees, which is used as an ointment on wounds'. I have heard *bana* used as a general term for sap, and this was the only time it was *bala bana* (instead of the usual *balan bana*).

(d) Fighting. A number of nouns which refer to fighting take the class II gender marker *balan*.

Most common nouns referring to places take *bala*. They include *bala mija* 'hut, camping place, tract of country', *bala jindigal* 'spirit home', *bala jalba* 'hole where a bandicoot lives', *bala jajar* 'bird's nest', and the like. But the term for a 'fighting ground', where inter-group corroborees were regularly held, is of gender II, *balan buya*. When a number of groups came together for a corroboree each would establish its camping place, *bayan*, just outside the *buya* (and in the direction from the *buya* towards which its territory lay). There was here a dialect difference in gender assignment; speakers of Jirrbal and Girramay said *balan bayan* (gender II, like *balan buya*) whereas speakers of Mamu, Wari, and Ngajan said *bala bayan*.

Fighting to settle a grievance was a ritualised matter, with a small group of men on each side, or else just single combat. The weapon of attack was generally *balan baŋgay* 'spear' and that of defence *balan bigin* 'shield', both of gender II by association with fighting. There were a number of specific varieties of spear, also *balan*; for example, *balan yanbara* 'spear which has echidna quills stuck with wax around the top'. However, a multi-prong spear used for impaling fish (and not for fighting) is *bayi jirrga*, probably taking class I marker *bayi* because fish do so (*bayi* is also used with fishing line and hook).

An unusual gender assignment is found with *bala* (not *balan*) *bagur* for 'duelling sword' (see chapter 1). I know of no explanation for this.

(e) Edible plants. Gender class III, *balam*, has the most straightforward semantic content. It covers all and only types of plant food—fruit, berries, vines, bulbs, grasses, root crops. Living in the rainforest, speakers of Dyirbal had access to around two hundred varieties of edible plants. *Balam* is also used for introduced plant foods (mangos, sugarcane, flour, jam, and much more). And, as just mentioned, alcoholic drinks—since these are made from plants. Honey, both that from the several species of native bees and also from the introduced English bee, is *balam girñjal*, being *balam* since it is made (by bees) from plant blossom.

There is a generic term, *balam wuju* 'plant food', which is coextensive with *balam*: everything which is *wuju* is *balam*, and vice versa. *Wuju* is useful for referring to a collection of several kinds of plant food. (In the 'mother-in-law style', Jalnguy, there is no equivalent for *wuju*; one just says *balam*. See section 5.4.4)

A tree can have several uses, and there may then be a different gender marker for each. For instance, the parasitic fig *Ficus pleurocarpa* has fruit which can be eaten when ripe; these are called *balam gabi*. But when referring to its timber or its bark (which was used for blankets), it is *bala gabi*. (It is interesting to note that the English name of this plant, *karpe*, is a loan from Dyirbal *gabi*.)

Generic terms *yugu* 'tree, timber, stick' and *wuju* 'plant food' can be used with the name of a specific tree, plus the appropriate gender marker:

(22)   bala yugu muja 'the timber of a bush guava tree (*Eupomatia laurina*)',
            which is used for spear shafts, and sometimes for firesticks
        balam wuju muja 'the pear-shaped fruit of the bush guava', which can be
            cooked and eaten in small quantities (too much may burn your mouth)

Of course one could just say *bala muja* and *balam muja*, which would clearly indicate that the reference is to timber and fruit respectively. Adding generic terms *yugu* and *wuju* serves to emphasise this.

(f) **Flesh food.** Somewhat parallel to the contrast in (22), we get

(23)   bayi rubiñ 'any edible fauna (including most fishes and some snakes)'
        bala jalgur 'meat and fish, including the edible parts of shellfish'
            (prototypically used for lean meat)

When something is alive it is *bayi rubiñ*, providing that its flesh can be eaten once it is dead. We see that *rubiñ* takes *bayi*, the default gender marker for non-human animates. Once it becomes flesh food, gender marker *bala* is used. Note that *bala* is also used in *bala jami* 'fat (of meat)', *bala gimirri* 'gravy', and *bala jalgiñ* 'human flesh (in cannibalism)'.

(g) **Proper names of places.** Just as the proper name of a person is often accompanied by noun marker *balan* or *bayi*—illustrated in (21)—so the name of a place (location, mountain, valley, etc.) is often accompanied by the class IV marker *bala*. One of several versions recorded of the story of the creator being Girugarr—see also (10) and (21)—includes:

(24) $\underline{bala}_O$ $\underline{ba\text{-}ngu\text{-}l}_A$ Dundubila$_O$ jarra-n
        THERE.ABS.IV THERE-ERG-I Dundubila   give.name-PAST
        He (Girugarr) gave the name Dundubila (to the mountain)

Note that this is another example of discontinuity, the two words of the O NP, *bala* and *Dundubila*, being separated by the A NP which here consists just of ergative noun marker *baŋgul*.

(h) Body and other parts. A body-part noun generally occurs in an NP with a noun referring to the whole of which it is a part. There is just one noun marker, and this shows the gender of the whole. Thus, with *jina* 'foot':

(25) bayi bugiba jina   'old man's foot'
      balan jambiba jina 'old woman's foot'

However, a body-part noun can occur alone, and then takes gender IV marker *bala*. If someone should see just a foot poking out from beneath a bush, and have no idea whose foot it might be, they might exclaim:

(26) ŋaja$_A$ [bala   jina]$_O$ bura-n
      1sg.NOM THERE.ABS.IV foot   see-PAST
      I saw a foot

If a severed foot were encountered, it would be described as *bala jina*. (And see the use of *bala diŋgal* for a severed head, in (20) above.) Note that *bala* could not be included in either of the NPs in (25).

Almost all body-part terms take *bala* when they are used alone. Many of them have extended meanings for parts of a geographical feature, or of an implement; they still take *bala*. For example, *guwu* 'nose' is also used for the peak of a mountain, *bala muɲan*, for the prow of a bark canoe, *bala gugay*, and for the point of a spear, *balan baŋgay*. Referring to a point on a spear, one would say *balan baŋgay guwu*, with *baŋgay* selecting gender II marker *balan*. But a broken-off spear point would be *bala guwu*.

Some body-part terms are also used for water features, and then they take *balan*, the gender II marker used for anything to do with water. Thus:

(27) bala garrgal 'upper arm on person'
      bala garrgal 'branch of tree'
      balan garrgal 'small river (tributary of larger one)'

Another example is *bala buŋgu* 'knee on a person' and *balan buŋgu* 'wave on the water'. *Balan binda* is 'waterfall' in all dialects, related to *bala binda* which is 'shoulder' in dialects N, W, M, and A (J and G have *bala baŋgal* and *bala bigil* respectively for 'shoulder').

Most names for genitalia are, like other body parts, *bala*. This applies to terms for vagina, vulva, clitoris, hymen, and penis. There is a single exception: 'scrotum' is *bayi galun* with *bayi*, used for human males. This presumably indicates that the scrotum is the focal point of male sexuality. (The penis isn't, since it is also used for urinating.)

What, one might ask, about testicles? These are a part of the scrotum, and so take *bala*. We find *bala bambu* used for testicle, eyeball, and bullet of a gun. Plus *balan bambu* 'egg' (*balan* like birds) and *bayi bambu* 'frog spawn' (*bayi* like frogs).

As mentioned before, 'female breast' is *balan ŋamun*, taking *balan* because of the drinkable liquid which it gives. There is one other small set of terms taking *balan*, for which I have no explanation. These are *balan guna* 'bowels, faeces', *balan gugun* 'dog faeces' and *balan buji* 'fart air'. (However, terms for bird droppings take *bala*.)

2.4 General principles

In terms of the basic concepts, non-human animates take *bayi*, plants with no edible parts take *bala*, and so on. There are exceptions, most of which can be explained in terms of general principles A–C.

PRINCIPLE A. **Gender assigned on the basis of legend and belief**

(a) **Birds.** It is believed that birds are, as a class, the spirits of dead human females. Thus, instead of taking *bayi* on the basis of their actual non-human animate status, they take *balan*, the marker for femininity, on the basis of belief.

However, out of the total set of about 140 birds that I have identified, there are around twenty which featured as male and female creatures in tribal legends, and have gender assigned on this basis. The willy wagtail (*Rhipidura leucophrys*) is *bayi jigirrjigirr* since he is thought of as the metamorphosis of a legendary man; the way in which the bird wiggles his bottom is reminiscent of how men dance in a corroboree.

One story tells of how the spirit of a dead man returned from the spirit home and was shown his own decaying head—following on from (20) above. He then returned permanently to the spirit home, never to return, and told all the people that they would—when their turn came—follow him. This, I was told, was the origin of death. Two birds play a role in the tale, and are both *bayi* because of their association with the dead man. *Bayi guŋgaga* 'laughing kookaburra (*Dacelo gigas*)' heralds his coming back from the spirit home, and *bayi galbu* 'black butcher bird (*Cracticus quoyi*)' calls out on his final return there.

In creation times, *balan muɲarra* 'scrub turkey (*Alectura lathami*)' was a female creature (hence *balan*), with white feathers, and *bayi gayambula* 'white cockatoo (*Cacatura galerita*)' was a male one (hence *bayi*), with black feathers. After bathing, they took off their feathers and put them on a flat rock to dry while they slept. The cockatoo woke first, took a fancy to the white feathers, and put them on. He flew so high that the turkey could not catch him; she had to don the black feathers and now can fly only just above the ground. There are similar stories about the other birds who are assigned gender on the basis of their male or female status in legends.

As mentioned in chapter 1, one should be maximally specific when speaking the everyday style of Dyirbal. There is for example, no generic term 'frog', since it is always possible to identify a frog—by size, colour, behaviour, and call. However, there is a general term *balan dundu* 'bird'. It may be employed to describe a conglomeration of birds of different sorts. Or for a single bird (typically a small one) which is far off and cannot be identified. *Balan dundu* can be employed of the general run of birds (which are all *balan*), but it may not be used of those birds which have an individual role in legends.

(b) Other animates. Most insects are just that, and come under the non-human animate gender, *bayi*. In one legend the dragonfly, *bayi yirriñjila*, was a creature who made the pool at the base of Murray Falls by fanning with his wings; this insect is *bayi* by being a human male in legend. The half-dozen terms for crickets and grasshoppers are *balan*, since these are regarded as 'old ladies'. (However, cicadas are simply insects, and thus *bayi*.)

Turtles have a legendary role, as women, and so are *balan*. Dangerous snakes are all *bayi*, except for *balan bima* 'death adder (*Acanthophis antarcticus*)' who is also a legendary woman. In one story, the blue-tongue lizard had the only water in the world. Animal after animal made a fruitless attempt to get it until the smallest animal of all succeeded. This is *balan galu*, a tiny mouse, who is *balan* by association with *balan bana* 'water', whereas all other rats and mice are *bayi*.

(c) Body part. An important creation legend tells how a boil formed on the calf of the first man. He squeezed the boil, it burst and the first child came out, a boy. Man and boy were both called *bayi ŋaga-ŋunu* (literally, 'calf-FROM'). And 'boil' is accorded the human male gender marker, *bayi burrubay*. (In contrast, sores, warts, wrinkles and rashes are *bala*, like body parts in general.)

(d) Artefacts. Most artefacts, other than those to do with fighting, are *bala*: axes, knives, digging sticks, grindstone, traps, nets, bags, baskets, blanket, clothing, canoe, and recently-introduced guns. However, 'boomerang' was a legendary man and is thus *bayi waŋal*. One legend tells of a frightening man, called *bayi wungumali*, who whirled around his head what is in English called a bullroarer, a flat piece of wood, on a string. All the men ran away from the deafening noise it produced, and Wungumali was able to steal a young girl for his wife. (Later her father rescued the girl and killed Wungumali.) The bullroarer, which is also called *bayi wungumali*, became a sacred artefact employed on ritual occasions.

(e) Natural phenomena. The sun was believed to be a woman and the moon her husband: hence, *balan garri* and *bayi gagara* respectively. The star cluster Seven Sisters (or Pleiades), *balan gurburru*, is believed to be a woman who came down to earth with a dilly-bag filled with all the varieties of snakes. The shooting star, *bayi jigubina*, is a man who swallowed a piece of burning coal; he used to chase people around, frightening them, and trying to kill them.

Bayi guñjuy 'thunder, thunderstorm', *bayi mayjala* 'lightning', and *bayi gambal* 'rain' are thought of as men, and hence *bayi*. However, terms for hailstorm, wind, cyclone, cloud, sky, and fog are all *bala*.

Perhaps the most powerful spirit in this region—and over much of Australia—is the rainbow, *bayi yamani*, who is a man. The rainbow can transform himself into the multi-hued scrub python (or carpet snake, *Morelia amethistina*), *bayi maguy*, who is thus also *bayi* (although other carpet snakes are *balan*—see the discussion below under Principle C). The colours in the rainbow are described as *bala girri*; this is *bala*, like other nouns for parts of things.

PRINCIPLE B. Gender assigned on the basis of physical association

We can distinguish three kinds of association. This first, (a) pairing, involves assigning different genders to complementary terms, while (b) physical purpose and (c) physical similarity assign the same gender to related terms.

(a) Pairing

- Fruit and vegetable food, *balam wuju*, is produced by plants, which are *bala*. Honey, *balam girñjal*, is produced by bees, and—because of this congruence— bees are *bala* (they are the only animates which are not *bayi* or *balan*). For example, *bala gandirri* 'small yellow native bee in forest', *bala guburr* 'big black native bee in scrub', and *bala mayi* for the introduced English bee.
- The spear, a fighting implement, is *balan baŋgay*. A spear may be held in the hand, or thrown from the hand, or thrown with the aid of *bayi jumala*, a woomera (or spear-thrower); this is a piece of wood which notches onto the end of the spear and helps to propel it further. Since the woomera is complementary to the spear, it is *bayi* to the spear's *balan*.
- When children are being trained, a piece of bark fashioned into a circle is thrown into the air and the novice attempts to project a spear through this moving target. Since the bark target is complementary to the spear, which is *balan*, it is *bayi gugandal*, with *bayi*.

(b) Physical purpose

- Matches (and a match box which holds them) are *balan* since they produce fire, which is *balan*. The saffronheart or jitta tree (*Halfordia scleroxyla*) is *balan jidu* since its timber is used for a flaming torch at night; it also bears fruit which are *balam jidu*. (Note that the English name *jitta* is based on Dyirbal *jidu*.)
- Anything to do with water is *balan*. This includes a bamboo tube for sucking up water, leaf spouting used to direct a stream of water onto some foodstuff in order to flush the poison out of it, and the introduced bottle.

- *Bayi milga* is a 'rain-maker', a pear-shaped piece of timber (generally made from a Queensland maple or red carabeen tree), placed in a river and spoken to, telling it to bring rain. It is, naturally, *bayi*, the same gender as rain.
- *Bayi wilam*, the 'blue jay (*Cracina novaehollandiae*)' is said to call out when rain is imminent; it takes *bayi*, like rain.
- Most fish are *bayi* and so are implements used to procure them: *bayi yarra* 'fishing line', and *bayi warugay* 'fishing hook'.

(c) Physical similarity

- The scorpion, *balan mala-yigarra*, is said to look like a crayfish (*balan yigarra*) with a hand (*mala*) attached. It is thus in *balan* gender, like the crayfish.
- The sting of the hairy mary caterpillar is said to smart like sunburn. Because of this, it shares the same name and gender as the sun, *balan garri*.
- Like most fish, the stingray, *bayi yadar*, is *bayi*. Its poisonous serrated tail, *balan wargaja*, is said to be like a spear and thus takes gender marker *balan*, like *balan baŋgay* 'spear'. (In Jalnguy, a single form, *balan waybay*, corresponds to both *balan baŋgay* and *balan wargaja* in the everyday style.)
- The firefly, *balan yugiyam* is *balan* whereas most other insects are *bayi*. This is because the flashes of light it emits are similar to sparks from a fire (although they are not hot).
- Terms for song and dance styles, and all sorts of noises, are *bala*. When guns were introduced, their sound was felt to be like the metronymic boomerang-upon-boomerang accompaniment for the song style *bala gama*. The generic term for 'gun' is *bala gama* in the northern dialects N, W, M, and A. (In southern dialects, J, U, and G, 'gun' is *bala marrgin*, a loan from English *musket*.) Note that the gun was not seen as a fighting weapon (which would place it in the *balan* gender), but simply an instrument for murder.

PRINCIPLE C. **Gender assignment to highlight an important property**

If a set of nouns has gender X, and a subset has some particular property, then this subset may be assigned a gender other than X. Three kinds of important property have been identified.

(a) **Can be eaten**

—(1) Pythons (or carpet snakes) are the only snakes which are eaten by speakers of Dyirbal. They are thus *balan*, to distinguish them from other snakes which are almost all *bayi*. Note that the generic term, *bayi wadam* 'snake', does not include pythons.

Examples include *balan gabul* 'diamond python (*Morelia spilota*)' and *balan yunba* 'water python (*Liasis fuscus*)'. However—as mentioned under (e) for principle A—the scrub python (*Morelia amethistina*) is believed to be a transmogrification of the rainbow, *bayi yamani*, and thus has the same gender, *bayi maguy*.

—(2) Invertebrates are almost all *bayi*. However, snails and slugs have the special property of being considered edible, and are thus *balan*.

—(3) Bandicoots are easy to catch, and provide good eating. There was a restriction that only old men were permitted to hunt them; this was described to me as 'like an old-age pension'. To mark this property, bandicoots are *balan*, setting them off from most other mammals, which are *bayi*.

(b) What they eat
—(4) Whereas most birds are *balan*, and are included under the generic term *balan dundu*, birds of prey are not covered by *balan dundu* and are given gender marker *bayi*. I was told that this is because 'they eat *dundu*'. Some (but not all) birds of prey have a role as men in legends, this providing a second reason for their being *bayi*; for example *bayi gurrijala* 'eaglehawk (*Aquila audax*)', as in (6).

—(5) Most mammals—kangaroos and wallabies, possums, etc.—are *bayi* and are vegetarian. Three of the species of bat only eat fruit, and are also *bayi*. But the remaining two types of bat consume insects, and take gender marker *balan* to mark this property.

(c) Being harmful to humans
—(6) Most fishes are—as non-human animates—*bayi*, and fall under the generic term *bayi guya*. But there are three species which are not covered by *bayi guya* and take gender marker *balan*. This is because of their harmful character. Eating the toad fish, *balan juruŋun*, can be fatal. The jellyfish, *balan jawayi*, has tentacles that can inflict a serious sting. And the freshwater stonefish, *balan jaŋgan*, has venomous spines which give painful wounds if stepped on.

—(7) There are four plants, all in the Urticaceae family, which are *balan* because of their harmful property—if a leaf is stroked in the wrong direction, the hairs on it will inflict a sting that persists for months. Two are stinging trees, *balan duŋan* (*Dendrocnide moriodes*) and *balan giyarra* (*D. photinophylla*) and two are stinging vines, *balan bumbilan* (*Urtica incisa*) and *balan biŋgilgayi* (*Tragia novae-hollandiae*).

It is interesting to summarise the gender-assigning effect of Principle C:

(28)

GENDER OF MAIN SET	GENDER OF SUBSET	
I, bayi	II, balan	(1), (2), (3), (5), (6)
II, balan	I, bayi	(4)
IV, bala	II, balan	(7)

Six of these involve non-human animates, for which the default gender is *bayi*. Since all animates are *bayi* or *balan* (Principle D), the gender assigned to the subset with an important property has to be *balan*, as in (1–3) and (5–6). However, for birds the default gender is *balan*, and the subset thus takes *bayi*, as in (4). Only for (7) is the main set inanimate, and thus *bala*. The subset could have been *bayi* or *balan*. It may be that *balan* was used since a number of trees are *balan* for other reasons—the tree from which the fire-making stick is fabricated, that whose timber is used for a flaming torch (both because of the association with fire, which is *balan*), and that whose bark is used to make a water-carrier (because of the association with a drinkable liquid, which is also *balan*).

2.5 Summing up

The grammatical category of gender can provide referential specification which is achieved through lexemes in other languages. Both English and Dyirbal have two terms for offspring. In English, they show the sex of the child, *daughter* and *son*. In Dyirbal they reflect the sex of the parent: *daman* 'child of mother (or of mother's sibling)' and *galbin* 'child of father (or of father's sibling)'. To these are added gender markers *balan* and *bayi*, which distinguish between sons and daughters.

(29)   balan daman 'mother's daughter'   balan galbin 'father's daughter'
       bayi daman   'mother's son'   bayi galbin 'father's son'

Gajin is used both for a long pointed stick used for digging up yams and for a young girl. However, the yamstick is *bala gajin* and the girl *balan gajin*. The blossom on a tree is *manga*—it is *balam manga* for blossom which will develop into an edible fruit and *bala manga* for other blossom.

Gender is especially appropriate for disambiguation in Jalnguy, as can be seen in:

(30)   IN EVERYDAY STYLE   IN JALNGUY STYLE
       'rainbow'   bayi yamani   bayi gagilbarra
       'wompoo pigeon'   balan bagamu   balan gagilbarra
       'flame kurrajong' bala dila   bala gagilbarra

In Jalnguy the wompoo pigeon (*Ptilinopua magnificus*) is given the same name as the rainbow since its colour is like the green of the rainbow. The flame kurrajong tree (*Brachychiton acerifolium*) is held to be sacred to the rainbow snake, and is similarly named. But contrastive gender markers serve to distinguish the three items.

For any system of genders, it is relevant to enquire concerning formal and functional markedness. The 'residue' gender, IV, is formally unmarked since it involves a zero suffix, opposed to -*m* for III, -*n* for II, and -*l* or -*yi* for I. However, in functional terms I have not been able to discern any markedness. In most European languages, the masculine gender is (or was) used in neutral circumstances. For Dyirbal, I tried to investigate every possibility. For a group of people of mixed sex it seems that either *bayi* or *balan* may be used. There may be a tendency to use *balan* if most of the group are female, of if the senior member is a woman, and similarly for *bayi* and men. But these are only tendencies.

What about a baby in the womb whose sex is not known? In English, the pronoun *it* is often used here (as in, *It is starting to kick*). *Bala* could not be employed, since in Dyirbal animates are confined to *bayi* and *balan* (Principle D). I enquired about this and was told that as soon as a baby was conceived the parents would think of it as male or female, thus referring to it by *bayi* or *balan*.

Gender assignment is pretty constant across dialects, with one exception. The most northerly dialect, Ngajan, shows a number of systematic differences:

- All bats are *balan*, whereas in other dialects fruit-eaters are *bayi* and insect-eaters *balan*.
- Birds of prey (including the eaglehawk) are *balan*, like most birds, whereas in other dialects they are *bayi* (because 'they eat other birds').
- Fishing line and hook are *bala*, like most non-fighting artefacts, whereas in other dialects they are *bayi*, because of the association with *bayi guya* 'fish'.

We have shown how the great majority of gender assignments, summarised in table 2.1, are explainable in terms of the basic concepts and general principles. But not all are. I know of no reason why *balan* is used for prawns and crabs, for the two egg-laying mammals (platypus and echidna), and for the dingo or native dog. (There are a number of other individual eccentricities.)

The ways in which genders are allocated to loan words are generally quite clear. Most artefacts are *bala*, introduced foodstuffs are *balam*, pipe and matches are *balan* because of the connection with fire, while tobacco is *balam* since it is leaves which are consumed. Tea leaves are *bala* since they are not consumed as such; the drink made from them is *balan*.

The pig, *balan bigibigi*, is the same gender as *balan gumbiyan* 'echidna' because the bristles on a pig are perceived as similar to the echidna's spines. These two animals share the same name, *balan ginga*, in Jalnguy. We also find that introduced horses and goats are seen as linked with dogs and hence are *balan* like dogs (and have the same Jalnguy correspondent).

One entirely new article was money. Here the gender varies between dialects. I do not know why it is *bala mani* in Ngajan and Mamu, but *bayi mani* in Jirrbal.

There may have been further legends and beliefs, which I did not become familiar with, that would help explain more about gender assignment. And there could be legends which had been forgotten but left in their wake some special gender specifi-cation. As in any judicious enquiry into the semantic basis of a grammatical system of genders, a lot can be explained—but not everything.

In summary, it has been shown that the semantic basis of gender in Dyirbal is not simply taxonomic, but involves principles for transferring gender membership, and that an understanding of it depends on a close cultural knowledge—the people's rep-ertoire of beliefs and legends. Three of the genders are positively specified, in terms of definite concepts, whereas the fourth class is only negatively specified, as 'everything else'. It may be that in any system of three or more genders there will always be one 'residue' class, similar to the *bala* gender in Dyirbal.

So as not to over-complicate the presentation, I have in this chapter generally used forms from Jirrbal. There are in some cases variant forms in other dialects. For instance, 'wompoo pigeon' and 'flame kurrajong' are *balan bagamu* and *bala dila* in Jirrbal (as quoted above) but *balan ŋirriwuɲal* and *bala giwan* respectively in Mamu.

An earlier, and much briefer, account of genders in Dyirbal (then called 'noun classes') was in my paper 'Noun classes' (1968b), a revised version of which became a chapter (pp. 159–83) of the volume, *Where have all the adjectives gone, and other essays in semantics and syntax* (1982a). There was also discussion on pages 306–11 of the 1972 grammar.

A note concerning Lakoff's misrepresentation

On the basis of my 1968b/1982a chapter, Lakoff (1987) presented a mangled account of what he called 'clas-sifiers' in Dyirbal, putting forward speculative views which go against what speakers said. I was explicitly told there was no implication that, because (say) women and certain harmful things are assigned to the same gender, there is any cultural association between them. (See further comment on this in the appendix to chapter 16.) Lakoff is free to speculate, but when his speculations go against cultural beliefs, these specu-lations must be regarded as harmful.

I had always stated that Principle C (then called 'Rule (2)') related to a subset having an important prop-erty which was often—but not exclusively—'harmfulness'. Lakoff seized on the fact that harmful fishes are *balan* (rather than default fish gender *bayi*) and that stinging plants are also *balan* (rather than *bala*). He then essentially took 'harmfulness' as a basic concept for the *balan* gender—which is highly misleading—and called his book *Women, fire and dangerous things, what categories reveal about the mind.*

However, *dangerous* (a word I did not use in this connection) and *harmful* are not synonymous. For example, *dangerous* could not be substituted into *His words were harmful and upset me mightily*, nor *harm-ful* into *It's dangerous to jump to glib conclusions.* But I suppose that *Women, fire and harmful things* (which would have been better, but still misleading) wouldn't have helped Lakoff's book reach the bestsellerdom it has achieved.

3

Classifiers in Yidiñ

Yidiñ shows signficant differences in grammar from its southerly neighbour Dyirbal. While Dyirbal employs a system of four genders, Yidiñ has a set of about twenty noun classifiers which serve to categorise things in the world.

A noun phrase in Yidiñ will typically include both a specific noun and an appropriate generic classifier. One would not generally say in Yidiñ 'the girl dug up the yam', or 'the wallaby is standing by the black pine'; it is more felicitous to include classifiers and say 'the person girl dug up the vegetable yam', or 'the animal wallaby is standing by the tree black pine'. That is:

(1) [mayi   jimirr]$_O$ [bama:-l   yaburu-ŋgu]$_A$ jula:-l
     vegetable yam   person-ERG girl-ERG   dig-PAST
     The person [CLASSIFIER] girl dug up the vegetable [CLASSIFIER] yam

(2) [miña   gangu:l]$_S$ jana-ŋ   [jugi:-l   gubuma-la]$_{LOCATIVE}$
     animal wallaby   stand-PRESENT tree-LOC black.pine-LOC
     The animal [CLASSIFIER] wallaby is standing by the tree [CLASSIFIER] black pine

Factors conditioning vowel length in Yidiñ are discussed in section 14.6.5.

3.1 How classifiers are used

It is good style in Yidiñ to include both classifier and specific noun in some, but not all, noun phrases; always to include them both would be unbearably pedantic, never to combine them would be to talk like a foreigner who had learnt the grammar but not the conventions of usage. A specific noun can be used without a classifier and a classifier can, quite freely, constitute a complete noun phrase.

There are a number of situations in which classifier and specific noun can alternate— one is in the construction of felicitous discourse, while another concerns relative clause constructions.

In addition to their considerable grammatical, phonological, and lexical differences, Dyirbal and Yidiñ also show markedly different strategies of discourse construction.

Dyirbal discourse is highly elliptical with maximum deletion of words that would either repeat information given in a previous sentence, or which can be inferred from the context; this applies both within a single utterance and in consecutive statement–response or question–reply involving a number of speakers. A polar question can be answered just by *ŋa* 'yes' or *yimba* 'no', while an information-seeking question will often receive a single word reply; *miña-gu ŋinda yanu-li baŋgay-bila* 'why are you going out with a spear?' could be answered by just *barrgan-gu* ('wallaby-DATIVE') 'for wallabies'.

In Yidiñ, on the other hand, the normal conversational style is for a response to repeat the question that is being answered—or the statement that is being commented upon—as fully as possible. For example:

(3) QUESTION ñundu$_S$ dugu:r-mu gada:-ñ
　　　2sg.NOM house-ABL come-PAST
　　　Have you just come from the house?

(4) ANSWER (yiyi) ŋayu$_S$　bulmba-m gada:-ñ
　　　yes, 1sg.NOM camp-ABL come-PAST
　　　(Yes), I've just come from the camp [CLASSIFIER]

It would not be normal to answer simply *yiyi* 'yes' to a question such as (3). In fact, *ŋayu bulmba-m gada:-ñ* is the main response, *yiyi* being just an optional extra which can be supplied, for emphasis, at the beginning but is more frequently omitted.

The consultants regarded it as their main task, in teaching me Yidiñ, to explain the construction of dialogue: 'if someone tells you so-and-so, how would you answer him back?' And, in fact, there is a considerable art to felicitous discourse in Yidiñ. For the response must be a complete sentence, as full and informative as the original statement or question—so that a listener who heard only the response would perfectly understand it—but it must *not* simply repeat all of the lexical and grammatical elements of the original utterance. There must be some, but not too much, lexical or grammatical variation (in addition to automatic alternations such as *you/I*).

This variation is achieved through a variety of devices (see Dixon 1977a: 114–18), one of the most productive being the interchange of specific noun and classifier. Thus (4) substituted the classifier *bulmba* 'camp, place' for the specific noun *dugur* 'house, hut', which it semantically subsumes. Alternatively, if a statement or question used a classifier, the response could substitute an appropriate specific noun.

Turning now to relative clause constructions, we can note that these are marked by a special inflection on the verb of the relative clause (full details are in Dixon 1977a: 322–57). There must be a noun phrase common to main and relative clauses and it must be in intransitive subject, S, or transitive object, O, function in each of the two clauses (corresponding to absolutive case, with zero inflection, for a noun). Various syntactic derivations are available to put a noun phrase into one of these functions (see chapter 7). The relative clause follows the main clause:

(5)   [ŋuŋu buña]$_S$ juŋga-ŋ,   badi-ñunda
       THAT woman run-PRESENT cry-RELATIVE
       That woman, who is crying, is running (along)

(6)   [bama:-l   waguja-ŋgu]$_A$ baja:-r,
       person-ERG man-ERG   leave-PAST
       gaña:rr$_S$ bila-ñunda   jabu-:
       crocodile go in-RELATIVE ground-LOC
       The man left the crocodile, who went into (a hole in) the ground

The noun phrase that is common to the two clauses may be stated in the main clause, as in (5), or in the relative clause, as in (6). Note that in (5) *ŋuŋu buña* 'that woman' is in S function for both clauses, whereas in (6) the common argument *gaña:rr* 'crocodile' is in O function for the main clause, which is transitive, and in S function for the relative clause, which is intransitive.

There is a further possibility, to include part of the shared noun phrase in the main clause and another part in the relative clause. Commonly, the specific noun may be stated in the main clause, and its classifier in the relative clause, as in (7), or vice versa, as in (8):

(7)   ŋayu$_A$ gangu:l$_O$ buga:-ñ, ñundu$_A$ miña$_O$ baga-lñunda
       1sg.NOM wallaby eat-PAST 2sg.NOM animal spear-RELATIVE
       I ate the wallaby, which animal [CLASSIFIER] you speared

(8)   ŋayu$_A$ bana$_O$ banji:-l, bugun$_S$ bayi-lñunda
       1sg.NOM water find-PAST spring come.out-RELATIVE
       I found some water [CLASSIFIER], which spring was coming out (of the ground)

3.2 Criteria for recognising classifiers

Working on classifiers in Yidiñ was a journey of discovery. I found that *miña* did not cover all animals, but only those considered edible. Thus *yalburr*, a grey frog species, is *miña*, but a smaller frog, *jidin*, is not. The white-tail rat, *durrgim*, can be eaten—and is included under *miña*—whereas a small mouse, referred to by the species name *mugiñ*, is not. It appeared that *miña* refers to 'edible animals', just as *mayi* covers 'edible plants'.

I also found that whereas *anything* burning (including even 'hot smoke') is *buri*, only certain liquids are describable as *bana*. The classifier *bana* applies to waterfalls, steam, and dew, but not to blood, urine, spittle, snot, semen, or sweat. *Bana* appeared to be basically 'any drinkable liquid' (although the use of *bana* with *birriñ* 'salt water' was puzzling).

A number of new classifiers were uncovered at this stage of the investigation— *mangum* refers to *all* frogs (whether edible or not) and *jarruy* to *all* birds (except for the flightless cassowary). *Walba* 'stone' is used with specific nouns referring to any type of stone or rock or rocky feature:

walba malan   'flat rock'
walba bunda   'mountain'
walba burray   'cave'
walba yirriy   'type of slatey stone'

And *jabu* 'ground, earth, dirt' is used with specific nouns such as mud, sand, white clay, dust, and so on.

Bulmba, which occurs in sentence (4), refers to any type of hut or windbreak or camp, or even to a potential camping-place. *Bulmba* can be used with the proper name of any habitable place, and also with a variety of specific nouns:

bulmba dugur   'house'
bulmba dabul   'beach'
bulmba buluba   'fighting ground'
bulmba burray   'cave'

Note that *burray* can occur with *walba* or with *bulmba*, further suggesting that the classifiers are not strictly exclusive of each other. We could have, in fact, a noun phrase containing *bulmba walba burray* (just as we could also have *miña mangum yalburr* 'edible-animal frog-genus grey-frog-species').

But the conditions on co-occurrence of these terms appeared, on investigation, not to be straightforward. For instance, we can have *wirra walba*, but not *wirra bunda. And whereas *jugi* can mean 'tree', 'wood', or 'stick', *wirra jugi* must be referring to a stick, not a growing tree. Similarly, *wirra jabu* is a possible collocation for describing a handful of dirt, but *wirra* cannot be used with *jabu* when it refers just to 'ground'. It seemed that *wirra* could only be applied to something that was movable.

It was plainly necessary to take stock, and try to discern what the semantic basis of the classifiers was. It was also becoming hard to decide exactly which words should be considered classifiers. *Jama*, for instance, is used to refer to anything harmful— dangerous snakes, centipede, stinging trees, strong drink, opium (or, I was told, medicine—presumably classed as *jama* because of its unpleasant taste). It is used most

often to refer to snakes and sometimes seemed to be a generic term 'snake'. Was *jama*
to be regarded as a classifier, like *miña, walba, jarruy*, and the rest? Some criterion was
obviously needed for deciding what was a classifier.

A criterion emerged by chance. I had also been having trouble with the inanimate
interrogative-indefinites *wañi* and *wañirra*; both had been glossed as 'what' or 'something'. I could not find any difference in their meaning or use, but the reaction of consultants made me feel that they were not free variants. Finally, I discovered that *wañi* is
used to refer to an object concerning which nothing is known—it enquires about the
genus. In contrast, *wañirra* is used when it is known which generic classifier the object
comes under, and the actual species name is being sought. *Wañi* is 'what (genus)?';
wañirra is '(genus being known) what (species)?' A typical exchange involving these
forms would be:

(9) PERSON A wañi$_S$ gali-ŋ
               WHAT.GENUS go-PRESENT
               What is that going (along there)?

    PERSON B miña$_S$ gali-ŋ
               animal go-PRESENT
               It's an animal [CLASSIFIER] going (along there)

    PERSON A [wañi:rra   miña]$_S$ juŋga-ŋ
               WHAT.SPECIES animal run-PRESENT
               What sort of animal [CLASSIFIER] is it running (along)?

    PERSON B [miña gangu:l]$_S$ warri-ŋ
               animal wallaby   jump-PRESENT
               It's an animal [CLASSIFIER] wallaby jumping (along)

I checked instances of *wañirra* in my corpus of texts and found that almost every one
occurred with a classifier: *wañirra mayi* 'what type of vegetable?', *wañirra jarruy* 'what
species of bird?', and so on. Further checking showed that a criterion for whether a
word belonged to the set of classifiers was whether it could occur with *wañirra*. (*Jama*
was found to be excluded.)

Note the alternation of verbs in the utterances of (9), to create a felicitous discourse:
gali-ŋ 'go', *juŋga-ŋ* 'move fast, run', and *warri-ŋ* 'jump'.

3.3 Semantic basis of classifiers

Classifiers are of two distinct types.

[I] Those classifying specific nouns according to the INHERENT NATURE of their
     referents—*bama* 'person', *mangum* 'frog', *jugi* 'tree', *buri* 'fire', *walba* 'stone', *jabu*
     'solid inanimate matter other than stone or wood', and so on.

[II] Those classifying specific nouns according to the FUNCTION or USE of their referents: edible flesh food (*miña*), edible non-flesh food *(mayi)*, drinkable liquid (*bana*), habitable place (*bulmba*), purposeful noise (*gugu*), or movable thing (*wirra*).

Before discussing each classifier in turn we can, in diagram 3.1, show the way in which these two types of classificatory term divide up the universe. The dots at the extreme left refer to specific nouns; 'inherent nature' classifiers are in the left-hand column, and 'function/use' classifiers on the right. Many-to-one relations between specific terms and classifiers are shown schematically (rather than quantitatively. In total around eighty names of bird species are known, all—except for cassowary—included under *jarruy*, for instance). Where there is a natural grouping of species for which there is *no* inherent nature classifier in Yidiñ, a dash is shown in the left-hand column (for instance 'possums'). Note that in many of these cases there *is* (only) a generic term in the Yidiñ Jalnguy style, justifying recognition of a taxonomic grouping. Where a specific term appears not to be grouped with anything else—as with 'dog', 'sun', 'moon', and 'boomerang' for instance—a single horizontal line is shown.

Diagram 3.1 is intended to illustrate the scope of the score or so classifiers, rather than just to list all types of Yidiñ nouns. Dots are freely used to indicate areas for which classifiers are lacking. (Generally, just a few sample types are quoted for the non-classifier sectors—thus to 'kangaroos/wallabies' and 'possums' should be added 'snakes', 'lizards/goannas', 'turtles', 'bats', and so on.)

I. INHERENT NATURE CLASSIFIERS

(a) *waguja* 'man, human male, masculine'
(b) *buña* 'woman, human female, feminine'
(c) *bama* 'person'

This is the only instance of a hierarchy among classifiers. A noun phrase can contain *bama*, and *waguja* or *buña*, together with a specific noun, as in:

(10) ŋañji$_A$ [bama waguːja wurgun muyŋga]$_O$ gundaː-lna
    1pl.NOM person man pubescent.boy cicatrice cut-PURPOSIVE
    We should cut cicatrices (tribal marks) on the person [CLASSIFIER] man
    [CLASSIFIER] pubescent boy

The NP in O function for (10) includes two classifiers, *bama* and *waguja*, the specific noun *wurgun*, and the inalienably possessed noun *muyŋga*. There is another illustration at example T11.1 within section 7.3.1.

Beyond *bama buña* and *bama waguja*, all occurrences of two classifiers in a noun phrase must involve one 'inherent nature' term and one 'function/use' classifier.

INHERENT NATURE CLASSIFIERS   FUNCTION/USE CLASSIFIERS

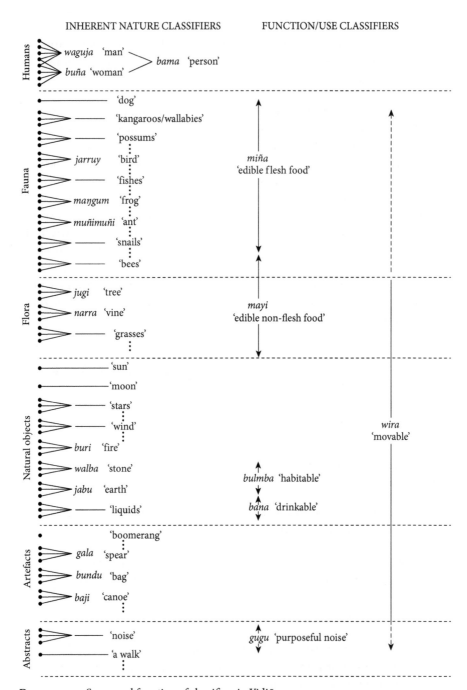

DIAGRAM 3.1 Scope and function of classifiers in Yidiñ

First published in Dixon, R.M.W (1977) *A Grammar of Yidiɲ* (Cambridge: CUP)

These three classifiers can be used with terms referring to stages of life—'baby', 'adult man', 'old woman', etc.—and with kin terms; and with proper names of people. Animals are believed to have once been 'people' and, in dreamtime legends referring to this era, the name of an animal can co-occur with *bama*. The names for ghosts and spirits (for anything not living) do not fall within the scope of *bama*.

Gaja 'spirit of a man' is also used to cover 'white man', and *guyngan* 'spirit of a woman' for 'white woman'. But whereas in the spirit senses *gaja* and *guyngan* can *not* occur with *bama* (and are restricted to the 'use' classifier, *wirra*—see below), in the 'white person' sense they *are* classified as *bama*.

Waguja and *buña* can be used, in marked circumstances, to specify the sex of an animal—thus *buña gangu:l* 'female wallaby' *waguja gangu:l* 'male wallaby' (similarly for 'dog', 'bird' etc.). In these cases *bama* could *not* be included with *waguja/buña*.

Note that there are no classifiers for body parts (or parts of any other object). A noun like *jina* 'foot' will normally be shown as inalienably possessed by some person or animal, and it is the possessor that selects the classifier.

There are only three classifiers for non-human animates in Yidiñ. Note particularly that there is no term 'fish' (in this Yidiñ differs from its neighbours, and in fact from most Australian languages); the term *miña* is employed, the context usually making it clear that it is *aquatic* edible creatures that are being referred to.

(d) *jarruy* 'bird'. This covers all birds except the giant flightless cassowary (emus do not occur in this region). Note that *jarruy* does include *jarruga* 'scrub-hen', *wawun* 'scrub-turkey' and various birds with distinct mythic roles, which are not included under the generic *dundu* in Dyirbal.

(e) *mangum* 'frog'. This classifier covers all twelve species of frog for which I have collected names. (When I asked the Yidiñ term for 'cane toad', a fairly recent invader, a consultant said that it had not yet been given a Yidiñ name but that it would certainly be called *mangum*.)

(f) *muñimuñi* 'ant'. Of the fifteen or so types of ant and termite (or white ant), each with its own species name, all but one can be classified by *muñimuñi*—thus *muñimuñi gaju:* 'black tree ant', *muñimuñi burrbal* 'red jumping ant'. The exception is *jilibura* 'green ant'; this insect has a special place in Yidiñ culture because of its medicinal properties, and it may be for this reason that it is not regarded as a type of *muñimuñi*.

Most plants are included under *jugi* 'tree' or *narra* 'vine'. Note that although there are half-a-dozen specific terms for types of grass (and a few more for types of tree-fern, weed, and seaweed) there are no classifiers applicable here.

(g) *jugi* 'tree'. The semantic extension of this term appears (as far as can be determined) to be about coextensive with the English noun 'tree'. Thus *jugi* covers even fairly low plants such as *nulugun* 'small pandanus' (which would not be included within the scope of the generic noun 'tree' in Dyirbal, for instance). Harmful plants—such as the stinging tree *giya:r*—are also regarded as a type of *jugi*.

(h) *narra* 'vine'. This classifier is used with more than a dozen specific nouns, including the vines of ground vegetables such as yams, and vines growing on trees—for instance, *mudi* 'thick black edible lawyer vine (*Calamus moti*, the species designation being based on the Yidiñ name)'.

There are three classifiers referring to types of natural phenomena. Note that there are no classifiers dealing with celestial objects or meteorological events.

(i) *buri* 'fire'. As indicated above, anything burning is included within the scope of *buri*. Thus we can have:

buri birmar '(hot) charcoal'
buri mimi   'a flying spark'
buri ŋañjal 'a light (from a burning torch)'

and even *buri wuñju* '(hot) smoke'. The class of *buri* nouns makes up almost the whole set of possible subjects for *guba-n* 'burn', a transitive verb that requires an inanimate subject (there is another verb *waju-l* 'burn, cook' which takes a human subject). The exception is *buŋan* 'sun' which can be the subject of *guba-n*, although it is not included under *buri*. (Note also that 'lightning' is not regarded as a type of *buri*.)

(j) *walba* 'stone'. This classifier can be used for any movable rock or pebble, or for a geographical feature made of stone; thus:

walba bayŋga   'a stone heated in the fire and thrust inside a dead animal
                in kapamari (earth oven) cooking'
walba jarruway 'a small hill, or island'
walba garbi   'an overhanging mountain ledge'

(k) *jabu* 'ground'. This term is complementary to *walba*. Any type of terrain that is not covered by *walba* is describable as *jabu*. Thus *jabu* can be used with a noun describing any type of earth or ground:

jabu gabuju   'white clay'
jabu jalmbul 'mud'
jabu gulgi   'sand'
jabu ŋumbun   'heaps of soft sand'

Or a place that is characterised by a particular sort of ground: *jabu dabul* 'beach'.

There are three classifiers referring to types of implement. Note that these only cover a fraction of the traditional artefacts known to the Yidiñji. There are no classifiers for woomeras (just two specific names *jarin* 'straight woomera' and *balur* 'curved woomera'), yamsticks, axes, knives, or traps (quite apart from items like boomerang and shield, which do not naturally group with anything else).

(1) *gala* 'spear'. There are half-a-dozen types of spear, all with rather specific uses. They include *gala baŋgur* 'multi-prong fish-spear' and *gala birji* 'small hook spear'.

(m) *bundu* 'bag'. This is apparently a classifier for any type of traditional basket. Only two hyponyms are known *bundu dugubil* 'bark bag' and *bundu jurbal* '(small) woven grass basket'. But note that *bundu* is used by itself as the specific name for a dilly-bag plaited from lawyer-cane (the commonest type of carrier for the olden-times Yidiñji). *Bundu* does not extend to metal containers, such as *biligan* 'billy can'.

(n) *baji* 'canoe'. It seems likely that this was a classifier. It has been encountered with only two specific nouns *baji bida* 'bark canoe' or 'bark trough' (for soaking nuts, etc.) and *baji ginu* 'dug-out canoe' (I was assured that *ginu* is not a loan).

There are two other terms that might possibly be regarded as 'inherent nature' classifiers—*jiguːrr* 'thunderstorm' and *jaŋga* 'hole'. On balance of evidence it seems that they should not be placed in the set of classifiers. Discussion will be found in Dixon (1977a: 488–9).

II. FUNCTION/USE CLASSIFIERS

(a) *miña* 'edible animal'. This term is used for anything animate that is habitually eaten by the Yidiñji. Some species covered by *muñimuñi* 'ant' are eaten, while others are considered inedible; thus *gajuː* 'black tree ant' and *burrbal* 'red jumping ant' are *miña*, but *gujin* 'bull ant' and *balawa* 'sugar ant with red head and black body' are not. Similarly for *mangum* 'frog'. It appears that all birds—included under the 'inherent nature' classifier *jarruy*—are edible.

It is interesting that an edible animal will not be referred to by *miña* in a context in which its being eaten is not the point at issue. One story tells how a woman who was bathing in a river came to be seized by a crocodile, but was later rescued. If a crocodile were being hunted for its meat, it would be referred to as *miña*. But in this story the crocodile is the aggressor—it is a question of the crocodile eating the woman, rather than the Yidiñji people eating the reptile—and it is nowhere referred to as *miña*.

An animal may only be described as *miña* when it reaches a size sufficient to warrant killing and eating. Any dish made from meat—for instance, 'stew'—is also *miña*. Egg, *diñal*, is regarded as a type of flesh food, and is also included within the scope of *miña*.

The class of *miña* includes all kangaroos/wallabies, possums, bandicoots, bats, turtles, goannas, grubs, eels, most fishes, and some snakes, lizards, frogs, rats, snails, as well as echidna (porcupine), platypus, and cow. Note that—for speakers of Yidiñ—some (but not all) poisonous snakes are eaten, as is the potentially harmful gar-fish (but the stone-fish and toad-fish are not considered edible). The remaining classes of insects—flies, leeches, grasshoppers, spiders, worms, cockroaches, etc.—are never eaten. One potential source of meat, the dog, could never be called *miña*; people in all parts of Australia felt a close relationship to the dog (sometimes including it within the kinship system—Thomson 1945: 166)—and certainly the Yidiñji would never have considered eating a dog. (Horses are, perhaps for similar reasons, also excluded from the class of *miña*.)

(b) *mayi* 'edible plant'. This term covers all sorts of non-flesh food. In Yidiñ the same name may be applied to, say, a tree and to anything obtained from it—*badil* is both a rickety nut, and the rickety nut tree. Generally, *jugi badil* would be used to describe the timber of this tree, while *mayi badil* refers to the fruit (although *jugi mayi badil* is perfectly normal—referring to the tree and its fruit). *Mayi* terms comprise a subset of *jugi* 'tree', a subset of *narra* 'vine' and also a number of plant species that are not included under any 'inherent nature' classifier—for instance *jalgaram* 'flat bottle fern'.

The most interesting aspect of *mayi* (to a speaker of English) is that it also covers bees and honey. As in Dyirbal, honey is classed as a non-flesh food, coming within the scope of *mayi*, and in Yidiñ the bees that make the honey are placed in the same category. Thus, among others:

mayi muruy   'slatey-grey native bee (and its honey)'
mayi banga   'small black native bee (and its honey)'
mayi yiŋgilibiy 'English bee (and its honey)'

Jumbagi 'tobacco' is not regarded as *mayi*, although it can be chewed as well as smoked. Yidiñ here differs from Dyirbal, which does place 'tobacco' in its 'non-flesh food' gender.

(c) *bana* 'drinkable liquid'. This is used as the unmarked term for referring to 'fresh water' (just as *miña* can, when it occurs without any other noun, often be translated as 'meat' and *mayi* as 'vegetables', and *buri* used alone indicates 'fire'). *Bana* is also used as a classifier with a noun referring to a water feature: spring, creek, lake, rain, dew, steam, and so on. It cannot be used with blood, sweat, urine, spittle, or any other type of liquid that is not normally consumed.

The use of *bana* with nouns referring to 'salt water' might be thought to constitute an exception to the 'drinkable' criterion. However, study of the meaning and use of the adjective *gilga* sheds some light on this apparent anomaly. *Gilga* is used to indicate anything imperfect or inadequate for its purpose—'soft wood (that will break easily if made into an implement)'or 'a weak (easily breakable) fishing line'. 'Salt water' is characterised as *gilga*—the consultant stressed that it is 'soft' just like 'soft wood'. *Birriñ* is thus regarded as 'contaminated or inadequate *bana*'. Just as a soft wood will be described as *jugi*, although it could not be used for anything, so salt water is included under *bana*, although it could not be drunk.

Salt water is thus held to belong to the same category as fresh water, but to be an imperfect instance of it. It contrasts with blood, urine, semen, etc., which are assigned to a quite different category.

Bana is also used with nouns such as *gulbul* 'wave' (which can of course occur on freshwater lakes as well as on the sea) and *bajagal* 'tide'.

(d) *bulmba* 'habitable place'. This classifier can be used with a noun referring to a hut or type of structure; for example:

> bulmba yiwan   'shelter for one person'
> bulmba dugur   'hut holding two or three people'
> bulmba jimu:rr 'hut holding from half-a-dozen to ten people'

Or with a description of any geographical feature at which one might camp (some examples were given in section 3.2). For instance, a consultant said that *bulmba walba* only made sense if it were *bulmba walba malan*—one could only camp at a rock *(walba)* if it were a flat rock *(malan)*.

Bulmba, used without any other noun, can be translated 'place'—it can refer either to an actual camping-site (so that if one says 'I'm going back home to sleep', *bulmba* would be used for 'home') or else to any past or potential camping place. *Bulmba* also has a more general meaning, 'the world' (as in 'God made the world')—here 'the world' is effectively identified as the complete set of places at which people can live. (The sky above a place is also regarded as part of that *bulmba* 'place'.)

Just as *bama* commonly occurs with the names of people, so *bulmba* can be used with place names. Similarly, *bana* occurs with the names of lakes, rivers, and creeks; and *bunda* 'mountain' or *jarruway* 'island, small hill'—both hyponyms of *walba* 'stone'—with the names of rocky features.

(e) *gugu* 'purposeful noise'. Yidiñ has more than two dozen specific nouns for referring to different types of noise. Some are animal or language noises:

> gugu gawal   'a call'
> gugu gugulu   'a recitative mourning style used by men'
> gugu gayagay 'a whisper'
> gugu ñurrugu 'the sound of talking a long way off (when the words
>   cannot quite be made out)'
> gugu jubun   'squeaky noise made by young animal'

while others are noises of banging or clapping or sawing, and so on:

gugu maral   'the noise of a person clapping their hands together'
gugu mida   'the noise of a person clicking their tongue against the
                       roof of their mouth, or the noise of an eel hitting the water'
gugu gada   'the noise of sticks being banged together for dance
                       accompaniment'
gugu dalŋudalŋu 'the noise of a bell ringing'

It appears that *gugu* is used with the name of any sound that results from some person or animal *purposefully* making a noise. That is, this classifier covers all controlled
attempts at communication (including, of course, all types of language and para-
language activity e.g. *gugu* occurs with *gurru:n* 'language'). It can be used with the
name of an animal, to describe the noise it makes—for instance, *gugu jigirrjigirr* 'the
call of a willy wagtail bird'.

However, *gugu* does not cover 'involuntary noises', that are side-effects of
some other activity. That is, the following nouns are *not* included in the scope of
gugu:

yuyururŋgul 'the noise ("shshshsh") of a snake sliding through grass'
gaŋga   'the noise of some person approaching, e.g. the sound of
                   their feet on leaves or through the grass, or even the
                   sound of a walking-stick being dragged along the ground'
duŋur   'reverberations caused by someone walking over
                   floorboards, or treading heavily over the ground outside'

(f) *wirra* 'movable object'. This is perhaps the most difficult and most interesting classifier. It is translated as 'thing' by consultants and occurs most frequently with the
names of artefacts like 'boomerang', 'shield', 'saddle', and also 'stick', 'stone', and so on. I
was told that *wirra* could only be used of something movable—*wirra walba* could be
a stone, but not a mountain, *wirra jabu* a handful of soil or sand, but not the ground
itself, and *wirra jugi* a stick but not a tree. It can be used for the sun and moon which
certainly move in the sky, and for wind and cloud.

Wirra cannot be used for anything that is describable as *miña*, *mayi*, or *bana*
(since the Yidiñji did not camp on anything movable, it is impossible for *wirra*
and *bulmba* to be applied to the same object). It does thus appear to be defined as,
in a way, a residue set—*after* all other nature/use classifiers have been assigned.
Most things that are not included under *miña*, *mayi*, or *bana* can—if movable—be
classed as *wirra*. Thus *wirra* covers non-drinkable liquids (like blood) and inedible
fruits; and even noises (like *gaŋga*) that are not *gugu*. It can be used for inedible
insects and reptiles (although it is not too frequent in this sense) but would not be

employed with a noun like *gudaga* 'dog'. *Wirra* is used with severed body parts, and with excretions (faeces and urine). It occurs with the names of spirits, such as the rainbow-serpent.

Wirra also has a quite different use; it is a crude term for referring to female genitalia, with very similar overtones to the English term 'cunt'. It appears that these two senses of *wirra* did not cause confusion, the context indicating whether the speaker was employing a nominal classifier (probably a feature of good style) or whether they were swearing. (The two senses are certainly related—compare with the use of 'thing' for genitalia in colloquial English.)

Some specific nouns can co-occur with two distinct classifiers (there are no examples of occurrence with more than two). Leaving aside *bama buña* 'person woman' and *bama waguja* 'person man', these cases always include one 'inherent nature' and one 'function/use' classifier. Examples involving animals (*miña* plus *mangum*, *muñimuñi* or *jarruy*) and plants (*mayi* plus *jugi* or *narra*) have already been quoted, as has *burray* 'cave' with *walba* 'stone' and/or *bulmba* 'habitable place'.

A piece of hot charcoal (*nirrgil*), say, can be described as *buri* and as *wirra*, and a plot of ground as both *jabu* and *bulmba*. Some co-occurrences are less predictable: a tree species, *diwiy*, holds water inside its bark (which can be tapped and drunk) yielding *bana diwiy* in addition to *jugi diwiy*.

Finally, loan items are sometimes dealt with through unusual combinations of classifier and specific noun: *gulgi* 'sand' normally falls within the scope of *jabu* 'ground'—referring to a patch of sand—or of *wirra* 'movable object'—referring to a handful of sand. In recent times 'sugar' has been described as *mayi gulgi*—it looks and feels like sand, but it is edible.

In other cases introduced items may, in the absence of any appropriate specific term, be described simply by a classifier. I recorded the story of the first aeroplane sighted in Cairns; the plane was simply described as *wirra* throughout the text. Similarly, in one text *gurru:n* was used to refer to the English language, in the absence of any specific name. And we mentioned earlier that the cane toad could be described only as *mangum*.

Most (or perhaps all) languages north of Yidiñ in the Cape York Peninsula have sets of classifiers, on a similar pattern to Yidiñ. In the grammatical introduction to his *Yir-Yoront lexicon*, Alpher (1991: 72–7) lists a set of 'generics' and provides fine exemplification of them within the dictionary; however, he gives little information concerning their grammatical functioning. Extending the work by Hall (1972: 70–1), Gaby (2006: 81–3, 279–83, 334–6) lists eighteen generics for Kuuk Thaayorre; she provides an outline of their semantics, and useful information concerning functions within the grammar.

Some information has been made available by Thomson (1945: 165–7) on Wik-Monkan, by Sutton (1978: 273–4) on Wik-Ngathana, and by Sommer (1972: 74–80) on Oykangand. Although these three writers each list a dozen or so classifiers, none has attempted a full listing or semantic study.

For further discussion of generics and classifiers in Australian languages, see Dixon (2002a: 449–60).

3.4 Comparing Dyirbal genders and Yidiñ classifiers

The system of four genders in Dyirbal and the set of twenty or so noun classifiers in Yidiñ each encodes a great deal of semantic information but in dissimilar ways, due to their different roles in the language.

Dyirbal does have a few generic nouns ('tree', 'snake', 'fish', 'bird') but only occasionally includes them in a noun phrase with a specific noun. They are used in general statements ('there are lots of fishes in this river') or when the identity of some referent cannot be further determined ('I saw a snake's tail disappearing'). In contrast, a classifier will generally occur in an NP together with an appropriate specific noun.

Consider a type of tree which has the same name in the two languages: *wuray* 'Davidson plum (*Davidsonia pruriens*)'. Either the timber or the fruit can be referred to, this being achieved through a classifier in Yidiñ and by a gender marker in Dyirbal:

(11)   in Yidiñ   in Dyirbal
       referring to timber: jugi wuray   bala wuray
       referring to fruit: mayi wuray balam wuray

Dyirbal does have generic terms *yugu* 'tree' and *wuju* 'non-flesh food', roughly corresponding to *jugi* and *mayi*. As illustrated at (22) in the preceding chapter, these could be added to the NPs in (11) for special emphasis, but the gender markers should be retained: *bala yugu wuray* and *balam wuju wuray*.

Every noun in Dyirbal relates to a gender (only a few relate to more than one). In contrast, not all nouns in Yidiñ come under the scope of a classifier (*gudaga* 'dog' does not, for instance), and a good few of them can occur with two classifiers, sometimes simultaneously.

One similarity is the way in which both genders and classifiers help to distinguish between the word classes Adjective and Noun. As shown in (7) of the previous chapter, in Dyirbal an adjective can generally occur with any of the four gender markers whereas a noun is restricted to one (just occasionally, two). In Yidiñ, an adjective can co-occur with any classifier—subject to semantic plausibility—whereas a noun may occur with no classifier at all, or with just one or two.

Neither Dyirbal nor Yidiñ has any 3rd person pronouns. The anaphoric role played by 3rd person pronouns in other languages is in Dyirbal partly fulfilled by gender-specified noun markers—see the discussion of example (6) in chapter 2. Classifiers in Yidiñ also play an anaphoric role—see example (4) above—although more restricted than that of noun markers in Dyirbal.

It will be useful briefly to survey a number of semantic fields, examining the ways in which they are treated in the two languages.

(1) **People.** Classifiers *waguja* and *buña*, and genders *bayi* and *balan*, refer to men and women, and can also be extended to indicate male and female animals. But whereas

bayi and *balan* are also used for male and female spirits and legendary people, *waguja* and *buña* are restricted to living entities.

(2) **Fire.** Classifier *buri* covers things burning and hot, which is one of the basic concepts associated with the *balan* gender.

(3) **Drinkable liquids.** Classifier *bana* has roughly the same scope as another basic concept of the *balan* gender, 'drinkable liquids', both languages including seawater as a deficient type. However 'dew' is included under classifier *bana* in Yidiñ, whereas in Dyirbal it takes gender marker *bala* rather than *balan*.

(4) **Fighting.** Another basic concept associated with the *balan* gender is 'fighting'. The fighting ground is *balan buya*, contrasted with the general term for any other kind of place, *bala mija*. Yidiñ has no special indicator for fighting; the fighting ground, *buluba*, is like all other places, within the scope of classifier *bulmba* 'habitable place'. And there is in Yidiñ no indicator for which implements are fighting weapons.

(5) **Non-human animates.** Dyirbal does have a generic term *dundu* 'bird' but this does not include about twenty birds which were characters in legend (including the cassowary), or are birds of prey. In contrast, the Yidiñ classifier *jarruy* appears to cover all birds except the flightless cassowary (which does not have a classifier).

It is interesting to note that Dyirbal does have generic nouns 'snake' and 'fish', for which there are no corresponding classifiers. And that Yidiñ has classifiers 'frog' and 'ant', for which there are no generic terms in Dyirbal.

(6) **Plant food.** Yidiñ classifier *mayi* has very similar scope to the *bala-m* gender in Dyirbal. (Indeed, gender suffix *-m* is likely to have had its origin in *mayi*.) Both include honey; a difference is that in Dyirbal honey is *balam* and the bees which produce it are *bala*, whereas in Yidiñ the same name is used for a bee and its honey, all under *mayi*.

(7) **Flesh food.** Dyirbal makes a clear distinction between *bayi rubiñ*, for anything living which could be eaten once it is dead, and *bala jalgur*, for the meat of a dead animal. Yidiñ uses classifier *miña* for both.

The dictionary of Yidiñ (Dixon 1991a) attempts to specify for every plant whether or not it is edible, and comes under classifier *mayi*. Exactly the same information is provided in the Dyirbal dictionary (in preparation) through a notation for each plant name concerning whether it is *balam*.

The Yidiñ dictionary also attempts to specify, for every animate creature, whether it falls under classifier *miña*; that is, whether it is edible. In this respect Yidiñ is superior to Dyirbal. There is in the latter language no grammatical marking for animates being edible, nothing that would automatically be included in a dictionary (unless it were extended to be something of an encyclopaedia).

Classifiers such as *gugu* 'purposeful noise' and *wirra* 'moveable object' also supply information which is missing from Dyirbal. But, on the other side of the ledger, Dyirbal stands apart in the subtleties of its principles of gender assignment and transfer— showing that sun and moon are husband and wife, that the rainbow is a legendary man, that birds are the spirits of dead women, that certain snakes are edible, that a number of fishes are harmful, and much more.

A major difference is that the organisation of classifiers in Yidiñ is essentially taxonomic, whereas the semantic basis for gender classes in Dyirbal involves principles of association and highlighted contrast. Legends and cultural beliefs play a significant role in the assignment of gender in Dyirbal. There is no evidence that legends and belief play any similar role in Yidiñ.

Whereas chapter 2 is a considerable expansion and revision of my previous writings on gender in Dyirbal, the facts and discussion of Yidiñ classifiers, in this chapter, are basically the same as in that section of the grammar (Dixon 1977a: 480–96), repeated in slightly revised form as a chapter in Dixon (1982a: 185–205). There has been some up-dating and adjustment for the present chapter, and section 3.4 is almost entirely new.

Part II

Kin Relations and How to Talk with Them

An indigenous Australian society was one large family. In Dyirbal, for instance, there were twenty-five categories of kin, and each member of the tribe would belong to one of them, with respect to ego. A series of algorithmic-type rules determine kin relations; for instance, a woman's sister and a man's brother count as equivalent to that woman and that man, respectively. The kin term *bayi gaya* has primary reference to mother's younger brother, but also encompasses mother's father's younger brother's son, mother's mother's younger sister's son, and so on. If there were about 500 people in a tribe, there would be around twenty in each of the twenty-five kin categories (such as *bayi gaya*) with respect to ego.

'Family' has a different connotation for indigenous Australians from that which it has in western society. Our family includes both consanguineal kin (blood relations)—such as grandparents, parents, siblings, children—and also affinal kin (those related through marriage)—spouse, and all the in-laws. Relationships in indigenous Australian society were entirely consanguineal (a 'classificatory kinship system'). There were no affinal categories per se; potential affines were determined consanguineally. One should marry the child of a woman who was classed as *balan waymin*; this 'potential mother-in-law' category includes mother's elder brother's daughter, father's elder sister's daughter, and so on.

That is, a woman does not become a man's mother-in-law by virtue of his marrying her daughter (an affinal link). Instead, he is allowed to marry her daughter by virtue of the fact that she is in the *balan waymin* category to him (a consanguineal link). Details of the kinship system for Dyirbal are set out in chapter 4.

Social responsibilities were established by kin relationships—who should be responsible for overseeing a boy's initiation, what role each person should play in organising someone's funeral. The kin relation between two people determined how they could behave together. There was a trusting and convivial rapport between a woman and her *bayi gaya* 'mother's younger brother, etc.' Ego would have a normal, neutral relation with parents, with siblings, and with 'parallel cousins' (mother's sisters' and father's brothers' children), who were named and treated as siblings.

But the children of 'cross-cousins' (mother's brothers' and father's sisters') were to be avoided. Cross-cousins through an elder-sibling link in the parent's generation are *balan waymin* 'potential mother-in-law' and *bayi ñubi* 'potential father-in-law'. Those through a younger-sibling link in the parent's generation are *balan guyugan* 'potential daughter-in-law' and *bayi wuribu* 'potential son-in-law'. None of these 'avoidance' categories of kin should be looked at, and they should not be spoken to directly.

A special speech style, Jalnguy (colloquially, 'mother-in-law' style), had to be used in the presence of avoidance kin, the potential affines. Phonetics, phonology, and grammar are identical between Jalnguy and the everyday language style. However, every verb, adjective, and noun (save for four grandparent terms) is different. The many-to-one correspondences between lexemes in the everyday style and Jalnguy were illustrated in section 1.2. There is, in chapter 5, a full account of when and how Jalnguy was used, its semantic organisation, the structure of its words, and the nature of correspondences with the everyday style.

When I began serious work on Yidiñ, in 1971, it had slipped further towards oblivion than had Dyirbal. It was not possible to ascertain the full kinship system (see Dixon 1991a: 146–8). However, two old speakers were able to remember about 190 lexemes in their avoidance style, also called Jalnguy (as against the more than 600 items I had been able to collect for Dyirbal Jalnguy). Chapter 6 is a comparative investigation of the avoidance vocabularies in the two languages, examining their nature and origins.

Unfortunately, the last couple of old speakers of Warrgamay were unable to remember the kinship system, or the avoidance vocabulary, although they did recall that there had been one.

4

The Dyirbal kinship system

Speakers of Dyirbal have an unusual (and possibly unique) kinship system. Marriage takes place with someone not from ego's own generation but a generation above or below. A cross-cousin through an elder-sibling link at the parents' generation (i.e. mother's elder brother's child, father's elder sister's child) is a potential mother-in-law or father-in-law; ego may marry the child of such a relation. It follows from this that ego may also marry the child of a younger opposite-sex sibling of a grandparent (e.g. mother's mother's younger brother's child). The system is quite symmetrical with regard to sex; similar results are obtained whether one starts with a male or female ego, and whether one traces relationships through father or through mother.

Following exposition of the rules of the kinship system, we examine how these are actually put into practice. Justification for the kin categories is also provided by linguistic observations on (i) the possible subjects of 'verbs of begetting'; (ii) dual forms of kin terms; (iii) the correspondences in the Jalnguy (or 'mother-in-law') speech style; (iv) the kinship basis of the two 1st person dual pronouns.

This is a classificatory kinship system in which consanguineal links determine whom ego may marry. There are twenty-five kin categories with respect to ego. Although they are glossed with what consultants consider to be the primary denotatum (e.g. MeB), it must be borne in mind that many other kin are included in accordance with well-known Australian principles of classification (Radcliffe-Brown 1930–31).

It was possible to gather kinship data from speakers of the Ngajan, Mamu, Jirrbal, and Girramay dialects. The same basic kinship system appears to have applied across the whole language area. There were some dialectal variations, and these will be mentioned below when they shed light on a particular analytic point. The fullest data come from Jirrbal speakers and, unless stated otherwise, Jirrbal terms are used.

I gathered extensive genealogies—extending two or three generations back—for about a dozen extended families (including over 200 individuals) and worked through these with six elderly people who had a full grasp of the kinship system. I asked each consultant what they would call each person on each chart, and also enquired how various other, younger, people should properly address certain relatives. A complete picture of the rules of the Dyirbal kinship system was built up inductively, over a period of several years.

The manner in which consultants answered questions was often revealing of the inner workings of the system. Andy Denham, when asked how he would address some far-off relative, sometimes thought aloud: 'let me see, my mother would call that person's father "elder brother" so that means that . . . '. It was in this way that I first became aware of the importance of the elder- versus younger-sibling distinction.

At a later stage I again went through the basic data, focusing now on what appeared to be 'exceptions'. In every case, consultants recognised the validity of my query, and offered an explanation. For instance, Bessie Jerry said that Jack Muriata should be *gaya* (MyB) to her, in terms of consanguineal linkage, but she called him *ñurra* since he was married to her sister, and a sister's husband is normally expected to be in the *ñurra* class.

Standard abbreviations are used: M, mother; F, father; B, brother; Z, sister; S, son; D, daughter; W, wife; H, husband; Sib, sibling; Ch, child; Sp, spouse; e, elder; y, younger; ♀, female ego; ♂, male ego.

4.1 The basic kin terms

It is convenient to divide the basic Dyirbal kin terms into nine sets, A to I.

A. Grandparents and grandchildren

gumbu   MM, MMB, MMZ; MFW, MFBW, MFZH, etc; ♀DCh
ŋagi   MF, MFB, MFZ; MMH, MMBW, MMZH, etc; ♂DCh
babi   FM, FMB, FMZ; FFW, FFBW, FFZH, etc; ♀SCh
bulu   FF, FFB, FFZ; FMH, FMBW, FMZH, etc; ♂SCh

Speakers state that the primary denotation of *gumbu* is MM, *balan gumbu*; MMZ are also *balan gumbu* and MMB are *bayi gumbu*; we can say that the prototypical gender of *gumbu* is *balan*, and the extended or non-prototypical gender is *bayi*. *Bayi ŋagi* covers MF and MFB while MFZ is *balan ŋagi*. The spouse of *gumbu* is expected to be called *ŋagi*, and vice versa. That is, the husband of *balan gumbu* is *bayi ŋagi* and the wife of *bayi gumbu* is *balan ŋagi*. Exactly the same comments apply to *babi* and *bulu*. We shall see later that particular significance attaches to those grandparent terms that have non-prototypical gender—*bayi gumbu*, *balan ŋagi*, *bayi babi*, and *balan bulu*.

Each of these four terms is its own reciprocal—if a child calls a grandparent *gumbu* then the grandparent will call the child *gumbu* (*bayi gumbu* for a male and *balan gumbu* for a female grandchild), and so on.

B. Father and his siblings

bayi ŋuma   F, FyB, MH, MyZH; FFyBS, FMyZS, etc.
balan ŋalban FyZ, MyBW; FFyBD, FMyZD, etc.
bayi bimu   FeB, MeZH; FFeBS, FMeZS, etc.
balan bimu   FeZ, MeBW; FFeBD, FMeZD, etc.

C. Mother and her siblings

balan yabu	M, MyZ, FW, FyBW; MFyBD, MMyZD, etc.
bayi gaya	MyB, FyZH; MFyBS, MMyZS, etc.
balan mugunan	MeZ, FeBW, MFeBD, MMeZD, etc.
bayi mugu	MeB, FeZH; MFeBS, MMeZS, etc.

A *yabu* who is not an actual mother can be referred to as *yabu jarraga*, which can be shortened to just *jarraga*. Similarly, a *ŋuma* who is not the actual begetter is, more specifically, *ŋuma galŋan*. *Jarraga* and *galŋan* were glossed by bilingual consultants as 'step-mother' and 'step-father' respectively.

Note that *bayi ŋuma* should be married to *balan yabu*, *balan ŋalban* to *bayi gaya*, *bayi bimu* to *balan mugunan*, and *balan bimu* to *bayi mugu*.

The children of same-sex siblings of grandparents will always be named from sets B and C—maternal grandparents; nephews and nieces from set C, and those of paternal grandparents from set B. If the grandparent's sibling is older than the grandparent then their children will be referred to by the term for an older uncle or aunt, and so on. Thus MFeBS = MeB, *bayi mugu*; FMyZS = FyB, *bayi ŋuma*.

In the northern dialects, Ngajan and Mamu, there are only two basic terms for father and his siblings, and two for mother and her siblings. Quoting the Mamu forms, *ŋuma* covers F and all FB, *ŋalban* is used for all FZ, *yabu* is M and all MZ while *gaya* is all MB. (The northern dialects do use *bimu*, *mugu*, and *mugunan*, but only as optional 'polite' terms at the Nyalal level—see section 4.2 below.)

D. Children

galbin	♂Ch, BCh, etc.
daman	♀Ch, ZCh, etc.

Terms for offspring code the sex of the parent, not of the child. The child's sex is of course indicated by the gender marker—*bayi daman* is a woman's son and *balan daman* her daughter.

The sisters and brothers of a man will refer to his children as *galbin*, just as he does; similarly, the sisters and brothers of a woman will refer to her children as *daman*, just as she does. Thus, the reciprocal of the terms under B (*ŋuma*, *ŋalban*, and *bimu*) is *galbin*, and the reciprocal of those under C (*yabu*, *gaya*, *mugunan*, and *mugu*) is *daman*.

E. Siblings

jurgay	Sib; MZCh, FBCh; SpSibSp; etc.
bayi mugirray	eB; MeZS, FeBS; WeZH, HeZH: etc.
bayi yabuju	yB; MyZS, FyBS; WyZH, HyZH; etc.
balan yayin	eZ; MeZD, FeBD; WeBW, HeBW; etc.
balan jaman	yZ; MyZD, FyBD; WyBW, HyBW; etc.

Bayi/balan jurgay is a generic term referring to all siblings—both true siblings and also classificatory siblings such as the children of mother's sisters and of father's brothers ('parallel cousins'). It can be used interchangeably with the appropriate specific term for elder/younger brother/sister. *Bayi mugirray* refers to one's own **elder** brother, or to the son of mother's **elder** sister or father's **elder** brother, and also to the husband of a spouse's **elder** sister, whether or not that cousin, etc. is himself older or younger than ego, i.e. it is the relative age of the **actual** sibling link that counts. Similarly for the other three terms.

The reciprocal of a *jurgay* term is also a *jurgay* term, in the pairs: *mugirray/yabuju*, *mugirray/jaman*, *yayin/yabuju*, *yayin/jaman*.

F. Potential spouse

balan bulgu (a) ♂FeZChD, ♂MeBChD; ♂MMyBD, ♂FMyBD,
              ♂MFyZD, ♂FFyZD; etc.
           (b) W, WZ, ♂BW

bayi wirru (a) ♀FeZChS, ♀MeBChS; ♀MMyBS, ♀FMyBS,
              ♀MFyZS, ♀FFyZS; etc.
           (b) H, HB, ♀ZH

These two terms can be defined either consanguineally, in terms of parent and sibling links, as in (a), or affinally, in terms of marriage links, as in (b). It is a major thesis of this chapter that the consanguineal specification, under (a), is primary. For any man there is a set of *bulgu* 'potential wives', and these include the grand-daughters of MeB, FeZ; etc.

The reciprocal of *balan bulgu* is always *bayi wirru*, and vice versa. It is worth noting that in the Ngajan dialect a single term, *muɲun*, corresponds to both *bulgu* and *wirru* in other dialects, the gender marker serving as a sufficient differentiator—*balan muɲun* 'potential wife' and *bayi muɲun* 'potential husband'.

G. Potential spouse's opposite-sex sibling

ñurra (a) ♀FeZChD, ♂FeZChS, ♀MeBChD, ♂MeBChS; ♀MMyBD,
          ♂MMyBS, ♀FMyBD, ♂FMyBS, ♀MFyZD, ♂MFyZS
          ♀FFyZD, ♂FFyZS; etc.
       (b) WB, HZ, ♂ZH, ♀BW

Bulgu/wirru and *ñurra* differ only in that *bulgu/wirru* must be of the opposite sex to ego, whereas *ñurra* must be of the same sex. *Ñurra* is an opposite sex sibling to ego's *bulgu/wirru*, and vice versa; that is, *ñurra* is someone who would be a potential marriage partner if they were of the opposite sex. *Ñurra* is the most familiar of all relationships. It is always its own reciprocal.

H. Cross-cousins through a parent's elder sibling/potential parents-in-law

balan waymin (a) MeBD, FeZD; etc.

(b) HM, WM; HMZ, HFZ, WMZ, WFZ

bayi ñubi (a) MeBS, FeZS; etc.

(b) HF, WF; HMB, HFB, WMB, WFB

As with *bulgu, wirru,* and *ñurra,* these two terms may be defined either (a) consanguineally or (b) affinally. We shall show that the consanguineal specification is prior. All cross-cousins through a parent's elder sibling are classed as *waymin* if female and *ñubi* if male; the daughter of such a kinsperson is classed as *bulgu* (for a man), and a man's wife should come from the *bulgu* class. Thus *waymin/ñubi* is a potential mother-in-law/father-in-law, as indicated under (b).

I. Cross-cousins through a parent's younger sibling/potential children-in-law

balan guyugan (a) MyBD, FyZD; etc.

(b) SW, BSW, ZSW

bayi wuribu (a) MyBS, FyZS; etc.

(b) DH, BDH, ZDH

As with sets F, G, and H, we suggest that *guyugan* and *wuribu* are primarily defined on a consanguineal basis, as the child of a cross-cousin with a younger-sibling link in the parent's generation, i.e. as the child of MyB or FyZ. *Guyugan* and *wuribu* are classes from which ego's own child may choose a spouse—they are 'potential daughter-in law' and 'potential son-in-law'.

Waymin and *guyugan* refer only to females, *ñubi* and *wuribu* only to males. This contrasts with the terms for ego's children, where it is the sex of the parent, not the sex of the child, that is marked in the kin term. The reciprocal of *waymin/ñubi* must be *guyugan/wuribu,* and vice versa.

This classificatory kinship system continues recursively for unlimited generations up and down, repeating the same terms. This is possible because the grandparent/grandchild terms function as their own reciprocals, and are treated as equivalent.

Consider first grandchildren—say, the child of a *gumbu.* Now *gumbu* refers to a female ego's daughter's child and also to a mother's mother. The child of a female ego's daughter's child (the child of a *gumbu* grandchild) is treated as the child of a mother's mother (the child of a *gumbu* grandparent), i.e. as mother's sibling. Thus the child of *gumbu* (or of *ŋagi,* ♂DCh, MF) is *balan yabu* (M, MyZ) if female and *bayi gaya* (MyB) if male. Similarly, the child of *babi* (♀SCh, FM) or of *bulu* (♂SCh, FF) is *bayi ŋuma* (F, FyB) if male and *balan ŋalban* (FyZ) if female.

We showed under B and C that there are different terms for parents' elder and younger siblings. But in the case of a great-grandchild there is no elder-/ younger-sibling link from which to choose whether, say *gumbu*'s son should be called MeB *(bayi mugu)* or MyB *(bayi gaya)*. It is the terms for parents' younger siblings (MyB, MyZ, FyB, FyZ) that are employed. This correlates with the situation in northern dialects, described above, where terms restricted to parents' younger siblings in the southern dialects are used for all parents' siblings, without regard for a younger/older distinction.

The parents of a grandparent are labelled, in a similar way, as the parents of the corresponding grandchild. So MMM and MMF (parents of a *gumbu*, MM, grandparent) are classed like the parents of a *gumbu* grandchild as *daman* 'classificatory female ego's child'. The parents of *babi*, FM, are also *daman*, while the parents of *ŋagi*, MF, and *bulu*, FF, are *galbin* 'classificatory male ego's child'.

One might expect that, alongside MMM as *daman* 'classificatory daughter', MMF should be *wuribu* 'potential son-in-law'. This is not the case; all great-grandparents are labelled simply as *daman* or *galbin*. This is in fact necessary in order to provide the correct reciprocals for the great-grandchild terms, described above. For instance, a male ego's daughter's daughter's son (♂DDS) is called *bayi gaya* by ego, and that kinsman will call ego (his ♂MMF) *bayi daman*. *Gaya/daman* is an established reciprocal pairing—see D above.

It will now be useful to summarise the gender possibilities of Dyirbal kin terms, set out in table 4.1. Most relate to just one gender while others may occur with either gender marker, depending on the sex of the referent. This can be critical. Consider *bimu* which is used for all of father's elder siblings. There is a striking contrast in the way one behaves towards the children of *bayi bimu*, FeB, who are parallel cousins, named and treated like siblings (terms in set E), and the childen of *balan bimu*, FeZ, who are cross-cousins (terms in set H), and in whose presence the Jalnguy style must be used. (Indeed, these are treated as distinct in the numeration of twenty-five kinship categories.)

We have now described the complete basic set of Dyirbal kin terms. Every person in the tribal community would be classified under one or other of these terms with respect to ego. This is likely also to apply for a visitor from a neighbouring tribe. There would have been some intertribal marriages, which would enable the visitor to be 'placed' within the local kinship matrix.

If two people were discussing a third then it would be most usual for the speaker to use the kin label appropriate to the addressee. A wife discussing with her husband their children would be most likely to say 'your *galbin*' (she **could** say 'my *daman*', but could never say 'our children'); the husband would be likely to reply 'your *daman*'. An exception might be when a young person was addressing an older one—a child would say to its father 'my *yabu* (mother)' in preference to 'your *bulgu* (wife)', etc.

TABLE 4.1. Gender membership for basic kin terms

	I, bayi (male humans)	II, balan (female humans)	both bayi and balan
A	—	—	gumbu, ŋagi, babi, bulu
B	ŋuma	ŋalban	bimu
C	mugu, gaya	yabu, mugunan	—
D	—	—	galbin, daman
E	mugirray, yabuju	yayin, jaman	jurgay
F, G	wirru	bulgu	ñurra
H	ñubi	waymin	—
I	wuribu	guyugan	—

The next two sections deal with some more specific kin terms, and then a number of linguistic features that relate to the kinship system. After that, section 4.4 (the central part of the chapter) explains the structure of Dyirbal kinship, especially the marriage rules.

4.2 Nyalal, the more specific or 'polite' kin terms

Dyirbal has a number of verbs that relate directly to the kinship system. The intransitive verb *maya-y* describes someone calling someone else by their kin label. Thus, if I called out to someone '*ŋinda, ŋuma*' ('hey you, father') this could be referred to by someone else through the sentence *bayi maya-ñu* ('he call.kin.term-PAST'). The transitive verb *ñala-l* refers to someone (the transitive subject) telling a second person (in dative case) what—basic or Nyalal—kin relation (transitive object) a third person (also transitive object) is to the second person. For example:

(1) ŋaja$_A$ bala-n$_O$ ŋinun-gu ñala-n   waymin$_O$
1sg.NOM THERE.ABS-II 2sg-DAT call.relation-PAST kin.term
I told you she is your waymin

There is a further set of kin terms described as Nyalal /ñalal/ (this is a participial form of the verb *ñala-l*). Alternatively, speakers would describe them, in English, as 'polite' forms. They are more detailed specifications of some of the basic kin terms, and are optionally used—in the appropriate circumstances—for reference, in place of the corresponding basic terms.

It was mentioned, under B/C in section 4.1, that in the northern dialects *bayi gaya* is the basic kin term for all MB. Here *bayi mugu* is a Nyalal term for MeB that can optionally be used in place of *bayi gaya*; there is no Nyalal term for MyB, only *bayi gaya* being used. Similar remarks apply to *balan mugunan*, MeZ, *bayi/balan bimu*, FeB/Z. (Only a few, very old speakers remained for the northern dialects and I was unable to ascertain whether *bayi mugu*, etc. were restricted to particular addressees, or whether they could be used with any addressee.)

Other Nyalal terms, in southern and some northern dialects, could be used instead of a basic kin term when addressing a certain type of kinsfolk. Some Nyalal terms occurred in texts and others were carefully explained to me by the oldest speakers, when I was working on the kin system in the 1980s. A selection (of the *circa* twenty-five Nyalal terms gathered) is included here:

(a) *bayi/balan juway* '(my) elder sibling', used in place of basic kin terms *bayi mugirray*, eB, and *balan yayin*, eZ, when talking to a parent or parent's sibling. (The parent or parent's sibling would use '(your) *mugirray/yayin*' in reply.)

(b) *bayi/balan mirray* '(my) younger sibling', used in place of *bayi yabuju*, yB, and *balan jaman*, yZ, when talking to father or father's sibling (*yabuju/jaman* used in reply).

(c) *bayi/balan gananunu* '(my) younger sibling', used in place of *bayi yabuju*, *balan jaman*, when talking to mother or mother's sibling (again, *yabuju/jaman* are used in reply).

(d) *bayi jabaymagi/balan yayinmagi* 'elder brother/sister', used in place of *bayi mugirray/balan yayin* if talking to a sibling or to a grandparent (the sibling or grandparent would use *jabaymagi/yayinmagi* in reply).

(e) *bayi malŋarra/balan wurana* 'younger brother/sister', used in place of *bayi yabuju/balan jaman* if talking to a sibling or to a grandparent (*malŋarra/wurana* would be used in response).

(f) *Bayi yindala/balan garriŋan* '(your) son/daughter', used in place of *bayi/balan daman* when MM or MF of the referent is addressing M of the referent (in reply she will use *gumbu*, ♀DCh, to her mother, and *ŋagi*, ♂DCh, to her father). Note that no special Nyalal term is used by a grandparent talking to a father about his child.

It is evident from these specifications that (i) parents and parents' siblings constitute a natural grouping; (ii) a generation two distant from ego's is grouped with ego's generation as opposed to a generation one distant—compare (a–c) with (d–e); (iii) the elder-/younger-sibling distinction, which plays a vital role in the Dyirbal kin system, is maintained in Nyalal terms (a–e).

In connection with (ii), we can usefully employ the terms 'harmonic' (same generation, or two apart), and 'disharmonic' (one or three generations apart) due to Hale (1966).

4.3 Some linguistic features

Before entering into an examination of the structure of the kinship system, it will be useful to describe the two verbs of begetting, the kinship duals, how kin terms are rendered in Jalnguy, and the basis for use of the two 1st person dual pronouns in northern dialects.

Verbs of begetting. There are two transitive verbs whose meanings point to a natural grouping of kin terms:

(i) *bulmbi-y* 'be the male progenitor of, beget' typically has 'father' as subject and his 'child' as object. But extensions are possible from this pattern: the subject can be FeB or FyB; or FeZ or FyZ. The full meaning of *bulmbi-y* is thus 'beget as a father does, either directly or through a brother'.

(ii) *gulŋga-l* is glossed by bilingual consultants as 'breastfeed' and it is most frequently used to describe a mother suckling her child. There are two ways in which the meaning is extended from this prototype. First, *gulŋga-l* can be used to refer to someone feeding solid food to a baby (just so long as the baby is being fed by someone else, rather than feeding itself). As a further extension in the same direction, a Dyirbal speaker once observed two friends giving each other bites of their respective ice creams, and he said *balagarra gulŋgal-gulŋgal-barri-ñ* 'those two are feeding each other', employing the reciprocal form of *gulŋga-l.*

The other meaning of *gulŋga-l* is to indicate that a woman has given birth to a child, maternal begetting. The subject is of course normally *yabu* 'mother'. But when used in this sense the subject of *gulŋga-l* can be MeZ or MyZ, or MeB or MyB. This meaning of *gulŋga-l* is 'give birth to, as a mother does, either directly or indirectly through a sister'.

These two verbs provide yet another instance of the grouping together of father and father's siblings, and of mother and mother's siblings.

Duals. There are a number of special expressions for referring to two people who are in a reciprocal kinship relation (cf. the 'dyadic' terms of Merlan and Heath 1982). These are set out in table 4.2.

TABLE 4.2. **Dual kinship terms**

Two people in a relationship of:			Can be referred to by the dual term:
A + A	gumbu/gumbu	(MM/♀DCh)	gumbu-jirr
	ŋagi/ŋagi	(MF/♂DCh)	ŋagi-jirr
	babi/babi	(FM/♀SCh)	babi-jirr
	bulu/bulu	(FF/♂SCh)	bulu-jirr
B + D	ŋuma/galbin	(F/Ch, FyB/♂eBCh)	ŋumay-girr
	ŋalban/galbin	(FyZ/♀eBCh)	
	bimu/galbin	(FeB/♂yBCh, FeZ/♀yBCh)	
C + D	yabu/daman	(M/Ch, MyZ/♀eZCh)	gina-girr
	gaya/daman	(MyB/♂eZCh)	
	mugunan/daman	(MeZ/♀yZCh)	
	mugu/daman	(MeB/♂yZCh)	
E + E	jurgay/jurgay	(Sib/Sib)	ŋalman-girr
F + G	wirru/bulgu	(H/W, etc.)	ŋaybirr, *or* mulba
G + G	ñurra/ñurra	(WB/♂ZH, HZ/♀BW, etc.)	dadiñ-garra
H + H	waymin/guyugan	(MeBD/FyZD, etc.)	duŋgarr-jirr
	waymin/wuribu	(MeBD/FyZS, etc.)	
	ñubi/guyugan	(MeBS/FyZD, etc.)	
	ñubi/wuribu	(MeBS/FyZS, etc.)	

There is one Nyalal-type alternative: two people who are in *mugu/daman* or *mugu-nan/daman* relationship (child plus MeB/MeZ) can be described as *gina-girr* or as *mugu-jirr* (never as *mugunan-jirr*); and two people who are in *bimu/galbin* relationship (child plus FeB/Z) can be described as *ŋumay-girr* or as *bimu-jirr*.

Forms *gina*, *ŋalman*, and *duŋgarr* are not known outside these dual expressions. I have heard *dadiñ* (without *-garra*) as an alternative to *ñurra*. (The Girramay dialect has *gibay* in place of *ñurra* and here the dual is *gibay-jirr*.) Dual suffixes *-jirr* and *-girr* are likewise unknown outside these expressions; *-garra* is a productive suffix, referring to 'a pair' (see section 11.1.1 and Dixon 1972: 230).

These duals provide further demonstration that a parent and the parent's siblings are grouped together. They also show the unity of the elder-linked cross-cousin (*waymin*, *ñubi*) / younger-linked cross-cousin (*guyugan*, *wuribu*) relationship; the same dual form, *duŋgan-jirr*, is used whatever the sex of the two people involved.

Kin terms in the Jalnguy style. The many-to-one correspondences between lexemes in the everyday language style and in Jalnguy, the avoidance style, applies also to kin terms:

A—Grandparents and grandchildren. *Gumbu*, *ŋagi*, *babi*, and *bulu* occur in both the everyday and Jalnguy styles. They are the only lexemes I know of that carry over into Jalnguy.

B, C—Parents and parents' siblings. A single lexeme, *bayi/balan wayuburr*, is used in the Jalnguy style of the Jirrbal tribe, corresponding to all of *ŋuma*, *ŋalban*, *bimu*, *yabu*, *gaya*, *mugu*, and *mugunan*. (For Ngajan and Mamu Jalnguy I was told that *balan ŋarmbu* is M, MZ; *bayi bamba* is MB; *bayi ŋabil* (lit. 'back (anatomical)') is F, FB; the term for FZ was not remembered.)

D—Children. There is no special Jalnguy noun; the adjective *wumbarr* 'little' is used as correspondent for *galbin* and *daman*.

E—Siblings. A single term in Jalnguy (of the Ngajan dialect), *bayi/balan warrgurraa*, corresponds to *jurgay*; there are no specific terms referring to elder/younger brother/sister.

F, G—Potential spouse and their siblings. The Jalnguy term *bayi/balan gulba* corresponds to all of *balan bulgu*, *bayi wirru*, and *bayi/balan ñurra*.

H, I—Cross-cousin/potential in-laws. There appear to have been no Jalnguy correspondents for *waymin*, *ñubi*, *guyugan*, or *wuribu*. The Jalnguy speech style was used for talking in the presence of such relations, and there may have been little need to refer to a relative from these classes when talking Jalnguy. If reference was required, an ad hoc descriptive label could be used; for example, Jalnguy *balan ñuri-marri-muŋa* lit. 'she who watches a lot' for *balan waymin* 'potential mother-in-law'.

It is noteworthy that the verbs *gulŋga-l* 'suckle; give birth to as a mother does, either directly or through a sister' and *bulmbi-y* 'beget as a father does, either directly or through a brother' do have unique Jalnguy correspondents, *gaba-l* and *galñja-y* respectively.

First person dual pronouns. All Dyirbal dialects make a distinction between singular, dual, and plural in both first and second person. The southerly dialects have a single first person dual pronoun, *ŋali,* referring to 'me and someone (anyone) else'.

Just the northerly dialects Mamu, Wari, and Ngajan contrast two first person dual pronouns, *ŋali* and *ŋanaymba*. They are used according to the relationship between the 'other person' and ego:

> *ŋali*   classificatory grandparent (A), sibling (E), cross-cousin/parent-in-law or child-in-law (H, I).
>
> *ŋanaymba*   classificatory parent or parent's sibling (B, C), child (D), potential spouse (F), potential spouse's opposite-sex sibling (G).

Diagram 4.1 shows the distribution of these two sets of pronouns in terms of a European-oriented kinship system, in which spouse and their relations are shown by affinal links. Those kin that demand the use of *ŋanaymba* are circled; there seems, from diagram 4.1, to be no rhyme or reason to the distinction between the two dual pronouns—*ŋanaymba* is used with some (but not all) kin from ego's own generation, and from the generations above and below.

However, when we place the 'potential in-law' and 'potential spouse' terms (*waymin, ñubi, guyugan, wuribu, bulgu, ñurra*) on a kinship chart according to their consanguineal definitions, as in diagram 4.2 of section 4.4, it becomes immediately apparent that *ŋanaymba* is used for all disharmonic kin (one generation above or below ego) and *ŋali* for all harmonic kin (same generation as ego, or two generations above or below). This kind of pronoun alternation is found in other Australian languages (see Hale 1966).

4.4 Rules for choosing a spouse

The Dyirbal kinship system appears very complicated if *bulgu, waymin,* etc. are shown as, primarily, W, WM, etc. (as in diagram 4.1). If, however, the consanguineal definitions of such terms (line (a) for each in section 4.1) are taken as prior, as in diagram 4.2, the system is seen to be built on straightforward principles. As already mentioned,

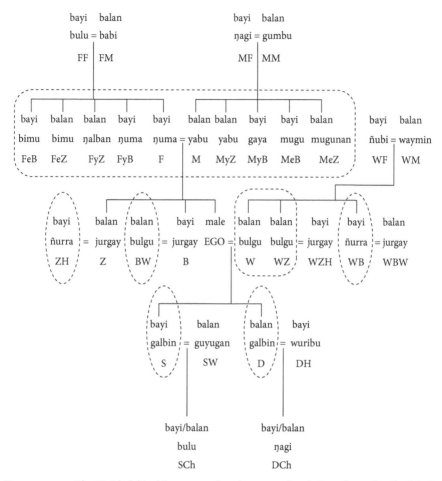

DIAGRAM 4.1 The Dyirbal kinship system showing spouse's relatives through affinal links (an exactly analogous chart applies for female ego). The relatives which require use of *ŋanayamba* as first person dual pronoun are circled; for all other relatives *ŋali* is used

the kin who demand use of the dual pronoun *ŋanaymba* are then all those in a disharmonic generation. The interesting feature of diagram 4.2 is that potential marriage links go diagonally, between ego and ego's spouse, and between ego's children and their spouses.

The criterial features of the Dyirbal kinship system are whether a sibling link involves people of the same or different sexes, and which sibling is older. It would be most efficient to talk simply of 'parent', 'parent's elder sibling of the opposite sex', etc. But it may be easier for the reader if we continue to talk in terms of 'father', 'father's elder sister', etc. It should be borne in mind that FeZ is exactly equivalent to MeB as a linking relative, MMyB to FFyZ, and so on. Diagram 4.2 deals just with male ego and

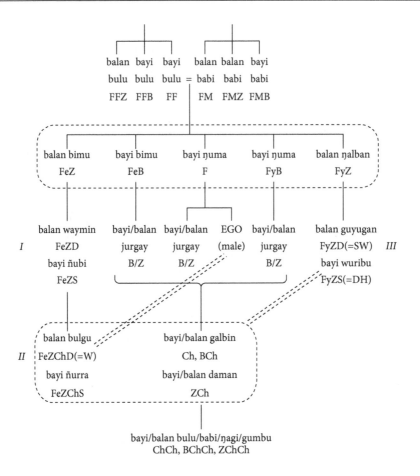

DIAGRAM 4.2 The Dyirbal kinship system showing all relatives of father through consanguineal links. Potential marriage links are shown by = = = =. The relatives which require use of *ŋanayamba* as first person dual pronoun are circled; for all other relatives *ŋali* is used

relatives through father; three corresponding charts can be constructed for female ego, and dealing with relatives through mother.

The normal procedure was that one of ego's *ñubi* (one of his potential fathers-in-law) would promise his daughter in marriage to ego when she was still a baby and ego a young boy. Once ego had grown up, gone through initiation, proved himself a good hunter able to provide for his promised bride and also her mother, he could claim his bride as soon she attained puberty. There were also established procedures for a girl to go to her promised husband if, by a certain time, he had not claimed her (*julbungan* refers to a woman claiming her promised spouse, at a stage when he should by then have claimed her).

Turning now to the structure of the kinship system, we find in fact that the whole system follows from any one element of it. Let us take as starting point (the sole initial 'axiom'):

I FeZD, MeBD, *balan waymin*, is potential mother-in-law;
   FeZS, MeBS, *bayi ñubi*, is potential father-in-law

Ego can always (in theory) marry the child of a *ñubi* or *waymin*. It then follows that:

II FeZSD, FeZDD, MeBSD, MeBDD is *balan bulgu*, potential wife
    (to a male ego), or *balan ñurra* (to a female ego);
    FeZSS, FeZDS, MeBSS, MeBDS is *bayi wirru*, potential husband
    (to a female ego), or *bayi ñurra* (to a male ego)

Since *I* (FeZCh, MeBCh) is potential father/mother-in-law to ego, then ego must be potential son-/daughter-in-law to *I*. The relationship between *I* and ego is the same as that between ego and *III* on diagram 4.2 (cross-cousins through younger-sibling link in parents' generation). Thus:

III FyZD, MyBD is *balan guyugan*, potential daughter-in-law;
     FyZS, MyBS is *bayi wuribu*, potential son-in-law

Ego's *galbin* and *daman* (actual and classificatory children) may marry *III*, and the children of such a marriage will then be the classificatory grandchildren of ego.

Diagram 4.2 is conventionally organised, with members of a single generation on the same horizontal level. We can redraw it in a different way, so that potential marriage partners are level with each other. To achieve this, elder and younger different-sex siblings of a parent are placed along a diagonal, as in diagram 4.3.

Now if *II* in diagrams 4.2 and 4.3 is a possible marriage partner for ego, so must ego be for *II*. To *II* ego is (from diagrams 4.2 and 4.3) FMyBS or MMyBS. If the grandparent of *II* were MeB to ego, then ego would be, to *II*, MFyZS or FFyZS.

It thus follows that the child of a younger sibling of a grandparent, who is of the opposite sex to the grandparent, will also belong to the class *bulgu* (if female) and will be a possible marriage partner, exactly like the grand-daughter of a FeZ or MeB. This is shown on diagram 4.3′, an extended version of diagram 4.3. Note that, for both parents' and grandparents' generation, a younger sibling of the opposite sex lies on a sloping line; this aligns all potential marriage partners on a horizontal.

It thus follows, as a further inference from our original axiom, that:

IV MMyBD, MFyZD, FMyBD, FFyZD is *balan bulgu*, potential wife
    (to a male ego) or *balan ñurra* (to a female ego)
    MMyBS, MFyZS, FMyBS, FFyZS is *bayi wirru*, potential husband
    (to a female ego) or *bayi ñurra* (to a male ego)

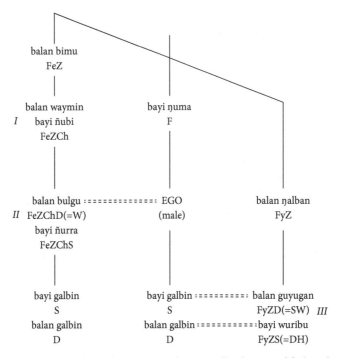

DIAGRAM 4.3 The Dyirbal kinship system, showing all relatives of father through con-sanguineal links, with generations along a diagonal and potential marriage partners lined up horizontally. (Note: a parent's same-sex siblings will be on the same horizontal as the parent; it is only opposite-sex siblings who are on a higher or lower level, depending on whether they are older or younger than the parent.) Potential marriage links are shown by = = = =

In section 4.1 we mentioned that each grandparent term has a prototypical gender marker, e.g. *balan babi* with primary denotatum FM. *Balan babi* also applies to FMZ, whose children will be classed like father's own siblings as *bimu* (FeB/Z), *ŋuma* (FyB), and *ŋalban* (FyZ). And, most significantly, FMB are *bayi babi*. It is grandpar-ent terms with marked gender (*bayi babi*, FMB; *balan bulu*, FFZ; *bayi gumbu*, MMB; *balan ŋagi*, MFZ) that are critical in calculating kin links and possible marriage partners.

In section 4.1 we mentioned that *bayi ñubi* could be defined consanguineally as (a) MeBS, FeZS, or affinally as (b) HF, WF, etc. But now we see that ego may marry the daughter of a *ñubi* or *waymin* (cross-cousin through an elder-sibling link) or the daughter of *bayi babi*, etc. (grandparent's opposite-sex younger sibling). If ego mar-ries the daughter of *bayi babi*, ego will still refer to his spouse's father as *bayi babi*, not as *bayi ñubi*. This provides further support for our taking consanguineal links as primary—*ñubi* refers to a sub-class of cross-cousins and this is **one sort** of potential

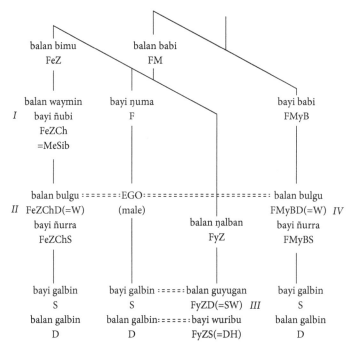

DIAGRAM 4.3′ Extension of diagram 4.3 to also include grandparents' younger siblings of the opposite sex, and their children. Potential marriage links are shown by = = = =

father-in-law. That is, the possible affinal classes are definable in terms of consanguineal classes, not vice versa.

Note also that the Jalnguy style was used in the presence of a *waymin, ñubi, guyugan,* or *wuribu,* but not to or in the presence of a *bayi babi,* etc. It is, most exactly, a 'cross-cousin speech style' (rather than an 'in-law-style', even though the term Jalnguy was translated for me, by bilingual consultants, as 'mother-in-law language'). In fact, the relationship between ego and a relative from grandparents' generation—whether *balan babi,* FM, or a *bayi babi,* FMyB, who is a potential father-in-law—is one of great intimacy, far removed from the deferential relationship that holds between cross-cousins.

What now of a grandparent's elder sibling of the opposite sex? We could predict, extrapolating from diagram 4.3′, that they should be at the end of a line sloping upwards. Where would this place the child of a grandparent's elder sibling of the opposite sex? One could infer, from the pattern of the chart, that they would be in the same horizontal line as a straightforward grandparent.

The status of this type of kinsperson can be inferred from the basic premises of the kinship system. Consider two people related as in diagrams 4.4a and 4.4b. Diagram 4.4a shows the relationship taking person *u* as ego; diagram 4.4b takes person *z* as ego.

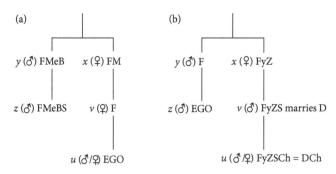

DIAGRAM 4.4 Grandparent's elder sibling of the opposite sex

In diagram 4.4b, person *v* is FyZS to ego *(z)* and must thus be *bayi wuribu* 'potential son-in-law'. Ego's daughter can marry *v* and *v*'s child (whether this marriage takes place or not) will be classed as *z*'s daughter's child. That is, *u* will call *z bayi ŋagi*, MF, and *z* will respond by calling the child *bayi/balan ŋagi* (since all grandparent/grandchild terms are their own reciprocal).

We see from diagram 4.4a that *z* is FMeBS to *u*. And from diagram 4.4b, that *u* and *z* call each other *ŋagi*. If we adjust the diagrams so that *z* is female, then she will be FMeBD to *u*, and they will call each other *gumbu*, MM.

Calculating in this way all the varieties of children of an older sibling of the opposite sex to a grandparent, we find that:

V MFeZS, MMeBS are *bayi bulu* (FF)
FFeZS, FMeBS are *bayi ŋagi* (MF)
MFeZD, MMeBD are *balan babi* (FM)
FFeZD, FMeBD are *balan gumbu* (MM)

There is a straightforward algorithm for calculating what type of classificatory grandparent a child of a grandparent's elder sibling of the opposite sex is. If we have a term *LMN* where *L* is M or F, *M* is FeZ or MeB, and *N* is S or D, then this is equivalent to *PQ*, where:

if *L* is M, then *P* is F; if *L* is F, then *P* is M;
if *N* is S, then *Q* is F; if *N* is D, then *Q* is M

That is, mother and father are interchanged in the first element, *L/P*, and son/daughter becomes father/mother in the final element, *N/Q* (sex being retained), with the middle portion (MeB or FeZ) being dropped.

Once this new information is added to diagram 4.3′ we get diagram 4.3″. Just as the child of a younger different-sex sibling of a grandparent is effectively one generation down (and a possible marriage partner), so the child of an elder different-sex sibling of a grandparent is effectively one generation up (and is a classificatory grandparent).

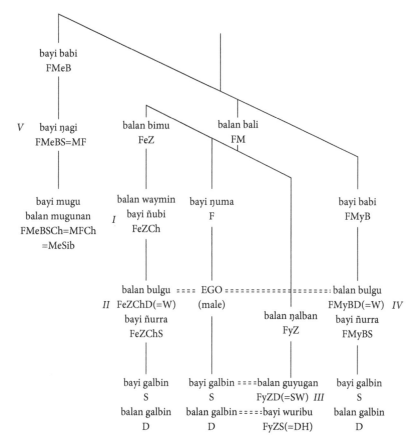

DIAGRAM 4.3″ Extension of diagram 4.3′ to also include grandparents' younger and older siblings of the opposite sex, and their children. Potential marriage links are shown by = = = =

Note that the term next to *V* in diagram 4.3″ does have its prototypical gender membership. The children of *V* are calculated according to this label. Thus FMeBS is *bayi ŋagi*, a classificatory MF, and his children (FMeBSCh) are classed as *bayi mugu* (MeB) and *balan mugunan* (MeZ) just like the children of a *bayi ŋagi* who is in fact MFeB. (The terms for parents' **elder** siblings are used, since there is an elder-sibling link, at the grandparent generation.)

There is one additional point worth noting. It is in most cases possible to tell what kin label you would use for person X from knowing how you refer to X's parents. Thus if ego calls X *bayi bimu*, FeB, then ego will call X's daughters *balan yayin*, eZ; but if ego calls X *bayi ŋuma* (*galŋan*), FyB, then ego must call X's daughters *balan jaman*, yZ.

Dyirbal lacks separate terms for the elder and younger siblings of a grandparent. Gender marking does distinguish, for example, *bayi ŋagi*, MF/MFB, whose children will be *mugu, mugunan, yabu*, or *gaya* (MeB, MeZ, MyZ, MyB) from *balan ŋagi*, MFZ, whose children will be *bulu, babi, bulgu/wirru,* or *ñurra* (FF, FM, W/H, SpSib). How-ever, if ego only knows that a certain relative is *bayi ŋagi,* this does not provide enough information to infer what their children should be. Ego must ascertain whether the relative in question is the elder or younger brother of ego's actual MF; this can be dis-covered by finding out what ego's mother calls the relative. If ego's mother uses the term *bayi bimu* (FeB) for the relative then ego should call the relative's children *bayi mugu* and *balan mugunan* (MeB, MeZ); but if ego's mother calls the relative *bayi ŋuma* (FyB) then ego must refer to that person's children as *bayi gaya* or *balan yabu* (MyB, MyZ).

A similar situation arises with *balan ŋagi* (MFZ) and here it is vitally important that ego ascertain whether an elder or a younger sibling link is involved—if the latter, that relative's children will be potential marriage partners; if the former, they will be clas-sificatory grandparents. Again, this can be resolved by discovering what ego's parent calls ego's grandparent's sibling—if mother uses the term *balan bimu* (FeZ) then ego calls that *balan ŋagi*'s children *bayi bulu* and *balan babi* (FF, FM), whereas if mother calls the relative *balan ŋalban* (FyZ) then ego must call the relative's children *balan bulgu* (potential wife) and *bayi ñurra,* if ego is male, or *bayi wirru* (potential husband) and *balan ñurra,* if ego is female.

4.5 The system in practice

The Dyirbal kinship system, like any other, is an ideal against which actual practice is measured and compared. It is likely that in pre-contact times most marriages accorded fully with the system set out here: a girl being 'promised' by their fathers when very young and later going off with the appointed husband (who would, generally, be six to ten years older than her). (There is a term *bayi/balan ŋalma* 'intended spouse' referring to a person of the *bayi wirru* 'potential husband' or *balan bulgu* 'potential wife' classes who has been promised to ego.)

Marriages were arranged as part of the social network of reciprocal obligation, and the forging of alliances. A daughter from family X would often be promised to a man (in the appropriate relationship) from family Y, with a clear understanding that a cer-tain man from family X would in due course be promised a wife from family Y.

There would, however, always have been elopements with proscribed kin. Indeed, there is a vocabulary for describing this. *Bayi/balan ŋalgiya* refers to ego's illicit spouse or lover or intended lover. In addition, the term *ñirri* (literally 'bird shit') describes a wrong marriage, e.g. to a parallel cousin, and the more extreme term *ñirririmu* is used for a very wrong marriage, e.g. to a classificatory daughter.

During the past hundred and forty years, after tribal numbers were reduced through murder by European settlers and by introduced diseases, it has been less easy to find a spouse of the right kin classification, and there have been more 'wrong' mar-riages. Still, people agree as to what is 'correct' and what not, and are clear about what a couple's official relationship was (they will comment: 'she married her [classificatory] son, and that wasn't right').

We have stressed that terms such as *bulgu* (♂FeZChD, ♂MMyBD, etc.) and *waymin* (MeBD, FeZD) are to be defined on a consanguineal basis. There can be exceptions in the case of a 'wrong marriage'. If two people in an unacceptable relationship do marry, they will be known as *bulgu/wirru* (W/H) to each other, these labels replacing their former consanguineal labels. The couple's parents would, however, still be referred to by their original consanguineal labels (that is, these would not be likely to be replaced by *waymin* 'mother-in-law' and *ñubi* 'father-in-law').

In a marriage that was perfect according to 'the law', I was told, the kin status of a child should be the same whether calculated through father or through mother. But there are many deviations from perfection. Consultants told me that, where there is any discrepancy, relationships should properly be calculated through the father. They would then add that they themselves preferred in some cases to work out relationships through the mother. For instance, Bessie Jerry said that she should 'by law' (as she put it) call Nancy Biran *ñurra*, since Nancy's father was *ñubi* to Bessie, but in fact Bessie calls Nancy *galbin*, calculating the relationship through Nancy's mother.

There is no doubt that the Dyirbal kinship system has a consanguineal basis. But, just as a relationship may sometimes be calculated through mother rather than through father, so it may occasionally be motivated by an affinal link. The wife of a *ñubi* would normally be expected to be a *waymin*; but it is quite possible for the wife of a *ñubi* not to be a *waymin* (according to consanguineal calculation)—in this case she may be called *waymin* or she can be called by the proper consanguineal term (depending on which of these alternatives is adopted by the two participants, and accepted by the rest of the community). To take another example, Andy Denham told me that Mary Ann Murray was *yayin* to him, 'by blood link', but that in fact he called her *ŋalban* because she was married to his *gaya* (the wife of a *gaya* being normally expected to be a *ŋalban)*.

Nowadays, of course, people marry from outside the tribe. I asked of one woman whose daughter had married an Aborigine from a distant place (whom the daughter called *wirru* 'husband' and the mother referred to as *wuribu* 'son-in-law') what kin terms would be appropriate for his parents, should they come to visit. She shook her head and said: 'Nothing. They don't belong to us.'

It must also be stressed that although the Dyirbal people have definite kinship rules, these can be adapted to circumstances. Bessie Jerry informed me that when young she had been told to call Paddy Biran *bayi mugu*, MeB, when he should really have been *bayi gaya*, MyB, since he was classificatory younger brother to Bessie's mother; Bessie doesn't know the reason for this. However, she does call Paddy's children *bayi wuribu* and *balan guyugan* (MyBS/D), recognising the inherent *gaya* relationship between her and Paddy.

On another occasion Andy Denham told me he called Willie Murray *bayi gaya* but then referred to Willie's children as *bayi ñurra* and *balan bulgu*. I raised my eyebrows at this (since the children should properly be *bayi wuribu* and *balan guyugan* to Andy); Andy volunteered that Willie Murray had told him, just before he died, to call them this way, since Willie wanted Andy to marry one of his daughters (although in fact he never did).

Feelings of social delicacy can also play a role. Consider the case of two sisters—the younger being the true daughter of her mother's husband but the elder having a different father. Most of my consultants used the same kin term for both girls, calculated through the mother's husband. One man, though, told me that he called the younger sister *daman* but the elder one *galbin*—he had to use this label since her father had been his own younger brother. In this case the actual relationship was so close that it **had to be** acknowledged, taking precedence over feelings of delicacy (under which the two girls would have been accorded the same kin label).

There can be other, complicating factors at work. I once asked Paddy Bute how he referred to Mary Muriata, the daughter of Jack Muriata (Paddy's *yabuju* 'classificatory yB') and Jack's second wife Jessie (Paddy's *jaman* 'classificatory yZ'). Much to my surprise, he replied *gumbu* (MMB, ZDCh). Paddy explained that Jack Muriata's first wife, Ethel, had been his *daman* (ZCh) and he had correctly called the children of Ethel and Jack by the label *gumbu*, calculating this through their mother. Since the children of Jack Muriata's first marriage called Paddy *gumbu* he had told Mary, the child of the second marriage, to address him in the same way (although if the relationship had been calculated through Mary's father it would be *galbin/bimu*, BCh/FeB, or through her mother *daman/mugu*, ZCh, MeB).

Schebeck, Hercus, and White (1973: 50–3) described how for Adnjamathanha, from South Australia, the preferred marriage for a male ego is with a classificatory MBD or FZD who is younger than ego; it is forbidden to marry an older cross-cousin. However, an alternative marriage possibility is with the daughter of such an elder cross-cousin. Thus, for the Adnjamathanha the preferred marriage is with someone of ego's own generation, the alternative being to marry into an adjacent generation.

Elder and younger siblings of a parent are treated differently in some tribes from the Cape York Peninsula, north of Dyirbal (Thomson 1972). There are also examples of marrying into a lower generation: McConnel (1950) reports that the Yaraidyana marry FZDD (MBDD is taboo) whereas the Nggamiti can marry FZDD and MBD; Thomson (1972: 21) reports that among the Tjungundji a man may marry his MMBD, FFZSD, or FZDD (see also Alpher 1982: 24–5). These show some similarity to the Dyirbal system, but for the Nggamiti and Tjungundji ego is allowed to marry into an adjacent generation or into his own generation, and none of these systems is symmetrical with regard to sex.

There is no kinship system like the Dyirbal one mentioned in the standard literature on Australian kinship: Radcliffe-Brown (1930–1), Elkin (1964), Scheffler (1978), Heath, Merlan, and Rumsey (1982). Nor have I been able to find anything of this type on any other continent.

5

Jalnguy, the 'mother-in-law' speech style in Dyirbal

5.1 Orientation

The languages of indigenous Australians have a rich aesthetic texture. Alongside the everyday language style, there is typically:

(a) A special register employed in the poetry of songs. This may include archaic words, some lexemes particular to the song style, modified grammatical conventions, plus distinctive rhythmic patterns and voice timbre.

(b) A mode of speech associated with male initiation. This may be taught to youths at initiation, and used by them then. It may also be used by initiated men in ceremonial contexts. A notable example of this, from Central Australia, involves a word being replaced by its opposite; for example, one says, literally, 'another is standing' in the initiation style to mean 'I am sitting' (Hale 1971). An even more remarkable instance comes from the Lardil tribe of Mornington Island, whose initiation register involves sounds not found in the everyday style—nasal clicks, an ingressive lateral, ejective stops, a bilabial trill (Hale 1973; Hale and Nash 1997).

(c) A respectful register, used in the presence of avoidance relatives. This typically involves a limited number of avoidance lexemes which are substituted for some of the most common words of the everyday style. Otherwise, everyday words are used unchanged in the avoidance style. McGregor (1989, 1990: 18) recorded 'only slightly over one hundred distinct avoidance lexemes' in Gooniyandi, and for Bunuba, also from Western Australia, Rumsey (2000: 125) had 'about two hundred'. Only for Dyirbal and Yidiñ do speakers maintain that *no* everyday lexemes are used in the avoidance style. (Some avoidance styles show minor differences in grammar.)

Dixon (2002a: 91–5) deals with special speech styles, and includes references to the literature on these, including those which show minor phonological and grammatical differences.

The Dyirbal-speaking tribes had a rich repertoire of five styles of song poetry, each with its own metrical pattern, and linguistic and musical characteristics. Dixon and Koch (1996a) provide a thorough study of 174 songs. Of the *circa* 820 non-grammatical words in these songs, about one-third comprise special song words, the remainder being everyday style lexemes.

The focus of this chapter and the next is on the so-called 'mother-in-law' speech style, Jalnguy. Its main use was to mark the relationship of avoidance between cross-cousins; prototypically potential mother-in-law and potential son-in-law. Jalnguy also had a role in initiation; after their tribal cicatrices had been cut, initiands were required to speak only in Jalnguy to their carers.

Dyirbal culture was severely impacted by the European invasion in the late nineteenth century. The last initiation took place in the 1920s. I was told that Jalnguy ceased in active use about 1930. However, when I commenced fieldwork in 1963, there were about ten old people who remembered Jalnguy and were eager to share it with me.

For the remainder of this chapter, and the next, 'Ja' will be used as an abbreviation for 'the Jalnguy style' and 'Ev' for 'the everyday language style' (termed Guwal in southern and Ngirrma in northern dialects).

It was possible to record four texts in Ja—a monologue from Chloe Grant, a dialogue between Chloe and Rosie Runaway (both in 1963), and two dialogues between Chloe and George Watson (in 1967). In addition, I went through a corpus of more than 2,000 lexemes in Ev, enquiring about the Ja correspondent of each. Three consultants worked with enthusiasm on this—Mollie Raymond (c1890–1992) on the Ngajan dialect (N), George Watson (c1899–1991) on Dulgubarra Mamu (M), and Chloe Grant (c1903–1974) on Jabunbarra Jirrbal (J). In 1967 we assembled a committee (a sort of Dyirbal Academy) to assist Chloe with Ja equivalents for some of the more esoteric Ev words; this included Ida Henry, Rosie Runaway, Rosie Onearm, and Tommy Springcart.

Virtually every open class lexeme—nouns, adjectives, time words, verbs, adverbals—has a different form in the Ev and Ja styles. Yet Ja has only about one-quarter as many lexemes as Ev. This is achieved through many-to-one correspondences between the two vocabularies. As illustrated in section 1.2, Ja has just a generic term relating to twenty names of frog species in Ev, one adjective for two adjectives of taste, one verb corresponding to seven or eight verbs for types of piercing, and so on.

Basically, there is a single underlying semantic system, which is projected onto the lexicon at two levels of generality. It is appropriate, when talking in the presence of an avoidance relative, to be vague. In other circumstances one should be as specific as possible.

Ja has a minimal set of words, just enough so that it is possible to express in Ja everything which can be said in Ev. Note that—should it be considered necessary—any required level of specificity can be achieved in Ja through adding modification and qualification to the basic Ja word (this is illustrated later in the chapter).

Correspondences between Ev and Ja lexemes can indicate the underlying structure of the lexicon. For example, at an early stage of research I had been given one-word glosses for some verbs, including:

(1) nudi-l 'cut'
     gunba-l 'cut'
     bañi-l 'cut'

However, when attention was directed towards Ja, different correspondents were given:

(2) Ev   Ja
     nudi-l   jalŋga-l
     gunba-l jalŋga-l
     bañi-l   bubama-l

Further investigation revealed that the Ja verb *jalŋga-l* has the meaning 'cut', and corresponds to several verbs in Ev, including:

(3) nudi-l 'cut deeply, sever, cut down (a tree)' (this is the nuclear correspondent
             of *jalŋga-l*; see section 5.3)
     gunba-l 'cut to medium depth, cut a piece out of'
     rulba-l 'split a piece of timber along the grain, with an axe'
     yaga-l 'open something up by cutting it (e.g. open up the belly of a fish);
             plough the ground'

And it was discovered that the Ja verb *bubama-l* means 'set something in motion in a trajectory, holding on to it (it may or may not impact on something else)'. This verb corresponds to a number of Ev verbs, including:

(4) baygu-l 'shake (e.g. one's head), wave (a flag), bash (e.g. pick up a goanna
             by the tail and bash its head on a tree to kill it)' (this is the nuclear
             correspondent of *bubama-l*)
     jinda-l 'gently wave or bash, e.g. blaze the bark of a tree to indicate which way
             one has gone, sharpen the end of a stick or pencil'
     darrbi-l 'shake a blanket to remove dirt or crumbs which have gathered on it'
     bañi-l 'split a soft or rotten log by embedding an axe in it, picking it up by
             the axe handle, and bashing it on a tree so that the log splits and the
             edible grubs it contains can be extracted'

It is seen that, although *bañi-l* has a similar result to cutting, it is basically regarded as an act of bashing the embedded-axe-plus-rotten-log on a tree. This is clearly shown by the Ja correspondent.

Before embarking on the detailed discussion, it will be useful to illustrate the nature of Ja through a fragment of text in Mamu Ja given by George Watson, taken from a dialogue with Chloe Grant. The Jalnguy (Ja) is given first, followed by the corresponding clause in everyday style (Ev), and then morpheme-by-morpheme analysis. Ja lexemes are underlined.

(5) Ja [ŋali   Girrñjañ-garra]$_S$ <u>ganba</u>   <u>wuyuba-rri-ñu</u> . . .
    Ev [ŋali   Girrñjañ-garra]$_S$ gala   wurrba-ñu
        1du.NOM <name>-one.of.pair earlier.today talk-PAST
        Earlier on today I and Girrñjañ (Jimmy Murray) (lit. I and someone else,
            Girrñjañ and someone else) were talking . . .

(6) Ja ŋaja$_A$ bayi$_O$ <u>baṉarrmba-n</u>
    Ev ŋaja$_A$ bayi$_O$ ŋanba-n
        1sg.NOM THERE.ABS.I ask-PAST
        I asked him:

(7) Ja baŋum wuñja-rri   bayi$_S$ <u>bawalbi-n</u>
    Ev baŋum wuñja-rri   bayi$_S$ yanu
        THEN   WHERE-DIRECTION THERE.ABS.I go.PAST
        in which direction he went then,

(8) Ja ba-ŋgu-l$_A$ ŋaygu-na$_O$ <u>wuyuba-n</u>
    Ev ba-ŋgu-l$_A$ ŋaygu-na$_O$ buwa-ñu
        THERE-ERG-I 1sg-ACC   tell-PAST
        He told me:

(9) Ja <u>mugilmbarram</u>-gu <u>bawalbi</u>-n bayi$_S$
    Ev girñjal-go   yanu   bayi$_S$
        honey-DATIVE   go.PAST   THERE.ABS.I
        he had gone for honey.

We can now comment on the nature of Ja, from this excerpt.

(a) All affixes are the same as in Ev: derivational suffix *-garra* 'one of a pair' in (5), nominal dative case *-gu* in (9), and verbal past tense inflection with allomorphs *-ñu* in (5), and *-n* in (6–9).

(b) Grammatical words, belonging to small, closed classes, are the same as in Ev. This includes pronouns—*ŋali* in (5), *ŋaja* in (6), *ŋayguna* in (8)—and noun markers—*bayi* in (6), (7), and (9), *ba-ŋgu-l* in (8). Alongside noun markers there are verb markers which are also the same in Ja; *ba-ŋum* is basically 'THERE-FROM' but in (7) it has a temporal sense 'from that time, then'.

There is also a small class of about sixteen 'particles'. All but three are the same in the two styles, including the most common one of all, *gulu* 'not', and also *biya* 'an event which could well have happened but in fact didn't', and *yamba* 'maybe'. Those that differ are 'in turn', *ŋurri* in Ev, *ŋurriñji* in Ja; 'inappropriate S or O argument', *warra* in Ev, *warranda* in Ja; and 'couldn't help it happening', *mugu* in Ev, *mumba* in Ja for Mamu and *buba* in Ja for Ngajan.

All interjections are the same in the two styles except for the most common one, 'no'. Corresponding to *yimba* in Ev, the Ja forms are *jagin* in Jirrbal, *jilbu* in Mamu, and *gamañjal* in Ngajan.

(c) Proper names, of people and of places, are unchanged in Ja, as shown by *Girrñjañ* 'Jimmy Murray' in (5).

(d) All lexemes have a different form in Ja—nouns such as 'honey', time words such as 'earlier today', verbs such as 'talk', 'ask', 'go', and 'tell', and also adjectives and adverbals.

In Ev there are separate verbs for 'talk' and 'tell'. However, these have the same basic content, differing only in transitivity. In keeping with its parsimonious profile, Ja has a single verb root, *wuyuba-* 'tell' and forms an intransitive stem from it through adding the reflexive derivational suffix *-rri-*, here functioning as a general intransitiviser:

(10)   transitive   'tell' Ev buwa-y   Ja wuyuba-l   in (8)
        intransitive 'talk' Ev wurrba-y Ja wuyuba-rri-y in (5)

There are other pairs like this; see section 5.8.1.

In every language, interrogative words have a pan-basic-word-class profile. While sharing a common 'questioning' character (and some grammatical properties), they essentially relate to a variety of word classes. For Dyirbal, 'where' forms are either noun markers or verb markers and, like them, are unchanged in Ja; this is illustrated by *wuñja-rri* 'in which direction' in (7).

'Who' relates to the grammatical category of pronouns. Like 1sg and 2sg pronouns in the Girramay dialect, it has separate forms for the three core syntactic functions: *waña* for S, *wañuna* for O, and *wañju* for A. Like 1st and 2nd person pronouns, 'who' is unchanged in Ja. However, 'what' patterns like nouns, inflecting on an absolutive-ergative pattern. Like nouns, 'what' has different forms—*miña* in Ev, and *mindirr* in Ja.

Along with other adverbals, *wiyama-y/-l* 'do what, do how' has a different form in Ja, *wiyaba-y/-l*. 'When' relates to the lexical class of time words and 'how many' to the adjectival subset of number words. In keeping with their lexical character, these two interrogatives have different forms in Ja, in fact the same form:

(11)   'when'   Ev miñay ⎫
        'how many'   Ev miñañ ⎬ Ja minay

Whereas the avoidance speech style is called *jalŋuy* across all dialects of Dyirbal, and also in Yidiñ, the term for Ev varies. Southern dialects of Dyirbal (A, J, U, Y, and G) use *guwal*, while further north we find *ŋirrma* in M and W, and *ŋiRma* in N. Yidiñ has no name for Ev; one would just speak of 'talking in Yidiñ', as opposed to 'talking in Ja'. Because of this variation, we prefer to refer just to 'Ev' (rather than to Guwal or Ngirrma).

As will be shown in the next chapter, there is more variation of lexical form between dialects for Ja than for Ev. This chapter concentrates on the principles of organisation for Ja. Where different dialects share the same principle of Ja organisation but differ in forms then—in order not to complicate the exposition—just the form in one dialect is, in most cases, quoted. This is generally J, sometimes M when slightly fuller information is available for that Ja.

5.2 When it was used

Ja was used in the context of avoidance relationships. The kin categories involved were:

- **balan waymin** father's elder sisters' daughters (FeZD), mother's elder brothers' daughters (MeBD), FMeBSSD, etc. potential mother-in-law
- **bayi ñubi** father's elder sisters' sons (FeZS), mother's elder brothers' sons (MeBS), FMeBSSS, etc. potential father-in-law
- **bayi wuribu** father's younger sisters' sons (FyZS), mother's younger brothers' sons (MyBS), etc. potential son-in-law
- **balan guyugan** father's younger sisters' daughters (FyZD), mother's younger brothers' daughters (MyBD), etc. potential daughter-in-law

The strongest degree of avoidance was between a man and his *waymin*, the next between a woman and her *wuribu*, the next that between *ñubi* and *guyugan*; these are all different-sex pairs. There was also a significant—but weaker—relationship of respect between cross-cousins of the same sex: *waymin* and *guyugan*, *ñubi*, and *wuribu*. For the strongest kind of avoidance relationship, the use of Ja was absolutely obligatory. For the weaker kinds—between cross-cousins of the same sex—the use of Ja was desirable but not absolutely essential.

A speaker of Dyirbal should not look directly at an avoidance relation, and should not speak directly to them. Instead, communication would be through a third party. Sitting as far as possible from his *waymin*, a man could say to his wife, in Ja: 'Would your mother like some more meat, from the wallaby which I just killed?' The *waymin* would respond through the same channel. The avoidance relationship was always reciprocal: if X used Ja in the presence of Y, then Y should use it in the presence of X.

To the best of my knowledge, there were no special phonetic or paralinguistic features associated with Ja. That is, it appears to have been spoken in the same tone of voice as Ev, the entirely separate lexicon being sufficient to mark it as a respect register.

I was told that Ja was learnt in a natural way, like Ev but a few years behind it. Since this was a classificatory kinship system, each person would have, from birth, a full set of avoidance relations, potential 'in-laws'. A boy would hear Ja spoken around him and would be encouraged to use it himself—by the age of eight or so—in the presence of any woman who was in *waymin* relationship to him. By the onset of puberty, it would be obligatory to do so.

I once asked Chloe Grant—in my blinkered European manner—what might be the consequence if a man spoke in Ev within hearing of a *waymin*. Would he be speared for this offence? Chloe shook her head: 'Oh no, he be so 'shamed, he feel such shame.' The social make-up of Dyirbal society was such that no one would deliberately flout the avoidance conventions.

Whereas some Australian peoples have a separate speech style for use in male initiation ceremonies, for the Dyirbal-speaking tribes this was a secondary function of Ja. The ceremony involved the incision of two or three cicatrices across the belly. As soon as the cuts were made, some older men would go out in search of eels, leaving the newly initiated youths with a number of guardians. For two or three days the initiands were not permitted to speak. Then the elders would return with eels, give the flesh to the youths to eat, and anoint the wounds with grease from pieces of chewed eel. During the two- or three-day-long eel ceremony, the initiands could talk to the older men, but only in Ja (note that these were not avoidance kin); they would be answered in Ev. It appears that this was the only circumstance in which the use of Ja was not reciprocal.

For Guugu Yimidhirr—next language but two to the north of Yidiñ—Haviland (1979a, b, c) has described an avoidance style which he calls 'brother-in-law language'. Like Dyirbal and Yidiñ, it has the same phonology and grammar as Ev. Some Ev lexemes are replaced by avoidance style lexemes, generally on a many-to-one basis. However, unlike Dyirbal and Yidiñ, some Ev lexemes were retained in the avoidance style, which was spoken in an especially soft, slow, and respectful manner. Again unlike Dyirbal and Yidiñ, the avoidance style was used only by men, typically in the presence of a brother-in-law, who was in an avoidance relationship (in Dyirbal, brother-in-law, *ñurra*, was the most familiar of relationships). Haviland also reports that, in the olden days, if a man did not speak in the avoidance style when it was appropriate to do so, he might be speared.

5.3 Semantic organisation

There were two ways in which a lexeme from the everyday speech style could be rendered in Ja.

(I) Directly, by a Ja word, generally of the same word class. For example, *bayi yuri* 'big grey kangaroo' is *bayi yuŋga* in Ja, and verb *nudi-l* 'cut' is *jalŋga-l*. There is generally—but not always—a many-to-one relationship. Thus *bayi yuŋga* is used for nine types of kangaroo and wallaby (each with a specific name in Ev) and, as seen in (3), *jalnga-l* is used for four Ev verbs.

Even with the many-to-one correspondences, Ja does not quite have a direct equivalent for each Ev lexeme. In these circumstances, a different technique is employed:

(II) By a description, in Ja, of what the referent of the lexeme does or is associated with. This is used primarily for nouns relating to various varieties of fauna (chiefly—but not exclusively—those that are not eaten).

(a) Based on an intransitive verb; for example:
- The bird known in English as 'kookaburra' or 'laughing jackass' is *bayi gungaga* in Ev, and in Ja *bayi yirrgunji-muna* 'he who laughs a lot'. *Yirrgunji-y* is the Ja verb 'laugh', corresponding to *miyanda-y* in Ev. Agentive nominalisations are formed either with suffix *-y* (after *a* or *u*)/zero (after *i*) or *-muna*.
- *Bayi gilgarri-muna* 'he who jumps a lot' is the Ja name for three grasshoppers (each with a specific name in Ev).

(b) Based on a transitive verb; for example:
- *Bayi ñanbal-muna* 'he who pierces a lot' is the Ja description for the stonefish, for several types of hawk, and for all species of wasps and ticks.
- *Bayi guyjul-muna* 'he who bites a lot' is the Ja for the mosquito, for march flies, for several types of biting ants, and for the centipede.
- A small brown rat with a sharp nose, who bores holes in trees to extract grubs, which he eats, is *bayi yugaba* in Ev and in Ja *bayi mayaja-yulmi-yulmi*, involving reduplication of *yulmi-y* 'eat' and incorporated noun *mayaja* 'edible grub'; literally 'he who is always eating grubs'.
- The examples just given relate, in a straightforward manner, to the A argument of a transitive verb. A more intricate instance involves the Ja correspondent of Ev noun *bala yabala* 'a flat place'. This is *bala naynu-rri-yarra-muna*, literally 'that which begins to throw itself out', involving transitive verb *naynu-l* 'throw' (corresponding to *mada-l* in Ev) plus reflexive suffix *-rri-y*, derivational suffix *-yarra-y* 'start to do', and nominaliser *-muna*.

(c) Based on a noun; for example:
- There are quite a few Ja nouns which involve suffix *-barra* 'associated with'. This is added to Ja noun *jinbay* 'ground' to form *balan jinbay-barra*, the name for several species of bird, all of whom lay their eggs on or near the ground, and also *bayi jinbay-barra* for several kinds of crickets, which do the same.

  The Ja name for three wagtail birds is *bayi burula-barra* 'associated with the fighting ground', from *balan burula*, Ja for 'fighting ground' (*balan buya* in Ev). They are characters in myth, and are said to dance like men at a corroboree.

- A single man, beyond usual marrying age, is *bayi yalŋgay* in Ev and in Ja *bayi muñju-ŋaŋgay* 'woman-WITHOUT'. Similarly, a single woman, beyond usual marrying age, is *balan yalŋgay-gan* in Ev and *balan bayabay-ŋaŋgay* 'man-WITHOUT' in Ja.

(**d**) Identical to another noun, but with different gender:
- As illustrated at (30) in chapter 2, Ja has *bayi gagilbarra* for 'rainbow', *balan gagilbarra* for 'wompoo pigeon', and *bala gagilbarra* for 'flame kurrajong tree'.
- *Bala jinbay* is Ja for 'ground, earth', and three species of termite are *bayi jinbay*, because they build nests on the ground.
- The candlenut tree (*Aleurites moluccana*) is *balam gaburra* in Ev and *balam mayaja* in Ja, since it harbours edible grubs, which are *bayi mayaja* in Ja.
- The Ja term for eel is *bayi balbiji* (corresponding to half-dozen specific names in Ev). The storm bird or channel-billed cuckoo (*Scythrops novaehollandiae*) is *balan balbiji* in Ja, because it has a long tail rather like an eel.

(**e**) Named by an adjective:
- As mentioned in section 4.3, the Ev kin terms *bayi/balan galbin* 'man's son or daughter' and *bayi/balan daman* 'woman's son or daughter' are both rendered in Ja just by the adjective 'little': *bayi/balan wumbarr*.
- The stump of a tree is *bala burumba* in Ev and *bala ñingal* in Ja, where *ñingal* is the Ja adjective 'short' (corresponding to *gundun* in Ev).
- Ja adjective *ŋilu* 'cold' is the basis for three Ja nouns: *bala ŋilu* 'wintertime' (*bala birrgil* in Ev), *balan ŋilu* 'nautilus pearl shell' (*balan gubaguba* in Ev), and *balan/ bayi ŋilu* 'widow/widower' (*balan/bayi bilmbu* in Ev).

The overarching principle is that everything which has a name in Ev also has a name in Ja, and this must be exclusively in terms of Ja lexemes. No Ev lexeme may be used in Ja (the only exception appears to be the four grandparent/grandchild terms).

Ev accepted many loan words from English in the late nineteenth and early twentieth centuries. These were allocated correspondents in Ja by drawing on the existing Ja lexicon. For example:

- *Balan jarrababarrañ*, the Ja term for scrub turkey (*balan guyjarri* in Ev), was extended to cover, in Ja, the European hen, described in Ev as *balan jugi* (a loan from *chook*).
- *Bala diŋun*, the Ja correspondent for *bala diban* 'stone' in Ev, was also used for the Ev loan *bala ŋayan* 'iron'.
- Ev loans *balam ŋarriñji* 'orange', *balam mandarriñ* 'mandarin', and *balam mayŋgu* 'mango' were included under *balam gumalam*, the existing Ja term for a couple of dozen fruit which can be eaten raw.
- Watermelon is *balam milin* in Ev and in Ja simply *balam jujamu*, based on Ja *balan jujamu* 'water' (corresponding to *balan bana* in Ev).

- Ev loan *balam juga* 'sugar' is *balam warruň* in Ja, based on the existing Ja noun *bala warruň* 'sand' (because of a similar consistency).
- Handkerchief was described by the loan *bala ŋaŋgija* in Ev. Its name in Ja is descriptive: *bala jurmbay-barri-muŋa* 'that which habitually rubs'.

As mentioned in section 2.4, the loan word *mani* 'money' takes gender marker *bala* in the Ngajan and Mamu dialects but *bayi* in Jirrbal. All dialects render it as *walba* in Ja. As far as I can tell, *walba* was not an existing lexeme in Dyirbal Ja. However, neighbouring language Yidiň had, in its Ev, *walba* for 'stone', extended after the invasion to 'coins'. It seems that *walba* was adopted from Yidiň Ev into Dyirbal Ja to describe this new commodity (quite unlike anything known before).

Having spent some pages exemplifying (II) descriptive labels, we can now examine (I), direct naming in Ja. My field technique was in two stages. First, the Ja equivalents were elicited for each of more than two thousand Ev lexemes. The directionality was then reversed; for each Ja form, I enquired what its Ev correspondent(s) would be. There were two different kinds of result.

At stage 1, *bayi yuŋga* had been given as the Ja name for a number of types of macropods (kangaroos and wallabies). In stage 2, I asked what *bayi yuŋga* corresponded to in Ev, and Chloe Grant simply listed the Ev species names: *bayi barrgan* 'sand wallaby', *bayi bungil* 'red scrub wallaby (pademelon)', *bayi jabali* 'whip-tail kangaroo', *bayi yuri* 'eastern grey kangaroo', and so on. No one of these was regarded as more central than the others as the Ev correspondent for Ja *bayi yuŋga*. Similar results were obtained with terms for possums, frogs, pythons, lizards, snails, bees, fruits, grasses, and more.

A different kind of result was obtained in other instances. For example, stage 1 produced:

(12)   Ev balan buni   'fire'   Ja balan yibay
        Ev balan yiŋgiň 'flying spark' Ja balan yibay

In stage 2, I asked what the Ev correspondent was of *balan yibay*, and was told: '*Balan buni*.' 'Anything else?' 'No, just *balan buni*.' 'What about *balan yiŋgiň*?' 'Oh yes, that's *balan yibay* too.' Then I asked: '*Balan buni* and *balan yiŋgiň* are two separate words in Ev, how can this difference be brought out in Ja?' The following revised correspondences were then provided:

(13)   Ev balan buni   Ja balan yibay
        Ev balan yiŋgiň Ja balan yibay gilgarrin-ja-ŋu 'fire which jumps a lot'

Balan buni can be called a 'nuclear word'. It is the central correspondent of Ja *balan yibay*. In contrast, *balan yiŋgiň* is a non-nuclear item, which is defined in terms of the nuclear one by adding the qualification 'which jumps a lot'.

A number of other nouns have nuclear status, including 'water' and 'stone'. But the nuclear/non-nuclear distinction shows up most clearly in the Ja correspondents of Ev verbs. In stage 1, about seven hundred Ev verbs were gone through separately with Chloe Grant and George Watson, and their Ja correspondents elicited (in almost every instance, the two consultants gave identical correspondents).

At this stage, about a hundred and fifty Ja verbs were obtained (more came later), almost all occurring several times as correspondents of different Ev verbs. For example, the Ja transitive verb *ñuriman* (quoting present tense citation form) was given as correspondent of (among others) the following transitive verbs in Ev:

(14)   buran   'see, look at, notice, read'
       waban   'look up at/for (e.g. a bee's nest up a tree)'
       rugan   'watch [someone] going, watch go out of sight'
       wamin   'watch someone without their being aware they are being watched,
               take a sneaky look'

Then a short time later, in stage 2, the Ja verb *ñuriman* was put to the consultant, and they were asked what the Ev correspondents were. A single Ev word was given in response, *buran*—nothing else. I enquired about *waban* and it was confirmed that that was also *ñuriman* in Ja. Then I asked: 'You've got two words in Ev, *buran* and *waban*, with different meanings. How can you bring out this difference in Ja?' 'Well, *buran* be just *ñuriman*, and for *waban* you draw it out a bit, say *ñuriman yalugala*.'

There was a similar response for other pairs. The nuclear verb, *buran*, was always given as *ñuriman*, nothing more, while an expanded correspondent was provided for each of *rugan* and *wamin*. My field notebook then read:

(15)   ñuriman
       buran   *just* ñuriman (*nuclear verb*)
       waban   ñuriman yalugala
       rugan   ñuriman bawalbiŋu
       wamin   jubuñju ñuriman

The following had been added to *ñuriman* in definitions for the three non-nuclear verbs of seeing:

- For *waban*, verb marker *yalu* 'to a place here' plus suffix *-gala* 'up'; that is, 'look towards a place up here'.
- For *rugan*, verb *bawalbi-l* 'go' (the Ja for Ev *yanu-l*) in relative clause inflection, *-ŋu*; that is, 'look at [someone] who is going'.
- For *wamin*, adjective *jubuñ* 'quiet, soft' (the Ja correspondent of Ev *yubay*) in instrumental inflection, *-ju*; that is, 'look at quietly/sneakily'.

After going through stage 2 with Chloe Grant, a few days later I followed the same procedure with George Watson, and obtained identical results. When I asked concerning the Ev correspondent of *ñuriman*, just *buran* was given, nothing else. On further enquiry, definitions were provided for the three non-nuclear verbs, *waban*, *rugan*, and *wamin*, while *buran* was consistently left just as *ñuriman*. The definitions were not precisely the same between consultants, but they were pretty similar.

The same results were obtained for every other Ja verb. It appears that what is happening is the following. Of the verbs in Ev, some are nuclear verbs with others being non-nuclear hyponyms of them. Ja has just nuclear verbs. When an Ev correspondent is sought for a Ja verb, the matching nuclear verb is given, nothing else.

Non-nuclear verbs can be defined in terms of their nuclear counterparts. The nuclear verbs are the basic building blocks; they cannot be defined in terms of each other. Ja has just nuclear verbs, the minimum inventory such that it is possible to express in Ja everything which can be said in Ev.

There is further discussion of nuclear verbs, and definitions of non-nuclear verbs, in sections 5.6–5.8. Meanwhile we examine nouns, adjectives, and time words in Ja.

5.4 Nouns

Ja terms for kin relations were presented in section 4.3. We can now briefly consider further semantic fields.

5.4.1 Body and other parts

There is typically a Ja noun for a number of Ev nouns describing adjacent or related parts of a human or animal body. For example (all take gender marker *bala*):

(16) Ev jina   'foot of person, goanna, crocodile, bird;
                  foot marks, animal tracks; that end of a
                  boomerang which is held in the hand'
           ŋuru   'heel, heel mark'   } Ja jurrmbur
           gadam 'sole of foot'
           magal 'back paw of wallaby, kangaroo'
           murun 'paw of dog; hoof of goat, pig, cattle, horse'

(17) Ev ŋangu 'mouth of person, bag, cave; doorway, door'
           mulin 'lips'   } Ja jawa
           buŋun 'marsupial pouch'

In Ev there are separate terms for phlegm (*galgi*), spittle (*ñumba*), and nasal mucus (*ñurray*); all are rendered by *ŋuju* in Ja. Ev has specific names for ten or so bones: clavicle (collar bone), shoulder blade (scapula), breast bone (sternum), true ribs, floating ribs, radius and ulna in the forearm, tibia and fibula in the lower leg, together with a general term *wurrmburr* 'bone'; all are rendered by *jigir* in Ja. There are in Ev four words for tail—of a snake (*jirri*), of a crocodile (*bugu*), of a fish or eel (*biri*), and of a mammal (*wana*). All are represented by *jibubu* in Ja, and this is also the correspondent of *wundu* 'penis'.

There appear to be just a few one-to-one correspondences. These include Ja *gumari* for Ev *waguli* 'blood', Ja *gurru* for Ev *jiba* 'liver', Ja *jumbuy* for Ev *diŋgal* 'head'. Almost all body parts are in the *bala* gender; one exception is 'scrotum' which is *bayi galun* in Ev, *bayi jibu* in Ja (see the end of section 2.3).

5.4.2 Age group terms

Ja has one-to-one correspondents for the general terms 'man' and 'woman', but *bayi bugiba* 'old man' is rendered by *bayi ŋundayba* and *balan jambiba* 'old woman' by *balan ŋundayba*. Another many-to-one correspondence is:

(18)   Ev bayi/balan malay   'new born baby'
       bayi/balan jaja   'child, up to about five'   } bayi/balan ñalmaru
       bayi/balan ñalŋga 'child, any age to puberty'

There was a unique correspondent, Ja *bayi rumbin*, for Ev *bayi gubi* 'wise man' (see section 1.1). But *bayi mularri* 'initiated man' was rendered by a descriptive label *bayi wadirr-ba* 'cicatrices-WITH'.

When the Europeans arrived, with the colour of skin one sees on a corpse, they were at first thought to be the returning spirits of dead ancestors. *Bayi waybala* 'white man' (a loan from *white fellow*) was included under *bayi gumirriñ*, the existing Ja for Ev *bayi guwuy* 'spirit of a dead man'. Similarly, *balan mijiji* 'white woman' (a loan from *missus*) was linked with Ev *balan guyŋgun* 'spirit of a dead woman' as Ja *balan muguyŋgun*. (Dyirbal-speaking peoples soon realised their error of identification, as the invaders ravished both land and women, and shot many of the men; but the Ja terms survived.)

5.4.3 Fauna

Under (f) in section 2.3, we mentioned Ev terms *bayi rubiñ* 'any edible fauna (including most fishes and some snakes)' and *bala jalgur* 'meat and fish, including the edible parts of shellfish' (prototypically used for lean meat). There is no Ja term corresponding to *bayi rubiñ*; one has to state what kind of edible animal is at issue. Nor is there a regular correspondent for *bala jalgur*. I was given only *bala jagarri-ŋangay* 'fat-WITHOUT', referring to its secondary sense of 'lean meat'.

As mentioned earlier, some types of fauna have a descriptive label in Ja—'he who pierces/bites a lot', and so on. There are also many direct Ja correspondents, most on a many-to-one basis. Table 5.1 illustrates this where there is no generic term in Ev.

TABLE 5.1. Only specific terms in Ev, just a generic term in Ja

Everyday style (Ev)	Jalnguy style (Ja)
bayi barrgan 'agile wallaby', bayi bungil 'pademelon wallaby', bayi yuri 'eastern grey kangaroo', and 6 other species of macropods (wallabies and kangaroos)	bayi yuŋga 'macropods'
bayi midin 'ringtail possum', bayi yabi 'brush-tail possum', and 9 other possums	bayi jibuñ 'possums'
bayi jaraba 'brown frog', bayi wurrŋul 'Leseur's frog', bayi ŋabambul 'tadpole', and about 20 other frogs	bayi guwaga 'frogs'
balan maguy 'scrub python', balan gabul 'diamond python'	balan gundaya 'pythons'
bala bayal 'small native bee', bala jurrugan 'black native bee', bala mayi '(introduced) English bee', and 2 other bees, plus balam girñjal 'honey'	bala mugilmbarran 'bees'
	balam mugilmbarran 'honey'
bayi jambun 'long wood grub', bayi gaban 'grub in acacia tree', bayi mandija 'grub in milky pine tree', and 4 other edible grubs	bayi mayaja 'edible grubs'
bayi jaban 'spotted eel', bayi girriŋan 'black eel', and 3 other eels	bayi balbiji 'eels'

There are also generic terms in Ja for 'lizards' (relating to 11 specific terms in Ev), 'bandicoots' (2), 'bats' (3), 'rats' (5), 'turtles' (4), 'shrimp and crayfish' (2), 'ticks' (4), 'edible snails' (2), 'worms' (3), and 'leeches' (4).

There are a couple of instances of there being a generic term plus a bevy of specific names in Ev, and a generic term in Ja:

(19)   Ev bayi wadam 'dangerous snakes',
            plus bayi ŋumbulu 'black whip snake',   Ja bayi jumbiñ,
            bayi guñjiwurru 'taipan', and more   'dangerous snakes'
            than 12 other names for snake species
        Ev bayi jabu 'non-harmful fishes',
            plus bayi bugal 'black bream', bayi   Ja bayi guya
            jubar 'barramundi', and more than 25   'non-harmful fishes'
            other names for fish species

We also find a few one-to-one correspondences, including Ja *bayi jugabay* for Ev *bayi garan* 'gar-fish'. *Balan ginga* was originally the Ja term just for *balan gumbiyan* 'echidna' (colloquially known as 'porcupine'). As noted towards the end of chapter 2, the bristles on a pig were perceived as similar to the echidna's spines, and *bayi ginga* in Ja was extended to also cover the Ev loan name *balan bigibigi* 'pig'.

In olden days, *balan jiŋgu* was the Ja correspondent for *balan ganibarra* 'wild dingo' and *balan guda* 'tame dingo (later extended to European dog)'. Then there came another tame animal, *balan jarraman* 'horse' (a loan from a contact pidgin; see Dixon et al. 2006a: 80–1), and this was also rendered in Ja by *balan jiŋgu*. And so too were goats.

It was mentioned in chapter 2 that birds, as a class, are believed to be the spirits of dead women and are thus *balan*. The generic term *balan dundu*, which covers all birds that do not have an individual role in legends, is rendered in Ja by *balan muguyŋgun* 'female spirit'. I was told that if one wanted in Ja to distinguish a bird from an actual female spirit, one could say *giñan-dayi muguyŋgun*, adding demonstrative *giñan* and suffix *-dayi* ('a short distance up'); 'this female spirit on high'.

Almost all birds with a role in legends (and a few others) have a name in Ja. Many are descriptive labels, as illustrated in section 5.3. Some are directly named, on a many-to-one basis. For example:

(20)   Ev balan gabirri 'emu'   ⎱ Ja balan mundin
          balan gunduy 'cassowary'   ⎰   'giant flightless birds'
       Ev bayi gayambula 'white cockatoo', ⎱ Ja bayi waŋgulay
          bayi gidila 'black cockatoo'   ⎰   'cockatoos'

5.4.4 Flora

Every language has maximal lexical resources in areas of greatest cultural importance. This applies no less to the Ja style. A number of staple foods—all requiring lengthy preparation—each have a unique correspondent in Ja. These include:

(21)   Ev balam mirrañ 'black bean'
          (*Castanospermum australe*)   Ja balam dirraba
       Ev balam jubula 'black pine'
          (*Prumnopitys amarus*)   Ja balam manji
       Ev balam guway 'brown walnut'
          (*Endiandra palmerstonii*)   Ja balam gadaginay

The Ja term *balam gumalam* is used for several kinds of fig, for wild raspberry, for wild strawberry, for bush guava, for wild cucumber, and for more than a dozen other fruits which may be eaten raw (plus introduced varieties). There is one Ja term covering several specific names in Ev for types of yams, and another for five varieties of edible lawyer vine.

Important plants without edible fruit also have many-to-one Ja correspondents. For example, *bala gurruŋun* covers four oak trees (all of the Protaceae family), appreciated for their hard timber. Half-a-dozen varieties of non-edible but useful vines are rendered in Ja by *bala galgul*; their domain of use varies—for weaving baskets or nets, for stunning fish, and for producing a medicinal rub. The two stinging trees and two stinging vines are all *balan waɲarrwaɲarr* in Ja.

There are also descriptive labels. Since torches are made from the saffronheart or jitta tree, *balan jidu* in Ev, the tree is given the same Ja name as Ev *balan ñara* 'flame, bright light'—*balan ŋarrgana*. The bark of four fig trees was used to make olden-times blankets and so these trees are called in Ja simply *bala muyñarri*, the Ja correspondent of Ev *bala gambila* 'blanket'. The fruit of the silver ash (*Flindersia bourjotiana*), *bala dubaldubal* in Ev, is eaten by white cockatoos and so the tree is named in Ja *bala waŋulay*, based on the Ja term *bayi waŋulay* 'cockatoos'; see (20).

As mentioned under (e) in section 2.3, there is no lexeme in Ja corresponding to Ev *balam wuju* 'edible plant food' from Ev. In Ja it is perfectly adequate—and more economical—to just say *balam*, which has the same semantic content as *wuju*.

5.4.5 Other nouns

There are direct Ja names for 'swamp', 'river', 'river bank', 'sun', 'moon', 'earth, ground', 'mud', 'place, house', 'scrub, jungle', among others.

Balan/bala jujamu in Ja covers Ev nouns *balan bana* 'water' plus *bala durbu* 'dew', *bala gayŋgir* 'tears', and *bala jurbul* 'sweat'. *Bala garrmban* in Ja is used for *bala garran* 'smoke' and *bala jawuy* 'steam' in Ev. *Bala jaŋan* in Ja corresponds to Ev nouns *bala muŋan* 'mountain', *bala julga* 'ridge', and *bala yirrgal* 'side of a hill'.

Descriptive labels include *bala yuwal-ŋa-ñ* 'that which breaks' for both *bala gimbirr* 'gale' and *bala gambarra* 'cyclone' in Ev, and *bala gimbura-rri* 'that which blows' for *bala gulubu* 'light wind, breeze'.

Turning to artefacts, there is one Ja term covering several varieties of spear (and also stingray tail) in Ev, one for kinds of boomerang, one for various types and sizes of dilly-bags, one covering both 'fish net' and 'turkey net'. And one-to-one correspondents for 'shield', 'sword', 'woomera', 'clothing', among others.

The descriptive label *bayi ŋarŋgalan* is used in Ja for both *bayi yarra* 'fishing line' and *bayi warugay* 'large fishing hook' in Ev; this is based on Ja *bala ŋarrŋgalan* 'nose'. Ev *bala barri* 'stone axe' and *bala mugay* 'grinding stone' are both *bala diŋun* in Ja, the same as *bala diban* 'stone' (and, nowadays, *bala ŋayan* 'iron' and *bala waya* 'wire') in Ev.

The loan word *bala buwu* 'fork' is rendered in Ja simply as *bala manburu* 'hand'; *bala bunjurru* 'boot, shoe' is in Ja *bala winarra* 'foot'; *bala gabarra* 'hat' is in Ja *bala gajaga* 'head'; and loan *bala jarruja* 'trousers' is in Ja *bala jabarra* 'thigh'.

Dyirbal Ev style has a rich repertoire of words for types of noises and sounds, and there are just a few in Ja. We find *bala wurmburr* in Ja corresponding to *bala gubil* 'whistle' in Ev. There is a many-to-one correspondence with *bala duɲurr* in Ja relating to three terms in Ev: *bala gada* 'noise of someone chopping, noise of twigs breaking as someone walks over them', *bala muŋga* 'the noise of a gun or dynamite going off, of a motor car approaching, of banging feet on floorboards (e.g. in time to music)', and *bala ramburr* 'a loud noise that shakes the earth'.

Many noises just carry descriptions in Ja. For example, 'snore', *bala buŋgurray* in Ev, was given the Ja rendering *bagu bayi nayɲul-ŋa-ñu yulmba-ŋu*, which is, literally, 'having lain down, he throws it out'.

5.5 Adjectives and time words

In traditional times, Dyirbal-speaking peoples did not have any habit of counting. There was, however, a small set of quantitative adjectives—numbering five in the Ev style of the J dialect, four in the Ev of M, and three in the Ja of both dialects:

(22) 'one'   Ev JM yuŋgul   Ja JM ñungul
      'two'   Ev JM bulayi   Ja JM ginaynjarran
      'three'   Ev J garbu, M warrañuŋgul ⎤
      'many'   Ev J mundi, M garbu   ⎬ Ja J guwarra, M warrañ
      'very many' Ev J muɲa, M garbu   ⎦

In the Ev column, note that *garbu* is 'three' in J and '(very) many' in M. The word for 'three' in M, *warrañuŋgul*, appears to be made up of *warra*, which is a particle whose usual meaning is 'inappropriate referent of pivot argument (S or O)'—see Dixon 1972: 118, and section 11.5—plus a linker -*n*- and *yuŋgul* 'one' (*n* and *y* coalescing into *ñ*). 'Three' is perhaps being described, in M, as 'odd one', in terms of an even/odd conception of number.

There is similarity of form between 'one' in the two columns, but in fact Ja *ñungul* is probably based on the Ev term for 'one' in Warungu, Dyirbal's neighbour to the west (see section 6.6.7). The Ja word for 'two' is fascinating. It appears to be made up of two affixes (plus linker -*n*-); nominal suffix -*ginay* means 'full of, covered with' while -*jarran* is 'two, each of two' (see section 11.1.1 and Dixon 1972: 223–4, 228–30). This is discussed further in section 6.6.2.

The majority of Ev adjectives do not have a direct correspondent in Ja, and require a descriptive label. However, there are more than a hundred adjectives in my Ja corpus. These are, basically, correspondents for the most central (and most frequent) adjectives in Ev. Those for dimension include:

(23) 'big'   Ev bulgan Ja gagir
      'small' Ev midi   Ja wumbarr
      'long'   Ev jalŋgay Ja wuganday
      'short' Ev gundun Ja ñingal

Dyirbal has one area of unusual lexical complexity; there are about a dozen terms for 'big' with respect to some specific type of fauna. These include: *wulmbin* 'big of kangaroo/wallaby', *wayja* 'big of water goanna', *yuɲuy* 'big of python' and *ŋarrbu* 'big of dingo or dog'. All are rendered by *gagir* in Ja.

Physical property, colour, and value terms include:

(24) 'hot'   Ev biŋgir   Ja ñigala
      'cold'   Ev dinu   Ja ɲilu
      'heavy'   Ev ñañjal   Ja ñañjarray
      'light in weight' Ev yagar   Ja walŋgu
      'rotten'   Ev buga   Ja gundum
      'black'   Ev gingin   Ja wirrin
      'white'   Ev burgala Ja ŋarrñjal
      'good'   Ev jigil   Ja ŋundarriñ
      'no good'   Ev wuygi   Ja maŋgay

There are many specific terms in Ev which are rendered in Ja through these nuclear adjectives, most often the value ones. For example, Ev adjectives 'alright', 'straight', 'intact (with no holes)', 'ripe', and 'clean' (among others) were all rendered as *ŋundarriñ* 'good', while those for which *maŋgay* 'no good' was given include 'crooked', 'stale', and 'coarse'.

Corporeal and human propensity adjectives include:

(25) 'hungry for vegetables'   Ev ŋamir   ⎫
      'hungry for meat or fish' Ev marrgiñ ⎬ Ja gabir
      'full up after eating'   Ev mañjay   ⎫
      'pregnant'   Ev muygam   ⎬ Ja duwurrba
      'fat'   Ev jami   Ja jagarri
      'acting quietly'   Ev yuray   Ja jubuñ
      'stupid, half-witted'   Ev banjar   Ja waɲul

Note that *bala duwurr* is the Ja correspondent of Ev *bala bamba* 'stomach', and *-ba* is the comitative suffix 'with'. Both 'full up after eating' and 'pregnant' are, literally, 'with stomach' in Ja. (And see (31–33) of section 6.4.)

A great many corporeal and human propensity adjectives in Ev are rendered just by value terms in Ja. *Maŋgay* 'no good' was given for, among many others, 'crippled' (adding the Ja noun for the body part affected), 'emaciated', 'shaky', 'introspective', 'sulking', 'promiscuous', 'lazy', 'tired', 'cunning', 'cheeky', 'offended', 'ashamed', 'bad-tempered', 'jealous', 'grumbling', 'telling lies', and 'forgetful'. A few Ev adjectives were rendered in Ja by *ŋundarriñ* 'good'; for example, 'feeling lively', 'feeling happy or pleased', 'kind, generous', and 'behaving well'. These value terms can have further specification added, as appropriate.

Correspondences between Ev and Ja lexemes for 'relative time' are again on a many-to-one basis:

(26) 'the other day'   Ev ŋudaŋga   Ja ganba-gabun
     'yesterday'   Ev ŋumbuŋga   Ja ganba-gabun
     'earlier on today' Ev jañjarru J, gala M ⎤
     'later on today'   Ev gilu   ⎬ Ja ganba
     'tomorrow'   Ev ŋulga   Ja ganba-gabun

The same Ja form, *ganba*, is used for both earlier and later on today. How can one tell which is intended? By the tense on the verb. In example (5), from the short Ja text extract at the beginning of this chapter, *ganba* is used in a sentence with a verb in past tense and is thus translated into Ev as *gala* 'earlier on today'. Like every human language, Ev incorporates a good deal of redundancy, indicating 'time referred to' by both tense and the time lexeme. In keeping with its parsimonious nature, Ja eliminates the redundancy. Nominal suffix *-gabun* indicates 'another' (see section 11.1.1 and Dixon 1972: 288); *ganba-gabun* refers to time before or after today.

5.6 Across word classes

In most instances, the Ja correspondent of an Ev lexeme belongs to the same word class—noun for noun, adjective for adjective, verb for verb, adverbal for adverbal. However, there are some exceptions. In the discussion of descriptive labels, in section 5.3, examples were given of some Ja correspondents for Ev nouns being based on a verb—through use of agentive nominalisers *-y* (after *a* or *u*)/zero (after *i*) and *-muŋa*—and others being identified by an adjective.

There are also correspondents of a verb or adverbal which are based on a noun or adjective. In Dyirbal, an intransitive verb stem is formed from a noun or adjective through derivational suffix *-bi-l* and a transitive verb stem through adding *-ma-l/ -(m)ba-l*. An example of a verb derived from a noun within Ja is:

(27) noun   'flame' Ev ñara   Ja ŋarrgana
     transitive verb 'set fire to' Ev maba-l Ja ŋarrgana-mba-l

That is, 'set fire to' is rendered as 'make a flame'. An example of an adverbal derived from an adjective is:

(28) adjective   'finished' Ev binirr Ja garrmirri
     transitive adverbal 'finish off' Ev jayŋu-l Ja garrmirri-mba-l

Adjective *binirr* means 'finished, all gone, nothing left'. Adverbal *jayŋu-l* refers to 'finishing something off, so that there is nothing left on which the action could be performed' (for example, pulling all the leaves off a branch, eating all the food in a house); it is rendered in Ja by 'make be finished'.

An adjectival participle can be formed from a verb by adding suffix *-ŋu* or *-nmi*. These are employed in deriving an adjective from a verb within Ja, as in:

(29) transitive verb 'cook'   Ev ñaju-l Ja durrma-l
      adjective   'cooked' Ev ñamu Ja durrma-nmi

The nuclear Ev verb *ñaju-l* refers to the act of cooking; its participle *ñaju-nmi* could describe something being cooked a bit or a lot, not enough or too much. In contrast, the non-cognate Ev adjective *ñamu* means 'cooked to perfection, ready to eat'. In Ja, this subtle and important meaning difference is lost, with Ev adjective *ñamu* being rendered by the verbal participle *durrma-nmi*.

Another example of adjective derived from verb within Ja is:

(30) transitive verb 'break'   Ev bana-l Ja yuwa-l
      adjective 'broken into pieces' Ev janu   Ja yuwa-rri-ŋu
      adjective 'shattered'   Ev muñi   Ja yuwa-yuwa-rri-ŋu
                                                 (+ wumbarr-wumbarr-bi-n)

Adjective *janu* 'broken into pieces' is rendered by a participle based on the intransitivised form (by suffix *-rri-y*) of Ja verb *yuwa-l* 'break'. Verbal reduplication indicates 'do to excess' and this is used in the Ja rendering for Ev adjective *muñi* 'shattered, smashed, crunched up into small pieces'. An extension was added to this, *wumbarrr-wumbarr-bi-n* ('REDUPLICATED-small-BECOME-PAST') 'became lots of small pieces' (reduplication of a noun or adjective indicates plurality).

5.7 Some verbs of motion

The way in which Dyirbal describes motion up or down or across a river, and up or down a hill or tree, shows considerable redundancy. That is, essentially the same information is coded in grammar and through lexemes. We can repeat, from section 2.1, the paradigm of bound forms which may—in both Ev and Ja—be added to a noun or verb marker (noting that the *-bayj-* and *-day-* forms refer to anything other than a river; that is, up or down a hill, or a cliff, or a tree, or up in the air). We can refer to this as the 'uphill/downriver' paradigm.

(31) -bayj-i   'short distance downhill'   -day-i   'short distance uphill'
      -bayj-a   'medium distance downhill'   -day-a   'medium distance uphill'
      -bayj-u   'long distance downhill'   -day-u   'long distance uphill'

      -balb-ala 'medium distance downriver' -daw-ala 'medium distance upriver'
      -balb-ulu 'long distance downriver'   -daw-ulu 'long distance upriver'
                          -guya 'across the river'

                -bawal 'long way (in any direction)'

Ev has verbs with similar reference (except for the degree of distance). In keeping with its principle of parsimony, Ja renders these by the intransitive verbalising suffix *-bi-l* applied to forms from (31), as shown in the first five rows of:

(32) 'move up hill, etc.'   Ev wayñji-l Ja dayi-bi-l
      'move down hill, etc.' Ev buṇa-l   Ja bayju-bi-l
      'move upriver'   Ev wandi-l   Ja dawulu-bi-l
      'move downriver'   Ev dada-y   Ja balbulu-bi-l
      'cross river'   Ev mabi-l   Ja guya-bi-l
      'go'   Ev yanu-l   Ja bawal-bi-l
      'come'   Ev bani-y   Ja yali-bi-l

It can be seen that the 'long distance' forms from (31) are used except for 'up hill' where it is the 'short distance' form (I do not have any non-ad-hoc explanation for this).

In the sixth row of (32) we see that 'go', the commonest verb of all, involves *-bi-l* added to *-bawal* 'long way in any direction'; this is used in (7) and (9) above. Verb 'come' is rendered by *-bi-l* added to verb maker *yali* 'towards here' (see paradigm (15) in section 2.1).

There are some intransitive/transitive pairs of verbs of motion which are rendered by intransitive verbaliser *-bi-l* and transitive verbaliser *-mba-l* added to the same form from (31):

(33) intransitive 'go'   Ev yanu-l   Ja bawal-bi-l
      transitive   'lead' Ev munda-l Ja bawal-mba-l

(34) intransitive 'move downriver'   Ev dada-y Ja balbulu-bi-l
      transitive   '(flood) washes away' Ev danga-l Ja balbulu-mba-l

Each of the lexemes in (32–34) is a nuclear verb; some have a number of non-nuclear verbs associated with them. For instance, in stage 1 of the elicitation, *dayibin* was given as the Ja correspondent of *wayñjin* 'move up anything other than a river', and also of *biliñu* 'climb a tree, branch by branch', and of *bumirañu* '"walk" up the smooth trunk of a tree with the aid of a loop of lawyer-vine thrown around the tree and continually jerked up' (for a full account of this, see Lumholtz 1889: 89–90). When, at stage 2, Ja verb *dayibin* was put to consultants, they gave just the nuclear verb *wayñjin* as its Ev correspondent. Further enquiry yielded more detailed renderings (what we can call 'definitions') for the two non-nuclear verbs:

(35) dayibin
              wayñjin   *just* dayibin (*nuclear verb*)
              biliñu   dayibin dandu-ṇga ('tree-LOCATIVE')
              bumirañu dayibin juyi-bila ('lawyer.vine-WITH')

5.8 Other verbs

Ja employs a number of stratagems for allowing it to express, with a minimum of special lexemes, everything which can be said in Ev. We saw in the previous section that a number of verbs of motion are manufactured by using a root which is primarily a suffix, from the uphill/downriver paradigm, (31), and adding to it an intransitive or transitive verbaliser.

5.8.1 Transitive/intransitive pairs

There are a number of pairs of Ev verbs which have essentially the same semantic content and differ only in transitivity. Relating to these, Ja has a single verbal root, which is always transitive, and uses the intransitivising suffix -*(ma)rri-* to create a correspondent for the intransitive member of the Ev pair.

There are two varieties of such transitivity pairs. One has subject of the intransitive (S) corresponding to object (O) of the transitive, as in

(36)   transitive   'put (something) standing' Ev jarra-l Ja dinda-l
         intransitive 'stand'   Ev jana-y Ja dinda-rri-y

(37)   transitive   'break (something)' Ev bana-l Ja yuwa-l
         intransitive '(something) breaks' Ev gayñja-y Ja yuwa-rri-y

Other pairs with this syntactic orientation include 'take (something) out' and 'come out'.

The other variety of transitivity pair has S corresponding to transitive subject (A), as illustrated in (10) above. The intransitive verb has an obligatory S argument and an optional second argument, e.g. 'X_S talks (to Y)'. These relate to the obligatory A and O arguments of the transitive verb: 'X_A tells Y_O'. Further examples include:

(38)   transitive   'follow (O: person, river, track)' Ev banja-l Ja gañjama-l
         intransitive 'follow' (plus optional dative   Ev marri-l Ja gañjama-rri-y
                      NP: person, river, track)

(39)   transitive   'eat (O: food)'   Ev jaŋga-y Ja yulmi-y
         intransitive 'eat' (plus optional   Ev mañja-y Ja yulmi-marri-y
                      instrumental NP: food)

In some (perhaps all) instances, the transitive and intransitive members of a pair have only approximately the same meaning. In (39), transitive *jaŋga-y* refers to any type of eating, whereas intransitive *mañja-y* would be used of someone who eats a substantial quantity of food to appease hunger (it was glossed by a consultant as 'having a feast'). The rather particular meaning of *mañja-y* is quite lost in the routine Ja rendering *yulmi-marri-y*. This is reminiscent of the subtle distinction between Ev adjective *ñamu* 'cooked to perfection' and verb *ñaju-l* 'cook'—see (29) in section 5.6—being lost in the Ja renderings. There are no doubt many other examples of Ja conveying an Ev meaning only in a rather rough-and-ready manner.

5.8.2 Kinds of definitions

Ja has a verbal root corresponding to each nuclear verb in Ev. Consultants agreed that it should be possible to render in Ja the meaning of each non-nuclear Ev verb. To achieve this, they offered 'definitions', which are of various kinds. A sample of these follows.

(a) Morphological addition to a nuclear Ja verb

- Reduplication of the first two syllables of a verbal root indicates 'do to excess'. Nuclear verb *wuga-l* 'give' in Ev is rendered by *jayma-l* in Ja. The non-nuclear Ev verb *gibi-l* is used when a hunter cuts up his kill and gives it to relatives. A young man would make an ostentatious show of presenting choice portions of meat to his promised wife and her mother, as an assurance that he could provide for them and should now be permitted to claim his bride (see section 4.4). In keeping with this, the Ja rendering of *gibi-l* involves reduplication of the nuclear verb: *jayma-jayma-l*.

- Adding an aspectual-type suffix to a nuclear Ja verb. Suffix *-ja-y* indicates that an action applies to many instances of the referent of the O argument of a transitive verb. Nuclear Ja verb *maŋga-l* 'pick up' is rendered by *mulwa-l* in Ja. And Ja has *mulwal-ja-y* for the Ev non-nuclear verb *naŋgi-y* 'scrap around (on the floor, or in a dish or bag), picking up every last crumb of food'.

(b) Syntactic addition to a nuclear Ja verb

- Adding a modifier within a core NP. In (35), *juyi-bila* 'lawyer.cane-WITH' is added to the S argument for Ja rendering of Ev verb *bumira-y* 'climb with the aid of a lawyer cane loop'.
- Adding a relative clause within a core NP. Ev nuclear verb *jurra-l* 'rub' is rendered by *jurrmbayba-l* in Ja. There is a related non-nuclear Ev verb *yiji-l* 'a gubi (Aboriginal doctor) rubs a sick person—often, with armpit sweat—to cure them'. The Ja correspondent of this was given as *maŋgay-bi-ŋu durrmbayba-l* 'rub [someone] who is sick'. The Ja adjective *maŋgay* 'no good' covers—among many other things—being sick; it takes intransitive verbaliser *-bi-l* plus relative clause ending *-ŋu*. There is a further relative clause example in (15).
- Adding a peripheral element. We saw in (32) that Ja uses *guya-bi-l* for Ev *mabi-l* 'cross river'. For Ev *balŋga-l* 'cross river by walking across on a log', Ja has *guya-bi-l dandu-ŋga-rru* ('log-LOCATIVE-ALONG'). There is a similar example in (35).
- Adding a verb marker—see example (15) above.

(c) Definition in terms of two nuclear items

- This is illustrated by the following transitive verbs and adverbals (quoting them in present tense citation forms):

(40) nuclear verb   'hit with rounded   Ev bijin   Ja jubumban
                           implement'
      nuclear adverbal 'try/test (something)' Ev ŋunbiran Ja ŋurbin
      non-nuclear   'bang on a log to see Ev ruljun   Ja ŋurbin jubumban
      verb   whether it is hollow'

That is, Ja adverbal and verb are juxtaposed—just as they can be in Ev—producing *ŋurbin jubumban* 'test by hitting with a rounded implement'. The O argument would be 'hollow log' *(murjañ* in Ja, corresponding to *yugari* in Ev), this making the meaning clear.

- Alternatively, a non-nuclear Ev verb can be rendered in Ja by two nuclear verbs in syntactic construction. In the J dialect we find:

(41) nuclear verb   'see, look at'   Ev buran   Ja ñuriman
      nuclear verb   'pick up'   Ev maŋgan Ja mulwan
      non-nuclear verb 'find (what has   Ev jaymban Ja ñuriman mulwali
                           been looked for)'

The Ja rendering for *jaymba-n* 'find-PRESENT' is thus *ñurima-n mulwa-li* 'see-PRESENT pick.up-PURPOSIVE', 'see to pick up' (which is what one generally does to a lost thing when it has been found). (Mja has *jawaymba-l* for 'find'; see table 6.4 in section 6.4.)

(d) Adding paralinguistic material

- Contrasting voice timbre may play a role. *Burrmbuñma-l* was given as Ja correspondent for two Ev verbs with totally different emotive overtones. *Buybu-l* is 'spit at, typically spit a curse at someone' and *ñuñja-l* is 'kiss in traditional manner, delivering a raspberry-like smack on the cheeks when reunited with relative or friend'. When I wondered whether ambiguity might arise on the use of *burrmbuñma-l* in Ja, Chloe Grant explained that a warm, inviting timbre would be employed for the 'kiss' sense and a harsh, angry one for the 'spit at' meaning.
- Although seldom sufficiently acknowledged, gesture and mime play a considerable role in language-based communication; these have an enhanced role in Ja. As mentioned under (b) just above, *jurrmbayba-l* is the Ja correspondent for Ev nuclear verb *jurra-l* 'rub'. It was also given, in stage 1 of the elicitation, for non-nuclear verbs *baŋga-l* 'paint or draw with a finger (and, nowadays, write)' and *ñamba-l* 'paint with the flat of the hand'. How to distinguish these in Ja? Noun

bala mala in Ev, *bala manburu* in Ja, covers both hand and fingers. That is, there is no way of distinguishing 'with a finger' and 'with the flat of the hand' within Ja. To remedy this, a mime would be added to *jurrmbayba-l*: using a finger, or using the palm of the hand.

Another example involves *gundum-ma-l* which was given, in stage 1, as the Ja for two Ev verbs. One is nuclear verb *bugama-l* 'run down, chase after to catch, e.g. a naughty child, your wife's lover, a stray cow'. The other is non-nuclear *julma-l* 'squeeze, e.g. squeeze a boil, squeeze fruit to extract the juice, knead flour mixture in baking'. To specify this in Ja, Chloe Grant added Ja transitive adverbal *yalaba-l* 'do like this' to *gundum-ma-l*, plus a mime of grasping the hands together.

5.8.3 Some semantic parameters

Dyirbal lexicon and grammar are structured in terms of a number of semantic contrasts. Some underlie the semantic organisation of virtually every human language: 'motion/rest', 'to/from', and 'here/there'. 'Up/down' is found in many other languages spoken in hilly country. 'Water/not water' plays a role in suffixes attached to noun and verb markers, and in verbs of motion, illustrated at (31–32) above. Two other contrasts are of particular interest.

(i) A 'visible/non-visible' distinction is shown in the first element of noun and verb markers, as set out in of section 2.1. In addition, there are separate verbs for 'spear at something which cannot be seen' and 'spear something which can be seen'; these were listed in the first illustration given of Ja—at (3) in section 1.2. There is also (as in most languages) a contrast between nuclear verbs *bura-l* in Ev, *ñurima-l* in Ja, 'gain sense impression visually; i.e. see, look at', and *ŋamba-l* in Ev, *ŋarrmi-l* in Ja, 'gain sense impression auditorily, i.e. hear, listen to'.

(ii) A contrast 'hold on to/let go of' is pervasive through the Dyirbal lexicon. For example:
- An important distinction is that between *balga-l* in Ev, *duyi-l* in Ja, 'hit with a long rigid implement (e.g. a stick) held in the hand; kill' and *minba-l* in Ev, *bilju-l* in Ja, 'hit with a long rigid implement (e.g. stick or boomerang) which is thrown; lightning strikes, shoot with a gun'.
- As also illustrated at (3) in section 1.2, there are different verbs for 'spear something holding onto the spear' and 'spear something, throwing the spear'.
- There is in Dyirbal a basic concept 'put in motion in a trajectory'. This is combined with 'hold on to' and 'let go of' in the following transitive nuclear verbs:

(42)   'put into trajectory, holding onto;   Ev baygu-l Ja bubama-l
        shake, wave or bash'; see (4) in
        section 5.1 above
        'put into trajectory, letting go of;   Ev mada-l Ja naɲɲu-l
        throw'

During stage 1 of elicitation, I asked George Watson and his wife Ginnie how they would render, in Ja, the Ev non-nuclear verb *darrbi-l* 'shake a blanket to remove dirt or crumbs which have gathered on it'. This set off an argument as to which was the most appropriate Ja verb, and emphasised for me the importance of the 'let go of/hold on to' parameter. George suggested *bubama-l* on the grounds that the blanket is held onto, whereas Ginnie preferred *naɲɲu-l* since the crumbs are thrown off. It really boils down to the question: what is the O argument for *darrbi-l*? Most often the O is the blanket, supporting *bubama-l* as Ja correspondent—as shown in (4) above—but sometimes the crumbs or whatever make up the O NP, supporting *naɲɲu-l* as the Ja rendering.

5.9 Envoi

On every occasion, speakers emphasised to me that each word (that is, each lexeme) in Ja must be different from Ev (the only exception appears to be the four grandparent/grandchild terms). It would be a considerable mental burden to have to master a second vocabulary, the same size as that of Ev. In fact, Ja has about a quarter as many lexemes as Ev. We have seen some of the strategies which Ja employs to get by with a reduced lexicon. There may be just a transitive verb root in Ja corresponding to a transitive/intransitive pair (with similar meaning) in Ev. The main feature of Ja is that it operates on a more general level than Ev. There is a full set of nuclear verbs, of generic nouns, and of the most central adjectives; more specific lexemes can—should the occasion arise—be rendered in Ja by 'definitions' based on the nuclear and generic terms.

Ja is purposely vague. This is consistent with its social role: to mark the avoidance relation between certain categories of kin, and to be used by youths just after they have been initiated. In everyday speech one should be as specific as possible; in avoidance circumstances it is appropriate to speak in generic terms. The semantic system of Dyirbal is, in effect, mapped onto vocabulary at two levels of generality. Investigation of the relationship between the two levels allows us to extrapolate the character of the underlying system.

Ja has the same grammatical possibilities as Ev but it exploits some of them rather more in order to minimise its inventory of lexemes. This is seen in the employment of descriptive labels utilising derivational suffixes, such as 'he who laughs a lot' for the kookaburra bird, and 'associated with the fighting ground' for three wagtail birds (type II in section 5.3 above).

One of the craftiest devices in Ja is creating locational verbs by adding verbalisers -*bi-l* and -*mba-l* to erstwhile suffixes for 'uphill', 'downriver', and the like, described in section 5.7. The uphill/downriver paradigm set out in (31) is unusual; nothing quite like it is found in any other Australian language. It plainly predates the expansion of Ja vocabulary, since Ja verbs are based on it. The most northerly dialect, Ngajan, has -*ba:ndu* as the 'long way (in any direction)' form, corresponding to -*bawal* in other dialects. In keeping with this, the correspondent for Ev *yanu-l* 'go' is *ba:ndu-bi-l* in Ngajan Ja, as against *bawal-bi-l* in the Ja of southern dialects.

The question of where Ja lexemes came from is a fascinating one. This is pursued in the next chapter, for the Ja of both Dyirbal and its neighbour Yidiñ.

There was a fairly full study of Ja in the last part (pp. 230–433) of my 1968 PhD thesis. The 1972 monograph, *The Dyirbal Language of North Queensland* was essentially a revision of the grammar which made up the first half of the PhD, plus summary information on Jalnguy (pp. 32–34. 292–306, 311–14, 320–7). Fuller material on Ja was published in 'The semantics of giving' (1973) and especially in 'A method of semantic description' (1971). Slightly revised versions of these two studies were included in the volume *Where have all the adjectives gone? and other studies in semantics and syntax* (1982a). Examples additional to those given in the present chapter can be found in the 1968 thesis and the 1971/1982a paper. Note, though, that some of the data and analyses in these early works have been refined in the light of further fieldwork, which continued from 1970 until 2002.

While this book was already in press, a subtle grammatical difference between Jja and J came to light. As reported in section 11.4.1, the reflexive derivational suffix on the -l conjugation in J is

- -*yirrí-y* when next but one after a stressed syllable
- -*rrí-y* elsewhere

Neighbouring dialects W, M, Y, and G have -*rri-y* everywhere.

Jja differs from J, and is like the Ev style of other dialects, in having -*rri-y* everywhere.

6

The origin of 'mother-in-law' vocabulary in Dyirbal and Yidiñ

The last chapter dealt with the semantic organisation of Jalnguy—the 'mother-in-law' style—illustrated for Dyirbal, for which there is the fullest data. We can now expand our scope to investigate differences between dialects of Dyirbal, and the relationship between Ja (Jalnguy) styles in Dyirbal and in Yidiñ. It will be seen that Dyirbal dialects show more differences in Ja than in Ev (everyday) vocabulary, and that the Ja styles of Dyirbal and Yidiñ are more similar than their respective Ev styles. We then study the origins of Ja lexemes in the two languages. Some appear to have been created from an Ev lexeme by phonological deformation, some are identical to an Ev form in another dialect or language, and some have been borrowed from Ja to Ja. For the latter, we investigate the direction of borrowing—from the Ja of Dyirbal into that of Yidiñ or vice versa.

Information on Ja is available for three dialects of Dyirbal, and we also examine Ev lexemes in these dialects. The following abbreviations will be used:

in dialect:	Ngajan	(Dulgubarra) Mamu	(Jabunbarra) Jirrbal
Ev lexeme	N	M	J
Ja lexeme	Nja	Mja	Jja

For Yidiñ we have Ev lexemes in both tablelands and coastal dialects, but information on Ja could only be obtained in the tablelands variety. Abbreviations used here are:

in dialect	tablelands	coastal
Ev lexeme	t	c
Ja lexeme	tja	—

6.1 The data base

6.1.1 In Dyirbal

Forms quoted in the last chapter were all from the Mamu and Jirrbal dialects, which have two rhotic phonemes and a system of just three short vowels. The most northerly dialect, Ngajan, has undergone the following phonological changes (where *V* is any vowel and *C* any consonant).

1. A contrast between short and long vowels has developed through the following changes. At the end of a syllable, *Vl* became *V:*, original *Vr* also became *V:*, *ay* became *a:*, and *uy* became *i:* (there were no syllable-final *iy*). Thus Ngajan has *ya:ga:* 'road' and *wagi:* 'sand' where other dialects have *yalgay* and *waguy*.
2. The contrast between two rhotics—apico-alveolar *rr* and apico-postalveolar *r*—was neutralised in Ngajan; the single rhotic in this dialect (an alveolar continuant) is written as *R*. The changes involved were:
   • A sequence *CVrV* became *CV:RV*
   • All other *r*, and all *rr*, simply became *R*
   For example, *bu:Ru* 'elbow' and *buRu* 'rhinoceros beetle' correspond to *buru* and *burru* in other dialects.

The Wari dialect, between N and M, retains a rhotic distinction but has developed long vowels through just some of the changes which have applied in N; full details are in chapter 13. Since no Ja data was obtained for Wari, this dialect is only marginally relevant for the present chapter.

As is illustrated in table 6.1, there was considerably more variation in the forms of Ja lexemes, than for Ev forms, across the N, M, and J dialects. In rows (a–e), the Ev forms are all the same (save for the regular long vowel adoption in Ngajan). The Ja

TABLE 6.1. Some corresponding Ev and Ja forms across N, M, and J dialects of Dyirbal

(a)	'sit'	NMJ ñina-y		Nja majiRabi-l, Mja, Jja majirrabi-l	
(b)	'hungry'	N ŋami:, MJ ŋamir		Nja danum	Mja, Jja gabir
(c)	'fat'	NMJ jami		Nja jagaRi, Mja jagarri	Jja ñunjan
(d)	'cool'	NMJ dinu		Nja gungi	Mja ŋilu	Jja gungi
(e)	'chest'	NMJ jindi		Nja magu	Mja windi	Jja mimbarra
(f)	'anus'	N ga:ñjan	MJ munu	Nja, Mja, Jja gumbu	
(g)	'pull'	NM yambu-l	J yilmbu-l	Nja yi:mbu-l	Mja, Jja yilwu-l

correspondents coincide in (a) but differ for the other four rows. Mja and Jja are the same in (b), Nja and Mja in (c), Nja and Jja (although geographically distant) are the same in (d), while in row (e) all of Nja, Mja, and Jja differ. In row (f) there is one Ev form for N and another for M and J, but the same Ja for all three dialects. For the last row, Ev forms fall together for N and M while Ja forms do so for M and J. (And note that the Ev form in J is identical to the Ja form in N, allowing for the vowel length change.)

I carried out a lexical comparison, across the Ev and Ja styles, for those items in N, M, and J for which monomorphemic Ja correspondents had been given:

(1)   THE SAME Ev LEXEME

N

208/278 = 75%	M	
128/197 = 65%	183/222 = 82%	J

(2)   THE SAME Ja LEXEME

Nja

192/278 = 69%	Mja	
75/197 = 38%	109/222 = 49%	Jja

It can be seen that M is closer to J than to N in terms of Ev lexemes; this would be expected since J and M are contiguous, whereas the W dialect intervenes between M and N. What is of particular interest is that, when Ja lexemes are examined, Mja is much more similar to Nja than it is to Jja.

It is likely (see Dixon 1972: 351) that the Dyirbal language was originally spoken by a single tribe in the southern part of its present territory. Speakers of Dyirbal then expanded north, the original tribe split into a number of separate tribes, and the modern dialects gradually evolved. It seems probable that the Ja vocabulary grew to its present size quite recently—after the dialects split—and has done so in different ways in different dialects. The figures in (2) suggest that the M and N dialects developed their Ja partly as a joint venture, whereas the J dialect has pursued a more separate course.

The organisation of Ja in the dialects is similar, but not absolutely identical. In section 5.8.1 we saw a number of instances of there being a single transitive verb in Ja for a transitive/intransitive pair in Ev. The examples given at (36), (38), and (39) in chapter 5—among others—apply across all three dialects. However, in a couple of cases there is a Ja intransitive verb just in the J dialect. We can expand (10) from the preceding chapter:

(3)

		NMJ	Nja, Mja	Jja
transitive	'tell'	buwa-y	wuyuba-l	
intransitive	'talk'	wurrba-y	Nja wuyuba-:Ri-y, Mja wuyuba-rri-y	jalguba-y

The J dialect has an intransitive verb *jalguba-y* 'talk' in its Ja, while Nja and Mja make do with an intransitivised form of *wuyuba-l* 'tell'. In the following example, involving intransitive verbs, Jja has *barrga-y* as correspondent for non-nuclear verb *manma-y* 'shift camp' while Mja defines this in terms of the nuclear verb *bawalbi-l* 'go' plus *nangu-ŋunu* 'camp-FROM'.

(4)

		MJ	Mja	Jja
nuclear	'go'	yanu-l	bawalbi-l	
non-nuclear	'shift camp'	manma-y	naŋgu-ŋunu bawalbi-l	barrga-y

(There is no verb *manma-y*, or anything with the same meaning, in N.)

Although they were remembering back thirty or forty years to a time when Ja was still in active use, the three main Ja consultants—Mollie Raymond for N, George Watson for M, and Chloe Grant for J—showed remarkable powers of recall. As we went systematically through two thousand or so Ev lexemes, they seldom failed to come up with a Ja rendering. Concentration was combined with sagacity. It was frequently instructive to observe the manner in which consultants thought.

Jubumba-l was given as the Mja equivalent of Ev nuclear verb *biji-l* 'hit with a rounded implement (either held in the hand or thrown)' and also non-nuclear verbs such as *bara-l* 'hit with a rounded implement, the blow coming downwards from a distance (for example, drive a nail in)' and *jilwa-l* 'kick with the foot, shove with the knee'. Then we moved on to another Ev verb, *nuga-y* 'grind (an axe, or food, etc.)'. George Watson thought for a good while. At first, he wondered whether *nuga-y* might also be *jubumba-l* in Mja, but wasn't too happy with this. Then he did remember the correct word for 'grind' in Mja: *yurrwi-y*. What this shows is that there is a close association, in Dyirbal semantics, between *biji-l* 'hit with a rounded implement' and *nuga-y* 'grind'.

6.1.2 In Yidiñ

The coastal and tablelands dialects of Yidiñ have a contrast of vowel length, but on a quite different basis from that in the adjacent Ngajan dialect of Dyirbal. There is a full description in section 14.6.5 of a number of phonological changes which have taken place; for present purposes the following outline should suffice:

1. A word with three syllables had the vowel in its second syllable lengthened. For example,*gudaga* 'dog' > *guda:ga*,*malanu* > *mala:nu* 'right hand'.
2. The final vowel was omitted if the preceding consonant was one which is permitted at the end of a word (a nasal, lateral, rhotic, or *y*, not a stop or *w*). Thus *guda:ga* stayed as is but *malanu* reduced to *mala:n*. It contrasts with *malan* 'flat rocks', thus establishing a distinction between long and short vowels.

There is also a small set of lexemes with a final long vowel, such as *gaju:* 'black tree ant' in Ev, and *buya:* 'fighting ground' in Ja. As mentioned in section 1.4.5, all long vowels in Yidiñ bear stress.

When I began work on it, the Yidiñ language was further along the path towards oblivion than was Dyirbal. The main consultant for the coastal dialect, Dick Moses, knew no Ja. However, Tilly Fuller and Pompey Langdon—speakers of the tableland dialect—remembered a fair amount. Similarly to speakers of Dyirbal, they maintained that no Ev lexeme could be used when speaking Ja. And they searched their minds back to remember a good deal of Ja.

It was not practicable to ask the Ja equivalents for as many Ev items as I had done for Dyirbal. However, a fair number of key Ja lexemes were volunteered (I attempted to check these between the two speakers), and Tilly Fuller—casting her mind back— produced a spontaneous text in Ja (see Dixon 1991a: 122–4).

Just like Dyirbal, there are direct Ja correspondents for nuclear verbs and the most central nouns and adjectives, and also descriptive labels as correspondents for more specific Ev lexemes. For example:

- 'Spear' is *gala* in Ev and *biŋgal* in Ja. 'Echidna' is *yagunuñ* in Ev and in Ja *biŋgal-damba*, involving derivational suffix *-damba* 'covered in, with a lot of'. Literally 'covered with spears', describing the spines on an echidna's back.
- 'Ground' is *jabu* in Ev and *gayi* in Ja. Like Dyirbal (and many other languages of the region), Yidiñ has derivational affix *-barra* 'associated with'. The Ja description *gayi-barra* 'associated with the ground' was given for both 'short-nosed bandicoot', *gayay* in Ev, and 'worm species', *wugun* in Ev.

Also like Dyirbal, there are instances of Ja having just a transitive verb corresponding to a transitive/intransitive pair in Ev. Example (36) from the last chapter is replicated in Yidiñ with (unusually) identical verb roots:

(5)			Ev	Ja
	transitive	'put	N jaRa-l, MJ jarra-l	Nja, Mja, Jja dinda-l
		standing'	tc jarra-l	tja dinda-l
	intransitive	'stand'	NMJ jana-y	Nja dinda-:Ri-y, Mja dinda-rri-y,
				Jja dinda-yirri-y
			tc jana-n	tja dinda-:ji-n

The -y conjugation for Dyirbal corresponds to the -n conjugation for Yidiñ. The intransitivising/reflexive suffix has forms *-:Ri-y*, *-rri-y*, and *-yirri-y* across the dialects of Dyirbal (see section 11.4.1); the corresponding suffix in Yidiñ is *-:ji-n* (see Dixon 1977a: 217–19).

We saw in section 5.7 of the preceding chapter how Dyirbal creates verbs of motion in Ja from bound forms in the uphill/downriver paradigm, and from a verb marker. Yidiñ has no such bound forms and uses regular roots for the Ja of verbs of motion. For example:

(6) 'come'   Ev gada-n   Ja munda:ji-n
     'go'   Ev gali-n   Ja barma-n
     'walk up' Ev maginda-n ⎫
     'climb up' Ev madi-l   ⎬ Ja gilmada-n
     'go down' Ev jada-n   Ja buŋgula-n

Yidiñ has a special way of creating Ja forms corresponding to locational lexemes in EV—it simply adds *ŋulañ* as first element to the Ev form (effectively producing a sort of compound):

(7) 'up'   Ev waŋgi   Ja ŋulañ-waŋgi
     'down'   Ev jilŋgu   Ja ŋulañ-jilŋgu
     'across the river' Ev guya   Ja ŋulañ-guya
     'east'   Ev naga   Ja ŋulañ-naga
     'west'   Ev guwa   Ja ŋulañ-guwa
     'north'   Ev guŋga:r ⎫
     'northern'   Ev jaŋgir   ⎬ Ja ŋulañ-guŋga:r
     'south'   Ev ŋara   ⎫
     'southern'   Ev guñin   ⎬ Ja ŋulañ-ŋara

Note that *guya* 'across the river' is identical to the bound form *-guya* 'across the river' in the uphill/downriver paradigm for Dyirbal—see (16) in chapter 2, and (31) in chapter 5. *Jaŋgir* 'northern' and *guñin* 'southern' function as adjectives (Dixon 1977a: 158); in Ja they are grouped with compass point labels *guŋga:r* 'north' and *ŋara* 'south' respectively.

The formative *ŋulañ* does play a role in the Ja of just the N and M dialects of Dyirbal. It is inserted between a noun or verb marker and a form from the uphill/downriver paradigm or from the up/down/out-in-front paradigm—(16) and (18) in chapter 2. For example:

(8) NMJ, Jja bala-n-dayi   Nja, Mja bala-n-ŋulañ-dayi
          THERE,ABS-II -SHORT.WAY.UPHILL

(9) NMJ, Jja bala-y-gala   Nja, Mja bala-y-ŋulañ-gala
          THERE-AT-UP.VERTICALLY

6.2 Lexemes between dialects and between languages

The remainder of this chapter examines the nature and origin of monomorphemic Ja lexemes (that is, excluding derived forms). There are 191 of these for the t dialect of Yidiñ, and 622 across the N, M, and J dialects of Dyirbal.

I carried out a lexical comparison between the two languages for those items for which Ev and monomorphemic Ja forms were known (163 items in all), parallel to the count given in (1–2) between dialects of Dyirbal. The number of lexemes which are identical or nearly identical between corresponding styles of the two languages are:

(10)   Ev   Ja

    Yidiñ and the adjacent N dialect of Dyirbal   38/163 = 23%   60/163 = 37%

    Yidiñ and all dialects of Dyirbal   42/163 = 26%   66/163 = 40%

We can see that Yidiñ and Dyirbal are more similar in Ja than in Ev lexemes. In light of the intra-Dyirbal figures in (1–2), it was suggested that the northern dialects of Dyirbal—M and N—developed their Ja partly as a joint venture, whereas the J dialect pursued a more separate course. The figures in (10) indicate that, as Ja vocabularies grew, there was a good deal of borrowing between Yidiñ and neighbouring dialects of Dyirbal.

In example (11), both Ev and Ja coincide for the two languages, in (12) just Ev do, and in (13) just Ja do.

(11) 'thigh'   N jaRa, MJ jarra   Nja jabaRa, Mja, Jja jabarra
                   tc jarra   tja jabarra

(12) 'sit'   NMJ ñina-y   Nja majiRabi-l, Mja, Jja majirrabi-l
                   tc ñina-n   tja ñiya:rji-n

(13) 'lie down'   NMJ bungi-l   Nja yu:mba-y, Mja, Jja yulmba-y
                   tc wuna-n   tja yulmba-n

In a few instances, there is a difference of meaning between Ja lexemes in the two languages. Yidiñ has separate terms—in both Ev and Ja—for 'person', 'male person, man', and 'female person, woman' whereas Dyirbal only has the last two. Ja for 'male person, man' in Dyirbal is identical to that for 'person' in Yidiñ:

(14) 'person'   tc bama   tja bayabay
      'male person, man'   tc wagu:ja   tja bulañbay
                            N ya:Ra, MJ yara   Nja bayaba:, Mja, Jja bayabay

There are a number of possible sources for Ja lexemes. One is from the Ev style of another dialect of the same language. The t and c dialects of Yidiñ are lexically very close. I have found just three lexemes in tja which are identical to Ev lexemes in the c dialect:

(15) t jambal 'raft'   tja warrjan
      c warrjan

(16) tc waju-l 'burn, cook'   tja maba-l
      c maba-l 'light (a fire)'

(17) tc jajama-n 'jump'   tja burrwa-l
      c burrwa-l 'jump up onto'

There is rich data on Ev lexemes across ten dialects of Dyirbal, and 122 of the 622 Ja lexemes have a cognate in the Ev style of another dialect. Row (g) in table 6.1—the word for 'pull'—shows *yilmbu-l* in Ja and *yi:mbu-l* in Nja (with the regular long vowel development). The forms of two adverbals are particularly interesting. Each exists in both intransitive (-y conjugation) and transitive (-l conjugation) form:

(18) 'do like this'   J   yalama-y/-l   Jja   yalaba-y/-l
                        MN yalaba-y/-l   Mja, Nja yalama-y/-l

(19) 'do what, do how' J   wiyama-y/-l   Jja   wiyaba-y/-l
                        MN wiyaba-y/-l   Mja, Nja wiyama-y/-l

It is likely that these adverbals ended in *-mba- in proto-Dyirbal. Southern dialects then shortened this to -ma- and northern dialects to -ba-. When Ja developed, each dialect took the Ev form from the other as its Ja form. Another, more mundane, example of Ev–Ja correspondence is:

(20) 'hide' N   janma-l ⎫
            MJ buyba-l ⎬ Nja, Mja, Jja muymba-l
            G   muymba-l ⎭ <Gja not available>

The verb 'have a stomach ache, bilious attack, diarrhoea' has four different forms in the Ev styles of the various dialects. Three of the forms occur in the Ja's, but of course for different dialects:

(21) N ga:ñji-y   Nja daRmba-y
      M gayñji-y   Mja gaymbuli-y
      A darrmba-y   <Aja not available>
      J gabinba-y   Jja gayñji-y
      G gaymbuli-y   <Gja not available>

In this unusually intricate example, we have NM = Jja, A = Nja, and G = Mja.

Detailed examination of the vocabularies shows thirty-three of the Ja lexemes in Yidiñ are cognate with an Ev form in one or more dialects of Dyirbal, as illustrated in:

(22)   'mountain' NMJ muɲan   Nja, Mja jaɲan, Jja ŋarrgana
                 tc bunda   tja muɲan

And thirty-five of the Ja lexemes in Dyirbal are cognate with an Ev form in Yidiñ, as in:

(23)   'vine'   NMJ gamin   Nja ga:gu:, Mja, Jja galgul
                 t galgul, c narra tja gamin

Looking further afield, nine forms in tja are cognate with Ev lexemes in languages to the north—Ja:bugay, Kuku-Yalanji, and Guugu Yimidhirr—while twenty-one of the Ja forms in dialects of Dyirbal have cognates in the Ev style of other languages, including Warrgamay and Nyawaygi to the south, and Warungu to the west. For example:

(24)   'flood'   Ja:bugay gundan   tja gundan
       'sand'   Warungu warruñ   Jja warruñ

6.3 Sources of Jalnguy lexemes

The last speakers of Warrgamay and Nyawaygi, languages to the south of Dyirbal, recalled that there had been an avoidance speech style, called Jalnguy in each instance. Nothing of it was remembered for Nyawaygi, and only three words—rather tentatively—for Warrgamay, none cognate with Dyirbal forms (Dixon 1981a: 12–13).

Working with the last speakers of Ja:bugay, Yidiñ's northerly neighbour, Patz (1991) was unable to discover whether or not there had been an avoidance style. Patz (2002: 12) also worked on Kuku-Yalanji, the next language to the north, and states: 'There is evidence that an avoidance language was formerly used among certain in-law relations, although it is not clear to what relationships this applied. The last person to know this avoidance style died many years ago and no records of this speech style exist.'

The next language north was Guugu Yimidhirr. Haviland's (1979a, b, c) work with the last rememberers was mentioned in a note at the end of section 5.2. A number of lexemes in this 'brother-in-law' style are cognate with terms in the Ev styles of other languages (including half-a-dozen in Yidiñ and Dyirbal; see Dixon 1990c: 21). But not a single cognate was found between the Guugu Yimidhirr avoidance style and the Ja of Yidiñ and Dyirbal.

It appears that Ja lexemes in Dyirbal and Yidiñ evolved in the following ways:

(a) By phonological deformation of the corresponding Ev lexemes in the same dialect.
(b) By taking over an Ev lexeme with the same or similar meaning from another dialect of the same language, or from a different language.
(c) By borrowing a Ja lexeme from another language: Yidiñ from Dyirbal, or Dyirbal from Yidiñ. It is then interesting to try to ascertain the direction of borrowing.

The next three sections—6.4, 6.5, and 6.6—deal in turn with these paths of adoption.

6.4 Dialect-internal phonological deformation

I have emphasised that, in each dialect, corresponding Ev and Ja lexemes have distinct forms. They are usually very different and plainly non-cognate, as shown by the examples throughout this chapter and the last. However, for almost fifty of the 622 Ja lexemes across dialects of Dyirbal, there is phonological similarity with the corresponding Ev lexeme. This can involve change of one or more word-internal segments, simplification of a consonant cluster, or adding a syllable. These will be discussed in turn.

Table 6.2 has one example of vowel change, in row (n), and thirteen of change in one or more consonants. We can first note that changes go in either direction: $m \rightarrow b$ in (a), $b \rightarrow m$ in (b); $\eta \rightarrow g$ in (a), $g \rightarrow \eta$ in (c). In (a–c), (j), (l), and one change in (m), the place of articulation remains the same but manner is changed; the opposite applies in (e–f). Both place and manner shift in (d) and (g–i). In (k) an apico-alveolar lateral plus bilabial nasal becomes an apico-alveolar nasal. Note that the second syllable is omitted in (l). Only two of these forms have a cognate in Yidiñ; 'river bank' is *dangil* and 'finger/toenail' is *biguñ* in the Ev style.

Another example of internal deformation has a cognate in Warrgamay, the verb 'return to point of origin, go home':

(25)		Ev	Ja		Changes
	Warrgamay	bana-			
	AJG	banaga-y	Jja	walaga-y	$b \rightarrow w, n \rightarrow l$
	MUY	ŋurba-y	Mja	walaga-y	
	NW	ŋu:ba-y	Nja	wa:Raga-y	

It is likely that the verb in proto-Dyirbal was *ŋurba-* and that the form in AJG was borrowed from Warrgamay. In Warrgamay, imperative involves suffix *-ga* and in Dyirbal it is the plain stem. Warrgamay imperative form, *bana-ga* appears to have been borrowed into southern dialects of Dyirbal, and assigned root form *banaga-y*. The Jja form, *walaga-y*, was created from this by deformation of the first two consonants (but the third remained). This Jja lexeme was then borrowed into Mja. And Nja must have

TABLE 6.2. Word-internal phonological deformation

		Ev	Ja	Changes
(a)	'hungry'	MJ ŋamir	Mja, Jja gabir	ŋ → g, m → b
(b)	'shake a blanket'	MJ darrbi-l	Jja narmi-l	d → n, b → m
(c)	'stiff, dead (of body)'	MJ juŋgul	Mja julŋul	n → l, g → ŋ
(d)	'preoccupied'	MJ ñurrŋu	Jja gurrŋu	ñ → g
(e)	'temple'	NMJ yagin	Nja, Mja yadin	g → d
(f)	'rose gum tree'	N yagiRa, MJ yagirra	Mja yadirra	g → d
(g)	'call to'	NMJ gayba-l	Nja, Mja mayba-l	g → m
(h)	'river bank'	N dangi:, MJ dangil	Mja danmil	g → m
(i)	'forked stick'	MJ raba	Mja raja	b → j
(j)	'rub'	NMJ jubi-l	Nja yubi-l	j → y
(k)	'pretend'	J gajilmba-y	Jja gajinba-y	lm → n
(l)	'message about death'	J wuwawuwa	Jja buwuba	w → b twice
(m)	'finger/toenail'	NMJ biguñ	Jja birruñ	g → rr
			Mja wirruñ	b → w, g → rr
(n)	'catch fish in net'	J jaywa-l	Jja jaywi-l	a → i

adopted a slightly different form, *waraga-y*, which, by the regular changes, became *wa:Raga-y*.

In rows (a–d) of table 6.3 there are examples of a consonant cluster simply being shortened. In rows (e) and (f) there is also replacement of bilabial stops and nasals by w, as in (25).

The various forms of the word for 'tongue', across Warrgamay and dialects of Dyirbal, provide an intriguing picture:

(26)		Ev	Ja	Change
	Warrgamay	jalañ		
	UYL	jalay		
	MAJG	jalŋgulay	Mja jalŋulay	lŋg → lŋ
	N	jalŋgula:		

TABLE 6.3. Simplifying a consonant cluster

		Ev	Ja	Changes
(a)	'motionless'	NMJ mindun	Jja minun	nd → n
(b)	'green ant'	MJ ŋulbuñ	Jja ŋubuñ	lb → b
(c)	'tease, torment'	MJ ŋilwa-l	Jja ŋiwa-l	lw → w
(d)	'float'	N wa:ŋga-l, MJ walŋga-l	Mja walŋa-l	lŋg → lŋ
(e)	'pull'	NM yambu-l, J yilmbu-l	Mja, Jja yilwu-l	lmb → lw
(f)	'night time'	N ŋulmuRu, MJ ŋulmurru	Nja ŋuwuRu, Mja, Jja ŋuwurru	lm → w

It is likely this word was *jalañ* in proto-Dyirbal, as in Warrgamay. It was then com-pounded with a form *-gulay* (of unknown origin). The second, unstressed, vowel in *jalañgulay* was elided and the heterorganic cluster *-ñg-* made into homorganic *-ŋg-*. This scenario would explain the forms in N, where the long-vowel-creation rule has applied at the end of the word but not in the middle (we would expect *jalŋgulay* to have become *ja:ŋgula:*). The reduction *jalañgulay → jalŋgulay* must have taken place after operation of the long-vowel-creation rule in N. In other dialects of Dyirbal, *jalañ* has become *jalay* (there are other instances of this change). Finally, the M dialect created its Ja lexeme by consonant cluster reduction: *jalŋulay*. (Unfor-tunately, the N and J consultants could not remember the Ja terms for 'tongue' in those dialects.)

A lexeme in Ja can involve lengthening of the corresponding form in Ev, as exempli-fied in table 6.4. Rows (a–f) involve the addition of a final *-rra* or *-wa* or *-lgay* (none of these is a meaningful element in the language), plus a number of additional changes. In rows (g–i), *-bV-* or *-wV-* is inserted as second syllable, where *V* repeats the preceding vowel. Note that in row (i) there is a dialect difference, the Ja form in M being based on the Ev form in J. (For Jja, I was given *ñuriman mulwa-li* 'see to pick up'—see (41) in chapter 5.)

There are a couple of instances where Ja forms appear to involve the addition of an initial *CV-* to a corresponding Ev lexeme:

(27) 'spirit of a dead woman' N gi:ŋgan, MJ guyŋgan Jja muguyŋgun

(28) 'head hair'   Ev N muRa:, MJ murray   Nja jilmuRa:, Mja jilmurray,
                                                            Jja gumurray

TABLE 6.4. Adding a syllable

		Ev	Ja	Changes
(a)	'help'	NMJ miwa-l	Jja miwarra-l	add at end:-rra
(b)	'spank'	N wuRŋgi-y, M wurrŋgi-y	Nja wuŋgiRa-y, Mja wuŋgirra-y	-R/rrŋg- → -ng-; add at end: -R/rra-
(c)	'blow'	MJ gimbi-l	Mja gimburra-y	final -i → urra-
(d)	'heavy'	MJ ñañjal	Jja ñañjarray	final -l → -rray
(e)	'pour'	N ji:ŋga-l, MJ jilŋga-l	Mja, Jja jilŋguwa-l	final -a → uwa
(f)	'on one's own'	J ŋalma	Jja ŋalmalgay	add at end: -lgay
(g)	'thigh'	NMJ jarra	Nja, Mja, Jja jabarra	insert -ba-
(h)	'upper arm'	NMJ jurru	Mja juburru	insert -bu-
(i)	'find'	J jaymba-l (M warrayma-l)	Mja jawaymba-l	insert -wa-

Dyirbal has no prefixes, and initial *mu-*, in (27), does not recur in the language. Note also the vowel difference in the final syllable: *a* in Ev *guyŋgan* but *u* in Jja *muguyŋgun*. For 'head hair', the initial element is *gu-* (origin unknown) for Jja and *jil-* for Nja and Mja. Note that the long vowel rule applies at the end of the word in Nja but not in the middle; we would have expected *ji:muRa:*. This suggests that the Ja form may originally have been something like *jilVmurray*, with the *V* having been dropped after operation of the long vowel rule in N. Where could the *jilV-* have come from? There is *jili*, the word for 'eye' in the Ev style of Yidiñ, but difference of meaning between 'eye' and 'head hair' makes this not too likely a source.

Interestingly, *jilmurray* was given as 'head' in tja, corresponding to Ev form *dungu*. Yidiñ has *murray* for 'head hair' in the Ev style; the Ja for this was not remembered.

The Yidiñ corpus yields just a few instances of phonological similarity between Ev and Ja forms, similar to those just illustrated for Dyirbal:

				Changes
(29)	'light' (noun)	tc ŋañjal	tja ŋaljan	-ñj- → -lj-, -l → -n
(30)	'pick up'	tc gumbi-l	tja gumbirraŋa-l	add at end: -rraŋa-

Note that the tja form in (30) appears to involve addition of *-rra-* (similar to the Dyirbal examples in rows (a–d) of table 6.4), plus *-ŋa-*, which is identical to the suffix in Yidiñ which derives a transitive verb from a noun, adjective, or intransitive verb.

There is an example of phonological similarity between Ev and Ja forms in Yidiñ which extends to Dyirbal:

(31) 'stomach' tc duburr   tja duwurr   b → w
                 N bugi:, MJ bamba   Nja duwuR, Mja duwurr,
                                     Jja duwurrgu

(32) 'full after tc duburr-ji   tja duwurr-ji
      eating'   N mañja:, MJ mañjay Nja duwuR-ba, Mja duwurr-ba
                                     Jja waljirra

(33) 'pregnant' tc gujal   <tja not known>
                  N guja:, MJ muygam Nja duwuR-ba, Mja duwurr-ba
                                      <Jja not known>

In (31), it appears that *duwurr*, the Ja word for 'stomach' in Yidiñ, is created from *duburr*, the corresponding Ev lexeme, by changing *b* to *w*. The tja term *duwurr* was then borrowed into Nja and Mja, and also into Jja with the (unexplained) addition of final *gu*.

In (32) we see that in Yidiñ both Ev and Ja forms for 'full after eating' involve the suffixation of comitative *-ji* 'with' to *duburr* and *duwurr*, yielding *duburr-ji* and *duwurr-ji*, literally 'with stomach'. The comitative suffix in N and M is *-ba*, with just the Ja forms having an equivalent derivation, *duwuR-ba/duwurr-ba* 'with stomach'. As pointed out in (25) of chapter 5, *duwurr-ba* is also used for 'pregnant' in Nja and Mja.

Note that the W dialect of Dyirbal has *dubu:* for 'stomach'. By the regular rules of long-vowel-creation, this could have come from *dubul* or *dubur*, but not from *duburr*.

It is perfectly likely that not all of the Ja forms quoted in this section were 'created' by phonological deformation of the corresponding Ev lexeme in the same dialect. There are many gaps in our knowledge concerning Ja styles for other dialects of Yidiñ and Dyirbal, and for all surrounding languages, and also of Ev styles. There may have been other sources in a few cases, but overall there is no doubt that phonological deformation was a major process.

6.5 From an everyday style lexeme in another dialect or language

The most common source for a Ja lexeme is an Ev form in another dialect of the same language, or in a neighbouring language; this has been illustrated in (15–24).

There are a few examples of Ja-to-Ev correspondences which apply simultaneously in both directions between two dialects, or two languages. Cross-correspondences between dialects of Dyirbal are illustrated in (18–19), (21), and:

(34) 'hook (fish)'   NM badi-l   Mja dilba-l
                                 J dilba-l   Jja badi-l

(35) 'almond bark tree'   N dunu   Nja dugan
       (*Prunus turnerana*)   MJ dugan   Mja dunu

In other instances there is also a Yidiñ cognate:

(36) 'yellow walnut'   tc gaŋgi   tja waŋir
       (*Beilschmiedia bancroftii*) NW gaŋgi   Nja ba:Ra
                                 MJ bara   Mja gaŋgi

(37) 'Alexandra palm'   tc bibiya   <tja not obtained>
       (*Archontophoenix alexandrae*) NW bibiya Nja gubungaRa
                                 MJ gubungara   Mja bibiya

For (36) it is likely that *bara* was the original Dyirbal name and then the northern dialects, N and W, borrowed *gaŋgi* from Yidiñ. When Ja terms were required for this tree, each of N and M adopted the Ev term from the other dialect. Exactly parallel comments apply for (37).

Some Ja-to-Ev correspondences are more intricate; for example:

(38) 'dilly-bag' (generic term)   tc bundu   tja jawun
                                    N jañju   Nja, Mja biñu
                                    MJ jawun   Jja jajirra

(39) 'small dilly-bag'   JG biñu   Jja jajirra ñiwur ('small dilly-bag')

Only the J (and G) dialects have a specific label, *biñu*, for a small variety of dilly-bag, and this has been adopted by N and M as their Ja form for the generic term, while tja has taken the Ev term, *jawun*, from M and J.

Since there is a one-to-many semantic correspondence between the Ja and Ev styles of a given dialect, Ja lexemes tend to have a wider, more general meaning. Thus, what is a species name in an Ev style may be taken into the Ja of another dialect as a generic label. Consider the following example from Dyirbal.

(40) 'eastern water dragon'   J jijan   Jja bajirri
       (*Physignathus lesueurii*) NM bajirri   Nja,Mja: only generic label

(41) generic term for all   none in Ev styles   Nja, Mja jijan
      lizards and goannas

The specific term in J for one type of lizard is taken into Nja and Mja as the generic label, covering the eastern water dragon and also more than a dozen other kinds of lizards and goannas. (No generic label was obtained for Jja.)

A similar type of meaning shift involves an inter-language correspondence. All dialects of Dyirbal have *midin* as the specific name for the most familiar variety of possum, the common ringtail (*Pseudocheirus peregrinus*). *Midin* has been borrowed into tja as the generic term 'edible animal (including fish), meat'.

Meaning shifts of various kinds may occur between forms in Ev and Ja styles, or between the Ja's of two dialects or two languages, as illustrated in:

(42) 'fresh water'   tc bana   tja maday, maja:l
                          NMJ bana   Nja nuba, Mja, Jja jujamu

(43) 'bark water container' tc dugubil, dubal <tja not obtained>
                          N duguba   Nja numbuRum
                          MJ nuba   Mja duguba
                                            Jja dugurr 'bark'

(44) 'freshwater eel'   tc jaban   tja jujamu
                          NMJ jaban   Nja jujamu
                                            Mja, Jja balbiji

It is likely that *nuba* originated as the Ev term for 'bark water carrier' in the M and J dialects of Dyirbal, and was taken over into Nja as 'fresh water'. The form *jujamu* is Ja for 'eel' in Yidiñ and in the adjacent N dialect of Dyirbal, but is 'fresh water' in Mja and Jja. It is hard to tell how this originated, and the direction of borrowing.

6.6 From another Jalnguy

Of the 622 Ja lexemes collected across three dialects of Dyirbal, and the 191 for the t dialect of Yidiñ, 67 are held in common. Each of these words was presumably first used in the Ja of one of the two languages and then borrowed into the Ja of the other. For more than half of the common forms I can find no evidence to suggest which Ja it belonged to first. This applies to the Ja lexemes in examples (5), (11), (13–14), and:

(45) 'hand'   NMJ mala tc mandi   Nja manbuRu, Mja Jja manburu
                                     tja manburu

(46) 'stone' N ŋaŋga:, MJ diban   Nja, Mja, Jja diŋun
               tc walba   tja diŋun

There are, however, 26 instances of words which occur in the Ja styles of the two languages, where there is some evidence suggesting direction of borrowing. This can relate to (1) phonological change involving long vowels; (2) phonological form; (3) conjugation membership; (4) affixes; (5) semantics; (6) distribution across dialects and languages; and (7) geographic location. These are discussed, in turn, in the following subsections.

6.6.1 Evidence from phonological change

As outlined in section 6.1.1, the N (and W) dialects of N replaced syllable final *Vl* and *Vr* by *V:*, *ay* by *a:*, and *uy* by *i:*. This is illustrated in examples (21), (26–8), (33) and in the tables.

There are a fair number of instances where the original form occurs in Yidiñ and in central and southern dialects of Dyirbal, with the phonological change having taken place in N. Examples involving Ev lexemes include:

(47) 'cross a stream by   N ba:ŋga-l, MJ balŋga-l   tc balŋga-l
      walking across on a log'

A mix of Ev and Ja lexemes is shown in (23) and in the cross-correspondence example:

(48) 'breastfeed'   N gu:ŋga-l, MJ gulŋga-l   Nja, Ma, Jja gaba-l
                            tc gaba-l   tja gulŋga-l

In (13–14) there are examples involving Ja lexemes throughout. However, for neither of these is there any clue as to whether Dyirbal borrowed a Ja lexeme from Yidiñ, or vice versa.

Just a few correspondences appear to be phonologically anomalous, and these do suggest a direction of borrowing. Going back to (21) and quoting just the *gayñji-l* forms, we can extend this to Yidiñ:

(49) 'have bilious attack'   N ga:ñji-l, M gayñji-l   Jja gayñji-l
                             tc galñji-l

The question here is: why does Yidiñ have *galñji-l* while M and Jja have *gayñji-l*? A similar query arises for the Ja correspondents in:

(50) 'bite'   Nja gi:ju-l, Mja, Jja guyju-l   tja gilju-l

(51) 'tooth'   Nja ŋuñaŋi:, Mja ŋuñaŋuy   tja ŋuñaŋil

Why, in (50–51) does Yidiñ have *il* when the unreduced form in Dyirbal has *uy*?

Indigenous Australians were typically multidialectal and multilingual. When two people from different groups were communicating, each would be likely to speak in their own variety but would be able to understand the other. They would often have principled ideas about some particular structural difference between their dialect and another.

George Watson grew up speaking the Mamu (M) dialect and had a good knowledge of the closely related Wair (W) dialect. He was aware of the phonological changes which produced long vowels. As he described it, the W dialect 'drags it out more'. George would tell me what a W form was by taking the corresponding M word and applying the long-vowel-creating changes. The interesting thing is that George did this absolutely automatically.

There is a minority of lexemes in W which did not undergo the long-vowel changes (they may be post-change borrowings, or there may be other explanations). But George applied the changes to them all. Compare (further examples are in Dixon 1990c: 42):

		form in M	actual form in W	George's 'W form'
(52)	'cheek'	jagal	jaga:	jaga:
(53)	'forest cicada'	juwalnjuwal	juwalnjuwal	juwa:njuwa:
(54)	'flame'	jaŋgur	jaŋgu:	jaŋgu:
(55)	'sword'	bagur	bagur	bagu:
(56)	'cicatrices'	muyŋga	mi:ŋga	mi:ŋga
(57)	'female spirit'	guyŋgan	guyŋgan	gi:ngan

For George Watson, every occurrence of *Vl*, *Vr*, and *Vy* at the end of a syllable in M should be replaced by *V:* in W.

M and W were contiguous dialects of the same language, with about 90 per cent lexical cognates. In contrast, Yidiñ is a separate language with very different grammar and only about 23 per cent of its Ev lexicon (37 per cent of Ja lexicon) in common with the adjacent N dialect of Dyirbal. Speakers of Yidiñ would have been aware that some of their lexemes were cognate with forms in N which have a long vowel, but they may have had a more rudimentary realisation of the correspondences involved than George Watson did for W with respect to M.

Of the syllable-final sequences, *Vl* is far more common than *Vr* or *Vy* in both Dyirbal (Dixon 1972: 279) and Yidiñ (Dixon 1977a: 38). Bilingual speakers of Yidiñ would have been aware of correspondences such as *yu:mba-y* in Nja, *yulmba-n* in tja—in (13)—*ga:gu:* in Nja, *galgul* in t—in (23)—and similar ones in (33), (47–48), and so on. I suggest that they operated with a general principle:

(58)   *V:* in N corresponds to *Vl* in Yidiñ

If a lexeme in N (in either Ev or Ja style) involving a long vowel was borrowed into Yidiñ, principle (58) would be applied. In most cases the long vowel in N would have emanated from an original *Vl*, but in some it would have been a development from *Vr* or *Vy*, and these are what gave rise to the apparently anomalous correspondences.

Thus, for the Ja lexeme for 'bite' in (50), we can reconstruct an historical scenario:

(59)   original form, retained in Mja, Jja   guyju-l
        long-vowel-creation in Nja   gi:ju-l
        Nja form borrowed into tja, applying principle (58)   gilju-l

And similarly for the Ja lexeme in (51) and the Ev one in (49). This provides evidence for borrowing from Nja into tja for (50) 'bite' and (51) 'tooth' (and from N into t for (49) 'have bilious attack').

The Yidiñ corpus (both Ev and Ja) includes a small number of forms ending in *-iy*; for example *galbiy* 'catfish'. An underlying final *y* is needed to explain the allomorphs these roots take (for example ergative *-ñju*, which is the allomorph used after *ay* and *uy*, rather than *-ŋgu*, which is the form used after a vowel). However, the final /iy/ is pronounced as [i:] when no affix follows; thus /galbiy/, [galbi:].

Now consider:

(60)   'bird' (generic)   N maRaba   Nja jaRi:
                            tc jarruy   tja jariyiy

The following historical scenario is rather likely:

- *jarruy* originated as the Ev form in Yidiñ
- it was borrowed into Nja as *jarruy*
- regular phonological changes applied in N, creating *jaRi:*
- Yidiñ then borrowed *jaRi:* from Nja into its own Ja style as *jariyiy*, which would in absolute form be pronounced, with a very long final vowel, as [jari:::], similar to the pronunciation of *jaRi:* in Nja.

This is a further example of a form being borrowed from Nja into tja.

6.6.2 Evidence from phonological form

There are putative instances of phonological deformation between Ja and Ja, similar to those reported in section 6.4, between Ev and Ja:

(61) 'body' Jja buba   tja wuwa

(62) 'sand' Nja guyŋgaRi, Mja guyŋgari tja guyŋari

If the forms in (61) are cognate, then the lenitional change $b \rightarrow w$ is much more likely than the reverse, suggesting that the Jja form is older. In (62) we appear to have cluster simplification *-yŋg = → -yŋ-* in tja. The fact that the regular change *uy → i:* has not applied in N suggests that the original form was *guyŋgari* in Mja; this was borrowed by Nja after the long-vowel-creating rules had applied, and then taken into tja with the consonant cluster being truncated.

We can now examine Ja forms for two birds:

(63) 'white cockatoo'   NMJ gayambula tc waŋgulay Nja, Mja waŋgulay
      (*Cacatua galerita*)   Jja muluŋgurrñi
                                                              tja muluŋgurr

(64) 'scrub turkey'   NM muŋarra, J guyjarri   Nja gi:jaRi
      (*Alectura lathami*)   Mja, Jja jarrabarrañ
                            tc wawun   tja jarrabarra, muŋa:r

The Dyirbal Ja forms *muluŋgurrñi* and *jarrabarrañ* are longer than the tja forms *muluŋgurr* and *jarrabarra* (there are no suffixes *-ñi* or *-ñ* in either language). It seems more likely that something should be subtracted than that something should be added when borrowing between Ja's, suggesting that the Dyirbal Ja terms are the originals. The same goes for:

(65) 'two' NMJ bulayi   Nja gina:njaRan, Mja, Jja ginaynjarran
       tc jambu:l   tja ginay

In section 5.5, we commented on the unusual make-up of the Ja adjective *ginaynjarran* 'two', consisting of two nominal suffixes, *-jarran* 'two, each of two' (in all dialects) and *-ginay* 'full of, covered with' (in M and J, the N equivalent being *-damba*). This must be quite an old creation, presumably originating in Mja and Jja. It would have been an early borrowing into Nja, since the long-vowel-creating rule applies, giving *gina:njaRan*. Neither suffix occurs in Yidiñ and it appears that tja has just borrowed the Dyirbal Ja lexeme in shortened form, as *ginay*.

6.6.3 Evidence from conjugation membership

As stated in section 1.5, there is correspondence between the predominantly transitive conjugations in Dyirbal and Yidiñ, marked by -l in each language, and between the predominantly intransitive conjugations, marked as -y in Dyirbal and as -n in Yidiñ. Only in Yidiñ do we find a small third conjugation, marked by -r.

In almost every instance, if two verbs are cognate between Dyirbal and Yidiñ, their conjugation memberships coincide, -l with --l and -y with -n. There are just two -r conjugation verbs in the tja corpus; both have cognates in Dyirbal Ja, belonging to the -l class:

(66) 'throw'   NMJ mada-l   Nja, Mja, Jja nayŋu-l
                tc gilbi-l   tja nayŋu-r

(67) 'smell'   NMJ ñuma-l   Nja, Mja ñunju-l
                tc ñuma-l   tja ñunju-r

If *nayŋu-* and *ñunju-* had originated in the -l conjugation in Dyirbal, and then been borrowed into tja, they would have been expected to be placed in the -l class. The fact that they are in the -r class in Yidiñ suggests that they originated in that language and were borrowed into Dyirbal.

6.6.4 Evidence from affixes

There is an interesting pattern in the following four Ja-to-Ja transitive verb correspondences:

(68) 'dig'   Nja buRganba-l, Mja burrganba-l   tja burrganbaŋa-l

(69) 'put down' Nja ju:bamba-l, Mja, Jja julbamba-l   tja julbamaŋa-l

(70) 'pierce'   Nja ñiRinda-l, Mja, Jja ñirrinda-l   tja ñirrindaŋa-l

(71) 'tell'   Mja, Jja wuyuba-l   tja wuyubaŋa-l

For each of these, the tja root involves the addition of *-ŋa-* to the Dyirbal Ja root (plus cluster simplification *-mb-* → *-m-* in (69)). Yidiñ has a process for deriving transitive verbs by adding *-ŋa-l* to a noun, adjective, or intransitive verb in the -n conjugation, and by adding *-maŋa-l* to an intransitive verb in the -l or -r conjugation. It looks as if the four tja transitive verbs in (68–71) were created by adding *-ŋa-l* to the Dyirbal Ja word, perhaps working in terms of the Dyirbal imperative form, which is the plain root (*burrganba*, etc.).

6.6.5 Semantic evidence

Examination of the semantics involved in correspondences may also suggest a direction of borrowing. Consider the form *ŋabil* (*ŋabi:* for N) in:

(72) 'back (anatomical)'   NM juja, J mambu   Nja ŋabi:, Mja ŋabil, Jja juja
                          tc bawu: tja juja

(73) 'father'   N ŋuman, MJ ŋuma   Nja ŋabi:, Mja ŋabil
                       tc bimbi   tja ŋabil

When speakers of Dyirbal were discussing *ŋabil* with me, they stated that it was basically a body-part term, which was then semantically extended to also cover 'father'.
(This does seem more plausible than the reverse.) If it is correct, *ŋabil* must have originated in Dyirbal Ja as 'back', been extended to 'father', and then been borrowed into
tja with only the latter meaning.
   We can now examine the Ja lexeme *bijiliñ*, in

(74) 'sword'   N baguR, MJ bagur   Nja bulbaRi, Mja yilimbirr
                       tc bagur   tja bijiliñ

(75) 'penda tree'   NMJ julujulu   Mja bijiliñ
     (*Xanthostemon whitei*)   tc julujulu tja bijiliñ

In both languages, trees and other plants may be named after some artefact which is
made from them (for instance 'firestick'); this happens a little in the Ev style and a lot
in Ja. The most likely scenario here is for *bijiliñ* to have originated in tja as 'sword', being
extended in that language to also cover 'penda tree' (from whose hard wood swords
were made), and then borrowed into Mja as just the name for the tree.

6.6.6 Evidence from language/dialect distribution

Example (31) in section 6.4 provides an instance of a tja form created by phonological
deformation from a corresponding Ev term, and then the tja item being borrowed
into Dyirbal Ja. The Yidiñ Ev lexeme *duburr* 'stomach' gave rise to tja *duwurr*, which
was taken over by Dyirbal Ja. In (29) we suggested that the Yidiñ Ev noun *ŋañjal*
'light' may well have been deformed into tja *ŋaljan*; this would then have been borrowed into Mja and Nja as *ŋaljan*. (The fact that the Nja form is *ŋaljan* rather than
ŋa:jan indicates that it is a recent loan into Nja, after the long-vowel-creating rules
had applied.)
   The next three examples suggest a Dyirbal origin for cognate Ja terms.

(76) 'human faeces'   NMJ guna   Nja, Mja, Jja ñiri
                       tc janja   tja ñiri

(77) 'bird droppings' N diRgin; MJ ñirri Nja, Mja. Jja ñiri
                       <t not available>   <tja not available>

We can see that Dyirbal formed *ñiri*, a generic term in Ja for all types of faeces, by phonological deformation of the MJ Ev term *ñirri* 'bird droppings' (substituting an apico-postalveolar
for an apico-alveolar rhotic). This was then borrowed as the tja term for 'human faeces'.

There is information on Ev lexemes for dialects of Dyirbal beyond the three for which it was possible to record Ja items, and these often provide useful information, as in:

(78) 'place, home'   NWMJ mija   Nja yabanda:, Mja, Jja naŋgu
                        tc bulmba   tja yabanday

(79) 'grass mattress' N naŋgu, W yabanday, Nja yabanda:, Mja yabanday
                        MJ bulmban   <Jja not available>
                        t naŋgu   <tja not available>

If a form occurs in an Ev style, this is taken to be its origin. *Yabanday* would have begun as 'grass mattress' in W, been adopted as the Ja term for 'grass mattress' in M and N, with the Nja form (now *yabanda:*) being also used for 'place, home'. In this meaning, *yabanday* was borrowed into tja. Similar arguments apply for:

(80) 'ground'   N jabu, MJ jigay, YL gayi   Nja gayi, Mja jinbay
                  tc jabu   tja gayi

This suggests that *gayi* began as an Ev lexeme in YL, was adopted into Nja, and thence borrowed into tja.

6.6.7 Geographical evidence

Occasionally, we find a form which occurs in the Ja styles of both Dyirbal and Yidiñ and also—with the same or a similar meaning—in the Ev style of a nearby language, which is presumably its origin. The geographical placement of languages will suggest a direction of borrowing between Ja's.

- In Ja:bugay, to the north of Yidiñ, *gumbu* is 'urine'. This may be the source for *gumbu* 'anus' in tja, Nja, Mja, and Jja. If so, it would have been taken first into tja and from there into the Dyirbal Ja's.
- The Ev style of Yidiñ has intransitive verb *gunji-n* 'break, break up'. The tja correspondent of this was given as *yuwa:ji-n*; this has the form of an intransitivised derivation of transitive verb *yuwa-l* (which was not actually recorded as such). We find transitive roots *yuwa-l* 'bend' in Ja:bugay, and *yuwa-l* 'break' in Nja and Mja. This suggests that *yuwa-l* originated in Ja:bugay, being taken into tja and from there into Dyirbal Ja's.
- The verb *yimirri-* 'be glad' in Warrgamay (to the south of Dyirbal) may be cognate with the verbs 'cry, sob' in Ja styles: *yimirri-y* in Jja and Mja, *yimiRi-y* in Nja, and *yimirri-n* in tja. If these are indeed cognate, the form would have come from Warrgamay into Dyirbal Ja's and then into tja.
- Nyawaygi (Warrgamay's southerly neighbour) has verb *jayma-l* 'take away'. This may be the source for *jayma-l* 'give' in Jja, Mja, Nja, and tja. If so, it would have been adopted first by Dyirbal Ja's, and then borrowed by tja.

- Warungu, to the west of Dyirbal, has *ñungul* 'one', which is likely to be the source for Jja and Mja *ñungul* and Nja *ñungu:* 'one'. The Ja for 'one' in Yidiñ (which is further away from Warungu) is *ñunmul*, and this may be a deformation of the Dyirbal Ja form.

6.6.8 Summary

Table 6.5 summarises the tentative conclusions from sections 6.6.1–6.6.7 concerning directions of Ja-to-Ja borrowing. We have suggested that nineteen terms may have

TABLE 6.5. Direction of borrowing for Ja lexemes

Section			Ja lexeme originating in Dyirbal and borrowed into Yidiñ	Ja lexeme originating in Yidiñ and borrowed into Dyirbal
6.6.1	(50)	'bite'	guyju-l, gi:ju-l	
	(51)	'tooth'	ŋuñaŋuy, ŋuñaŋi:	$\longrightarrow$
	(60)	'bird'	jaRi:	
6.6.2	(61)	'body'	buba	
	(62)	'sand'	guyŋgari	
	(63)	'white cockatoo'	muluŋgurrñi	$\longleftrightarrow$
	(64)	'scrub turkey'	jarrabarrañ	
	(65)	'two'	ginaynjarran	
6.6.3	(66)	'throw'	$\longleftarrow$	nayŋu-r
	(67)	'smell'		ñunju-r
6.6.4	(68)	'dig'	burrganba-l	
	(69)	'put down'	julbamba-l	
	(70)	'pierce'	ñirrinda-l	$\longrightarrow$
	(71)	'tell'	wuyuba-l	
6.6.5	(72–3)	'back'	ŋabil $\longrightarrow$	
	(74–5)	'sword'	$\longleftarrow$ bijiliñ	
6.6.6	(31)	'stomach'	$\longleftarrow$	duwurr
	(29)	'light' (noun)		ŋaljan
	(76–7)	'human faeces'	ñiri	
	(78–9)	'place, home'	yabanday	$\longrightarrow$
	(80)	'ground'	gayi	
6.6.7		'anus'	$\longleftarrow$	gumbu
		'break'		yuwa-l
		'cry, sob'	yimirri-y	
		'give'	jayma-l	$\longrightarrow$
		'one'	ñungul	

been borrowed from Dyirbal Ja into Yidiñ Ja, and seven may have gone in the opposite direction. There are forty-one further cognates between the Ja styles of the two languages for which little evidence can be found concerning place of origin.

6.7 Conclusions

It is not a totally straightforward matter to produce figures for the different kinds of cognates for Ja lexemes. In (72), for instance, *juja* 'back' in tja could have been borrowed from the Ev styles of N and M, or from the Ja style of J. In such cases I have adopted the convention of counting the tja lexeme as primarily related to the Ev form in Dyirbal.

Approximate figures for cognation of monomorphemic Ja lexemes in the t dialect of Yidiñ are:

derived from the Ev style of the same dialect by phonological deformation	3
cognate in the Ev style of another dialect of Yidiñ	3
cognate in the Ev style of a dialect of Dyirbal	33
cognate in the Ev style of Ja:bugay	5
cognate in the Ev style of Kuku-Yalanji and/or Guugu Yimidhirr	4
cognate in a Ja style of Dyirbal	67
no cognates known	76
	—
Total	191

Approximate figures for monomorphemic lexemes in Ja styles across the N, M, and J dialects for Dyirbal are:

derived from the Ev style of the same dialect by phonological deformation	48
cognate in the Ev style of another dialect of Dyirbal	122
cognate in the Ev style of a dialect of Yidiñ	35
cognate in the Ev style of Warrgamay and/or Nyawaygi	12
cognate in the Ev style of Warungu	5
cognate in the Ev style of another language of the region	4
cognate in the Ja style of Yidiñ	67
no cognates known	329
	—
Total	622

There is less information available on the Ev vocabulary of surrounding languages—such as Ja:bugay, Warungu, and Warrgamay—than there is for Dyirbal and Yidiñ. Allowing for this, the figures just quoted do suggest that, in augmenting their Ja vocabularies, Dyirbal and Yidiñ had a greater tendency to borrow from the Ev style of each other, rather than from any other neighbour.

It may have been noticed that J lexemes are often longer than Ev items. We find:

- In the Ev styles of both Dyirbal and Yidiñ, 75 to 80 per cent of monomorphemic lexemes have two syllables, the remainder three or more.
- Of Ja lexemes for which an Ev style cognate is known, 74 per cent are disyllabic in Yidiñ and 68 per cent in Dyirbal.
- Of the remaining Ja lexemes, in both languages (those with a cognate in another Ja, and those for which no cognate is known), less than half are disyllabic.

In both languages, a number of Ja lexemes for which no Ev cognate is known have as their final syllable what appears to be a derivational affix, but the form before the affix has no independent existence; this applies to seventeen items in tja and sixty-four across Nja, Mja, and Jja. For instance, we saw in (12) that in the Ja styles of Dyirbal 'sit' is *majirrabi-l*. Suffix *-bi-l* is the inchoative verbaliser, used to derive intransitive verbs from nominals (see section 5.7); but *majirra* does not occur alone. Also in (12), 'sit' in tja is *ñiya:rji-n*. Suffix *-:ji-n* derives an intransitive stem from a transitive verb root; but *ñiya(r)-* does not occur alone. (See also final *-ŋa-l* in the tja forms of (68–71).) All this provides some explanation for why so many Ja lexemes are trisyllabic or longer.

The discussion in this chapter leads to the following conclusions:

At some time in the past, Dyirbal and Yidiñ had smaller avoidance vocabularies (similar in size to those in other Australian languages). There would have been special Ja equivalents for only some of the more important lexemes from the Ev style; other Ev words would have been used in the same form in Ja.

Each dialect then expanded its avoidance vocabulary so that there was no lexical material in common between the Ev and Ja styles (save for the four grandparent terms in Dyirbal). This process was achieved by:

- borrowing, from the Ev style of a neighbouring dialect or language, forms that were not in the Ev style of the dialect in question;
- creating Ja forms by phonological deformation of lexemes in the dialect's own Ev style;
- borrowing terms that were already in the Ja style of a neighbouring language or dialect;
- making full use of the grammatical mechanisms of the languages— creating descriptive labels in Ja such as *bayi guyjul-muŋa* 'he who bites a lot' for mosquito, march flies, biting ants, and centipedes; and for 'stand' using *dinda-rri-y*, the intransitivised form of *dinda-l* 'put standing' (see sections 5.3, 5.8.1, and 6.1.2).

In section 6.6, evidence was presented suggesting that nineteen loans were borrowed from a Ja of Dyirbal into tja, and seven in the other direction. This could be taken as an indication that an extensive Jalnguy vocabulary was first achieved in Dyirbal, with Yidiñ later following suit. Note, though, that the data on Yidiñ Jalnguy are rather skimpy; consultants Pompey Langdon and Tilly Fuller said that they were able to remember only a fraction of the full set of Yidiñ Jalnguy forms. I feel the evidence is too slight to attempt any such historical inferences. All that is clear is that the Jalnguy vocabularies grew to their present size at about the same time in Dyirbal and Yidiñ and that each influenced the other.

Knowledgeable speakers of Dyirbal and of Yidiñ were proud of the fact that 'everything is different' in Ja from what it is in Ev (with respect to the lexicon, that is). The present chapter has attempted to shed some light on how this was achieved.

We can now move on to examine and compare critical grammatical properties of Dyirbal and Yidiñ, and of Warrgamay.

This is a streamlined and slimmed-down revision—with argumentation and explanation improved—of a rather long paper 'The origin of "mother-in-law vocabulary" in two Australian languages' (Dixon 1990c). The paper includes more detail on Dyirbal dialects other than N, M, and J; plus a number of further examples, a few of them rather borderline.

Part III

Grammatical Studies

On the basis of the 1972 grammar, Dyirbal has gained renown as a language with 'ergative syntax'. For operations of coordination and subordination, S (intransitive subject) and O (transitive object) are identified. That is, Dyirbal uses an exclusively S/O pivot. The situation in Yidiñ is more complex; in some circumstances it employs an S/O pivot, and in others an S/A pivot ('accusative syntax'), with S then being identified with A (transitive subject). These different syntactic orientations are described in chapter 7, and explained—at least in part—in terms of the contrasting narrative techniques of the two languages.

There has been much written in recent years concerning 'serial verb constructions' (SVCs), whereby a predicate consists of more than one verb but is conceived of as describing a single action. Chapter 8 presents a full account of this feature in Dyirbal, recognizing both asymmetrical SVCs—involving a verb and an adverbal—and symmetrical SVCs—made up of two (or more) verbs. This chapter includes criteria for recognizing SVCs, plus the types of verbs taking part in SVCs, techniques for transitivity matching, inflectional possibilities, the occurrence of derivational suffixes and reduplication, and the range of meanings involved.

Dyirbal has no complement clause constructions per se, instead employing a number of other construction types as 'complementation strategies'—SVCs, relative clause constructions, and purposive constructions. Chapter 9 describes these mechanisms and the ways they operate, investigating which of them is appropriate for verbs which in other languages typically take complement clauses: 'see', 'hear', 'like', 'want', 'tell to do', 'finish', and others.

Most Australian languages make a clear distinction between intransitive and transitive verbs, and they also have a number of conjugations. As mentioned in chapter 1, there is generally a correlation—but not full coincidence—between conjugations and transitivity classes (for example, in both Dyirbal and Yidiñ most members of the -l class are transitive). In chapter 10, attention is directed to Warrgamay. A process of grammatical reanalysis is revealed, whereby the paradigm for the predominantly intransitive verbal conjugation was merged with that of antipassive derivations. This led to coincidence of conjugations and transitivity classes in the Warrgamay proper dialect, while a more typical Australian system was retained in the Biyay dialect.

7

Comparing the syntactic orientations of Dyirbal and Yidiñ

Grammar is the rich heart of each language. But it is not autonomous. In chapter 2 we first tried a 'grammar prior' approach, examining the semantic content of the four grammatical genders in Dyirbal, and attempting to explain their composition. This was not a fruitful tactic. But when we took a 'semantics first' stance, and studied the various ways in which real-world meaning contrasts are mapped onto the gender system, then the principles involved became clear. Much of the infrastructure of a grammar is determined by factors outside it.

A further example of this is provided in the present chapter. Dyirbal works exclusively in terms of an S/O syntactic pivot, whereas Yidiñ combines an S/O pivot with an S/A one. These contrasting syntactic orientations are explained, at least in part, by the different principles of discourse orientation in the two languages. Once again, we have a part of the infrastructure of the grammar being determined by a factor outside it.

7.1 The syntactic orientation of Dyirbal

Like many other Australian languages, both Yidiñ and Dyirbal have a 'split ergative/accusative' pattern for marking the functions of NPs in clauses. This is illustrated for Dyirbal in table 7.1.

1st and 2nd person pronouns have one form, nominative, for transitive subject (A) and intransitive subject (S) functions, and another form, accusative, for transitive object (O) function. There is a quite different system for nouns and adjectives: absolutive form—with zero marking—for S and O functions, and ergative form for A function. The major allomorph of ergative case is -ŋgu, as used here. It was shown in (5) of section 2.1 that noun markers inflect like nouns and adjectives.

Thus, at the morphological level, Dyirbal (and also Yidiñ) show an (absolutive-)ergative system for nominals (nouns and adjectives) and a (nominative-)accusative one for pronouns. (This can be explained in terms of the 'nominal hierarchy'; see Dixon 1994: 83–97.)

TABLE 7.1. **Marking of core syntactic functions in Dyirbal**

	1st and 2nd person pronouns		nominals (nouns and adjectives)	
	e.g. 1 singular	e.g. 1 dual	e.g. 'man'	e.g. 'old person'
transitive subject (A)	ŋaja (NOM)	ŋali (NOM)	yara-ŋgu (ERG)	wuygi-ŋgu (ERG)
intransitive subject (S)			yara (ABS)	wuygi (ABS)
transitive object (O)	ŋaygu-na (ACC)	ŋali-na (ACC)		

Pronouns behave in a slightly different way in Girramay, the most southerly dialect of Dyirbal. Girramay is like the neighbouring language Warrgamay in having different forms for each of the core functions A, S, and O, just for singular 1st and 2nd person pronouns. This is illustrated in table 1.2 of chapter 1. (Note that Girramay has accusative shown by -*ña*, while other dialects use -*na*, and 1sg accusative is *ŋaña*.)

The fact that each word in an NP has explicit case marking means that pronouns and nominals can be mingled together in one clause, and indeed in one NP, without any possibility of confusion. Consider, for example:

(1) [ŋinda   wuygi-ŋgu]$_A$ [ba-m   mirrañ]$_O$ babi
    2sg.NOM old.person-ERG THERE.ABS-III black.bean.ABS peel.IMP
    You, old person, slice the beans!

In Dyirbal, as in Yidiñ, almost every verb is either strictly intransitive or strictly transitive. In (1), *babi-l* 'peel' is transitive and so requires A and O NPs. The A NP, *ŋinda wuygi-ŋgu*, is made up of a nominative pronoun and an ergative noun, from the 'A row' of table 7.1, while the O NP, *bam mirrañ*, has noun marker and noun both in absolutive form.

7.1.1 Pivot, coordination, and antipassive

In every language, clauses and sentences may be linked together to create written paragraphs or spoken discourse. There is typically a 'common argument' which threads through the component clauses, connecting them. This is called a 'topic'. For example, in the following fragment of English discourse, the recurrent topic is underlined:

(2) Mary$_S$ came late, [a traffic hold-up]$_A$ delayed her$_O$,
    and then she$_S$ drove so fast that she$_A$ almost crashed [the car]$_O$

In some languages, the topic argument must be in a specified syntactic role in each clause. By examining a clause—taken out of the discourse context in which it occurred—one can see what the topic is. Such a grammatically determined topic is called a 'pivot'. Dyirbal is a language of this type. That is, its grammar includes the following principle:

(3)   Two clauses can only be coordinated if they share a 'common argument', which is in surface S or O function in each clause. (The occurrence of the common argument is generally omitted from the second clause.)

That is, Dyirbal has an S/O pivot for coordination. It is said to have an 'ergative' profile at the syntactic level.

We can now illustrate this. Consider clauses (4), with intransitive verb *miyanda-y* 'laugh' and (5) with transitive verb *bunju-l* 'slap':

(4)   [bayi   yara]$_S$ miyanda-ñu
      THERE.ABS.I man.ABS laugh-PAST
      The man laughed

(5)   [bayi   yara]$_O$ [ba-ŋgu-n   yibi-ŋgu]$_A$ bunju-n
      THERE.ABS.I man.ABS   THERE-ERG-II woman-ERG slap-PAST
      The woman slapped the man

There is a common argument, 'man', which is in S function in (4) and in O function in (5). The two clauses can thus be coordinated and the second occurrence of the common argument omitted (this being shown by Ø):

(6)   [bayi yara]$_S$ miyanda-ñu Ø$_O$ [ba-ŋgu-n yibi-ŋgu]$_A$ bunju-n
      The man laughed and the woman slapped him

The O argument is omitted from the second clause. Since Dyirbal works with an S/O pivot, this O argument is taken to be identical with the S argument of the first clause. Note that Dyirbal has no explicit coordinating conjunction, like English *and*. Coordination is marked by the whole of (6) constituting one intonation group (and by the omission of the second occurrence of the common argument).

The two clauses could be combined in the opposite order:

(7)   [bayi yara]$_O$ [ba-ŋgu-n yibi-ŋgu]$_A$ bunju-n Ø$_S$ miyanda-ñu
      The woman slapped the man and he laughed

The S argument is omitted from the second clause. In terms of the S/O pivot, it is taken to be identical with the O argument of the first clause; that is, it is the man—not the woman—who laughed.

Two clauses may of course be coordinated if the common argument is in S function in both, or in O function in both. Typically, narratives and discourse in Dyirbal involve long 'pivot chains', sequences of clauses where the pivot argument is in S or O function in each. The pivot will be stated in the first clause, and perhaps referred to again, every few clauses, by just a noun marker.

Compare sentence (7) in Dyirbal with the corresponding English coordination:

(8)   [The woman]$_A$ slapped [the man]$_O$ and Ø$_S$ laughed

A topic argument which links clauses in English can be in any function, then being shown by a pronoun. In (2) we had *Mary* in S function, *her* in O function, and then *she* in S and A functions. However, for ellipsis under coordination, English operates on an S/A principle. If a common argument is in S or A function in each of two coordinated clauses, then it may be omitted from the second. In (8) it is the S argument which is omitted from the second clause. In terms of English's S/A principle for ellipsis under coordination, this omitted S must be identical with the A argument of the first clause. That is—in contrast to (7)—in (8) it is the woman who laughed.

If the common argument is in O function in one clause of a coordination in English, then it may not be omitted. [*The man*]$_S$ *laughed* and [*The woman*]$_A$ *slapped* [*the man*]$_O$ share an argument, *the man*, but it is in O function in the second clause, and cannot be omitted from a coordination. That is, we cannot say *[*The man*]$_S$ *laughed and* [*the woman*]$_A$ *slapped* Ø$_O$. However, English has a syntactic device for dealing with this, the passive derivation. [*The woman*]$_A$ *slapped* [*the man*]$_O$ can be re-phrased as [*The man*]$_S$ *was slapped by the woman*. We now have *the man* in S function, available to be ellipsed under coordination: [*The man*]$_S$ *laughed and* Ø$_S$ *was slapped by the woman*.

Let us now return to Dyirbal, with its S/O pivot for coordination, and consider the means for linking (5) and:

(9)   [bala-n   yibi]$_S$ miyanda-ñu
      THERE.ABS-II woman.ABS laugh-PAST
      The woman laughed

There is an argument shared by the two clauses, 'the woman', but it is in S function in (9) and in A function in (5), thus not available as it is for coordination. Just as English has a passive derivation which puts an underlying O argument into surface S function (to satisfy the S/A principle for ellipsis under coordination), so Dyirbal has what is called an 'antipassive' derivation, which puts an underlying A argument into surface S function (to satisfy the S/O pivot for coordination, and for relative clause constructions, which are discussed in section 7.1.2):

(10)   ANTIPASSIVE DERIVATION

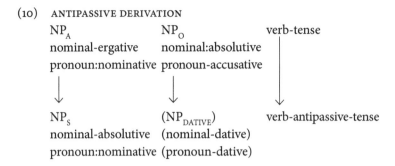

The verb of a transitive clause receives antipassive suffix *-ŋa-y* between root and inflection, and this serves to derive the antipassive, an intransitive construction. The underlying A argument goes into S function in the antipassive. And the original O argument becomes a peripheral constituent of the antipassive, marked by dative suffix *-gu*; as a non-core element, it may be either stated or omitted.

The antipassive version of (5) is thus:

(5-ap)   [bala-n   yibi]$_S$ [ba-gu-l   yara-gu]$_{DATIVE}$
          THERE.ABS-II   woman.ABS   HERE-DAT-II man-DAT
          bunjul-ŋa-ñu
          slap-ANTIPASSIVE-PAST
          The woman slapped the man

The argument shared by (9) and (5), 'the woman', is now in S function in each clause and they can be combined in either order, with the S/O pivot principle being satisfied:

(11)   [bala-n yibi]$_S$ miyanda-ñu Ø$_S$ [ba-gu-l yara-gu]$_{DATIVE}$ bunjul-ŋa-ñu
        The woman laughed and (she) slapped the man

(12)   [bala-n yibi]$_S$ [ba-gu-l yara-gu]$_{DATIVE}$ bunjul-ŋa-ñu Ø$_S$ miyanda-ñu
        The woman slapped the man and (she) laughed

There is an important difference between the English and Dyirbal examples just discussed. English has no pivot in the strict sense. Clauses can be combined with the topic NP in any function in each, and this may be shown by pronouns, as in (2). The S/A principle simply mediates the *omission* of a repeated topic argument. In contrast, Dyirbal *only permits* two clauses to be coordinated as one sentence (constituting a single intonation group) if they share an argument which is in S or O function in each. For example, a sequence of (9) followed by (5) could only be two sentences, each making up a separate intonation group.

As shown in table 7.1, nominals show ergative morphology (S linked with O), while pronouns show accusative morphology (S linked with A). The examples of clause coordination presented so far, with an S/O pivot (ergative syntax), have involved nominals. What about when the common argument is a pronoun? Would there then be an S/A pivot (accusative syntax) mirroring the S/A morphology of pronouns? A most fascinating feature of Dyirbal grammar is that this is *not* what happens. The S/O pivot is pervasive, applying irrespective of whether the common argument is a nominal or a pronoun.

Consider the following two clauses:

(13)   ŋaja$_S$ miyanda-ñu
      1sg.NOM laugh-PAST
      I laughed

(14)   ŋaygu-na$_O$ [ba-ŋgu-n   yibi-ŋgu]$_A$ bunju-n
      1sg-ACC   THERE-ERG-II woman-ERG slap-PAST
      The woman slapped me

The 1st person singular pronoun occurs in each clause. It is in S function in (13) and in O function in (14), satisfying the S/O pivot condition on coordination. These two clauses can thus be coordinated, in either order, with the second occurrence of the 1sg pronoun omitted:

(15)   ŋaja$_S$ miyanda-ñu Ø$_O$ [ba-ŋgu-n yibi-ŋgu]$_A$ bunju-n
      I laughed and the woman slapped me

(16)   ŋaygu-na$_O$[ba-ŋgu-n yibi-ŋgu]$_A$ bunju-n Ø$_S$ miyanda-ñu
      The woman slapped me and I laughed

The pronoun has different form in (13) and (14), nominative *ŋaja* in (13) and accusative *ŋaygu-na* in (14). This is irrelevant as far as coordination is concerned; all that matters here are syntactic functions (S and O).

We can now consider the coordination of (13) and:

(17)   ŋaja$_A$ [bala-n   yibi]$_O$ bunju-n
      1sg.NOM THERE.ABS-II woman.ABS slap-PAST
      I slapped the woman

The 1sg pronoun has the same form, nominative *ŋaja*, in (13) and (17). However, this is irrelevant as far as the rules of coordination are concerned. What matters is syntactic function and *ŋaja* is in A, a non-pivot function in (17). If (13) and (17) were spoken in sequence, with the second occurrence of *ŋaja* omitted, we would get:

(18)   ŋaja$_S$ miyanda-ñu [bala-n yibi]$_O$ bunju-n

This would *not* mean 'I laughed and slapped the woman'. It could only be interpreted as two separate sentences: 'I laughed. The woman was slapped (by someone else, not by me)'.

In order to coordinate (13) and (17), the latter must be cast in antipassive form:

(17-ap)   ŋaja$_S$ [ba-gu-n   yibi-gu]   bunjul-ŋa-ñu
           1sg.NOM   THERE-DAT-II woman-DAT slap-ANTIPASSIVE-PAST
           I slapped the woman

We now have *ŋaja* in S function in (17-ap), as it is in (13), and the two clauses can be coordinated in either order:

(19)   ŋaja$_S$ miyanda-ñu Ø$_S$ [ba-gu-n yibi-gu] bunjul-ŋa-ñu
        I laughed and (I) slapped the woman

(20)   ŋaja$_S$ [ba-gu-n yibi-gu] bunjul-ŋa-ñu Ø$_S$ miyanda-ñu
        I slapped the woman and (I) laughed

It is interesting to see the result of attempting to combine (17) 'I slapped the woman' and (13) 'I laughed', in this order, omitting the occurrence of *ŋaja* from the latter:

(21)   ŋaja$_A$ [bala-n yibi]$_O$ bunju-n Ø$_S$ miyanda-ñu

The S argument of transitive verb *miyanda-y* is omitted. By the S/O pivot principle, it is taken to be identical with the O argument of the first clause. That is, (21) is a bona fide coordination, meaning 'I slapped the woman and she laughed'. Note that (21) could *not* mean 'I slapped the woman and I laughed'. In order to express this, the first clause would have to be antipassivised: *ŋaja$_S$ [ba-gu-n yibi-gu] bunjul-ŋa-ñu Ø$_S$ miyanda-ñu.*

As mentioned in previous chapters, there is in Dyirbal freedom of ordering not only for phrasal constituents within a clause, but also for words within a clause (and, indeed, within a sentence). There are certain statistical tendencies (note that these are not hard-and-fast rules), including: (a) a nominative pronoun typically precedes an accusative one; (b) an absolutive nominal typically precedes an ergative one; (c) core arguments typically precede the verb and peripheral ones typically follow it (for fuller information see Dixon 1972: 291). However, almost any order of words is acceptable.

7.1.2 Relative clause construction

A relative clause modifies the head of an NP. There must be an argument within the relative clause which is identical with the modified head; this is the common argument.

In Dyirbal, a relative clause involves: suffix *-ŋu* onto the verb of the relative clause; followed by a case suffix indicating the function of its NP within the main clause. (The case suffix is zero for absolutive (as usual), *-rru* for ergative, *-gu* for dative, etc.) This can be illustrated by embedding (4), 'the man laughed', as a relative clause to the O argument 'the man' in (5) 'the woman slapped the man':

(22) [bayi   yara   [Ø_S miyanda-ŋu]_{RELATIVE.CLAUSE}]_O
     THERE.ABS.1 man.ABS   laugh-REL.ABS
     [ba-ŋgu-n   yibi-ŋgu]_A bunju-n
     THERE-ERG-II woman-ERG slap-PAST
     The woman slapped the man who was laughing

Or we could embed [*balan yibi*]_S *miyanda-ñu*, 'the woman laughed', as relative clause to the A argument in (5):

(23) [bayi   yara]_O [ba-ŋgu-n   yibi-ŋgu
     THERE.ABS.1 man.ABS THERE-ERG-II woman-ERG
     Ø_S miyanda-ŋu-rru]_{RELATIVE.CLAUSE}]_A bunju-n
     laugh-REL-ERG   slap-PAST
     The woman who was laughing slapped the man

As shown here, the common argument is stated in the main clause and omitted from the relative clause (its place and function there being indicated by Ø). Each constituent within an NP takes the appropriate case inflection. In (22), relative clause verb *miyanda-ŋu* is, like noun marker *bayi* and head noun *yara*, in absolutive form (with zero marking), and in (23) *miyanda-ŋu* takes ergative suffix *-rru*, agreeing in case with *baŋgun* and *yibiŋgu* within the same NP.

In Dyirbal there are the following conditions on the functions of the common argument in main clause and in relative clause:

(24) (a) In the main clause, the common argument can be in any of the core functions—A, S, and O—or in instrumental, dative, or locative peripheral function. The only restriction is that it cannot be in allative or ablative function. S function is illustrated in (22) and A function in (23); for the others see Dixon (1972: 99–105).
     (b) In the relative clause, the common argument must be in a pivot function, S or O.

It is a straightforward matter to embed (5) 'the woman slapped the man' as relative clause to 'the man' in (4) 'the man laughed' since the common argument is in O, a pivot function, in the relative clause:

(25) [bayi yara [Ø_O [ba-ŋgu-n yibi-ŋgu]_A bunju-ŋu]_{RELATIVE CLAUSE}]_S
     miyanda-ñu
     The man who was being slapped by the woman laughed

But suppose we wanted to say 'The woman who was slapping the man laughed'. The common argument is 'the woman', which is in A function in what we want to use as a relative clause. The antipassive derivation must be applied, producing (5-ap), which has 'the woman' in surface S function and can be the basis for a relative clause:

(26)   [balan yibi [Ø$_S$ [ba-gu-l yara-gu] bunjul-ŋu]$_{RELATIVE.CLAUSE}$]$_S$ miyanda-ñu
       The woman who was slapping the man laughed

Note that, as with coordination, exactly the same conditions apply for pronouns as for nominals. If the common argument is a pronoun, it must be in S or O function in the relative clause (irrespective of morphological form).

In summary, Dyirbal has split orientation at the morphological level, pronouns following an accusative and nominals an ergative system. However, it has an entirely ergative syntax, working in terms of an S/O pivot for coordination, and for the function of the common argument in a relative clause.

We can now turn to Yidiñ, which shows the same morphological split as Dyirbal, but is significantly different in its syntax.

7.2 The syntactic orientation of Yidiñ

Although they inhabited adjoining territories, Yidiñ and Dyirbal have very different vocabularies (sharing about one-quarter of the lexicon) and grammatical constructions and forms. However, Yidiñ is similar to Dyirbal—and many other Australian languages—at the morphological level, in having accusative inflection for pronouns and an ergative system for nominals. This is illustrated in table 7.2, which is similar to table 7.1 for Dyirbal. Note that ergative case (for A function on nominals) is basically -*ŋgu* on a root ending in a vowel, as in *waguja-ŋgu* 'man-ERGATIVE', but reduces to -:*ŋ* on a disyllabic root, as in *buña-:ŋ* 'woman-ERGATIVE'. Absolutive case, for S and O

TABLE 7.2. Marking of core syntactic functions in Yidiñ

	1st and 2nd person pronouns		nominals (nouns and adjectives)	
	e.g. 1 singular	e.g. 1 dual	e.g. 'man'	e.g. 'woman'
transitive subject (A)	ŋayu (NOM)	ŋali (NOM)	waguja-ŋgu (ERG)	buña-:ŋ (ERG)
intransitive subject (S)			wagu:ja (ABS)	buña (ABS)
transitive object (O)	ŋañañ (ACC)	ŋali-ñ (ACC)		

functions on nominals, is again zero. (Full details of rules for long vowels and related matters are in section 14.6.5.)

Coordination plays a relatively minor role in Yidiñ compared with its extensive usage in Dyirbal, and it will be expedient to first consider relative clauses in Yidiñ.

7.2.1 Relative clause construction

Yidiñ has a more restrictive condition than Dyirbal on the functions of the common argument in a relative clause construction:

(27)   The common argument must be in S or O function in the main clause and also in the relative clause.

Consider:

(28)   wagu:ja$_S$ maŋga-ñ
        man.ABS laugh-PAST
        The man laughed

(29)   wagu:ja$_O$ buña-:ŋ$_A$ wura-:ñ
        man.ABS woman-ERG slap-PAST
        The woman slapped the man

Since the common argument, 'the man', is in S function in (28) and in O function in (29), we could have (29) as main and (28) as relative clause, 'The woman slapped the man who was laughing', or the reverse:

(30)   wagu:ja$_S$ maŋga-:ñ   [[Ø$_O$ buña-:ŋ$_A$ wura-ñunda]$_{RELATIVE.CLAUSE}$]$_S$
        man.ABS laugh-PAST   woman-ERG slap-REL
        The man who the woman was slapping laughed

In Yidiñ the verb in a relative clause takes suffix *-ñunda* ~ *-ñu:n*. Since the common argument in the main clause can only be in S or O function, it must be in absolutive case, with zero realisation. That is, it is never followed by a non-zero case inflection as happens in Dyirbal.

The relative clause generally follows the main clause (so that the S NP is discontinuous), the whole sentence comprising one intonation group. This is in contrast to Dyirbal where the relative clause typically follows the noun it is modifying (although there can be variation on this pattern, in terms of the great freedom of word ordering in that language).

If the common argument has A as its underlying function in either main or relative clause, then—to meet the requirement of the S/O pivot—it must be placed in surface S function through application of the antipassive derivation. The antipassive derivation in Yidiñ has exactly the same form as that in Dyirbal, set out in (10). Yidiñ has dative case -*nda*, and verbal antipassive suffix -:*ji-n*.

Now consider (29) and:

(31)   buña$_S$ maŋga:-ñ
       woman.ABS laugh-PAST
       The woman laughed

These do share an argument, 'the woman', which is in S function in (31) but in A function—a non-pivot function—in (29). In order to combine these in a relative clause construction, (29) must be cast as an antipassive:

(29-ap)   buña$_S$ waguja-nda$_{DATIVE}$ wura-:ji-ñu
          woman.ABS man-DAT   slap-ANTIPASSIVE-PAST
          The woman slapped the man

We can now have (31) as main and (29-ap) as relative clause 'The woman who slapped the man laughed', or the reverse:

(32)   buña$_S$ waguja-nda$_{DATIVE}$ wura-:ji-ñu
       woman.ABS man-DAT   slap-ANTIPASSIVE-PAST
       [[Ø$_S$ maŋga-ñunda]$_{RELATIVE.CLAUSE}$]$_S$
             laugh-REL
       The woman who was laughing slapped the man

Exactly the same considerations apply for pronouns. Although they show an accusative morphology, pronouns follow the S/O pivot condition in relative clause constructions, just as nominals do. Consider:

(33)   ŋayu$_S$ maŋga-:ñ
       1sg.NOM laugh-PAST
       I laughed

(34)   ŋañañ$_O$ buña-:ŋ$_A$ wura-:ñ
       1sg.NOM woman-ERG slap-PAST
       The woman slapped me

There is an argument common to (33) and (34), the 1st person singular pronoun. Irrespective of its different forms—*ŋayu* for S function in (33) and *ŋañañ* for O function in (34)—the fact that it is in pivot function in each clause enables us to combine (33) as main and (34) as relative clause:

(35) ŋayu$_S$ maŋga-:ñ [[Ø$_O$ buña-:ŋ$_A$ wura-ñunda] $_{RELATIVE.CLAUSE}$]$_S$
     1sg.NOM laugh-PAST   woman-ERG slap-REL
     I, who the woman was slapping, laughed

Or, with (34) as main and (33) as relative clause:

(36) ŋañañ$_O$ buña-:ŋ$_A$ wura-:ñ [[Ø$_S$ maŋga-ñunda]$_{RELATIVE.CLAUSE}$]$_O$
     1sg.NOM woman-ERG slap-PAST   laugh-REL
     The woman slapped me, who was laughing

The 1st person singular pronoun has the same form, *ŋayu*, in (33) and in (37):

(37) ŋayu$_A$ buña$_O$ wura-:ñ
     1sg.NOM woman.ABS slap-PAST
     I slapped the woman

However, (33) and (37) cannot be combined in a relative clause construction since the common argument is in a non-pivot function, A, in (37). It is necessary to cast (37) as an antipassive:

(37-ap) ŋayu$_S$ buña:-nda wura-:ji-ñu
         1sg.NOM woman-DAT slap-ANTIPASSIVE-PAST
         I slapped the woman

We can now have (37-ap) as main and (33) as relative clause:

(38) ŋayu$_S$ buña:-nda wura-:ji-ñu
     1sg.NOM woman-DAT slap-ANTIPASSIVE-PAST
         [[Ø$_S$ maŋga-ñunda]$_{RELATIVE CLAUSE}$]$_S$
            laugh-REL
     I, who was laughing, slapped the woman

Or (33) as main and (37-ap) as relative clause:

(39) ŋayu$_S$ maŋga-:ñ [[Ø$_S$ buña:-nda wura-:ji-ñu:n]$_{RELATIVE.CLAUSE}$]$_S$
     1sg.NOM laugh-PAST   woman-DAT slap-ANTIPASSIVE-PAST
     I, who was slapping the woman, laughed

In summary, the S/O pivot condition applies strictly for both clauses in a relative clause construction in Yidiñ. However, things are rather different with respect to coordination.

7.2.2 Coordination

We saw, in section 7.1.1, that coordination in Dyirbal works in terms of an S/O pivot irrespective of whether the common argument is a nominal or a pronoun. Yidiñ is quite different. If the common argument for a coordination is a nominal (with ergative morphology) there is an S/O pivot (ergative syntax) reflecting the morphology. But an S/A pivot (accusative syntax) applies if the common argument is a pronoun, congruent with its accusative morphology.

We can first illustrate with nominals. (28) and (29) may be coordinated, in either order:

(40) wagu:ja$_S$ maŋga-ñ Ø$_O$ buña-:ŋ$_A$ wura-:ñ
      man.ABS laugh-PAST   woman-ERG slap-PAST
      The man laughed and the woman slapped him

(41) wagu:ja$_O$ buña-:ŋ$_A$ wura-:ñ Ø$_S$ maŋga-:n
      man.ABS woman-ERG slap-PAST   laugh-PAST
      The woman slapped the man and he laughed

As in Dyirbal, there is no explicit conjunction (similar to English *and*), with coordination being marked by the whole sentence making up one intonation group (and omission of the second occurrence of a common argument).

The 1st person singular pronoun is the argument common to (33), 'I laughed', and (37), 'I slapped the woman'. It is in S function in (33) and in A function in (37); this satisfies the S/A pivot condition for coordination when the common argument is a pronoun. Coordinating (33) and (37), in this order, we get:

(42) ŋayu$_S$ maŋga-:ñ Ø$_A$ buña$_O$ wura-:ñ
      1sg.NOM laugh-PAST   woman.ABS slap-PAST
      I laughed and (I) slapped the woman

The A argument is omitted from the second clause. Since the S argument in the first clause is a pronoun, it is identified with this, in terms of the S/A pivot condition for pronouns.

It is relevant to ask whether these two pivot principles—S/O for nominals and S/A for pronouns—ever interact. If all core arguments are nominals, or all are pronouns, there is never any difficulty. But ambiguity may arise when nominals and pronouns are mixed. Consider:

(43) ŋayu$_A$ buña$_O$ wura-:ñ Ø$_S$ maŋga-:ñ
      1sg.NOM woman.ABS slap-PAST   laugh-PAST

The S argument has been omitted from the second clause. It could be identified with the O argument in the first clause, which is a nominal, in terms of the S/O pivot applying for nominals. The sentence would then mean: 'I slapped the woman and she laughed'. Or the omitted S argument from the second clause could be identified with the A argument in the first clause, which is a pronoun, in terms of the S/A pivot applying for pronouns. The sentence would then mean: 'I slapped the woman and I laughed'.

Such occasional ambiguity would be resolved in terms of discourse or situational context. (It is the price to be paid for employing mixed pivots.)

Having now outlined the varying syntactic principles for coordination and relative clause constructions in Dyirbal and Yidiñ, we can move on to summarise these, and then make an attempt at explanation.

7.3 Summary and explanation

The varying pivot conditions in the two languages, for coordination and relative clause constructions, are summarised in table 7.3.

TABLE 7.3. Contrasting syntactic orientations for Dyirbal and Yidiñ

	COORDINATION function of pivot		RELATIVE CLAUSE CONSTRUCTION function of pivot in	
	nominal pivot	pronoun pivot	main clause	relative clause
Dyirbal	S/O		almost any	S/O
Yidiñ	S/O	S/A	S/O	

7.3.1 Types of discourse organisation

One noteworthy difference between the two languages lies in their techniques for discourse organisation. Non-autobiographical narratives in Dyirbal have much the same form as those in English. They are told in the 3rd person, with utterances of the participants quoted as direct speech; examples are in Dixon (1972: 368–82, 387–97).

Story-telling in Yidiñ is along rather different lines. Typically, the main character takes on the identity of narrator quite early in the story, with what follows being told from a 1st person perspective. This technique was employed in texts recorded by both of the main Yidiñ consultants, Dick Moses and Tilly Fuller. The entire corpus of Yidiñ texts is in Dixon (1991a: 28–124). For ease of reference, text and line numbers from the 1991 compilation are retained here.

Typically, there are one to four sentences setting the scene and introducing the main participant, who then takes over and recounts the rest of the story in 1st person. For example, text 11 is about Bindam, a legendary woman who ran away from her husband, Gamburrguman, and travelled around the tribal territory, naming places as she went. The story begins with a one-line introduction, and then Bindam speaks.

T11.1 [yiŋu bama, yiŋu bama buña   Bindam]$_S$, gali-:ñ
 THIS   person THIS person woman Bindam   go-PAST
  Gamburrguma:n-i-m   juŋga:-ñ
  Gamburrguman-GEN-ABL run-PAST
  This person, this person woman Bindam went off, she ran away from
  Gamburrguman who she used to belong to

T11.2 ŋayu$_S$ dabu:l-da ŋara gali-ŋ,   Jadi:-da bayii-:li-ñu . . .
  1sg.NOM beach-LOC south go-PRESENT Jadirr-LOC come.out-GOING-PAST
  I go south along the beach, I went and came out at Jadirr . . .

All the rest of the story is told in the 1st person, by Bindam.

 If the initial main character dies, or otherwise departs from the story, another character will take over, and continue the story from their perspective, in 1st person. Text 4 tells how the Yidiñji people first arrived in their present-day territory. Unusually, there is here no 3rd person introduction. The recording commences with Gulmbira, an old Yidiñji man, speaking:

T4.1   ŋayu$_S$ gana burrgi-:na   gali-:na . . .
  1sg.NOM TRY   go.walkabout-PURPOSIVE go-PURPOSIVE
  I tried to go walkabout, to go off . . .

For the next 38 lines, the story is told by Gulmbira, in 1st person. He travels around and meets Gindaja, the cassowary, who was a legendary man. Then Gulmbira dies; he describes this himself:

T4.37 ŋayu$_S$ gali-ñ, ŋayu$_S$ wula-:ñ
  1sg.NOM go-PAST 1sg.NOM die-PAST
  I've gone, I've died

T4.38 Gindaja-ŋgu$_A$ ŋañañ$_O$ buji-:ñ: 'ñundu$_S$ gali-n, wula-n'
  Cassowary-ERG 1sg.ACC tell-PAST 2sg.NOM go-IMP die-IMP
  Cassowary told me: 'You go!, die!'

T4.39 Ginda:ja$_S$ gali-:ñ
  Cassowary go-PAST
  Cassowary went on

T4.40 Baŋgilan-ña$_O$ wawa-:li-ñu   wala   gali-:ñ
       Baŋgilan-ACC look.for-GOING-PAST CEASED go-PAST
       Stopped looking for Baŋgilan, and went on

T4.41 ŋayu$_S$ yiŋgu guya   wuja-:na . . .
       1sg.NOM HERE across.the.river cross.river-PURPOSIVE
       I should cross the river here . . .

Gulmbira continues telling the story until line 38, when he recounts how Cassowary told him to die. Line 39 is in 3rd person, introducing the new narrator, Cassowary, who—from line 41—tells the next 18 lines of the story from his perspective, in 1st person.

(No subject is stated for line 40. It could either be taken to be 'he', with this line continuing the 3rd person linking from line 39. Or it could be taken to be 'I', commencing Cassowary's story-telling.)

As a consequence of this narrative style, 1st (and 2nd) person pronouns are extraordinarily frequent in Yidiñ narratives, occurring two to four times more often than pronouns in Dyirbal narratives. This must be a major factor in why coordination in Yidiñ uses an S/A pivot for pronouns and an S/O for nominals (reflecting the morphological marking of each) whereas Dyirbal uses an S/O pivot for everything.

There is also the fact that pivot chains in Yidiñ tend to be relatively short—seldom more than two or three clauses—whereas those in Dyirbal may extend over six or twelve clauses. For lengthy pivot chains to work effectively—with no danger of ambiguity—it is essential that Dyirbal should have a single pivot principle. This facilitates a homogenous grammar of coordination.

7.3.2 Common arguments in relative clause constructions

The question now to be addressed is: why, since Yidiñ has an S/A pivot for pronouns and an S/A one for nominals in coordination, does it not carry this through into relative clause constructions? The answer lies in the likelihood of a pronoun functioning as common argument in a relative clause construction.

In some languages no pronoun can be modified by a relative clause (see Dixon 2010b: 318–19). English may have a restrictive relative clause with a non-singular pronoun, as in: *You who voted for me will be rewarded, while you who voted against will come to regret it.* However, English may not have a relative clause to a singular pronoun. One can say *My father, who was mowing the lawn at the time, saw the escaped tiger run by*, but not *I, who was mowing the lawn at the time, saw the escaped tiger run by*. A different construction would have to be used, something like: *I saw the escaped tiger run by when I was mowing the lawn.*

Dyirbal and Yidiñ are unlike English in that a relative clause can be used with any kind of first or second person pronoun. In one conversation, a tape recording was being played back and Rosie Runaway exclaimed, in the Girramay dialect of Dyirbal:

(44) ŋamba   [ŋaña   [[Ø$_S$ wurrba-ŋu]$_{RELATIVE.CLAUSE}$]]$_O$
     listen.IMP 1sg.ACC   talk-REL.ABS
     Listen to me who is talking! (that is: Listen to my talking on the recording!)

A number of Yidiñ examples were given—in section 7.2.1—of a relative clause to a 1sg pronoun. Literal translations were provided: 'I, who the woman was slapping, laughed' for (35). However, this is not felicitous English. It would have to be re-phrased as a construction without a relative clause, such as 'I laughed as I was being slapped by the woman'. Similarly for (38) and (39).

In those languages for which any pronoun can function as common argument in a relative clause construction—such as Dyirbal and Yidiñ—this actually happens only rather rarely. That is, the great majority of common arguments are nominals. Yidiñ has a split pivot for coordination because pronouns are so common as a coordination pivot. For relative clause constructions, the pivot condition is always S/O— reflecting the ergative morphology of nominals—because pronouns are so rare as common argument.

In Dyirbal, pivot conditions are uniformly S/O. This applies for all types of coordination, and for the function of the common argument in a relative clause. However, in the main clause of a relative clause construction, the common argument may be in any core or peripheral function, other than allative or ablative. (In chapter 9 we shall see that relative clause constructions in Dyirbal have a further role, as a complementation strategy.)

7.4 Conclusion

The infrastructure of a grammar can best be understood if approached in terms of the role of the language within the culture which it serves. A 'semantics first' approach—in chapter 2—allowed us to explain the make-up of gender classes in Dyirbal. Similarly, in this chapter, the nature of discourse organisation in the two languages sheds light on why they employ differing syntactic pivots. The observation that Yidiñ uses a pronoun as common argument in coordination far more frequently than does Dyirbal helps explain why, while Dyirbal has an S/O pivot (ergative syntax) for all kinds of coordination, Yidiñ operates with a split system: an S/A pivot (accusative syntax) for pronouns and an S/O one for nominals. And the observation that 1st and 2nd person pronouns are only rather seldom modified by a relative clause is the key to understanding why the only pivot involved in relative clause constructions is S/O, its ergative syntax reflecting the ergative morphology of nominals.

This is a shortened and greatly revised version of a book chapter, 'The syntactic development of Australian languages' (Dixon 1977c). The argumentation has been refined, and out-dated notions discarded.

There are in fact two varieties of relative clause in the northern dialects of Dyirbal, and also two in Yidiñ, basically having the same syntax and differing in meaning, as the relative clause describes a continuing activity or a completed one. And there are further syntactic properties of relative clauses in the two languages. See Dixon (1972: 99–105; 1977a: 322–41).

In both languages, proper names and kin terms behave in some ways like pronouns, taking accusative suffix -*ña* for O function, as *Baŋgilan* does in T4.40. See Dixon (1972: 43–4; 1977a: 150–1).

8

Serial verb constructions in Dyirbal

A predicate in Dyirbal can include two or more verbals, which must agree in transitivity and inflection. This chapter examines the properties of such multi-verbal predicates, showing that they are serial verb constructions (SVCs), of both symmetrical and asymmetrical varieties.

8.1 Introductory

8.1.1 Word classes

As stated in section 1.5, there are four main open word classes:

$$\left.\begin{array}{l} \text{noun} \\ \text{adjective} \end{array}\right\} \text{nominal}$$
$$\left.\begin{array}{l} \text{verb} \\ \text{adverbal} \end{array}\right\} \text{verbal}$$

The lexicon which has been compiled includes a couple of thousand nouns, several hundred instances of verbs and of adjectives, and around forty adverbals.

Nouns and adjectives share the same morphological possibilities. They are distinguished by the fact that a noun relates to just one gender (very occasionally to two) whereas an adjective may be accompanied by a noun marker showing any gender (so long as this is semantically plausible). An adjective generally modifies a noun but it can be the only lexeme in an NP. It then has understood reference to a noun (which is not explicitly stated), and this determines the gender of the noun marker it is used with.

Verbs and adverbals also share the same morphological possibilities. Just as an adjective modifies a noun, so an adverbal modifies a verb. An adverbal does sometimes make up a predicate on its own but it is then understood to be modifying a verb (which is not explicitly stated).

Verbs and adverbals fall into two conjugations, in terms of their allomorphic choices for suffixes; these are indicated by -y and -l respectively on the citation form of each verbal. Almost all verbs are either strictly intransitive or strictly transitive. There is a correlation between transitivity and conjugation classes: most (but not all) -y verbs are intransitive, and most (but not all) -l verbs are transitive. (Derivational processes which change the transitivity of a verb are described in section 8.3, as are derivations which form intransitive and transitive verbal stems from nouns and adjectives, and also from time words and verb markers.)

Most adverbals are transitive (all belonging to the -l conjugations) or intransitive (all in the -y conjugation). However, there are five ambitransitives of type S = A. That is, they can be used both transitively (and then take -l conjugation allomorphs) or intransitively (taking -y allomorphs), with the transitive subject (A) corresponding to the intransitive subject (S). A sample of twenty adverbals is in table 8.1. (Where lexical forms vary between dialects, it is the J form which is given here.)

There is a closed class of 1st and 2nd person pronouns which have one form for A and S functions (nominative case) and another for O function (accusative case). This is

TABLE 8.1. A sample of adverbals in Dyirbal

Transitive only	Intransitive only	Transitive (-l Conjugation) & Intransitive (-y Conjugation)
ŋunbira-l try doing	wuda-y stop doing	wiyama-l/-y do how, do what
ŋurbi-l try, test, taste	ŋabi-y do again	yalama-l/-y do like this
nyunmi-l do sloppily	mumbi-y wait before doing	ginda-l/-y do with the aid of a light
ŋuyma-l do properly	ŋaramba-y tried and can't do	mumba-l/-y do on one's own
darra-l do badly	gurrma-y dawdle over doing	bulumba-l/-y do for no reason
jayŋu-l finish it off	gajilmbarri-y pretend to do	
gudi-l do too much		
nyinbi-l do too soon		
wirrja-l do quickly		

in contrast to the absolutive (S and O functions) versus ergative (A function) inflection of nouns, adjectives, and noun markers.

Dyirbal has no 3rd person singular pronouns per se. Noun markers, which are discussed in section 2.1, partly cover this role. Dialects differ with respect to non-singular 3rd person forms. Jirrbal and Mamu have complex forms 3dual *bala.garra* and 3plural *bala.maŋan*, which inflect on an absolutive-ergative pattern like nominals and noun markers. We find *bala.maŋan* '3plural.ABS' in S function in (24) below and *baŋgu. maŋan-du* '3plural-ERG' in A function in (42) and (44). Girramay has 3dual *bula* and 3plural *jana* which are like 1sg and 2sg pronouns—see table 1.2 in chapter 1—in having distinct forms for all three core functions; for example, 3 plural O form *jana-ña*, as in example (4), S form *jana*, and A form *jana-ŋgu*.

There is a small class of time words (including *ŋulga* 'tomorrow', *muguy* 'for a long time'). Verbalisations of inflected time words may occur in SVCs; see example (55) below.

Section 2.1 has full details of the important grammatical systems of noun markers, demonstratives, and verb markers, plus the systems of affixes indicating uphill, downriver, etc. which may follow them. Verbalised forms of locative and allative verb markers feature in many SVCs.

8.1.2 Verbal complexes

Corresponding to the predicate of each clause is what we can call a 'verbal complex'. This may include any number of verbs and/or adverbals, provided that (a) they agree in surface transitivity, and (b) they agree in inflection. For example, intransitive verbs *warri-y* 'fly' and *wayñji-l* 'move up' can each make up a complete predicate, or they may be combined in one predicate (verbs making up an SVC are underlined throughout):

(1) /ba-n$_S$ <u>warri-ñu</u> <u>wayñji-n</u>/
     THERE.ABS-II fly-PAST move.up-PAST
     She (the scrub turkey) flew up

All the examples in this chapter are taken from texts. In transcription, I use '/' to indicate an intonation break; an utterance could end at any place marked by '/'. A necessary criterion which I employ for recognising two or more verbs as making up an SVC in Dyirbal is that they should occur in one intonation group, between two instances of '/', as do *warri-ñu wayñji-n* in (1).

As explained in the previous chapter, Dyirbal works in terms of an S/O pivot ('ergative syntax'). A pivot NP may be stated (in S or O function) near the beginning of each pivot chain and then be the basis for a string of predicates. Generally, I shall only quote the intonation group with the SVC. The pivot, stated earlier, may be shown at the beginning in parenthesis. For example:

(2)   (ñaluŋga-ñaluŋga_s . . .) /buja-buja-ñu   mandala-ñu gamu-ŋga/
      REDUP-child   REDUP-bathe-PAST play-PAST   water-LOC
      Many children were playing and bathing a lot in the water

Full reduplication of a noun (here *ñaluŋga* 'child') indicates plurality. Reduplication of the first two syllables of a verb (here *buja-y* 'bathe') indicates 'action performed to excess'.

Dyirbal not only has free order of phrasal constituents in a clause, but in addition free order of words in a clause and also in a sentence. In about three-quarters of SVCs, the verbs occur next to each other, but in the remainder they are separated by one or more words (which can be any type of clausal constituent). For example:

(3)   /jiŋgali-ñu añja bayi_s   banaga-ñu/
      run-PAST NEW THERE.ABS.I go.back-PAST
      He ran back

Note that *añja* (the only word in the language commencing with a vowel) has a variety of functions (Dixon 1972: 117). Used sentence-initially it introduces a new pivot, as in example (37). If used before or in the middle of a verbal complex it indicates a new type of action involving an established pivot. It is shown in interlinear gloss as 'NEW'.

In examples (1–3), both verbs are intransitive. In (4), both are transitive. In all four examples, both verbs are in past tense, shown by suffix *-n~ -ñu*.

(4)   /[bala-n   jana-ña]_o/ galga-n   yubal-ja-ñu/
      THERE.ABS-II 3plural-ACC leave-PAST put.down-MANY-PAST
      Many of them (the snakes) were put down and left

Verbal derivational suffix *-ja-y* here indicates that the action involves many objects.

In (4), the two verbs describe a single activity 'put down and left'. If this could be separated into two actions, they would be 'put down' (first of all) and 'left' (following on from being put down). The fact that, in (4), *galga-n* 'left' precedes *yubal-ja-ñu* 'put many down' confirms that the predicate is viewed as depicting a single activity. The individual verbs within the SVC describe different aspects of the activity.

In the 1972 grammar I simply mentioned (pages 64–5) that a verbal complex in Dyirbal can include any number of verbs and adverbals provided that they agree in transitivity and inflection, and illustrated this with an example similar to (1).

Over the last few decades there has evolved the systematic study of predicates relating to two or more verbs, called 'serial verb constructions'. I have gone back to my corpus of texts (recorded between 1963 and 1998) and investigated the make-up of multi-verb predicates in Dyirbal. Before presenting these results, we need to consider the general nature of SVCs.

8.2 Characterisation of serial verb constructions

8.2.1 Cross-linguistic characterisation

During the late nineteenth century, it was noted that—in certain West African languages—adding a second verb to a predicate has a similar effect to an adverb of time or manner or a prepositional phrase of motion, position or instrument in a European language. In his grammar of 'Ashante and Fante' (or Twi), Christaller (1875: 69–73) provided an excellent description of the phenomenon, but the label 'serial verb' had not yet been coined. A half-century later, Balmer and Grant (1929: 115–28) produced another grammar of the same language and now referred to 'compound or serial verbs'.

Over the last few decades, serial verbs have been recognised as a construction type which occurs in a wide variety of languages—in West and South-west Africa, East and South-east Asia, Oceania, and South America, with a number reported from other regions, including Meso- and North America. They are also found in most (some would say all) creole languages.

The defining features of an SVC are:

A. The predicate of an SVC consists of two or more verbs, each of which could function as the sole verb in a clause.
B. There is no mark of coordination or subordination between the verbs in an SVC.
C. The SVC is conceived as describing a single activity or state.
D. The SVC functions as a single predicate. It generally falls within one intonation unit, so that no pause is likely in the middle of an SVC. Grammatical categories which apply to a predicate in the language of study have the complete SVC as their scope. These may include tense, aspect, evidentiality, modality, mood, negation, and markers of subordination (including relative clause). In most instances, only a complete SVC can be negated or questioned, not just one of its components.
E. There must be at least one core argument shared by all the verbs in an SVC. This is typically subject (embracing S and A functions). Sometimes all core arguments are shared.

The verbs making up an SVC may have varying transitivities, but the SVC itself will have a single transitivity value. In most languages, the verbs of an SVC occur next to each other; in some, other clausal constituents may intervene.

Aikhenvald (2006) distinguishes between two varieties of SVCs:

- An asymmetrical SVC involves two verbs of different status. There is a 'major member' (the head) which can be virtually any verb. Co-occurring with this is a 'minor member', chosen from a limited set of verbs of a certain semantic set. Amongst the semantic values which the minor member may specify are:

(a) direction—coming or going, up or down, across, back, etc.—or stance

(b) aspect, extent, and change of state, covering progressive, continuative, habitual, and the like

(c) obligation, necessity, probability

(d) starting, finishing, and continuing

- A symmetrical SVC combines verbs of any semantic types and no one verb may be recognised as head. The only restriction is semantic plausibility—for instance 'bathe' and 'play'—in example (2)—fit well together (whereas 'bathe' and 'reside' would scarcely be compatible).

Further discussion of the defining features of an SVC, together with a number of classes of exceptions, are in Aikhenvald (2006). That chapter also includes detailed references to the literature on SVCs.

8.2.2 Characterisation of serial verb constructions in Dyirbal

What I am putting forward as SVCs in Dyirbal satisfy criteria A–E. With respect to D, the verbs of an SVC fall within one intonation group (as mentioned above, this is one of my criteria for recognition) and there may be no pause between components. The verbs must agree in inflection (details are in section 8.3). Negation—see examples (19) and (27)—and questioning—see (29)— relate to the complete SVC. For criterion E, the verbs in an SVC are either all intransitive, and then share the same S argument, or all transitive, and then share the same A and O arguments.

With respect to criterion B, in Dyirbal coordination is shown simply by clausal apposition; there are no markers 'and', 'but', 'or', and so on. A relative clause is marked by verbal inflection, and this must apply to all the verbs in an SVC—see example (39). We have already mentioned the great freedom allowed for ordering of words in a sentence. In view of this, it is scarcely surprising that the verbs in an SVC do not have to occur in contiguity (although in fact they do in about three-quarters of instances). In example (3), both particle *añja* 'new type of activity' and noun marker *bayi* 'he' (the S argument) intervene between the two verbs of the SVC. The NP in A function, *yugu-ŋgu* 'tree-ERG', intervenes between verbs in the SVC of example (32). And similarly in ten further examples below.

We can recognise a division between asymmetrical SVCs, involving a verb (the major member, and head) and a member of the class of adverbals (the minor member), and symmetrical SVCs, involving just two or more verbs. The grammatical and semantic possibilities are fully explored in sections 8.4–8.6. But first we need to outline a few basic points of grammar.

8.3 Grammatical background

The corpus of SVCs is taken from texts (of varied genre) recorded from about fifteen speakers across three dialects—Girramay (G), in the extreme south of the language area, Jirrbal (J), just to the north of G, and Dulgubarra Mamu (M), a little further north. They have essentially the same grammatical system, but differ in the forms of some grammatical items and a few lexemes. For instance, the high-frequency verb 'return to point of origin, go back, go home' is *banaga-y* in J and G but *ŋurba-y* in M.

8.3.1 Verbal structure

Verbs and adverbals basically divide into intransitive and transitive subclasses (just one or two verbs, and five adverbals, may have either transitivity value). They also divide—by the allomorphic form of verbal affixes—into two conjugations. These are shown by quoting the verb root with a final *-y* or *-l*. For example, of the verbs in example (1), *warri-y* 'fly' belongs to the -y conjugation and *wayñji-l* 'move up' to the -l conjugation. There also is a single irregular verb, *yanu(-l)* 'go'.

A verbal (verb or adverbal) word has the following structure:

A. Root—obligatory
B. One or more derivational suffixes—all optional
C. One choice from the inflectional system—obligatory

There may also be reduplication (REDUP), whereby the first two syllables are repeated before the root, indicating 'action performed to excess, or state existing in excess'. For example, *buja-buja-ñu* 'bathe a lot', in example (2).

If a derivational or inflectional suffix has different forms they are quoted as '-y conjugation allomorph/-l conjugation allomorph'. For example, past tense is *-ñu/-n*, as shown on *warri-ñu wayñji-n* 'flew up' in example (1).

Derivational suffixes occur in the following order after the root (one may be chosen from each of slots 1, 2, 3, 4, and 5):

1. Valency-reducing derivations. Used with a transitive root or stem, forming an intransitive stem:
   - 1a. Antipassive (APASS), *-na-y/-(ŋ)a-y*;
   - 1b. Reciprocal, *-(n)barri-y*, together with reduplicating the first two syllables of the root. (There is no instance of this on an SVC in the present corpus, but there would be likely to be in a larger corpus.)

2. Aspectual-type derivations (used with verbs of both transitivity values and not affecting transitivity):
   - 2a. 'Do it quickly', form is *-nba-l* after transitive -l stems and *-gali-y* elsewhere (that is, with intransitive -l and with all -y stems).
   - 2b. 'Do repeatedly (over a longish period)', *-gani-y*.
   - 2c. 'Start to do', or 'do a bit more', or 'start to do a bit more', *-yarra-y*.

3. A fourth aspectual-type derivation (also used with verbs of both transitivity values and not affecting transitivity):
   - 3a. *-ja-y*. May indicate either (a) that an action is repeated many times within a short time span (often blindly, everywhere, in the hope of encountering a goal); or (b) that an activity involves many referents of the underlying S or O argument, as in example (4).

Note that each of the three suffixes in slot 2 (which are themselves mutually exclusive) may be followed by *-ja-y*, from slot 3. Interestingly, *-yarranja-y*, the combination of 2c *yarra-y* with 3a *-ja-y* has a special meaning 'doing habitually'.

4. A further valency-reducing derivation. Used with a transitive root or stem, forming an intransitive stem:
   - 4a. Reflexive (and general intransitiviser, REFL). On a -y verb: *-márri-y* after a root of two syllables, *-(m)bárri-y* on a longer form. On an -l verb: in G and M, *-rrí-y*; in J, *-yirri-y* when next but one after a stressed syllable, *-rrí-y* elsewhere.

5. Valency-increasing or -maintaining derivation:
   - 5a. Applicative (also general transitiviser, APPLIC), *-ma-l~ -mba-l ~ -ba-l*. With an intransitive root it creates a transitive stem; with a transitive root it maintains transitivity.

There are further complications in that the sequence can be threaded again after slot 4, so that we may have, for instance, ROOT-REFLEXIVE-APPLICATIVE-REFLEXIVE (see Dixon 1972: 246–7). Such extra details are not relevant for the present chapter.

Inflectional system. Each verb must select just one of the following eight choices:

1. Past tense *-ñu/-n*.
2. Future tense (FUT), *-njay/-ljay* in G; *-ñ* in J and M.
   The past suffix extends to present time in G and J, while future does so in M.
3. Positive imperative (IMP), ø (zero form).
4. Negative imperative (NEG.IMP): in G verbal suffix *-mu/-lmu* plus particle *ŋarru* placed anywhere before the verb; in J, verbal suffix *-m* plus particle *galga* placed anywhere before the verb; in M verbal suffix *-m* plus particle *ŋarru* placed anywhere before the verb.
5. Purposive (PURP), *y-gu/-l-i*. Used on a non-initial clause within a pivot chain, purposive indicates either 'in order to'—as in examples (5), (7), (15), (17), and (42)—or 'as a natural result of'—as in (16). In an initial clause it may mean 'should' or 'want to (because of some need)'—as in (26) and (53).
6. *-ŋurra*, indicating (a) that the S or O of the *-ŋurra* clause is coreferential with the A NP of the preceding clause, and (b) that the event of the *-ŋurra* clause follows immediately after the event of the preceding clause.

7. Apprehensive: *-bila* in J and G, *-ba* in M. As in *galga yanu-m ba-lu baji-bila* (DON'T go-NEG.IMP THERE-TO fall-APPREHENSIVE) 'don't go there lest you fall!' This is not attested occurring on an SVC in my corpus, but no doubt could so occur.

8. Relative clause suffix (REL) *-ŋu*. The verb(s) in a relative clause cannot take any of inflections 1–7, but are instead marked by *-ŋu*, followed by a marker agreeing with the case which the common argument receives in the main clause.

The irregular verb *yanu(-l)* uses root *yana* for positive and negative imperatives. Past tense form is *yanu* (rather than the expected **yanun*), with root *yanu-l* being employed elsewhere. Note that this is the most frequent lexeme in the language.

While inflection is a property of a whole SVC, and must apply to every one of its constituent verbs, derivational processes apply on an individual basis to verbs within an SVC. This is illustrated in section 8.5.1 for valency-changing derivations, and in section 8.5.3 for aspectual-type affixes (which do not affect transitivity) and reduplication.

8.3.2 Verbalisations

There are two productive processes for deriving verbal stems from non-verbal elements.

(i)   Creating an intransitive stem by adding inchoative (INCH) suffix *-bi-l*.
(ii) Creating a transitive stem by adding causative (CAUS) suffix *-ma-l* (to a stem of two syllables) or *-(m)ba-l* (to a longer stem).

The verbalising suffixes may be attached to:

(a) A plain adjective or noun. For instance, from adjective *guyi* 'dead' we get intransitive verb *guyi-bi-l* 'die (become dead)' and transitive *guyi-ma-l* 'kill (make dead)'. In example (46), an old man started to transform himself, *yamani-bi-li* (rainbow-INCH-PURP) 'so that he became a rainbow'. From noun *mulgu* 'noise' is derived transitive verb *mulgu-ma-l* 'make a noise'.

(b) A noun or adjective in allative or locative case (but not one in ablative case). We get noun *burba* 'swamp', allative form *burba-gu* 'to the swamp' and inchoative *burba-gu-bi-l* 'go to the swamp'. And noun *mija* 'camp', locative *mija-ŋga* 'at the camp', inchoative *mija-ŋga-bi-l* 'be at the camp'.

(c) Some time words may take suffix *-gu* 'until' or *-mu* 'since'. Just those ending in *-gu* may be verbalised. For example *ŋulga* 'tomorrow', *ŋulga-gu* 'until tomorrow' and inchoative *ŋulga-gu-bi-l* 'do it until tomorrow'. (See also causative *ŋulga-gu-mba-l* in example (55).)

(d) An allative or locative (but not an ablative) verb marker—see (15) in chapter 2—may undergo either of the verbalisations. For example, when I was recording a group outside the Murray Upper store, on a pension day in late 1963, Jimmy Murray told Rosie Runaway to turn to the front, so that the microphone would pick up her voice:

(5) /mirra ya-lu-bi   yabu/   wurrbay-wurrbay-gu/
     front HERE-TO.PLACE-INCH.IMP mother, REDUP-talk-PURP
     Face to the front, mother, to talk a lot

Verb marker *yalu* 'to here (towards a place)' takes inchoative *-bi* and then positive imperative (with zero marking).

Either verbalisation process can also apply to an allative or locative verb marker which is accompanied by a *-bayji-* or a *-gala-*type suffix. Verbalisations of verb markers make up a significant proportion of SVCs, and there are several instances in the examples below.

Dyirbal has a third, rather minor, type of verbalisation. The delocutive suffix *-(m)ba-y* (DELOC) derives an intransitive verb stem from institutionalised bird and animal cries, from some exclamations, from a number of grammatical particles, etc. (see Dixon 1977c). For example, the willy wagtail bird, *balan jigirrjigirr*, is said to call out 'jigirr-jigirr-jigirr' and this act is described by verb *jigirr-mba-y*. Three SVCs in the corpus include a delocutive verb—see example (43).

8.4 The serial verb construction in Dyirbal

8.4.1 Asymmetrical SVCs

The majority of SVCs are symmetrical, involving two (or more) members of the open class of verbs. There is also a significant number of asymmetrical SVCs, where a verb is accompanied by a member of the smallish class of adverbals. One common adverbal is the ambitransitive deictic *yalama-y/-l* 'do like this'. In (6) it is used, in its intransitive sense, with verb *wurrba-y* 'speak'; both adverbal and verb are in past tense inflection.

(6) /jañja <u>wurrba-ñu yalama-ñu</u>/
     now speak-PAST do.like.this-PAST
     (The man) now spoke like this: (followed by direct speech)

Example (7) is from a legend in which a man has been over-exploiting two women. They plan to get their own back by placing a rotten walnut in the fire, so that it will explode. The walnut was told to wait until the man was covering both women with his body, copulating with them, and then to explode, burning the man with its fiery fragments but not hurting the women who would be protected by his body. They address the walnut thus:

(7) /magul   miju   ba-ŋgu-l$_A$ ŋali-na$_O$
    MEANWHILE take.no.notice.IMP THERE-ERG-I 1dual-ACC
    garrju-li   guba-li   yuma-ru/
    do.properly-PURP cover-PURP body-INST
    Wait a while until he is covering us two up properly with his body

This begins with a command 'take no notice of us for the time being' and then a purposive clause 'until (lit. so that) he is covering us with his body'. Accusative pronoun
ŋalina 'us two' is in O function for both clauses. Adverbal *garrju-l* 'do properly' and
verb *guba-l* 'cover', making up the SVC, are both transitive, and both in purposive
inflection.

Example (30) below is another asymmetrical SVC, combining adverbal *jayŋu-l* 'finish it off' with verb *nudi-l* 'cut down', giving *nudi-n jaybi-n* 'finish cutting down (the
trees)'.

Each adverbal can co-occur with a verb or it can comprise a complete predicate.
One could say just *bayi yalama-ñu* 'He did like this' (accompanied by a mimed action)
or *baŋgul ŋalina garrju-li* 'So that he should do something properly to us' (where
the 'something' should be inferable from discourse context). Interrogative adverbal
wiyama-y means 'do what' when used alone—as in example (18)—and 'do X how'
when used with a verb meaning 'X', as in example (8) where both adverbal and verb in
the SVC are intransitive and inflected for future tense:

(8) /yaburri/   bala$_S$ wiyama-njay banda-njay/
    INTERJECTION THERE.ABS.IV do.how-FUT burst-FUT
    Oh dear! I wonder if (the pipe) is going to burst (lit. how it is going to burst)?

This comes from a story about the first contact between Aborigines and the white
invader, when the white man put a pipe in his mouth and lit it, engendering conster-
nation about what might happen.

It can be seen that the adverbal precedes the head verb in (7) and (8) but follows it
in (6) and (30). There does appear to be a tendency for the adverbal to come first—it
does so in about 70 per cent of textual examples—but little significance attaches to
this. For example, we encounter both *wurrbañu yalamañu* and *yalamañu wurrbañu*
for 'talk like this' with no difference in meaning or pragmatic import. As elsewhere in
Dyirbal, the order in which words are placed matters very little.

Sentences (14) and (16–20) of the next chapter are further examples of asymmetrical SVCs. More instances
are provided in Dixon (2006b).

It might be suggested that a further kind of asymmetrical SVC should be recognised, where the minor
member is a verb of motion (or of rest). However, such a line of analysis does not yield satisfactory
results. A verb such as 'return' appears to be a candidate to be a minor member in some instances of
an SVC and a major member in others. The only clear-cut asymmetrical SVCs are those involving an
adverbal.

8.4.2 The corpus of SVCs

We now examine the full gamut of both asymmetrical and symmetrical SVCs. Topics to be considered include: criteria for recognition, transitivity matching, inflectional possibilities, examination of the types of verbs in SVCs, and types of meaning engendered.

Scanning a collection of more than sixty texts—covering monologues of various genres, dialogues, and spontaneous conversation—across the Jirrbal, Girramay, and Mamu dialects, I assembled a corpus of 270 SVCs, 50 of them asymmetrical (that is, including an adverbal) and 220 symmetrical (made up just of verbs). In accord with criterion A in section 8.2.1, each component verb and adverbal could be used alone, making up a complete predicate.

And, in satisfaction of point C in section 8.2.1, each SVC is conceived of as describing a single activity or state. When George Watson recorded his life story, he said that since he was the consequence of rape by a white man, his mother had wanted to kill him at birth. However, her sister volunteered to rear George. After a few years, his mother wanted the child back and said:

(9) /ŋinda$_A$ [bayi   ŋaygu]$_O$ añja/ ŋurba-yarray-ma   wuga/
    2sg.NOM THERE.ABS.I 1sg.GEN NEW go.back-START-APPLIC.IMP give.IMP
    You give back my male one (son)!

Transitive verb *wuga-l* 'give' is combined with intransitive *ŋurba-y* 'go back, return'. The latter bears derivational suffix *-yarra-y* 'start to do'—this is difficult to render in the translation of (9)—and it requires applicative suffix *-ma-l*, which here serves just to ensure transitivity agreement with *wuga-l*. The two verbs of the SVC are in positive imperative form (with zero realisation). Verbs 'give' and 'return' combine to describe the activity 'give back'.

In example (10), intransitive verbs *jalmbi-l* 'dance' and *duŋgarra-y* 'cry' describe a group of people who are simultaneously dancing and crying:

(10) /jañja jalmbi-n   duŋgarra-ñu/
     now   dance-PAST cry-PAST
     (All the people) were now dancing and crying

The great majority of SVCs have just two components. However, there is one SVC consisting of four verbs—example (49) below—and eleven which contain three verbs (all these are symmetrical SVCs). We can illustrate with three examples of three-verb combinations, each describing a single activity (there is a further example at (24)).

(11) /[bayi   yuŋgurrun]$_S$ jiŋgali-ñu mija-gu-bi-n   ŋurba-ñu/
     THERE.ABS.I other   run-PAST camp-ALL-INCH-PAST go.back-PAST
     The other man ran back to the camp

The SVC in (11) involves two intransitive verbs, *jiŋgali-y* 'move fast, run' and *ŋurba-y* 'go back, return' plus inchoative verbalisation of noun *mija* 'camp' in allative inflection, *mija-gu* 'to the camp'. While the SVC in (11) is intransitive, that in (12) is transitive. It consists of transitive verb *budi-l* 'carry in hand', a transitivised form of *yanu(-l)* 'go', and transitive verbalisation of adjective *bulayi* 'two' giving *bulayi-mba-l* 'make two' or 'do twice' or 'do to two'.

(12) (nayi-jarran$_O$ . . .) /ba-ŋgu-l$_A$ <u>bulayi-mba-n</u> <u>budi-n</u>   <u>yanu-ma-n/</u>
      girl-PAIR   THERE-ERG-I two-CAUS-PAST carry-PAST go-APPLIC-PAST
      Then he carried the two (girls) off

Example (13) comes from a legend explaining the origin of death. A youth places a piece of wood on the fire and states that, when it has burnt down to nothing, he will die.

(13) /buni$_S$ añja <u>ganda-yarra-ñu</u>   <u>gundun-bi-n</u>   <u>wula-ñu/</u>
      firewood NEW burn-CONTINUE-PAST short-INCH-PAST disappear-PAST
      And the piece of firewood burned to be very short and vanished (i.e.
         burnt down to nothing)

The SVC in (13) involves two intransitive verbs, *ganda-y* 'burn'—which takes suffix *-yarra-y*, here indicating 'continue'—and *wula-y* 'vanish, disappear', plus inchoative verbalisation of adjective *gundun* 'short'. This combination of verbs describes the piece of wood burning down to be very short and then gone.

Criteria for recognising two or more verbs as making up an SVC in Dyirbal are (i) that they should occur in one intonation unit, marked by '/' at each end in transcription, and (ii) that they should bear the same inflection. Examining the corpus, verbs which satisfy (i) and (ii) in fact always turn out to satisfy criterion (iii), that they should agree in surface transitivity.

However, these criteria are not quite watertight. Special consideration is required when two verbs in purposive inflection occur in the same intonation unit.

8.4.3 Decisions about purposive

A verb in past or future inflection can be accompanied by one in purposive form; for example, 'X-PAST Y-PURP' meaning 'X is done so that Y should happen' or 'X is done and as a natural result Y happens'. Moreover, the two clauses 'X-PAST Y-PURP' can be within one intonation unit, as in:

(14) /bayi$_{S/O}$,   añja galga-n bungi-li   [bayi-n-bayji
      THERE.ABS.I NEW leave-PAST lie. down-PURP THERE.ABS.I-LINK-DOWN
         muŋa-gabun]$_{S/O}$/
      mob-ANOTHER
      Another mob were left to lie down a short distance downhill

The pivot argument, in absolutive case, is shown by *bayi* at the beginning and *bayi-n-bayji muŋa-gabun* at the end of the intonation unit. It is in O function for transitive verb in past tense *galga-n* 'left' and in S function for intransitive verb with purposive inflection *bungi-li* 'in order to lie down'. Note that no NP in A function is stated (it is understood to be ancestral hero Girugarr, whose journeyings are the subject of the text).

A further example involves two transitive verbs:

(15) /ŋana$_A$ jawun$_O$ buña-ñ   ŋurbay-yarra-ma-li   ba-gu-l/
      1plural.NOM dilly.bag weave-PAST return-START-APPLIC-PURP THERE-DAT-I
      We wove dilly-bags to make a return of them to him

The two clauses within one intonation unit in (15) share the same A argument, *ŋana* 'we', and O argument, *jawun* 'dilly-bag(s)'. The legend tells how a storytime character, Yamubili, brought nautilus shells up from the coast as a trade item, and the tablelands folk are now saying how they wove dilly-bags as exchange goods. From intransitive verb *ŋurba-y* 'return' (plus suffix *-yarra-y* 'start to do') a transitive stem is derived by adding *-ma-l*, giving *ŋurba-yarra-ma-li* 'to return with them'.

It is also possible to have an intonation group include two verbs, both in purposive inflection, which belong to two different clauses, 'X-PURP Y-PURP' 'as a result of something earlier, X, and as a natural consequence of X, Y', as in:

(16) /baŋanday-gu buga-bi-li/
      be.sick-PURP   dead-INCH-PURP
      (He was hit), as a result (he) got sick and as a further result (he) died

We thus see that if an intonation group includes two verbs each in purposive inflection, they may belong to different clauses (and not be an SVC). However, there are many examples of two (or more) purposive verbs which do make up an SVC, as in (7), (26), (42), (53), and:

(17) /banagay-mba-li   ya-li-gala   yambil-ma-li/
      go.back-APPLIC-PURP HERE-TO.PLACE-DOWN fly-APPLIC-PURP
      (The flying star spirit flew down south to get a painted basket) in order to fly
         back up here with it

Example (17) involves two intransitive verbs, *banaga-y* 'go back, return' and *yambi-l* 'fly' both in derived transitive form with applicative suffix *-ma-l*, *banagay-mba-l* 'go back with (it)' and *yambil-ma-l* 'fly with (it)'. The two verbs plainly describe a single activity 'fly back with it', and constitute an SVC.

If the inflection on each of two verbals within one intonation unit is any of (see section 8.3.1) past or future, positive or negative imperative, *-ŋurra* or the relative clause marker *-ŋu*, then they *always* constitute an SVC. If we have an adverbal and a verb both in purposive—as in (7)—then they must make up an SVC, since the adverbal will be modifier of the verb. But if there are two verbs in purposive inflection then they may either comprise an SVC, as in (17), or be two sequential clauses (and not an SVC), as in (16). Each instance has to be examined by the linguist on its own merits, to decide whether one activity is being described, or two. (The decision is not always an easy or a clear-cut one.)

8.5 Grammatical properties

8.5.1 Transitivity matching

Any verb or adverbal can be included in an SVC just so long as surface transitivity matches across the construction. We can have two intransitive verbs or two transitives. But if one verb is intransitive and the other transitive, then either the first must be transitivised or the second intransitivised. The possibilities will now be surveyed.

I. SVC is intransitive. This applies to slightly more than half the SVCs in the corpus. We can recognise four subtypes.

Ia. All verbals are simple underlying intransitives. Examples of this include (1–3), (6), (8), (10), (38), (40), (41), (49), (50), and:

(18) /jañja ñina-ñu wurba-ñu wiyamay-gu/
      now   sit-PAST talk-PAST do.what-purp
      (All the men) now sat around talking about what to do

The intonation unit includes an SVC in past tense, *ñina-ñu wurrba-ñu* 'sat around talking' and then a second clause consisting just of adverbal *wiyama-y* 'do what' in purposive inflection, *wiyamay-gu* 'in order to do what'.

Ib. The SVC includes an intransitive verbalisation, employing inchoative derivational suffix -*bi-l*. As described in section 8.3.2, -*bi-l* can be used with a variety of forms. First, a plain adjective or noun, as in (13), (53), and:

(19) /ŋarru ŋamir-ŋamir-bi-m   ñina-m/
      DON'T REDUP-hungry-INCH-NEG.IMP sit-NEG.IMP
      Don't sit around feeling very hungry!

We can have an SVC made up of two inchoatively verbalised adjectives. One Saturday in late 1963, Paddy Beeron had been waiting and waiting for his friend Mosley Digman to return home. Once he arrived, Mosley told Paddy:

(20) /maya-jilu-ban/   <u>burrun-bi-n</u>   <u>wagi-bi-n</u>/
      NO-INTENSIFIER-EMPHATIC busy-INCH-PAST working-INCH-PAST
      (I) couldn't help it, (I)'ve been busy working

Loan words are always taken over from English as nominals, never as verbals. Thus, from English *work* we get Dyirbal adjective *wagi* 'working'. This is verbalised as *wagi-bi-l* 'be working' and in (20) it is combined with inchoative verbalisation of adjective *burrun* 'busy', *burrun-bi-l* 'be busy'.

We can also have inchoative verbalisation of noun or adjective in allative or (more rarely) locative inflection, as in (11) and:

(21) (bayi$_S$ ...)   /<u>banaga-yarra-ñu</u>   ba-lu-dayi
      THERE.ABS.I go.back-START-PAST THERE-TO.DIRECTION-UP
      <u>muṇan-gu-bi-n</u>/
      mountain-ALL-INCH-PAST
      (He) started to go back a short distance uphill there to the mountains

An inchoative verbalisation may apply to an allative verb marker, as in (22), or (more rarely) a locative verb marker, as in (23):

(22) (Gudami$_S$ ...) /<u>ya-lu-bi-n</u>   <u>wayñji-n</u>/
      Gudami   HERE-TO.DIRECTION-INCH-PAST move.up-PAST
      (Gudami (a legendary dog)) travelled uphill in this direction

(23) ([bayi   ŋagi]$_S$ ...)   /<u>wula-ñu</u>   jañja
      THERE.ABS.I mother's.father vanish-PAST now
      <u>bala-y-jilu-bi-n</u>/
      THERE-AT-INTENSIFIER-INCH-PAST
      (Grandfather) vanished right there now (he went into a cave and the entrance closed up)

The inchoative verbalisation may also apply to an allative or locative verb marker plus a suffix from the -*bayji* set or the -*gala* set—see paradigms (16) and (18) in chapter 2—as in the three-verb SVC:

(24) (bala.maŋgan$_S$ ...) /baŋum gana <u>bani-ñu</u>   <u>ŋurba-yarra-ñu</u>
      3plural.ABS   THEN   TRY come-PAST go.back-START-PAST
      <u>ya-lu-bayju-bi-n</u>/
      HERE-TO.PLACE-LONG.WAY.DOWN-INCH-PAST
      (They) then tried to come back to a place a long distance downhill

Ic. **The SVC includes an underlying transitive verbal in detransitivised form.**
As pointed out in the discussion of verb structure in section 8.3.1, antipassive and
reflexive derivations may apply to a transitive form and derive an intransitive stem.
Either of them may be employed for transitivity matching with an intransitive
verb. Examples of reflexive (and general intransitiviser) *-(yi)rrí-y~ -márri-* include
example (39) and:

(25) /bala-y   bayi$_S$ <u>banaga-ñu</u> jañja <u>ṇamba-yirri-ñu</u> bayi$_S$/
       THERE-LOC THERE.ABS.I go.back-PAST now listen-REFL-PAST THERE.ABS.I
       Now he went back there thinking (as he went)

In (25) the reflexive form not only satisfies transitivity matching, it also has a semantic
role. The reflexive of transitive verb *ṇamba-l* 'hear, listen to' means 'think' (lit. 'listen
to oneself)'.

The antipassive intransitivising suffix *-na-y/-(ŋ)a-y* is used for transitivity matching
with intransitive verb *yanu(-l)* 'go' in:

(26) /gaji <u>bural-ay-gu</u>   <u>yanu-li</u>/
       TRY look.at-APASS-PURP go-PURP
       (We) should try to go on looking as we go

There is another instance in example (37).

It is, of course, possible to combine Ib and Ic, having an SVC which includes both
an inchoative verbalisation and an underlying transitive verb in detransitivised form.
George Watson explained that his maternal grandfather, Nyaywi, had an equable
disposition:

(27) (Ñaywi$_S$ . . .) /gulu <u>rañjarañja-bi-n</u>   <u>milgay-marri-ñu</u>/
       Nyaywi   NOT talk.in.harsh.voice-INCH-PAST grumble.at-REFL-PAST
       (Nyaywi) didn't talk in a harsh voice, nor did he grumble at people

A further instance of this is example (46).

Id. **The SVC includes two underlying transitive verbals each in detransitivised form.**
Any predicate can be placed in antipassive or reflexive form, by adding the appropriate derivational suffix. This can apply to a single-verb predicate, and equally to a
multi-verb one. The function of antipassive (and one function of reflexive) is to place
an underlying A argument into surface S function in order to satisfy Dyirbal's S/O
pivot condition. (Their differing semantic effects are discussed in Dixon 1972: 91–2.)
For example:

(28) /<u>nudil-ŋa-ñu</u>   bayi_S   <u>bañil-ŋa-ñu</u>   jambun-du/
cut-APASS-PAST THERE.ABS.I chop-APASS-PAST grub-INST
(The younger brother,) he was cutting and chopping out grubs

In the underlying transitive, 'he' would have been in A and 'grubs' in O function. Within the antipassive, (28), 'he' is the pivot, in S function, and 'grub' goes into instrumental case.

An example of an SVC in a polar question comes from an historical account of the last cannibalism (in 1940). A policeman asked one of the perpetrators:

(29) /ŋinda_S   <u>balgal-ŋa-ñu</u>   <u>nami-rri-ñu</u>/
2sg.NOM kill-APASS-PAST mix.up-REFL-PAST
Were you mixed up in the killing?

The SVC here consists of two transitive verbs, both in derived intransitive form: *balga-l* 'hit with a long rigid implement, held in the hand, kill' is in antipassive form, and *nami-l* 'mix up things which should be kept separate' takes reflexive suffix, here acting as a general intransitiviser.

II. SVC is transitive. This applies to slightly less than half the SVCs in the corpus. We can again recognise four subtypes, corresponding to Ia–Id.

IIa. All verbals are simple underlying transitives. Examples of this include (4), (7), (44), (48), (51), and (52). The SVC in (30) consists of a verb and an adverbal, while that in (31) has two verbs.

(30) /ba-ŋgu-l_A   <u>nudi-n</u>   yugu_O <u>jaŋu-n</u>/
THERE-ERG-MASC cut-PAST tree   finish.off-PAST
He finished chopping down the trees (i.e. he chopped down all the trees)

(31) ([bayi   gugar]_O . . .) /<u>bura-n</u>   <u>waba-n</u>   [ba-ŋgu-n
THERE.ABS.I black.goanna look.at-PAST look.up-PAST THERE-ERG-II
nayi-jarran-du]_A/
girl-PAIR-ERG
The two girls looked up (at the black goanna (up in the tree))

IIb. The SVC includes a transitive verbalisation, employing causative derivational suffix *-ma-l~ -(m)ba-l*. Examples involving transitive verbalisation of an adjective include (12), (45), (47), and:

(32) /bayi_O/   <u>balga-n</u> yugu-ŋgu_A <u>guyi-ma-n</u>/
THERE.ABS.I hit-PAST tree-ERG   dead-CAUS-PAST
(While he was chopping wood,) a tree (fell and) hit and killed him

There is causative verbalisation of an allative verb marker in:

(33)   /barrmi-n   ba-ŋgu-l$_A$ ya-lu-mba-n/
        look.back-PAST THERE-ERG-I HERE-TO.PLACE-CAUS-PAST
        He looked back towards this place

And of an allative verb marker plus suffix *-gala* 'vertically up' in (54) and:

(34)   ([ba-n   midi]$_O$ . . .) /ba-ŋgu-l$_A$ ya-lu-gala-mba-n
        THERE.ABS-II small   THERE-ERG-I HERE-TO.PLACE-UP-CAUS-PAST
        bura-n/
        look-PAST
        (The small woman (up the tree)) was seen by him (who was) looking up

The time word *ŋulga* 'tomorrow' plus affix *-gu* 'until' receives causative verbalisation in example (55).

IIc. The SVC includes an underlying intransitive verbal in transitivised form, shown by suffix *-ma-l~ -mba-l~ -ba-l*. Examples include (9), (12), (36), (42), and:

(35)   /giña-n-galu$_O$ /gila-rri   balba-n yanu-ma-n/
        THIS.ABS-II-IN.FRONT SOMEWHERE-TO.PLACE roll-PAST go-APPLIC-PAST
        This one (a round tank) out in front, was taken by being rolled to a place
           somewhere

The three-verb SVC in (12) combines IIb and IIc by including both causative verbalisation of adjective *bulayi* 'two', and underlying intransitive verb *yanu(-l)* 'go' in transitive form.

IId. The SVC includes two underlying intransitive verbals each in transitivised form. The applicative derivation, marked by suffix *-ma-l~ -mba-l~ -ba-l*, can apply to any intransitive predicate, whether involving one verb or an SVC. An example of an SVC in which both verbs are in applicative form is (17). Verbs *banaga-y* 'go back, return' and *yambi-l* 'fly' undergo the applicative derivation to become *banagay-mba-l* 'go back with' and *yambil-ma-l* 'fly with', the underlying S argument going into surface A function and the 'applicative argument'—which would have received comitative marking in the original intransitive construction—being now in O function (so as to be pivot in this segment of discourse).

There are fifty or more SVCs for each of types Ia, Ib, IIa, and IIb, a couple of dozen in each of Ic and IIc, and just a handful in each of Id and IId.

Dyirbal has two verbs 'follow' which appear to have essentially the same meaning but differ syntactically—*marri-l* is intransitive and *banja-l* is transitive. A textual sample has twenty-two instances of a predicate whose verb is *marri-*; six of them include a dative NP stating what is being followed (four a person, one a river, and one a track). And there are eighteen instances of a predicate whose verb is transitive *banja-*; the O argument is a river in five instances, a track in two, and a person or animal in eleven.

Interestingly, there are two instances of SVCs including both verbs. One SVC is transitive, so that *marri-l* has to be transitivised as *marril-ma-l*:

(36) /gundaya-gu$_A$ <u>marril-ma-n</u>   <u>banja-n/</u>
      carpet.snake-ERG follow-APPLIC-PAST follow-PAST
      (The blue-tongue lizard) was followed by the carpet snake

The other SVC is intransitive, and here *banja-l* bears antipassive suffix, giving *banjal-ŋa-y*:

(37) /añja [ba-n   yibi-jarran]$_S$/ ba-li-gayul   <u>marri-n</u>
      NEW   THERE.ABS-II woman-PAIR THERE-TO.DIRECTION-SAME follow-PAST
      <u>banjal-ŋa-ñu/</u>
      follow-APASS-PAST
      And two women followed (the river) in the same direction there

The combination of two verbs 'follow' in one predicate is a stylistic device to empha-sise the nature of the activity. A transitive combination is chosen in (36) because the creature who is being followed, the blue-tongue lizard, is the pivot of this part of the discourse. It is in O, a pivot function. And in (37) it is the women doing the follow-ing who are the pivot. They are underlying A (a non-pivot function), and within the intransitive SVC are placed in derived S (a pivot function).

A similar principle is followed in other instances. Transitivity matching types Ic and Id involve intransitivisation of a transitive verb because it is the underlying A (now surface S) that is pivot argument for the part of discourse in which the example sen-tence occurs. For instance, this is 'we' for (26) '(We) should try to go on looking as we go'. Similarly, in types IIc and IId an intransitive verb is transitivised because it is the O argument of the SVC which is discourse pivot.

8.5.2 Inflectional possibilities

The eight terms in the inflectional system on verbs in Dyirbal were listed in section 8.3.1. All save apprehensional *-bila~ -ba* are attested on SVCs (and this would no doubt occur if a larger corpus were to be assembled).

Past tense is most common, accounting for about 70 per cent of SVCs in the corpus. There are around three dozen purposives, twenty or so positive imperatives, a dozen relative clause SVCs, and just a handful of SVCs in future, in negative imperative, and in *-ŋurra* inflection.

Most SVCs in this chapter are in past tense. The other possibilities are:

- future—example (8)
- positive imperative—(9) and (55)
- negative imperative—(19)
- purposive—(7), (17), (26), (42), and (53)
- *-ŋurra*, with the unusual role of indicating that the S or O of its clause is coreferential with the A NP of the preceding clause (and also that the event of the *-ŋurra* clause follows immediately after the event of the preceding clause). George Watson recorded a short account of a spirit figure called Yugubarra who shouts 'giwu, giwu, giwu', warning people not to sleep too long or too deeply in case of an attack:

(38) /warrañuŋgul$_O$ ba-ŋgu-l$_A$ giwu$_O$ jarra-ɲu/   bayi$_S$
      three   THERE-ERG-I 'call' call.out-REL THERE.ABS.I
      añja gara-ɲurra   bani-ɲurra/
      NEW sneak-ɲurra come-ɲurra
      He having called out 'giwu' three times (lit. three giwu's), he came
      sneaking up

'He', referring to Yugubarra, is in A function (*baŋgul*) in the first clause of (38) and then goes into the pivot function S (*bayi*) in the second clause, this being marked by *-ŋurra* on both verbs in the SVC, *gara-l* 'sneak up' and *bani-y* 'come'.

- Relative clause affix. Verbs in the predicate of a relative clause take suffix *-ŋu*, followed by a marker of the case of the common argument in the main clause. Example (39) was used by Chloe Grant to describe seeing the large eyes of an owl shining out at her in the night. The common argument, 'big eyes', is in O function for the main verb *ŋarba-l* 'be frightened of' and thus takes absolutive case, which has zero marking. The relative clause to 'big eyes' is then also in absolutive case. It consists of locative noun *yidira* 'in the grass' and two verbs, intransitive *ñina-y* 'sit', and the reflexive form of transitive *buyba-l* 'hide', *buyba-yirri-y* 'hide oneself'.

(39) /[[yidi-ra   ñina-ɲu buyba-yirri-ɲu]$_{RC}$ gayga-bu bulgan]$_O$ ŋaja$_A$
      grass-LOC sit-REL hide-REFL-REL   eye-ONLY big   1sg.NOM
      ŋarba-n/
      be.frightened.by-PAST
      I was frightened by (seeing) just (two) big eyes which were sitting
      hiding in the grass

8.5.3 Aspectual-type suffixes and reduplication

The list of derivational processes applying to a verbal, in section 8.3.1, includes four aspectual-type suffixes, which have semantic effect and do not change transitivity. Three of them are attested in an SVC but, interestingly, they typically occur on just one of the verbs.

- *-ja-y-*, 'action is repeated many times within a short time span' or 'activity involves many referents of S or O argument'. There is a single instance in the SVC corpus, example (4), and here the suffix appears on just one verb.
- *-yarra-y-*, 'start to do' or 'do a bit more' or 'start to do a bit more'. It occurs in twelve examples in the corpus, and for each of them the suffix occurs on just one verb. See examples (9), (13), (21), and (24).
- *-gani-y-*, 'do repeatedly over a longish period'. Example (40) involves two intransitive verbs, *mamba-l* 'keep putting food into mouth until it is full', and *mañja-y* 'eat to appease hunger'. Just the first of them bears suffix *-gani-y-*.

(40) /mambal-gani-ñu   mañja-ñu/
      put.food.in.mouth.till.full-REPEATEDLY-PAST eat.to.appease.hunger-PAST
      (We) kept on stuffing our mouths, eating to appease hunger

There are four other SVCs in the corpus for which *-gani-* occurs on just one verb (they include example (52)), and two for which it is on both verbs. For example:

(41) (ba-n$_S$...)   /yanul-gani-ñu   balŋgal-gani-ñu/
      THERE.ABS-I   go-REPEATEDLY-PAST walk.along.branch-REPEATEDLY-PAST
      (She) kept going, kept edging along the branch (high up in the tree)

The process of reduplication also has just a semantic effect, 'action performed to excess, or state existing in excess'. Reduplication occurs on about three dozen SVCs in the corpus and, like the aspectual-type suffixes, it generally applies just to one verb, as in examples (2), (48), (50), (51), and (52). In example (19) the adjective within an inchoative derivation is reduplicated, and in (43) the exclamation within a delocutive verb is. For only three SVCs does reduplication apply to both verbs. George Watson explained how, when living on Palm Island, he had used a tractor to construct a dam, for water to be piped up to the settlement:

(42) (bana$_O$...) /baŋgu.maŋgan-du$_A$ guñja-guñja-li   ŋaba-ŋabay-ma-li/
      water   3plural-ERG   REDUP-drink-PURP REDUP-bathe-APPLIC-PURP
      For them all to drink (water) a lot and bathe in it a lot

Thus, while inflection is a property of a complete SVC (in effect, of a predicate), derivational affixes and reduplication apply to verbs on an individual basis. In (41), where the two verbs both show *-gani-*, and in (42), where they are both reduplicated, the derivation has applied to the verbs separately (and is not a property of the SVC).

8.6 Semantics

8.6.1 Types of verb in SVCs

It is interesting to see which verbs and adverbals occur most commonly as components of SVCs in the corpus. The nine most frequent are two transitive verbs (*bura-l* and *budi-l*), five intransitive verbs, and two ambitransitive adverbals:

- dialect variant verb *banaga-y*, in J and G (23 occurrences), *ŋurba-y*, in M (14), 'go back, return'—37 in all
- verb *yanu(-l)* 'go'—32
- verb *bura-l* 'see, look at, notice'—25
- verb *ñina-y* 'sit, stay'—17
- verb *bani-y* 'come'—15
- adverbal *wiyama-y/-l* 'do what, do how'—15
- verb *wayñji-l* 'move up'—14
- verb *budi-l* 'carry in the hand'—12
- adverbal *yalama-y/-l* 'do like this'—11

We can now examine how many of each type of verb occur in an SVC. Delocutive verbs were mentioned at the end of section 8.3.2. These involve the addition of *-(m)ba-y* to a bird or animal cry or an exclamation, etc., deriving an intransitive verb stem. There are three delocutive verbs in the SVC corpus, each combined with a verb of motion. For example:

(43) /bayi$_S$ baŋum yagay-yagay-ba-ñu   yanu/
      THERE.ABS.I THEN   REDUP-EXCLAMATION-DELOC-PAST go.PAST
      (He was badly burnt,) then he went off calling out 'yagay, yagay'
        (an exclamation to accompany some decisive happening)

We can adopt a rough classification of verbs as follows:

(a) Adverbals, occur in 50 SVCs
(b) Verbs of motion, in about 150
(c) Verbs of rest, in about 50
(d) Other verbs, in about 200
(e) Verbalised nouns and adjectives (in plain form or in allative or locative case), in about 50

(f)   Verbalised allative and locative verb markers (with and without suffix from the
      -bayji and *-gala* sets), in about 40

All kinds of combinations of verbs from (a–f) are encountered, except that (i) there
are no SVCs combining an adverbal with a verbalised verb marker; and (ii) there are
none combining verbalised noun or adjective with a verbalised verb marker.

The 'other' category, (d), covers a wide semantic range, including: verbs that imply a
physical effect on the O (hit, punch, spear, cut, paint, tie, burn), verbs of giving (give,
send), of attention (look, listen, examine, search for), of speaking (talk, ask, name,
grumble), corporeal verbs (eat, chew, drink, swallow, laugh, cry, be sick, swive), and
verbs of mental attitude (be frightened, show off). (I have not been able to perceive
any variety of verb which can *not* occur in an SVC.)

8.6.2 Meaning types

We can now survey the kinds of meanings conveyed by SVCs in Dyirbal.

One possibility is for the construction to consist of two verbs which have essentially
the same meaning, and differ just in their basic transitivity. The examples with 'follow',
in (36) and (37), are the only instances of this kind that I have noted in the corpus.
Transitivity must be matched for them to co-occur, by either transitivising one or
intransitivising the other.

What we sometimes get is a verb which has a rather general meaning, accompanied
by one of its hyponyms, providing further semantic specification. There are several
examples of this with the general verb *bura-l* 'see, look at, notice'. It is used together
with the more specific verb *waba-l* 'look up at' in example (31), and with *ŋarɲja-y* 'stare
at, watch steadily' in:

(44)   (baŋgu.maŋgan-du$_A$ . . .) /<u>bura-n</u>   <u>ŋarɲja-ɲu</u>/
       3plural-ERG   look.at-PAST stare.at-PAST
       (They (the Girramay people)) looked and stared at (Captain Cook's party)

Several SVCs involve transitive verb *baŋga-l* 'paint', accompanied by a second verb
indicating what sort of painting is being undertaken. In example (45), adjective *gingin*
'black' bears causative verbaliser *-ma-l*, giving *gingin-ma-l* 'make black'.

(45)   /jilin-du   <u>baŋga-n</u> bala-n$_S$ <u>gingin-ma-n</u>/
       charcoal-INST paint-PAST THERE.ABS-II black-CAUS-PAST
       She (the black snake) was painted black (lit. painted made black) with
          charcoal

Example (46) uses the reflexive form *baŋga-rri-y* 'paint oneself', combined with the
inchoative verbalisation of adjective *gijar* 'striped', giving *gijar-bi-l* 'become striped'.

(46) (bayi$_S$ ...)   /bala-y-ŋarru   <u>baŋga-rri-ñu</u>   <u>gijar-bi-n</u>/
    THERE.ABS.I THERE-LOC-BEHIND paint-REFL-PAST stripy-INCH-PAST
    yamani-bi-li/
    rainbow-INCH-PURP
    (He (the old man)) transformed himself), he painted himself (making
    himself) become striped behind there, so that he became a rainbow

We may get two verbs each of which describes a different aspect of motion. They include 'flew up' in (1), 'fly back' in (17), 'ran back' in (3) and (11), 'come back' in (24), 'came sneaking up' in (38), 'kept going edging along the branch' in (41), 'taken by being rolled' in (35), and 'carried off (i.e. carried going)' in (12). There are combinations of a verb of motion with an allative or locative verbalisation, such as 'go back to the mountain' in (21). Related to these are 'give back' in (9), 'went calling out' in (43), and 'put down and left' in (4).

Many SVCs indicate simultaneous activities (or states). We get 'sat talking' in (18), 'sit feeling very hungry' in (19), 'sitting hiding oneself' in (39), 'went back thinking' in (25), 'go looking' in (26), 'have been busy working' in (20), 'were bathing and playing' in (2), 'stuffing our mouths and eating' in (40), and 'hit and killed' in (32). Example (27) involves negation of an SVC consisting of verb 'grumble at' and verbalised adjective 'talk in a harsh voice', describing two rather similar aspects of Nyaywi's personality.

A further example of simultaneous happenings is:

(47) /bala$_O$ ba-ŋgu-l$_A$ yulba$_O$ <u>ñaju-n</u>   <u>gulgu-ma-n</u>
    THERE.ABS.IV THERE-ERG-I BRANCH burn-PAST merging-CAUS-PAST
    ba-ŋgu-l$_A$/
    THERE-ERG-I
    He burned the branch making it merge (with the fire; that is, lose its separate
    identity)

Adjective *gulgu* generally means 'join up with a group and become a part of it'. Here it indicates that the tree branch has burnt away, sublimating itself into the fire. Example (13), 'it burnt, became short, and vanished', is similar, except in that sentence there is an element of sequentiality between 'become short' and 'vanish'.

Note the discontinuous O NP, *bala . . . yulba* in (47) and repetition of ergative noun marker *baŋgul*. Both are normal features of Dyirbal discourse (in (25) and (49) absolutive noun marker *bayi* is stated twice).

The verbs in an SVC may describe related activities, which can be either simultaneous, as in (10), 'were dancing and crying', or interwoven, as in (28), 'was cutting and chopping', (42), 'drinking a lot and bathing a lot', and:

(48) /bala-y   balga-n   bunju-bunju-n/
      THERE-LOC hit-PAST   REDUP-spank-PAST
      (We) hit and spanked a lot (the old man) there

A classic example of interwoven activities is shown in the four-verb intransitive SVC:

(49) /yuṇarra-ñu bayi$_S$ mulma-ñu   ba-li
      swim-PAST THERE.ABS.I dive.deeply-PAST THERE-TO.DIRECTION
      bayi$_S$ yanu   gulgulba-ñu/
      THERE.ABS.I go.PAST dive.shallowly-PAST
      He went along in that direction swimming, diving deeply, diving shallowly

Verb *yanu(-l)* indicates that he was going along the river, with the other three verbs describing the manner of his going—*yuṇarra-y* 'swimming', *mulma-y* 'diving deeply' and *gulgulba-y* 'diving shallowly (like a platypus)'. The three activities would have been alternated as he progressed.

Some SVCs have a metaphorical overtone. For example:

(50) /[midi ba-n]$_S$ añja banda-banda-ñu miyanda-ñu/
      small THERE.ABS-II NEW REDUP-burst-PAST laugh-PAST
      Then the small (i.e. younger) woman burst out laughing

Dyirbal has a profusion of verbs for kinds of hitting. They include *balga-l* 'hit with a long rigid implement which is held in the hand; kill'—in (29), (32), (48), and (54)—*minba-l* 'hit with a long rigid implement, which is thrown; shoot', and *bunju-l* 'hit with a flexible implement, whip, spank'—in (48). There are also two verbs referring to hitting with a rounded implement, *bara-l* and *biji-l*.

We find *bara-l* used for a blow coming from above, such as driving a post into the ground and banging a nail in with a hammer. In the SVC of example (51) it joins up with *wadi-l* 'copulate with, swive':

(51) /bala-y-ju   ba-ŋgu-l$_A$ bara-bara-n   wadi-n/
      THERE-LOC-INTENSIFIER THERE-ERG-I REDUP-drive.in-PAST swive-PAST
      Right there he swived (the woman) driving in (his penis)

Verb *biji-l* is used for hitting with a stone (held onto or thrown), punching, banging on a drum, and heavy rain falling on a person. In (52), it combines with *ŋanba-l* 'ask':

(52) /ba-ŋgu-l$_A$ ŋanba-n/ biji-biji-gani-ñu ŋanba-n/
      THERE-ERG-I ask-PAST REDUP-punch-REPEATEDLY-PAST ask-PAST
      He asked (them), he bombarded them with questions (lit. he kept punching
        a lot asking)

Interestingly, the metaphorical SVCs in (50) and (52) can both be rendered by metaphorical expressions in English—*burst out laughing* and *bombard with questions*.

Finally, there are a few rather special meanings associated with SVCs. Adjective *jilbay* means 'expert at a task, experienced'. In (53), Jimmy Murray combines *wurrba-* 'speak' with the inchoative derivation *jilbay-bi-n* 'become expert', in telling Rosie Runaway to encourage her classificatory grand-daughter to speak in Dyirbal (rather than in English) implying that by so doing she will attain proficiency in the language:

(53) /jañja <u>jilbay-bi-li</u>   gumbu$_S$ <u>wurrbay-gu</u>/
     now expert-INCH-PURP granddaughter talk-purp
     (You) should let your granddaughter speak language and become clever

The next example has what was, for me, an unexpected translation:

(54) ([bayi . .   maguy]$_O$) /<u>balga-n</u> <u>ya-lu-gala-mba-n</u>
     THERE.ABS.I carpet.snake hit-PAST HERE-TO.PLACE-UP-CAUS-PAST
     yugu-ŋgu/
     stick-INST
     (He) raised the stick to hit the carpet snake with it

In example (34), the same causative derivation from verb marker *yalu-gala* 'towards a place up here' combines with *bura-l* 'see, look at, notice' to mean 'look up at'. I would have predicted that *balga-n yalu-gala-mba-n* in (54) should mean 'hit upwards'. In fact, I was told that the sentence should be translated 'raised the stick to hit (without necessarily bringing it down on the victim)'.

It was mentioned in section 8.3.2 that inchoative and causative verbalisations can apply to a time word marked by suffix -*gu* 'until', such as *ŋulga-gu* 'until tomorrow'. We can then get *ŋulga-gu-mba-l* 'make it be until/for tomorrow', as in:

(55) /<u>jaguma</u>   gaji <u>ŋulga-gu-mba</u>/
     tie.up.IMP TRY tomorrow-UNTIL-CAUS.IMP
     Try and tie up (the fishing line) for tomorrow (then it will be ready to be
       used tomorrow)

8.7 Summary

Dyirbal has a well-defined serial verb construction. Surveying a textual corpus of 270 SVCs, 50 are of the asymmetrical variety, where the minor member comes from the smallish class of adverbals (covering meanings such as 'do properly', 'do badly', 'do too soon', and 'do like this'). The remainder are symmetrical SVCs whose members can be verbs of any semantic hue. A high proportion of SVCs have at least one member referring to motion or rest.

An SVC falls within a single intonation group, with no pause between components. Its members can be simple or derived verbals, verbalised nouns or adjectives (in plain form or with allative or locative suffix), verbalised forms of allative or locative 'verb markers' (indicating direction or place with respect to 'there' or 'here'), or a verbalised time word with 'until' suffix. Each verb which can occur in an SVC may make up a predicate on its own. One SVC in the corpus has four members, eleven have three members and the remainder just two.

There are no marks of coordination or subordination between the words in an SVC. Dyirbal has generous freedom of ordering for words within a sentence. In keeping with this, the component verbs of an SVC do not have to be contiguous, although in fact they are in about three-quarters of instances. (Items placed between verbs in an SVC include all or part of an NP in S, O, or A function, a particle such as *gaji* 'try', a locational indicator, or any combination of these.)

An SVC is understood to be describing a single activity or state. It has the normal properties of a predicate; for example, negation applies to the whole SVC (as in examples (27) and (19)). The verbs in an SVC must agree in surface transitivity and inflection (covering tense, purposive, imperatives, etc.). The verbs in each SVC share the same S argument (if intransitive) or A and O arguments (if transitive). Aspectual-type suffixes, and reduplication—which have purely semantic import—sometimes apply to all verbs in an SVC but more often to just one of them.

SVCs have been reported for a number of languages from the central north of Australia; all appear to be just of the asymmetrical variety. These include Kayardild (Evans 1995: 302–12), Nakkara (Eather 2011: 398–415), Ndjébbana (McKay 2000: 286–9), Gurrgone (Green 1995: 259–85), Burarra (Green 1987: 76–82) and Djapu (Morphy 1983: 87–93).

Yidiñ is the only language besides Dyirbal for which both asymmetrical and symmetrical SVCs have been described. See the discussion of 'verb complexes' in Dixon (1977a: 252–4).

This chapter is a revised version of a paper 'Serial verb constructions in Dyirbal' (2012b). An earlier discussion of asymmetrical SVCs is in Dixon (2006b).

9

Complementation strategies in Dyirbal

Dyirbal lacks a complement clause construction. However, there are a number of other construction types which have secondary function as 'complementation strategies', covering the roles filled by complement clauses in other languages. Before delving into this, it will be useful to briefly survey the main types of clause linking.

9.1 Types of clause linking

There are three basic ways in which clauses can be combined to form a complex sentence. These are illustrated in diagram 9.1.

(a) Coordinate and non-embedded subordinate structures. Here, two clauses are immediate constituents of the 'sentence' node, as shown at (a) of the diagram. In English, the second clause is preceded by a linking word. This may be a coordinator such as *and*, in (1), or any of a varied set of subordinate linkers, such as temporal *after* or *when*, or the consequence linker *(in order) to*, as in (2).

(1)   John$_S$ went to the river and (he$_S$) bathed
(2)   John$_S$ went to the river (in order) to bathe

(b) Relative clause. This is a constituent of an NP, which is an argument of a clause, as shown at (b) of the diagram. A relative clause modifies the head of its NP, in much the way that an adjective does, helping to specify its reference, as in:

(3)   I$_A$ saw [the child [who was hanging in a cradle]$_{RELATIVE.CLAUSE}$]$_O$

(c) Complement clause. As shown at (c) of the diagram, a complement clause fills an argument slot in a higher clause—as in (4), (6), and (8)—instead of an NP doing so—as in (5), (7), and (9).

(4)   John$_A$ announced [that [his party]$_S$ had won]$_{COMPLEMENT.CLAUSE:O}$
(5)   John$_A$ announced [the election result]$_{NP:O}$
(6)   Mary$_A$ saw [[the volcano]$_S$ erupting]$_{COMPLEMENT.CLAUSE:O}$

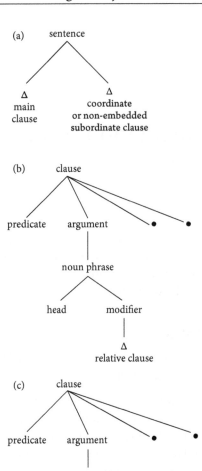

(a)   sentence

Δ
main
clause

Δ
coordinate
or non-embedded
subordinate clause

(b)   clause

predicate   argument

noun phrase

head   modifier

Δ
relative clause

(c)   clause

predicate   argument

Δ
complement clause

DIAGRAM 9.1 Types of clause linking

(7)   Mary$_A$ saw [the eruption]$_{NP:O}$
(8)   I$_A$ want [to eat [a mango]$_O$]$_{COMPLEMENT.CLAUSE:O}$
(9)   I$_A$ want [a mango]$_{NP:O}$

9.1.1 Complement clause constructions

The criteria for recognising something as a complement clause are: (i) it has the internal structure of a clause; (ii) it functions as a core argument of a higher clause; and (iii) it refers to a proposition.

There are three basic varieties of complement clause, according as the proposition which it describes is a **fact**, as shown by a *that* complement clause in English, in (4);

or an **activity**, as shown by an *-ing* complement clause in (6), or a **potential state**, as shown by a *to* complement clause in (8).

In every language in which they occur, complement clauses may function as O argument, as they do in (4), (6), and (8). In English they may also be A argument—as in [*That his party had won the election*]$_{\text{COMPLEMENT.CLAUSE:A}}$ *pleased John*$_{\text{O}}$—or S argument—as in [*That his party had won the election*]$_{\text{COMPLEMENT.CLAUSE:S}}$ *mattered a lot (to John)*.

In order to provide a perspective on the functioning of complement clauses, it is useful to distinguish between Primary and Secondary types of verbs, and then sub-divisions within these:

Primary verbs, which may be the complete predicate of a sentence, divide into:

Primary-A, whose core argument slots may only be filled by NPs, not by complement clauses. This covers verbs of MOTION ('walk', 'follow'), REST ('stand', 'put'), AFFECT ('kick', 'knit'), GIVING ('give', 'lend'), CORPOREAL ('drink', 'shiver', 'cure'), among others.

Primary-B. All argument slots may be filled by NPs, but at least one argument slot may be filled by a complement clause, as an alternative to an NP. The semantic types of verbs within Primary-B include:

- ATTENTION, including 'see', 'find', 'show', 'hear'
- THINKING, including 'think of', 'dream about'
- SPEAKING, including 'tell', 'grumble at', 'ask', 'encourage to do'
- LIKING, including 'like', 'dislike', 'regret', 'fear'

Languages vary as to what is expressed lexically and what is included within the grammar. Cross-linguistically, we can recognise a number of **Secondary concepts**, which serve to modify the meanings of Primary verbs. In some languages these concepts are expressed by derivational affixes to verbs, such as 'start to do', 'try to do', 'want to do', and 'make do'. In other languages, such as English, secondary concepts are expressed by **Secondary verbs**. They include:

Secondary-A verbs (the BEGINNING and TRYING types), that do not add to the core arguments of the Primary verb with which they are associated. Alongside *I*$_{\text{A}}$ *cut down* [*the trees*]$_{\text{O}}$, with Primary-A verb *cut*, we can have—adding Secondary-A verb *start*— *I*$_{\text{A}}$ *started* [*to cut down* [*the trees*]$_{\text{O}}$]$_{\text{COMPLEMENT.CLAUSE:O}}$. Note that syntactically *start* is the main verb and *cut* the verb of the complement clause. However, semantically 'cut' is the central notion and 'start' a modifier to it. Secondary-A verbs in English include *start, finish, continue,* and *try*.

Secondary-B verbs (the WANTING type), which include *want, hope,* and *plan*. These *do* add an argument to those of the primary verb they are associated with. Compare *John*$_S$ *will go,* and *I*$_A$ *want* [*John*$_S$ *to go*]$_{COMPLEMENT.CLAUSE:O}$. However, main clause subject and complement clause subject often coincide, and then the latter is omitted, as in *I*$_A$ *want* [Ø$_S$ *to go*]$_{COMPLEMENT.CLAUSE:O}$.

Secondary-C verbs (the MAKING type), which include *make, force,* and *cause*. These also add an argument to those of the Primary verb with which they are associated, as in *I*$_A$ *forced* [*John*$_S$ *to go*]$_{COMPLEMENT.CLAUSE:O}$. With Secondary-C verbs, complement clause subject is unlikely to coincide with main clause subject, and when it is it cannot be omitted. That is, one can only say *I forced myself to go,* not **I forced Ø to go*.

Cross-linguistically, there is a fair range of possibilities for which variety of complement clause may occur with which type of verb. However, we do find a number of recurrent associations. For example, Secondary-B verbs of WANTING typically take a potential state complement clause, as in *I*$_A$ *want* [*(Mary) to return home*]$_O$. Potential state complement clauses are also found with some SPEAKING verbs—such as *I*$_A$ *told* [*John to go*]$_O$—and some of the LIKING type—for example, *Charlie*$_A$ *likes* [*Uncle Tom to tell him stories*]$_O$.

Some verbs may take either a fact or an activity complement clause, with contrasting meanings. For instance:

(10)   John$_A$ heard [Mary('s) singing *Jerusalem*]$_{COMPLEMENT CLAUSE:O}$
(11)   John$_A$ heard [that Mary was singing *Jerusalem*]$_{COMPLEMENT CLAUSE:O}$

Sentence (10) states that John actually heard the activity of Mary's singing, whereas (11) indicates someone told him the fact that she was singing the song.

The chapter on 'Complementation' in Dixon (2010b: 370–421) provides fuller details concerning criteria for recognising complement clauses, their meanings and functions, and the associations between types of Primary-A and Secondary verbs and varieties of complement clauses.

9.2 Complementation strategies in Dyirbal

My 1972 description of Dyirbal described every grammatical pattern in a corpus of forty texts and much other material. A linguist who read the grammar wrote and asked why there was no mention of complement clauses. I knew about complement clauses in English and other languages, and I also knew the grammar of Dyirbal. The language simply has no complement clauses; that is, it has no clauses functioning as core arguments in a higher clause.

As I continued to work on Dyirbal through the 1970s and 1980s—gathering materials for a dictionary/thesaurus, recording and analysing more texts, and pursuing further grammatical study—the question nagged at me as to what Dyirbal might have which would correspond to complement clauses in other languages. Prototypical complement-clause-taking verbs cross-linguistically include 'see', 'hear', 'like', 'want', 'tell to do', and 'finish'. As time went by, I came to realise that in Dyirbal each of these verbs carries the expectation of entering into a certain grammatical construction—a purposive construction, a relative clause construction, or a serial verb construction. These constitute what I call 'complementation strategies', being roughly equivalent to complement clause constructions in other languages.

   In English, *see* commonly takes an ING complement clause as O argument, to describe an activity which is seen; this is (c) from diagram 9.1. In Dyirbal, verbs of seeing carry the expectation of including a relative clause within their O NP, as a way of referring to an activity which is seen; this is (b) from diagram 9.1., used as a complementation strategy. For example:

(12)   bura-n   ŋaja$_A$ [guyibarra [Ø$_S$ yambi- ŋu]$_\text{RELATIVE.CLAUSE}$]$_O$
        see-PAST 1sg.NOM curlew   fly-REL
        I saw the curlew flying

Whereas in English *want* is a transitive verb taking a (FOR) TO complement clause in O function, in Dyirbal verbs of wanting are intransitive, and carry the expectation of being linked to a further clause by an 'in order to' linker (purposive verbal inflection); this is (a) from diagram 9.1, used as a complementation strategy. For example:

(13)   ŋaygu-na$_O$ ba-ŋgu-l$_A$ ŋanba-n Ø$_S$ yanu-li
        1sg-ACC   THERE-ERG-I ask-PAST   go-PURP
        He asked me to go

And whereas in English *finish* takes a complement clause in O function, in Dyirbal adverbals of finishing occur with another verb in a serial verb construction. As described in the preceding chapter, the two verbals agree in transitivity and final inflection and have the same arguments. This is a third variety of complementation strategy. For example:

(14)   jaɲu   mara$_O$ burbi
        finish.IMPERATIVE leaf   pull.off.IMPERATIVE
        Finish pulling off the leaves! (i.e. Pull off all the leaves!)

Note that Dyirbal has no way of expressing the Secondary-C concept of making, neither a lexical verb nor a derivational affix to the verb. Quite simply, one must specify the mechanism of causation. Rather than the vague 'He made me laugh', a speaker of Dyirbal has to specify what was done to bring about this activity; for instance, 'She told me a joke and as a result I laughed' or 'He tickled me and as a result I laughed'.

(The nearest thing to a causative verb is *giga-l* 'tell to do, let do', which takes a purposive complementation strategy; see (43) in section 9.5.)

The concept 'start, begin' is realised only through one of the verbal derivational suffixes listed in section 8.3.1: -*yarra-y* 'start to do, do a bit more, start to do a bit more'. For example:

(15) bayi$_S$ jiŋgali-yarra-ñu
      THERE.ABS.I run-START.TO.DO-PAST
      He started to run

The complementation strategies will now be described one at a time—the serial verb, then the relative clause, and then the purposive strategy.

9.3 The serial verb strategy

In the discussion of serial verb constructions (SVCs), we described the asymmetrical type, which includes a member from the smallish class of adverbals, illustrated in table 8.1 of the last chapter. Some of the adverbals correspond to verbs which take complement clauses in other languages. Their use in SVCs constitutes one kind of complementation strategy.

This can be exemplified with transitive adverbals *ŋunbira-l* 'try doing' in (16) and *ŋurbi-l* 'try, test, taste' in (17). (As in the last chapter, verbs in an SVC are underlined.)

(16) ŋinda$_A$ <u>ŋunbira</u> bala$_O$ <u>maŋga</u>
      2sg.NOM try.to.do.IMP THERE.ABS.IV pick.up.IMP
      You try to pick it up!

(17) ba-ŋgu-l$_A$ <u>ŋurbi-n</u>   <u>guñja-n</u>   mayi$_O$/   garrja
      THERE-ERG-I try/taste-PAST drink-PAST English.bee alright
      He tasted (lit. tried drank) the English bee honey drink; (it was) alright

Examples of SVCs as a complementation strategy involving transitive adverbal *jaŋu-l* 'finish doing' are (14) above and (30) in chapter 8. The intransitive adverbal *gajilmbarri-y* 'pretend to do' features in:

(18) bayi$_S$ <u>gajilmbarri-ñu</u>   <u>yanu</u>
      THERE.ABS.II pretend.to.do-PAST go.PAST
      He pretended to go

If one member of a serial verb construction is basically intransitive and the other basically transitive, then—as described in section 8.5.1—either the intransitive member must be transitivised (by an applicative derivation) or the transitive member must be intransitivised (by an antipassive or other process). Sentence (19) links the intransitive adverbal *wuda-y* 'stop doing' with the transitive verb *bara-l* 'punch, bang nail in'; here the verb is made intransitive by the antipassive derivation.

(19) bayi$_S$ wuda-ñu   baral-ŋa-ñu
      THERE.ABS.I stop.doing-PAST nail-APASS-PAST
      He stopped nailing

In (20) the verb *mabi-l* 'cross river' is intransitive, and the transitive adverbal *jayŋu-l* 'finish doing' takes the reflexive suffix *-yirri-y-*, here simply functioning as an intransitiviser. The inclusion of *jayŋu-l* in (20) implies that both sons have crossed the river.

(20) [ŋaygu daman-jarran]$_S$ Dali-gu mabi-n   jayŋu-yirri-ñu
      1sg.GEN son-PAIR   Tully-ALL cross.river-PAST finish-REFL-PAST
      My two sons have finished crossing the river to Tully

9.4 The relative clause strategy

A relative clause must have an argument which is identical to the head of the NP it is modifying (this whole NP being an argument of the main clause). As described in chapter 7, for Dyirbal the common argument in the relative clause must be in S function, as in (21), or in O function, as in (22). This argument is not stated within the relative clause.

(21) ŋali$_A$ bayi$_O$ balga-n [[Ø$_S$ gulu yanu-ŋu]$_{RC}$]$_O$
      1dual.NOM THERE.ABS.I kill-PAST   NOT go-REL
      We two killed him who wouldn't go (we killed him because he was so lazy
          and wouldn't go out)

(22) ŋaja$_A$ [bala-n   baŋgay]$_O$ bural-ja-ñu
      1sg.NOM THERE.ABS-II spear   see-LOTS-PAST
      [[Ø$_O$ baŋgugarra-gu$_A$ galgal-ja-ŋu]$_{RC}$]$_O$
          3dual-ERG   leave-LOTS-REL
      I saw lots of spears which the two (men) had left

In each of these examples the relative clause is detached from the noun which it modifies; this is fairly common and in accordance with word order being remarkably free in Dyirbal. Both verbs in (22) include the derivational suffix *-ja-y* 'action involving many objects'.

Note that only a plain relative clause interpretation is possible for (21). For (22), taken out of context, a complementation strategy interpretation would be possible, referring to an activity: 'I saw the many spears being left by the two men'. But in the text from which (22) is taken, the storyteller comes across a pile of spears which two men had left, some time before, outside a house (and from this recognises it as the men's house). It is thus clear that a straight relative clause meaning is intended in this instance, rather than a complementation strategy.

Whereas the common argument must be in surface S or O function within the relative clause, it can be in almost any function in the main clause (any except for allative and ablative). In fact, for a relative clause complementation strategy, the common argument is only in S or O function in the main clause, as in the relative clause. Table 9.1 summarises the combination of possibilities, and examples they occur in.

Some verbs expecting the relative clause complementation strategy are intransitive; row (i) of table 9.1 is illustrated in (23), for which a little background is needed. A boy and girl were promised in marriage at an early age. When they had reached maturity, the man was expected to claim his promised wife once he had proved himself as a hunter and provider. But if he failed to do so, she would have to go to him, which she would feel shy about. She might say:

(23) ŋaja$_S$ ŋurji-ñu   [[Ø$_S$ ŋanbal-ŋa-ŋu ba-gu-l]$_{RC}$]$_S$
      1sg.NOM be.shy-PAST   ask-APASS-REL THERE-DAT-I
      I was shy and ashamed at having to ask him (to marry me) (lit. I who was
       asking him was shy)

The main clause has intransitive verb *ŋurji-y* 'be shy and ashamed'. Its S argument is pronoun *ŋaja* 'I', modified by a relative clause. The underlying form of the relative clause is *ŋaja*$_A$ *bayi*$_O$ *ŋanba-ŋu*, 'I ask him', with the common argument, 'I', in A

TABLE 9.1. Functions of common argument within a relative clause complementation strategy

	Function in main clause	Function in relative clause	Examples
(i)	S	S	(23)
(ii)	S	O	(24), (46)
(iii)	O	S	(12), (25–27), (44)
(iv)	O	O	(22), (28)

function. This is antipassivised, in order to get the common argument in the relative clause into S function, i.e. *ŋaja$_S$ ŋanbal-ŋa-ŋu ba-gu-l*.

Sentence (24) describes someone feeling ashamed because they have been grumbled at. Here the common argument, 'I', is in S function for the intransitive main clause verb *murri-y* 'feel ashamed of having done wrong', and in O function for the transitive relative clause verb *milga-y* 'grumble at'. This is row (ii) in table 9.1

(24) ŋaja$_S$ murri-ñu   [[Ø$_O$ ŋinda$_A$ milga-ŋu]$_{RC}$]$_S$
     1sg.NOM feel.ashamed-PAST   you.NOM grumble.at-REL
     I felt ashamed at having been grumbled at by you (lit. I, who was grumbled at
       by you, felt ashamed)

In each of (25–26), the common argument, 'him' is in O function in the main clause and in S function in the relative clause; this is row (iii) in table 9.1.

(25) ŋaja$_A$ bayi$_O$ ŋamba-n [[banaga-ŋu]$_{RC}$]$_O$
     1sg.NOM THERE.ABS.I hear-PAST   return-REL
     I heard him returning (lit. I heard him who was returning)

(26) ŋaja$_A$ jinga-ñu
     1sg.NOM tell.about-PAST
     [bayi   [Ø$_S$ rubi-ŋu ba-ŋgu   jalgu-ru]$_{RC}$]$_O$
      THERE.ABS.I   eat-REL THERE-INST.IV   meat-INST
     I told about his eating the meat (lit. I told about him who was eating the meat)

Alternatively, the relative clause may be underlyingly transitive, with the common argument in A function; this must then be placed in S function through the clause being recast in antipassive form, as in:

(27) ŋaja$_A$ bayi$_O$ dija-n
     1sg.NOM THERE.ABS.I meet.by.chance-PAST
     [[Ø$_S$ [ŋaygu   bulgu-gu] wadil-ŋa-ŋu]$_{RC}$]$_O$
       1sg.GEN wife-DAT copulate.with-APASS-REL
     I found him copulating with my wife (lit. I found him, who was copulating
      with my wife)

The common argument is *bayi*, 'him', which is in O function for the main clause verb *dija-l* 'meet by chance, encounter, find'. It is in underlying A function in the relative clause, 'He was copulating with my wife', and is placed in S function within an antipassive derivation.

The final possibility is for the common argument to be in O function in each clause, row (iv) of table 9.1. In one story about the olden days, a noise was heard outside the camp at night, said by the old people to be made by a frightening spirit called Dambun. A young girl ignored the old people's warnings and went out to look for the noise, bearing a lighted torch. On finding that the noise was made by a mopoke owl, sitting in the grass, she burst out laughing. Back at the camp, the old people heard this laughter and imagined that it resulted from the girl's being tickled by Dambun. In telling the story many years later, the girl says (this is in Dixon 1972: 387):

(28) baŋgu.maŋgan-du$_A$ ŋaygu-na$_O$ ŋunja-ñu
      3plural-ERG   1sg-ACC   blame-PAST
      [[Ø$_O$ Dambun-du$_A$ gidimba-ŋu]$_{RC}$]$_O$
      Dambun-ERG tickle-REL
      They all put the blame (for the laughing) on me being tickled by Dambun (lit.
      They blamed me who (they thought) was being tickled by Dambun)

9.5 The purposive strategy

The system of verbal inflections—set out in section 8.3.1—includes purposive, which is -*y-gu* on a verb from the -*y* and -*l-i* on one from the -*l* conjugation. This typically goes on the second (or later) clause of a coordination. As described in chapter 7, two clauses may only be coordinated if there is a common argument which is in S or O surface function in each; this is generally omitted from the second clause (or shown just by a noun marker).

A purposive construction involves one clause (C$_1$) whose verb bears tense or imperative inflection, and a second clause (C$_2$) whose verb takes purposive inflection. Either the activity of C$_1$ was done *in order that* that of C$_2$ should follow, or the activity of C$_2$ follows *as a natural consequence* of what was described in C$_1$. For example:

(29) [bayi   yara]$_S$ yanu
      THERE.ABS.I man   go.PAST
      Ø$_O$ [ba-ŋgu-n   yibi-ŋgu]$_A$ bura-li
          THERE-ERG-II woman-ERG see-PURP
      either The man went so that the woman should see him
      or The man went and as a result the woman saw him

In (29), the shared argument, *bayi yara*, is in S function in C$_1$ and in O function in C$_2$. In (30) this is reversed, with *bayi yara* being in O function in C$_1$ and in S function in C$_2$.

(30) ŋaja$_A$ [bayi   yara] bara-n   Ø$_S$ baji-gu
      1sg.NOM THERE.ABS.I man. punch-PAST   fall-PURP
      either I punched the man and as a result he fell down
      or I punched the man so that he should fall down

Purposive inflection can also occur on the verb of a main clause (although it is found less often in this position than in the second clause of a complex sentence construction such as (29–30)). For example:

(31)   ŋaja$_S$ yanu-li, I have to go

This implies that there is some reason for which I must go; for example, there may be no food for my family so that I have to go out to hunt. A sentence such as (31) can be translated as 'have to', 'ought to', 'need to' or even 'want to', but only when this implies a desire brought on by some external factors.

There are two constructions in English which are quite different in structure, but both include *to* in their marking. Compare:

(32)   I$_S$ came (in order) to dance
(33)   I$_A$ wanted [(John$_S$) to dance]$_{COMPLEMENT.CLAUSE:O}$

In (32), intransitive verb *come* is linked to *dance*, through the 'non-embedded subordinate' linker *in order to*, which can be shortened to just *to*; this is structure (a) in diagram 9.1. In (33), *want* is a transitive verb taking as its O argument the complement clause *John to dance*; this is structure (c) in diagram 9.1. The complement clause subject is omitted when it is the same as the main clause subject, giving *I wanted to dance*. The two sentences can become *I came to dance* and *I wanted to dance*, superficially similar but in fact entirely different in their structure.

Dyirbal lacks a verb with a wide general sense similar to English *want*. It does have verbs of wanting with more specific meanings, all intransitive; for example, *walŋgarra-y* 'want to do something to satisfy a persistent emotional worry or desire'. We can compare the following with (32–33):

(34)   ŋaja$_S$ bani-ñu   wuri-gu
       1sg.NOM came-PAST dance-PURP
       I came to dance

(35)   ŋaja$_S$ walŋgarra-ñu wuri-gu
       1sg.NOM want-PAST   dance-PURP
       I wanted to dance

Unlike (32) and (33), the Dyirbal sentences (34) and (35) *do* have the same grammatical structure; both are type (a) in diagram 9.1.

Each of *come* in English and *bani-y* in Dyirbal is a simple intransitive verb. *Want* in English is transitive, taking as its O argument either an NP (as in *I want an orange*) or a complement clause (*I want (Mary) to eat an orange*).

Walŋgarra-y in Dyirbal is an intransitive verb. But whereas one can just say *ŋaja bani-ñu* 'I came', **ŋaja walŋgarra-ñu* is not an acceptable sentence. *Walŋgarra-y* carries the expectation that it will be accompanied by a purposive clause, as in (35). Just as the transitive verb *want* in English takes a complement clause as its O argument, so the intransitive verb *walŋgarra-y* in Dyirbal requires an accompanying purposive clause. This is a purposive complementation strategy.

Transitive *ŋuymi-y* 'like to do' is another verb which expects the complementation strategy of a purposive clause. Generally, the purposive clause will also have a transitive verb, sharing A and O arguments with *ŋuymi-y*, as in:

(36)   ŋaja$_A$ [bala-m   ŋarriñji]$_O$ ŋuymi-ñu jaŋga-ygu
        1sg.NOM   THERE.ABS-III orange   like-PRES eat-PURP
        I like to eat oranges

One day, I wondered whether *ŋuymi-y* could be used in a similar way to *like* in English, and attempted to say:

(37)   ŋaja$_A$ [bala-m   ŋarriñji]$_O$ ŋuymi-ñu
        1sg.NOM   THERE.ABS-III orange   like-PRES
        I like oranges

Consultants did not reject this sentence outright, but they were not at all happy with it, suggesting that it would be better if *jaŋgaygu* were added. It is clear that transitive verb *ŋuymi-y* expects an accompanying purposive clause, in the same way that intransitive *walŋgarra-y* does.

The two clauses in a purposive construction must have a common argument, which is in S or O surface function in each. Table 9.2 summarises the combination of possibilities, and examples they occur in, just as table 9.1 did for the relative clause strategy.

TABLE 9.2. **Functions of common argument within a purposive complementation strategy**

	Function in main clause	Function in purposive clause	Examples
(i)	S	S	(35), (38), (47)
(ii)	S	O	(39)
(iii)	O	S	(13), (40)
(iv)	O	O	(36), (41–43)
(v)	A + O	S	(45)

The S–S linkage was illustrated by (35) 'I wanted to dance'. If the common argument is in underlying A function in the purposive clause, it must be put into surface S function through antipassivisation, as in:

(38) ŋaja$_S$ walŋgarra-ñu wuju-gu jaŋga-na-ygu
      1sg.NOM want-PAST   food-DAT eat-APASS-PURP
      I wanted to eat some food

Row (ii) of table 9.2 is illustrated in (39) where the common argument, *bayi* 'he', is in S function in the first clause, with the intransitive verb *wugi-l* 'show off', and in O function in the purposive clause, with the transitive verb *bura-l* 'see':

(39) bayi$_S$ wugi-n   yibi-ŋgu$_A$ bura-li
      THERE.ABS.I show.off-PAST woman-ERG see-PURP
      He was showing off, for the woman to see (and admire) him

There are also transitive verbs which expect a purposive clause. We can get main clause O identical with purposive clause S, which is row (iii) of table 9.2. This is illustrated by (13) 'He asked me to go' and by:

(40) ŋinda$_A$ ŋaygu-na ŋanba-n jigarin-gu   wugal-ŋa-ygu
      2sg.NOM 1sg-ACC ask-PAST cigarette-DAT give-APASS-PURP
      You asked me to give a cigarette (to you)

Here the purposive clause involves a transitive verb with the shared argument, 'me', in A function; it must thus be antipassivised. As in (13), the 1sg pronoun functions as O argument in the main clause, realised here as *ŋayguna*, and as S argument in the purposive clause (the S form *ŋaja* is here omitted).

It is also possible for the shared argument to be in O function in both clauses, row (iv) of table 9.2. We may also have the same NP in A function, as in (36) and:

(41) [bayi   yara]$_O$ [ba-ŋgu-n   yibi-ŋgu]$_A$ yajijarra-n   baga-li
      THERE.ABS.I man   THERE-ERG-II woman-ERG threaten-PAST spear-PURP
      The woman threatened to spear the man

Or we have identical Os and different As, as in:

(42) [bayi   yara]$_O$ [ba-ŋgu-n   yibi-ŋgu]$_A$ yajijarra-n
      THERE.ABS.I man   THERE-ERG-II woman-ERG threaten-PAST
      [ba-ŋgu-l   gubi-ŋgu]$_A$ baga-li
      THERE-ERG-I wise.man-ERG spear-PURP
      The woman threatened the man that the wise man would spear him

Another example of the same type is:

(43) ŋaja$_A$ bayi$_O$ giga-n   gubi-ŋgu$_A$ mawa-li
      1sg.NOM THERE.ABS.I tell.to.do-PAST wise.man-ERG feel-PURP
      I told him to be examined (lit. felt all over) by the wise man
        (Aboriginal 'doctor')

The verbs *giga-l* 'tell to do, let do' and *jabi-l* 'stop from doing, refuse to allow' have opposite meanings. Interestingly, they take different complementation strategies, the purposive strategy with *giga-l*, as in (43), and the relative clause strategy with *jabi-l*, as in:

(44) ŋaja$_A$ bayi$_O$ jabi-n   [Ø$_S$ [yanu-ŋu]$_{RC}$]$_O$
      1sg.NOM THERE.ABS.I stop-PAST   go-REL
      I stopped him from going (lit. I stopped him, who was going)

Note the similarity between the types of complement clause required by corresponding verbs in English: a *to* complement clause in *I told him to go*, and a type of *-ing* complement clause in *I stopped him from going*.

There is a further possibility, shown in row (v) of table 9.2, where the referent of the S in the purposive clause is the sum of the referents of A and O in the main clause:

(45) ŋaygu-na$_O$ ba-ŋgu-n$_A$ ŋiba-ñu
      1sg-ACC   THERE-ERG-II ask.to.do-PAST
      ŋali$_S$ yanu-li   wabu-ŋga-rru
      1dual.NOM go-PURP forest-LOC-THROUGH
      She asked me, for us two to go through the forest together

Here the S argument of the purposive clause is, necessarily, stated.

Just one verb in my corpus occurs with two complementation strategies. The intransitive *ŋarjarrmba-y* 'feel unsettled in mind, be unable to make up one's mind, try to plan' occurs with the relative clause strategy in (46), where the sense is 'feel restless', and with the purposive strategy in (47), where the meaning is 'can't decide'.

(46) ŋaja$_S$ ŋarjarrmba-ñu   [[Ø$_O$ bulgu-ŋgu$_A$ galga-ŋu]$_{RC}$]$_S$
      1sg.NOM feel.unsettled-PAST   wife-ERG   leave-REL
      I felt restless (couldn't settle to do anything) at having been left by (my) wife
        (lit. I, who had been left by (my) wife, felt restless)

(47) ŋaja$_S$ ŋarjarrmba-ñu   wuñja-rri yanu-li
      1sg.NOM can't.decide-PAST WHERE-TO go-PURP
      I couldn't decide where to go

9.6 Discussion

Table 9.3 provides an overview of some of the verbs in Dyirbal which expect a complementation strategy, and which strategy each relates to, plus reference to the examples each verb occurs in. (Eleven of the verbs in the table have different forms in some dialects; just one dialect form is listed here.)

We can now usefully survey the verbs which take each strategy.

I. SERIAL VERB STRATEGY. This is confined to adverbals expressing Secondary concepts of finishing and trying. They are the minor members of asymmetrical SVCs. Verbs in the SVC share core arguments—S if the whole SVC is intransitive, A and O if it is transitive.

II. RELATIVE CLAUSE STRATEGY. This is used for all verbs of attention and thinking for which a complementation strategy is applicable (all are transitive), for some verbs of speaking (both transitive and intransitive), and for intransitive verbs referring to human propensities.

This strategy is always optional. For instance, a transitive verb such as *bura-l* 'see' or *ŋari-l* 'answer' may have a simple NP in O slot, or may enter into a relative clause complementation strategy.

This strategy roughly corresponds to both 'fact' complement clauses, shown by *that*, and 'activity' ones, marked by *-ing*, in English. A consequence is that the semantic distinction between these two complement clause types in English is neutralised in Dyirbal. Referring to earlier example, (10), *John heard Mary('s) singing 'Jerusalem'*, describing an activity, and (11), *John heard that Mary was singing 'Jerusalem'*, detailing a fact, would receive identical translations in Dyirbal.

Employing a relative clause construction as a complementation strategy means that there is no formal difference between a relative clause per se and its use as a strategy. We noted that for example (22) one interpretation would be 'I saw lots of spears which the two men had left'—that is, I saw the spears, with the relative clause specifying which spears these were—and 'I saw lots of spears being left by the two men'—stating that I witnessed the activity of spear-leaving. The appropriate reading would have to be inferred from the context of utterance.

III. PURPOSIVE STRATEGY. This roughly corresponds to the 'potential state' type of complement clause in English, marked by *(for . . .) to*. It has varying properties with different semantic types of verbs:

(a) For verbs of speaking which take this strategy, it is optional. For example, transitive *yajijarra-l* 'threaten to do something bad to' can have a simple NP in O slot (as in *ŋaja bayi yajijarra-n* 'I threatened him'), or it may enter into a purposive strategy, as in (41–42).

(b) As pointed out in section 9.5, transitive verbs of liking—*ŋuymi-y* 'like to do', as in (36), and *jiwa-l* 'dislike'—may be used with a simple NP in O slot, but are preferred with a purposive strategy. Intransitive *wugi-l* 'show off, act proud' may be used alone

TABLE 9.3. **Verbs expecting complementation strategies**

	COMPLEMENTATION STRATEGY
ATTENTION AND THINKING	
transitive bura-l 'see, look at, read', in (12), (22) barmi-l 'look back at' walgi-y 'look round (something) at' duygi-y 'look under at' ruga-l 'watch someone/something going' wami-l 'look at clandestinely' jarmi-l 'look for something lost' jaymba-l 'find' dija-l 'meet by chance, encounter, find', in (27) ñula-l 'show' ŋamba-l 'listen, hear about, understand', in (25) ŋurrumi-l 'think of, imagine, have premonition about' yibirra-y 'dream about'	relative clause
SPEAKING	
transitive buwa-y 'tell' jinga-y 'recount, tell about', in (26) baya-l 'sing about' manja-l 'point out by a shout' ŋunja-y 'blame', in (28) jabi-l 'refuse to allow, stop someone doing', in (44) ŋari-l 'answer' banju-l 'won't answer' milga-y 'grumble at' *intransitive* wilimba-y 'call out in fright at'	relative clause
transitive ŋanba-l 'ask', in (13), (40) yumba-l 'invite to come over' yaja-l 'ask to accompany' nunga-l 'ask to help' ŋiba-y 'ask to do something', in (45) giga-l 'tell to do, let do', in (43) nurra-l 'encourage to do, give permission to' yajijarra-l 'threaten to do something bad to', in (41–2) *intransitive* waji-l 'promise to come'	purposive

TABLE 9.3. *continued*

	COMPLEMENTATION STRATEGY
LIKING AND OTHER PROPENSITIES	
transitive ŋuymi-y 'like to do something', in (36) jiwa-l 'dislike' *intransitive* wugi-l 'show off, act proud', in (39) ŋilwa-l 'tempt to fight'	purposive
intransitive gayga-ganda-y 'be jealous about' murri-y 'feel ashamed of having done wrong', in (24) murrŋgi-y 'feel sore (physically or mentally)' ŋurji-y 'be shy and ashamed', in (23)	relative clause
ŋarjarrmba-y 'feel unsettled in mind, be unable to make up one's mind, try to plan', in (46–7)	relative clause & purposive
WANTING	
intransitive walŋgarra-y 'want to do something to satisfy a . . . persistent emotional worry or desire', in (35), (38) garrgi-y 'want to go to a place' jananba-y 'be anxious/getting ready to do something'	purposive
FINISHING AND TRYING	
transitive jayŋu-l 'finish doing', in (14), (20) ŋunbira-l 'try something out', in (16) ŋurbi-l 'try, test, taste', in (17) *intransitive* wuda-y 'stop doing', in (19) gajilmbarri-y 'pretend to do', in (18)	serial verb

(as in *bayi wugi-n* 'he was showing off') or with a purposive strategy, as in (39). The same applies for *ɲilwa-l* 'tempt to fight'.

(c) Verbs of wanting are all intransitive, and all require a purposive clause as a complementation strategy. In the examples I have given, the purposive clause is intransitive, with its S argument being identical with the S of the wanting verb. We can thus have 'I wanted to dance', in (35), or 'I wanted to eat some food', in (38), where the purposive clause has been antipassivised in order to bring its underlying A argument into surface S function. I have not encountered any instance of an S–O linkage, something like 'I$_A$ wanted mother$_A$ to fetch me$_O$' (although this would not be excluded on syntactic grounds, in terms of the S/O pivot condition on clause linking).

It is interesting to enquire why verbs of wanting are intransitive in Dyirbal, whereas in English they are transitive. This relates to the matter of pivots. English works in terms of clause linkage where the common argument is in S or A function in each clause. We can thus have *John$_A$ wanted* [$\emptyset_S$ *to go*]$_O$ where *John* is in A function in the main clause and in S function (from which it is omitted) in the complement clause. In contrast, Dyirbal has a strict S/O pivot, and, to satisfy this, verbs of wanting are intransitive, with the 'wanter' in S function.

Since in Dyirbal there must be an argument common to two clauses which are to be syntactically linked, the language lacks constructions similar to English *I$_A$ wanted* [*John$_S$ to go to town*] or *I$_A$ wanted* [*Mary$_A$ to eat lunch$_O$*], where the core arguments of the *to* complement clause are different from the A argument of *want*. I was told by consultants that one would have to say something like 'I told John to go to town', using the verb *giga-l* 'tell to do, let do'.

In summary, although Dyirbal has no complement clauses per se, it does of course have verbs which correspond to those that take complement clauses in languages which have them. These verbs in Dyirbal carry the expectation of occurring in one of a number of construction types which we can call 'complementation strategies'. These are the purposive construction, the relative clause construction, and the serial verb construction. Which verb expects which strategy relates to the meaning of the verb, and the meanings of the construction types used as complementation strategies.

A complement clause construction is found in very few (if any) Australian languages. For Panjima, from Western Australia, Dench (1991: 196–201) describes a situation rather similar to that in Dyirbal. Relative clause constructions are used as a complementation strategy with verbs such as 'see' and 'hear', purposive constructions with 'want', and both strategies are available for 'tell'. There is general discussion of complementation strategies, cross-linguistically, in Dixon (2010b: 405–13).

Dixon (1995) dealt with complement clauses in English and Fijian, plus a first articulation of complementation strategies in Dyirbal. This was the introduction of the notion of complementation strategy, which has since achieved a degree of general usage (see, for example, Deutscher 2000). The present chapter is a revision and enlargement of Dixon (2006c).

10

Grammatical reanalysis
in Warrgamay

We now turn our attention to the Warrgamay language, adjacent to Girramay, the southernmost dialect of Dyirbal. The point of particular interest is that two kinds of morphological alternation, which were previously non-functional, have now been reanalysed so that they carry a functional load. One concerns case allomorphs (discussed in section 10.1) and the other a realignment of verbal conjugations so that they fully reflect transitivity (dealt with in the remainder of the chapter).

As outlined in section 1.3.2, when I began work in the region Warrgamay was closer to extinction than Dyirbal. However, between 1964 and 1980 I was able to gather significant grammatical and lexical data on the dialect called Warrgamay proper, spoken along the lower Herbert River, working primarily with John Tooth and Lambert Cocky. There was one speaker remaining—Nora Boyd—for the Biyay dialect ('Biyay Warrgamay'), spoken around Halifax, and she provided valuable information in 1973–5 (Mrs Boyd died in 1976). (Each of the three aged consultants had spoken Warrgamay as first language in their youth, but no one in future generations had fully acquired it.) The two dialects are very similar in lexicon and grammar, but a minor difference is illuminating, and critical for an understanding of the reanalysis which has taken place.

10.1 Making case alternations functional

10.1.1 Types of allomorphic variation

The function of any language is to communicate meaning from speaker to hearer in as efficient and straightforward a way as possible; most parts of the language system are oriented to this end. But every language does have a few irregularities which add complexity without in any sense assisting the communicative function. As languages evolve, there is always a tendency to eliminate such irregularities.

A morpheme may have alternative forms, 'allomorphs', each of which is used in particular circumstances; these may be phonologically or lexically determined.

(a) **Phonologically-conditioned allomorphy** is likely to make the articulation of forms easier, assisting the physiological aspect of the process of communication. In Warrgamay, for example, the ergative-instrumental case inflection is -*bu* after a stem ending in *m*, -*du* after *n*, *l*, or *rr*, and -*ju* after *ñ* or *y*. The form of the case suffix in each particular instance can be predicted on phonological grounds—it begins with a stop that is homorganic with the stem-final consonant. (After *l* the suffix is either -*du* or -*ndu*, also homorganic.) Sequences -*mb*- and -*ñj*- are certainly easier to pronounce than, say, -*md*- or -*ñd*-.

(b) **Lexically-conditioned allomorphy** means that a certain list of roots take one allomorph, another list take a second allomorph, and so on. It is normally impossible to predict, by any general principle, which allomorph a given form will select. Speakers just have to learn and remember, for each root, the variant that is used. For instance, one has to know that in English *care*, *dare*, and *fare* form past tense by adding /d/ whereas *bear*, *tear*, and *wear* change the stem vowel from /ɛə/ to /ɔː/ in past tense. Lexically-conditioned allomorphy is an extra complexity that carries no semantic load and does not make for easier articulation. It is, from the point of view of the communicative function of language, a useless alternation.

It is likely that all languages have alternations and irregularities of this type, that 'do no work'; they are usually the residue of past diachronic changes of various sorts. There is always a tendency to eliminate them. (But as fast as old irregularities are being smoothed out—by analogic remodelling and the like—so new ones may be entering the language, as the result of some new types of change.)

An interesting feature of Warrgamay, on which we focus in this chapter, is a marked propensity to get rid of non-functional alternations—reinterpreting them so that they do bear a semantic load. Warrgamay shows a much more pronounced tendency in this direction than any other Australian language I am familiar with.

10.1.2 Reassigning case allomorphs

It is common in Australian languages to have a single suffix which marks the following two cases (which can be distinguished syntactically):

- *ergative*, marking transitive subject function, as in 'John-ERG saw me'; and
- *instrumental*, marking a tool or body part used in an action, as in 'hit stick-INST' or 'kick foot-INST'.

And it is common to have another suffix which marks the two cases:

- *locative*, marking a position of rest ('at', 'in', or 'on'), as in 'swim water-LOC'; and
- *aversive*, indicating that some person or thing (marked by aversive case) is to be avoided, with the action described by the verb being directed towards this

avoidance, as in 'Hide policeman-AVERS', meaning 'Hide to avoid the police-man!'. Aversive case is also used with a verb like 'be frightened of', as in 'I'm frightened snake-AVERS'.

An interesting feature of Australian languages is that ergative-instrumental and locative-aversive typically have the same range of allomorphs, differing only in the final vowel: *-u* for the former and *-a* for the latter. For instance, in Warrgamay, locative-aversive is a homorganic stop plus *-a* after a root ending in a consonant: *-ba* after *m*, and so on.

Whereas allomorphs of ergative-instrumental and locative-aversive after a stem ending in a consonant are generally phonologically conditioned, those after a vowel-final root may be lexically conditioned. In a number of languages from north-east Queensland, a few vowel-final roots take *-lu/-la* while the majority take *-ŋgu/-ŋga*. (See Dixon 1980: 376, 495; 2002a: 158, plus, for example, Gaby 2006: 155 on these allomorphs).

In Warrgamay, as in Dyirbal, 'who' inflects like personal pronouns, whereas 'what' behaves like a nominal. Dyirbal forms for 'what'—*waña* in Girramay, *miña* in other dialects—inflect exactly like nouns and adjectives.

It is likely that, at an earlier stage of Warrgamay, *miña* 'what' took *-lu* for ergative-instrumental and *-la* for locative-aversive, whereas other vowel-final forms took *-ŋgu* and *-ŋga*.

(1) EARLIER STAGE

	ergative instrumental	locative aversive
miña 'what'	-lu	-la
other vowel-final nominals	-ŋgu	-ŋga

In modern Warrgamay the regular inflection *-ŋgu* has been analogised to apply also to *miña*; however, with *miña*, suffix *-ŋgu* only covers the primary function, ergative, *-lu* being retained for instrumental function. Similarly, *-ŋga* now marks locative with *miña*, and *-la* is confined to aversive function. That is, the present-day language shows:

(2) MODERN WARRGAMAY

	ergative	instrumental	locative	aversive
miña 'what'	-ŋgu	-lu	-ŋga	-la
other vowel-final nominals	-ŋgu		-ŋga	

Examples of *miña* with the four case forms are:

(3) miña-ŋgu$_A$ ŋaña$_O$ janba-y
     what-ERG 1sg.O hit.with.rounded.object-UNM
     What hit me? (said by someone sitting under a tree, when something fell from the tree on their head)

(4) miña-lu   ŋinda$_A$ burba-y   ŋaña$_O$
     what-INST 2sg.A   hit.with.long.rigid.object-UNM 1sg.O
     What did you hit me with?

(5) miña-ŋga ŋinba$_S$ ji:gi-bali
     what-LOC 2sg.S   sit-CONTIN.UNM
     What are you sitting on?

(6) miña-la   ŋinba$_S$ bi:ra-mbali
     what-AVERS 2sg.S   fear-INCH.CONTIN.UNM
     What are you frightened of?

This is a very normal type of change. Kuryłowicz (1964: 11) describes how when a given morpheme X has two functions, one of which can be regarded as 'primary' and the other as 'secondary', and another form Y is extended by analogy to cover just part of the functional range of X, then Y will take over the primary function, leaving the original morpheme, X, in just (what was) its secondary function. Ergative and locative are undoubtedly the primary functions, and the productive allomorphs -*ŋgu* and -*ŋga* have been extended to mark these with *miña*, confining -*lu* and -*la* to the more minor instrumental and aversive roles.

The important point about this change is that -*ŋgu* and -*lu*, -*ŋga* and -*la* were originally lexically conditioned, with *miña* taking -*lu* and -*la* and all other vowel-final forms taking -*ŋgu* and -*ŋga*. The alternation did not carry any semantic load. But now it does have a functional role—with *miña*, -*ŋgu* indicates just ergative and -*lu* instrumental, while -*ŋga* shows locative and -*la* aversive. In the earlier stage a single sentence could have been ambiguous between 'what hit me?' and 'what did [someone] hit me with?'; now *miña-ŋgu* would be used in the first case and *miña-lu* in the second. Similarly, 'what did you sit on?' and 'what did you sit down for fear of?' are now disambiguated through the use of *miña-ŋga* and *miña-la* respectively. The -*ŋgu*/-*lu* and -*ŋga*/-*la* lexical alternations have been assigned a functional load to distinguish, with the important item *miña*, between the core functions ergative and instrumental, and locative and aversive.

A possible next step would be for -*lu* and -*la* to be analogised to all vowel-final roots, as instrumental and aversive markers, generalising this semantic distinction and treating all vowel-final forms in the same way as *miña*.

10.2 Transitivity

Each clause is either intransitive or transitive, this being shown by (a) the forms of pronouns and nominals filling core argument slots, and (b) the inflectional ending of the verb.

TABLE 10.1. Marking of core syntactic functions in Warrgamay

	1st and 2nd person non-singular pronouns, e.g. 1dual	1sg, 2sg and all 3rd person pronouns, e.g. 1sg	Nominals (nouns and adjectives) e.g. 'girl'
Transitive subject (A)	ŋali NOMINATIVE FORM	ŋaja	gajiya-ŋgu ERGATIVE CASE
Intransitive subject (S)		ŋayba	gajiya ABSOLUTIVE FORM
Transitive object (O)	ŋali-ña ACCUSATIVE CASE	ŋaña	

We can first illustrate the marking of core syntactic functions, in table 10.1; this is similar to the paradigm for Girramay, set out in table 1.2. Nouns and adjectives inflect on an absolutive-ergative system while non-singular 1st and 2nd person pronouns show a nominative-accusative pattern. Unlike Dyirbal, there is a full set of 3rd person pronouns—in singular, dual, and plural numbers—and these are like 1sg and 2sg in having distinct forms for A, S, and O functions. As can be seen, some of the 1st and 2nd person pronominal forms are the same as, or similar to, those in Dyirbal.

These different case-marking possibilities do make it easy to decide on the syntactic function of any noun phrase in a sentence. We need only enquire whether the noun and pronoun forms which can fill a certain slot belong to the top row, the middle row, or the bottom row of table 10.1.

Most verbal suffixes have one allomorph for use in an intransitive clause, and another for a transitive clause. These are set out in table 10.2. (Note that there are no tenses per se in the Warrgamay system, only a set of aspectual-type terms.)

Note that continuative, negative imperative, and irrealis have longer forms in the transitive column, and begin with *-l-*. In contrast, the intransitive allomorph for purposive commences with *-l-*, and is longer than the transitive form. This is something to which we will return.

Continuative (CONTIN) is an optional derivational suffix which comes between root and inflection, indicating that an activity is extended in time.

The system of verbal inflections has seven members, and each verb must select one of these. We can briefly outline their nature.

- For *positive imperative* (POS.IMP) there are two phonologically conditioned allomorphs in the transitive column: *-ya* is used on a disyllabic root ending in *i* but ø (zero) is used in all other instances.
- Negative commands are marked by the *negative imperative* (NEG.IMP) verbal inflection, and also require a preverbal particle *ŋarru* 'don't'.

TABLE 10.2. Verbal suffixes in the Warrgamay proper dialect

	In intransitive clause	In transitive clause
DERIVATION		
continuative	-bali-	-l-gani-
INFLECTIONS		
positive imperative	-ga	-ya ~ ø
negative imperative	-ja	-l-ja
irrealis	-ma	-l-ma
purposive	-lagu	-gu
perfect	-gi	-ñu
unmarked	-y	-y
subordinate	-ñu	-ñu

- *Irrealis* can have unmarked reference to the future; it is also used in 'apprehensive' function, to indicate something unpleasant that might happen (similar to the aversive case with nouns, discussed in section 10.1). The irrealis verb will then normally be in the second clause of a sentence, with the first clause indicating action that can be taken to avoid this unpleasant possibility, e.g. 'You$_S$ hide, policeman$_A$ you$_O$ see-IRREALIS', meaning '. . . lest the policeman see you'.
- *Purposive* (PURP) can occur on the verb in a main clause, marking necessity or desire, e.g. 'I should go/I want to go'; it also has a very important role in marking the second verb in a purposive construction, e.g. 'I went there *to swim*', 'I took the woman *for her to cook the food*' (this is discussed in section 10.3).
- *Perfect* (PERF) indicates that an action is irretrievably finished.
- The most frequent verbal inflection is *unmarked* (UNM). It can be used in circumstances where none of the other inflections would be appropriate (such as for describing a present action) and also for referring to anything in the past or future, as an alternative to any of the other (non-imperative) inflections. The unmarked inflection has the same form, *-y*, in both columns. Since a sequence *iy* is not permitted at the end of a syllable, this suffix becomes ø after a stem ending in *i*.
- The *subordinate* suffix marks the verb in a relative clause. Note that it has the same form as perfect for a verb in a transitive clause.

An intransitive clause has one obligatory noun phrase, in S (intransitive subject) function; that is, the forms of the nouns, adjectives, and pronouns in this NP must be taken from the middle row in table 10.1. The verb takes inflections from the intransitive column in table 10.2. For example:

(7) ŋayba$_S$ yugarra-ma
     1sg.S   swim-IRREALIS
     I will swim

A transitive clause has an NP in A (transitive subject) function—with forms from the top row of table 10.1—and an NP in O (transitive object) function—with forms from the bottom row of table 10.1. The verb takes inflections from the right-hand column in table 10.2. For example:

(8) ñulaŋga$_A$ ŋaña$_O$ ŋunda-lma
     3sg.A   1sg.O   look.at-IRREALIS
     He will look at me

Note that the order of words in a clause is quite free in Warrgamay, as it is in Dyirbal. Examples are quoted as they were given by consultants.

10.2.1 Classes of verbs

Warrgamay verb roots fall into two classes.

I. **Intransitive roots.** These can only occur in intransitive clauses, with an S NP, and must take inflections from the intransitive column in table 10.2. This class includes *yugarra-* 'swim'—as in (7)—*gaga-* 'go', *wirga-* 'bathe', *bana-* 'return', and *wa:ji-* 'laugh', among many other members.

II. **Ambitransitive roots.** Verbs of this class occur predominantly in transitive constructions, with an A and an O NP, taking an inflection from the transitive column in table 10.2, as *ŋunda-* 'see, look at' does in (8). Other verbs in this set include *gunba-* 'cut', *ganda-* 'burn', *ñu:nja-* 'kiss', *muja-* 'eat', and *gi:ba-* 'scratch', among many others.

But although the verbs of set II have a basically 'two core argument' character, and the majority of their instances are in transitive clauses, it appears that all (or almost all) of them *can* also be used in an intransitive construction, with an S NP, and then take an inflection from the intransitive column in table 10.2. Thus a root like *ŋunda-* 'see, look at' is most often found in a transitive clause, such as (8) and (9):

(9) ŋaja$_A$ ma:l$_O$ ŋunda-lgani
     1sg.A man   look.at-CONTIN.UNM
     I'm looking at the man

But *ŋunda-* can also occur in an intransitive construction, with intransitive verbal inflection, and with the S argument corresponding to the A argument in its transitive use:

(10)   ŋayba$_S$ ŋunda-bali
       1sg.S   look.at-CONTIN.UNM
       I'm having a look

An intransitive construction featuring a basically transitive verb can be extended by an optional peripheral argument, corresponding to the O argument of the verb's transitive use as in:

(11)   ŋayba$_S$ ŋunda-bali   (ma:l-ndu)
       1sg.S   look.at-CONTIN.UNM man-INSTR
       I'm having a look (at the man)

Note that (9) and (11) were given as a 'minimal pair' by the consultant, with the English translations quoted here—'I'm looking at the man' for (9) and 'I'm having a look at the man' for (11). These provide a clue to the rather subtle distinction between a set II verb used in a transitive construction, as in (9), and in an intransitive one, as in (11).

When a set II verb is used in an intransitive construction, and the transitive O argument is included as a peripheral constituent, this is marked by either instrumental or dative case. Pronouns have no instrumental form, so only dative may be used with them. As far as nominals are concerned, either instrumental or dative may be employed if the verb bears purposive inflection (I do not know what conditions this choice), but just instrumental otherwise.

As mentioned before, set II verbs are most often used in transitive constructions. However, more than half of the set II verbs did also appear in intransitive clauses in my initial corpus. Checking a sample of the remainder, all were accepted in clauses of both transitivity types. This suggests that set II verbs are all ambitransitive, of type S = A.

There appear to be several reasons for using a set II verb in an intransitive construction. The first is a matter of focus: a transitive clause describes what A is doing to O, while an intransitive one highlights the fact that the referent of the S argument is undertaking some activity. This is illustrated in (9–11) and in (12–13). Once more, the English translations are as provided by consultants.

(12)   ŋaja$_A$ gungul$_O$ muja-lgani
       1sg.A vegetables eat-CONTIN.UNM
       I'm eating vegetables

(13)   ŋayba$_S$ (gungul-ndu)   muja-bani
       1sg.S vegetables-INST eat-CONTIN.UNM
       I'm having a feast (of vegetables)

Warrgamay operates with an exclusively S/O pivot. Within a relative clause construction, the common argument must be in S or O function in both main and subordinate clauses. And two clauses may only be linked under the sentence node if they share an argument which is in S or O function in each (it is then generally omitted from the second clause).

The second reason for a set II verb to be used in an intransitive clause is to satisfy this S/O pivot condition. If a common argument linking two clauses is in underlying A function in one (or both) clauses, then an intransitive construction is employed, placing the common argument into S function, which will satisfy the pivot condition. This is similar to the circumstances in which Dyirbal would use an antipassive derivation (as described in chapter 7). There is further discussion of all this in section 10.3.

The third circumstance for using a set II verb in an intransitive construction is when the speaker does not want to specify what the underlying O argument is. The O argument in a transitive and the S argument in a transitive clause are obligatory; they must be stated and cannot be omitted. If I wanted to say that I was eating, but didn't wish to specify exactly what I was eating, it would not be felicitous to use the transitive construction (12), and omit the O NP. I would instead use an intransitive construction:

(13′) ŋayba$_S$ muja-bani
       1sg.S   eat-CONTIN.UNM
       I'm eating

The fourth reason for using a set II verb in an intransitive construction is to code a reflexive relation. We can first exemplify *ganda-* 'burn' and *giːba-* 'scratch' used in transitive clauses.

(14) ŋaja$_A$ wagun$_O$ ganda-ñu
      1sg.A wood   burn-PERF
      I've burnt the wood

(15) maːl-ndu$_A$ gajan$_O$ giːba-lgani
      man-ERG grass   scratch-CONTIN.UNM
      The man is scratching up grass

If the underlying A and O arguments have identical reference (a reflexive relation), the verb is used in an intransitive construction, with underlying A = O as the S argument. A sentence such as *ŋaja ganda-gi* could be ambiguous between 'I've burnt (something unspecified)' and 'I've burnt myself'. To avoid this, the relevant body-part term is generally included in the S NP of the reflexive construction, as in,

(16) [ŋayba mala]$_S$ ganda-gi
      1sg.S hand burn-PERF
      I've burnt my hand

(17) [ma:l gambara]$_S$ gi:ba-bali
      man body   scratch-CONTIN.UNM
      The man is scratching his body

In each of (16) and (17) the S NP indicates inalienable possession, shown by apposition between 'whole' noun or pronoun and 'part' noun (see the end of section 1.5).

One interesting question concerns why, since set II roots—which are basically transitive—can also occur in intransitive constructions, set I roots cannot also be used in transitive constructions (e.g. 'laugh at', 'go with'). A diachronic explanation for this is proposed in section 10.4.

10.3 The purposive construction

A purposive construction involves two clauses. The verb of the first clause (C_1) may be in any inflection except purposive or subordinate, and the verb of the second clause (C_2) takes purposive. The meaning of the whole is 'C_1 in order that C_2'.
    In terms of the S/O pivot condition, the two clauses in a purposive construction must share an argument which is in S or O function in each.
    The possibilities can be illustrated one at a time. In (18) the common argument, *ŋayba* 'I', is in S function in both clauses, and in (19) the common argument, *muyma* 'boy' is in S function in the first clause and in O in the second.

(18) ŋayba$_S$ gaga-y Ø$_S$ wirga-lagu
      1sg.S go-UNM   bathe-PURP
      I went to bathe

(19) muyma$_S$ bana-y   Ø$_O$ gajiya-ŋgu$_A$ ñu:ñja-gu
      boy   return-UNM girl-ERG   kiss-PURP
      The boy returned to be kissed by the girl

The common argument, *balbay* 'bottle', is in O and S functions respectively in the two clauses of the purposive construction (20); and in (21) the common argument, *ji:jin* 'wallaby' is in O function in each clause.

(20) ŋaja$_A$ balbay$_O$ burmbi   Ø$_S$ bandali-lagu
      1sg.A bottle   throw.UNM   burst-PURP
      I threw down a bottle, so that it burst

(21) ŋinda$_A$ jiːjin$_O$ baba   Ø$_O$ ŋaja$_A$ gunba-gu
     2sg.A   wallaby spear.POS.IMP   1sg.A cut-PURP
     You spear a wallaby so that I can cut it up!

Suppose now that we wish to join together into a purposive construction two clauses which do share an NP, but it is in A function in one of the clauses. This clause must be recast in intransitive form, so that the underlying A NP takes on S function. Consider (22) and (23):

(22) muyma$_S$ bana-y
     boy   return-UNM
     The boy returned

(23) gajiya$_O$ muyma-ŋgu$_A$ ñuːnja-gu
     girl   boy-ERG   kiss-PURP
     The boy [wants] to kiss the girl

Sentence (23) has the common argument, *muyma* 'boy', in A function. This must be recast as an intransitive clause, so that *muyma* goes into S, a pivot function:

(24) muyma$_S$ ñuːnja-lagu gajiya-gu
     boy   kiss-PURP girl-dat
     The boy [wants] to kiss the girl

Sentences (22) and (24) can now be linked in a purposive construction, with the occurrence of the common argument omitted from the second clause:

(25) muyma$_S$ bana-y Ø$_S$ ñuːnja-lagu gajiya-gu
     The boy returned to kiss the girl

In more than half the instances I gathered of a set II verb being used in an intransitive clause, it has purposive inflection. This shows that the major function of the 'intransitive alternative' for set II verbs is to satisfy the S/O pivot condition on clause linking within a purposive construction.

10.3.1 Comparison with Dyirbal

There are a number of important points of difference between Warrgamay and Dyirbal.

(a) **Transitivity**. Every Dyirbal verb (save for two or three) is either strictly intransitive or strictly transitive. In Warrgamay, every verb which may be used in a transitive clause can also be used in an intransitive one; this is set II, of ambitransitives.

(b) **Conjugations.** Dyirbal has two conjugations which do *not* coincide with transitivity classes. (This is typical of Australian languages.) Most members of the -l conjugation are transitive but there is a significant minority of intransitives; for example, *bungi-l* 'lie down' and *wandi-l* 'motion up'. And most members of the -y conjugation are intransitive but there is a significant minority of transitives; for example, *jaŋga-y* 'eat' and *buwa-y* 'tell'. The two columns of table 10.2, for Warrgamay, could be said to represent conjugations, but one is used only in intransitive and the other exclusively in transitive clauses.

(c) **Conjugation markers.** A full account of verbal suffixes in Dyirbal, across all dialects, is in section 11.4. In the present context it is useful to display the Girramay forms for six of these, in table 10.3.

Many of the allomorphs in the right-hand column of the table commence with *-l-*, so this has been dubbed the '-l conjugation', and its roots written with a final *-l*; for example *ñunja-l* 'kiss'. Some of the corresponding allomorphs in the middle column begin with *-y*, a few with *-n*, and some have nothing corresponding to the initial *-l-* in the right-hand column. This is called the '-y conjugation' and its members written with a final *-y*; for example *banaga-y* 'return'. It is convenient to refer to the *-l* and *-y* as 'conjugation markers'; for instance, the applicative derivation involves the appropriate conjugation marker plus *-ma*, and the agentive nominalisation is the conjugation marker plus *-muɲa*.

We can compare this partial paradigm in Girramay with the Warrgamay allomorphs as set out in table 10.2. There are three instances of an *-l* conjugation marker in the transitive column, with zero corresponding to this in the intransitive column.

TABLE 10.3. Sample of verbal suffixes in the Girramay dialect of Dyirbal

	Onto -y stem	Onto -l stem
applicative derivation	-y-ma-l	-l-ma-l
reciprocal derivation	-y-barri-y	-l-(n)barri-y
agentive nominalisation	-y-muɲa	-l-muɲa
negative imperative inflection	-mu	-l-mu
future tense inflection	-n-jay	-l-jay
purposive inflection	-y-gu	-l-i

(d) **Antipassive.** Dyirbal has an antipassive derivation—stated at (10) in chapter 7—which puts what is basically a transitive clause into intransitive form, with the underlying A argument going into surface S function, in order to satisfy the S/O pivot condition.

Warrgamay does not have an antipassive. Indeed, it does not need one. We saw just above that if, in one clause of an intended purposive construction, the common argument is in underlying A function—as in (23) 'The boy [wants] to kiss the girl'—then this must be re-phrased as an intransitive, with 'the boy' now in S function. This is possible because *ñu:nja-* 'kiss' is an ambitransitive verb of set II, which can be used in both transitive and intransitive clauses, with an inflection from the appropriate column in table 10.2.

We can consider clauses in Dyirbal corresponding to (22) and (23) in Warrgamay. Cognate verbs are involved: intransitive *banaga-y* 'return' and transitive *ñunja-l* 'kiss'.

(26) [bayi   rugun]$_S$ banaga-ñu
      THERE.ABS.I boy   return-PAST
      The boy returned

(27) [bala-n   gajin]$_O$ [ba-ŋgu-l   rugun-du]$_A$ ñunja-li
      THERE.ABS-II girl   THERE-ERG-I boy-ERG   kiss-PURP
      The boy [wants] to kiss the girl

Dyirbal operates with an S/O pivot for clause linkage, just like Warrgamay. Clauses (26) and (27) can only be combined in a purposive construction if (27) is antipassivised, putting 'the boy' into S function:

(28) [bayi   rugun]$_S$ ñunjal-ŋay-gu [ba-gu-n   gajin-gu]
      THERE.ABS.I boy   kiss-APASS-PURP THERE-DAT-II girl-DAT
      The boy [wants] to kiss the girl

We can then link (26) and (28):

(29) [bayi rugun]$_S$ banaga-ñu Ø$_S$ ñunjal-ŋay-gu [ba-gu-n gajin-gu]
      The boy returned to kiss the girl

In order to meet the S/O pivot constraint, Warrgamay uses an ambitransitive verb in an intransitive construction. In corresponding circumstances, Dyirbal applies the intransitivising antipassive derivation to a strictly transitive verb. And note the similarity of form between the intransitive purposive inflection in Warrgamay *-lagu*, as in (24–25), and the ending on the corresponding Dyirbal verb in (28–29), *-lŋaygu*.

In fact *-lŋaygu* is the basic ending in Dyirbal, but in Girramay (the dialect adjacent to Warrgamay) it has reduced to *-laygu*. The forms across dialects of Dyirbal are:

(30) antipassive derivational suffix plus purposive inflection on *ñunja-l* 'kiss':
Mamu dialect   ñunja-l-ŋa-y-gu
Jirrbal dialect   ñunja-l-(ŋ)a-y-gu
Girramay dialect   ñunja-l-a-y-gu

The antipassive derivational suffix on verbs of the *-l* conjugation was undoubtedly *-ŋa-y* originally. The *-ŋ-* is optionally omitted in Jirrbal and generally omitted in Girramay.

The form in Girramay is similar to that in Warrgamay, but they differ in that the Warrgamay form consists of two morphemes:

(31) ñu:nja-lagu
kiss-PURP

In contrast, the Girramay form is analysed into five morphemes:

(32) ñunja-l-a-y-gu
kiss-CONJUGATION.MARKER-APASS-CONJUGATION.MARKER-PURP

In Girramay the root is followed by conjugation marker *-l-*, then antipassive *-a-*, followed by conjugation marker *-y-* and finally purposive *-gu*. Antipassive is a productive suffix, and the antipassive stem can take any of the verbal inflections. In Warrgamay *-lagu* is an unanalysable form; there is no occurrence of *-la-* outside this suffix.

It was noted earlier that, in table 10.2, three of the transitive allomorphs for Warrgamay commence with *-l-*, and that purposive is the only row in table 10.2 where the intransitive allomorph is longer than the transitive one. In addition, the intransitive purposive form commences with *-l-*, which typically comes at the beginning of transitive allomorphs.

All this suggests that we should look further to see if there is any historical relation involved.

10.4 Reconstruction of historical changes in Warrgamay

We can suggest that at an earlier stage what can be called pre-Warrgamay had the following characteristics.

(i) As in other Australian languages every (or almost every) verb was either strictly transitive or strictly intransitive.

(ii) Also like other languages, pre-Warrgamay had two verbal conjugations which correlated with, but did not fully coincide with, transitivity classes.

We can suppose that the verbal paradigm at this stage included:

(33)	PREDOMINANTLY INTRANSITIVE CONJUGATION	PREDOMINANTLY TRANSITIVE CONJUGATION
perfect	-gi	-ñu
irrealis	-mu	-l-mu
purposive	-gu	-gu

(iii) There was an S/O pivot for clause linking, just as in Dyirbal and modern Warrgamay. It order to satisfy this, pre-Warrgamay would have needed an antipassive derivation, *-l-a-*, which could be followed by the full range of intransitive allomorphs.

The increments to a verbal root would then include:

STAGE 1	INTRANSITIVE ROOT	DERIVED ANTIPASSIVE STEM	TRANSITIVE ROOT
perfect	-gi	-l-a-gi	-ñu
irrealis	-mu	-l-a-mu	-l-mu
purposive	-gu	-l-a-gu	-gu

Typical purposive constructions at this stage would have been:

(18′) ŋayba$_S$ gaga-y Ø$_S$ wirga-gu
1sg.S go-UNM bathe-PURP
I went to bathe

(25′) muyma$_S$ bana-y Ø$_S$ ñu:nja-la-gu gajiya-gu
boy return-UNM kiss-APASS-PURP girl-DAT
The boy returned to kiss the girl

Sentences (18′) and (25′) are parallel constructions, and in each case the purposive clause is intransitive at the surface level. We can suggest that the ending on the verb in (25′) was generalised to function also as the ending on the verb in (18′), so that *-lagu* replaced *-gu* as the purposive inflection for intransitive verbs. This gives:

STAGE II	INTRANSITIVE ROOT	DERIVED ANTIPASSIVE STEM	TRANSITIVE ROOT
perfect	-gi	-l-a-gi	-ñu
irrealis	-mu	-l-a-mu	-l-mu
purposive	-lagu ⟵——	-l-a-gu	-gu

A typical variety of purposive construction is one in which the underlying A NP of the purposive clause is coreferential with the S or O NP of the initial clause; thus -*lagu* would probably have been a common ending on a purposive verb. This would have been part of the explanation for why (under our hypothesis) -*lagu* was generalised to replace -*gu* in the left-hand column.

We can also note that -*gu* could scarcely have been generalised from the left-hand column to replace -*lagu* in the middle column without a form like *ñu:nja-gu* becoming irretrievably ambiguous between the interpretation as a simple verb in a transitive sentence, e.g. (19), and that as the verb in a derived antipassive construction, like (25′).

As this stage -*lagu* would be the purposive inflection on all verbs in intransitive clauses, whether underlyingly intransitive or derived intransitive (from an underlying transitive root). But note that in an antipassive clause -*lagu* is segmentable (into transitive conjugation marker -*l*-, plus antipassive derivational suffix -*a*-, plus purposive -*gu*), whereas with intransitive roots -*lagu* is functioning as a simple form, the (unanalysable) intransitive allomorph of purposive.

The next obvious generalisation (or, really, simplification) is to combine the first and second columns in the paradigm so that there is just one set of allomorphs for all verbs in intransitive clauses. We have suggested that antipassive -*lagu* was extended to the intransitive column, partly because of its greater frequency. But for the other verbal inflections (perfect, irrealis, and the rest) the intransitive allomorphs would be much more frequent than the antipassive variety; and, unlike purposive, all of the other inflections (leaving aside the unmarked ending -*y*, and subordinate -*ñu*) do have different forms in the left-hand and right-hand columns. We might thus expect that, for inflections other than purposive, the intransitive allomorph might be generalised to the second column, giving:

STAGE III	SET I ROOT IN INTRANSITIVE CLAUSE	SET II ROOT IN	
		INTRANSITIVE CLAUSE	TRANSITIVE CLAUSE
perfect	-gi		-ñu
irrealis	-mu		-l-mu
purposive	-lagu		-gu

This would only work if there were, at approximately the same time, a tidying up of the conjugation-transitivity correlation. We suggested that, at Stage I, Warrgamay (like very many other Australian languages) had a statistical correlation—and not a coincidence—between conjugation and transitivity classes. There would have been a few intransitive verbs in the -l conjugation and some transitive roots in the -ø class. It is interesting to see whether any verbs of these types in modern Dyirbal do have cognates in Warrgamay and, if so, what inflections they take.

We find that *bungi-l* 'lie down' is an intransitive member of the predominantly transitive -l conjugation in Dyirbal, and that the intransitive root *bungi-* 'lie down' occurs in Warrgamay. In Warrgamay proper it just takes intransitive inflection, from the left-hand column in table 10.2, like any other intransitive root. But in the Biyay dialect *bungi-*, although still intransitive, takes inflections from the right-hand column of table 10.2. For example:

(34)   Warrgamay proper Biyay
    Irrealis   bungi-ma   bungi-lma
    Purposive bungi-lagu   bungi-gu

We can infer that *bungi-* (with a few other exceptional verb roots) has been transferred from one class to the other in Warrgamay proper, to ensure that transitivity does coincide with conjugation. However, the process has not been completed in the Biyay dialect. Biyay does appear, in a number of ways, to be more conservative than Warrgamay proper (see the discussion in Dixon 1981a: 48–52).

With the replacement, from the middle column of the Stage II paradigm, of perfect *-lagi* by *-gi*, irrealis *-lama* by *-ma*, and so on, the justification for analysing *-lagu* into three morphemes would have disappeared. Since *-la-* only occurs in *-lagu*, it cannot be segmented out as a distinct morpheme. Now *-lagu* would be felt to be indivisible, simply the allomorph of purposive used in an intransitive clause, whether affixed to a set I or set II root.

This diachronic hypothesis explains the modern intransitive allomorph *-lagu* as being derived from the transitive conjugation marker *-l-*, plus *-a-* as a residue of an original antipassive derivational affix, plus the original intransitive allomorph of purposive, *-gu*.

Note that all other suffixes in Warrgamay—as in surrounding languages—have canonical forms commencing with a consonant, and it is likely that the antipassive suffix was originally *-Ca-*, where C represents a consonant, with the change *-l-Ca- > -l-a-* in Warrgamay paralleling *-l-ŋa > -l-a-* in Girramay. The antipassive suffix in Warrgamay *could* have been *-ŋa-*, identical to that in Dyirbal, but there is no way of verifying this. Dyirbal and Warrgamay do show striking similarities but there are also many differences, and—as already mentioned—there is simply not enough evidence to support a close genetic relationship.

It may seem a little surprising that the transitive allomorph of purposive is *-gu*, rather than *-l-gu*, which would parallel *-l-ma* and *-l-ja* in the transitive column of table 10.2. It is relevant to note that the verbal paradigm for Nyawaygi (see Dixon 1983: 470–90), Warrgamay's southern neighbour, shows some important similarities with the Warrgamay system. A number of inflectional allomorphs for the transitive -l conjugation in Nyawaygi do begin with *-l-* (e.g. irrealis *-l-ma*, negative imperative *-l-jam*) but in Nyawaygi—as in modern Warrgamay—the purposive inflection is just *-gu* in the transitive -l conjugation. This supports the suggestion that at Stage I purposive was *-gu* for *both* pre-Warrgamay conjugations.

In summary, we have suggested that Warrgamay had an antipassive derivational process that formed an intransitive stem from a transitive root, and that this was largely motivated by the S/O pivot condition on clause linking ('ergative syntax'). Through morphological generalisation—allied to an 'elimination of exceptions' that led to an exact coincidence of conjugation and transitivity classes—this has developed into the possibility of using basically transitive verbs in either transitive or intransitive clauses, with the appropriate inflectional allomorphs in each case.

Set II verbs occur most of the time in transitive constructions; it appears that all or almost all of them can also function intransitively. A transitive verb will generally only appear in an intransitive construction in marked syntactic circumstances—to signify a reflexive relation, or to satisfy the pivot constraint on purposive constructions, relative clause constructions, and so on. There is no syntactic reason for basically intransitive verbs to function transitively, and there has been no change to the original restriction that set I can occur only in intransitive constructions.

If, as we hypothesise, conjugations did not in Stage I coincide with transitivity classes, then they would have constituted an unnecessary complexity that served no communicative function. A speaker would have had to learn, for each verb, not just the transitivity—which does have syntactic-semantic relevance—but also the conjugation class of each verb—which does not have. Through the series of changes we have suggested, Warrgamay has taken the lexically-conditioned conjugational alternation and, by making transitivity exactly coincide with conjugation, given it an important syntactico-semantic role. The fact that this tidying-up has not fully taken place in the Biyay dialect confirms the supposition that pre-Warrgamay would have been like other modern Australian languages (e.g. Dyirbal) and had only a *degree* of correlation between conjugation and transitivity classes. Warrgamay proper has assigned a communicative role to this previously asemantic distinction.

This has, in turn, paved the way for a straightforward simplification in Warrgamay grammar, the loss of the antipassive derivation. By having inflectional allomorphs show transitivity (without any exceptions), modern Warrgamay is able to carry exactly the same syntactic and semantic load as pre-Warrgamay (of Stage I) and as modern Dyirbal, with one less morpheme. There is no need for an antipassive derivation and a suffix to mark it.

10.5 Possible future developments

Warrgamay would have ceased to be actively spoken sometime during the first half of the twentieth century. Between 1964 and 1980 I was able to work with the last rememberers. They have now all returned to the land of spirits.

It is fascinating to speculate on what might have happened if there had been no deadly invasion of Europeans. Left to itself, how might Warrgamay have developed?

We start with the transcendent notion of 'ergative syntax'—an S/O pivot condition which underlies clause linking.

(a) We suppose that originally each verb had fixed transitivity. As in table 10.1, nominals were in absolute form for S and O functions, and took ergative case to mark

A function. There was an antipassive process which applied to a transitive clause and derived an intransitive construction, with the underlying A argument going into surface S function (to meet the pivot constraint).

(b) Emanating out of the antipassive derivation, erstwhile transitive verb roots (our set II) could be used in plain form in either transitive or intransitive clauses, with A corresponding to S (and the underlying O being marked as instrumental, or dative in the intransitive construction). Set II verbs were still used more frequently in transitive than in intransitive clauses. This was the state of the language when it passed out of use.

(c) Suppose, as the next development, that set II verbs came to be used more often in the original intransitive than in the original transitive frame. Then, in the fullness of time, they were used only in the original intransitive frame (so that the original transitive frame fell out of use).

When a verb had one argument this would be shown as in the 'S row' from table 10.1. When there were two arguments, the underlying A would also be marked from the S row, with the underlying O taking either instrumental case—as in (11) and (13)—or dative case within a purposive clause—as in (24).

The 'S row' of table 10.1 (originally 'absolutive case' for nominals) would now be used for both S function in a one-argument clause, and for A function in a two-argument clause. It would be appropriate to now call it 'nominative case'. The case used to mark O function in a two-argument clause should be called 'accusative' (this would be the original instrumental). The earlier absolutive-ergative inflection of nominals would have been replaced by a nominative-accusative system.

Following through this line of development, the original S/O pivot would have now become an S/A pivot. This series of changes were motivated by the demands of a language with ergative syntax (reflecting the ergative morphology of nominals), and they naturally lead to the replacement of this with accusative morphology and accusative syntax.

However, this is simply speculation.

A number of other Australian languages seem to have followed developments rather similar to those we have outlined for Warrgamay; and in some instances—such as Lardil on Mornington Island, and Yinyjibarnrdi-Ngarluma in Western Australia—the changes have proceeded to their logical conclusion, with the evolution of an entirely nominative-accusative grammatical system. Fairly detailed discussions with examples and further references are in Dixon (1980: 449–57; 2002a: 530–46).

Fuller information on Warrgamay grammar is in Dixon (1981a). The present chapter is a thorough revision of a 1981 paper 'Grammatical reanalysis: an example of linguistic change from Warrgamay (North Queensland)'.

Part IV

Variation, Contact, and Change

There is always variation within language—sometimes between levels in a socio-economic hierarchy, often between generations, and typically between geographical locations. I have been able to investigate the last for the three languages dealt with in this volume.

A Grammar of Yidiɲ (Dixon 1977a) provided as full an account as I was able to gather of grammatical differences between the coastal (c) and tablelands (t) dialects. *Words of our Country* (Dixon 1991a) included a comparative vocabulary, adding entries for the Gunggay and Waɲurr dialects, for which only limited lexical data was available. In the case of Warrgamay, all available grammatical and lexical information across dialects is in Dixon (1981a).

Dyirbal was a larger language than the other two, with more dialects across a greater geographical area. There were also available more speakers and rememberers, with sound knowledge, than for Yidiɲ and Warrgamay. The next three chapters examine variation across the dialects of Dyirbal, on the basis of data which could be gathered by fieldwork from 1963 through 2002 (and some earlier manuscript materials).

Grammatical items—suffixes, and grammatical words such as pronouns, noun, and verb markers, and particles—are dealt with in chapter 11, with an account of their varying forms and functions across dialects. Chapter 12 takes a sample of 360 lexemes, examining whether there is just one form across all attested dialects, or two forms, or three. It also highlights meaning shifts. And attention is paid to cognates in adjoining languages.

The major phonological difference between dialects of Dyirbal is that regular changes have led to the evolution of contrastive vowel length in the most northerly dialect, Ngajan. Related to this, the contrast between two rhotic phonemes has been neutralised. Wari, next dialect to the south, has developed some long vowels (not so many as Ngajan) and has retained the rhotic distinction. Chapter 13 provides a detailed examination of these mechanisms of change, and puts forward explanation for them.

Our scope is extended in chapter 14. The Cairns rainforest region in north-east Queensland constitutes a distinct geographical zone and also a small linguistic area. This chapter focuses on contact involving Warrgamay, Dyirbal, Yidiñ, and also Ja:bugay, Yidiñ's northerly neighbour. There is discussion of how the languages have influenced each other in terms of demonstratives and related items, tense system, pronoun system, initial rhotic, and contrastive vowel length. In each instance, the likely direction of diffusion is examined.

11

Dyirbal grammar: Variation across dialects

This chapter expands on the information in my 1972 grammar *The Dyirbal Language of North Queensland*. It will be frequently referred to, by the publisher's abbreviation '*DDL*' followed by page number(s). Note that I am not, as a rule, repeating information given in *DDL*, but rather adding to it. There are a few new affixes and particles, plus a new clitic, which have come to light since *DDL*; these are described and exemplified.

DDL provided grammatical description of the Girramay (G), Jabun-barra Jirrbal (J), and Dulgu-barra Mamu (M) dialects; this has now been expanded. And to it has been added data on four further dialects, to the extent that this could be obtained. Just about every item is covered for Ngajan (N), most of them for Wari-barra Mamu (W), some for Gambil-barra Jirrbal (A), and a few for Jirru (Y). The 'Mourilyan' (P) and Walmal (L) dialects are only known from lists of lexemes (see section 1.3.1). There was one speaker, Joe Kinjun, who belonged to the group which spoke Gulngay (U); however, he was unreliable and mixed together dialects so freely that it was generally impossible to discern what was in fact Gulngay.

Long vowels have evolved in N and W, full details being set out in chapter 12. Within the context of the present chapter, it is relevant to note the occurrence of long vowels at the end of nominal roots and some grammatical words:

(1) Before a word boundary
    in both N and W: *Vl* > *V:*, *Vr* > *V:*
    just in N: *ay* > *a:*, *uy* > *i:*

Note that there is a minority of forms which do retain a final *l* or *r* or *y* in N, and a final *l* or *r* in W. These may have been loans after the operation of the long-vowel-creating changes, or there may be some other explanation for them; they are discussed in section 13.5.

The other significant phonological difference between dialects is that the two rhotics, apico-alveolar *rr* and apico-postalveolar *r*, have in N been collapsed into a single rhotic phoneme, written as *R*.

We will first deal with nominal derivation and inflection, then noun and verb markers, demonstratives, and the suffixes they take, followed by pronouns and interrogative/indefinites, verbal derivation and inflection, and finally particles, clitics, universal affixes, and interjections.

11.1 Nominals

The suffixes discussed here apply to both nouns and adjectives.

11.1.1 Nominal derivation

Full meanings, functions, and exemplification are in *DDL*: 221–33. The attested forms across dialects are:

(a)	NWMY	-ba	'with'
	AJG	-bila	
(b)	M	-barray	'with a lot of'
(c)	N	-ŋaŋga:	'without'
	WMAJY	-ŋaŋgay	
	G	-biday	
(d)	NW	-damba	'covered with, full of' (negative connotations)
	MAJG	-ginay	
(e)	NWMAJG	-ŋunu	'out of, from' (homonymous with ablative case)
(f)	N	-baRa	'belonging to, associated with'
	WMAJG	-barra	
(g)	MJG	-ŋarru	'like a'
(h)	MAJG	-bajun	'really, very'
(i)	NW	-wajan	comparative
	MAJG	-bara	
(j)	NWMAJG	-gabun	'another'
(k)	N	-jaRan	'a pair, a couple'
	WMAJG	-jarran	
(l)	N	-ñami:	'many, all of'
	N	-mumba:	
	MJG	-mumbay	

(m) N   -gaRa   'one of a pair'
     WMAJG   -garra

(n) NWMAJG   -maŋgan   'one of a group of more than two'

(o) MJG   -gayul   'the same'

(p) NWM   -ju   intensifier
     A   -julu
     JG   -jilu

The original form for (p) would have been *-jilu*, as in JG. There would then have been vowel assimilation giving *-julu*, as in A, and finally truncation to *-ju*, in NWM.

In two instances, when N and W have a form different from those in other dialects, there is a similar form in N's neighbour to the north, Yidiñ (see Dixon 1977a: 143–4, 244–5):

(d) derivational suffix *-damba* 'with a lot of' (unpleasant overtones)
(i) post-inflectional suffix *-wajan*, comparative meaning

It is likely that both of these were borrowed from Yidiñ into N and then into W.

G differs from other dialects in having *-biday* for (c) 'without'. There is a similar form in G's neighbour to the south, Warrgamay, derivational suffix *-biray* in one dialect and *-biyay* 'without' in another.

Three more derivational affixes have come to light since *DDL*:

(q) M -janga   'look like a'
     J -bulubulu
     G -jundujundu

This suffix is typically used in the complement NP of a verbless clause. An example from J is:

(2) [giña-m wuju]   [guway-bulubulu]
     THIS-IV vegetable black.walnut-LOOKS.LIKE
     This vegetable looks like a black walnut (*Endiandra palmerstonii*)

An illustration of (q) in three dialects is:

(3) M [giña-n ñalŋga] [yabu-janga]
     J [giña-n ñalŋga] [yabu-bulubulu]
     G [ɲiña-n ñalŋga] [yabu-jundujundu]
        THIS-II child   mother-LOOKS.LIKE
        This girl looks like her mother

It is instructive to compare this suffix with (g) -*ŋarru* 'like a'. It appears that -*janga/-bulubulu/-jundujundu* has a rather specific meaning 'look like a' whereas -*ŋarru* has wider scope. It can indicate 'be like a', or 'do like a'—as in 'the man dives like a platypus' (*DDL*: 225)—or 'look like a'.

(r)   J -garamu 'very big'

For example:

(4)   ŋayguna$_O$ bura-n   yara-garamu-gu$_A$
       1sg.ACC   see-PAST man-VERY.BIG-ERG
       The very big man saw me

This sentence demonstrates -*garamu*'s status as a suffix. If it were an adjective, then (4) would have ended *[*yara-ŋgu garamu-gu*], with ergative inflection on each item. (Note that in Warrgamay there is an adjective *garamu* 'huge'.)

   This suffix is typically used with body parts; for example *maŋa-garamu* 'very big ears', *guwu-garamu* 'very big nose', *bamba-garamu* 'very big belly'.

Alongside adjective *midi* 'small', there is, in NMAJG, *midi-jagan* which was said to be 'smaller than *midi*'. I know of no occurrence of -*jagan* outside this word.

Another affix which came to light after *DDL* is what appears to be the only prefix in the language. In NMJG *yuwu*- 'do X times' is attested only with number lexemes 'two', 'three', and 'many'. For example, *yuwu-garbu* 'do three (or a few) times', *yuwu-muŋa* 'do many times'. Interestingly, number word *bulayi* 'two' shortens to *bula* when prefixed with *yuwu*-, as in:

(5)   ŋaliji$_S$ yuwu-bula balŋgi-gu
       1sg.NOM TIMES-two turn.off-PURP
       We two will have to turn off the path twice

11.1.2 Genitives

The two genitive suffixes mark a possessor within an NP. They are, essentially, derivational, taking (like all other words in the NP) a case inflection showing the function of the NP in its clause.

(a)   simple genitive NWMJG -u after a nasal, -ŋu elsewhere
(b)   general genitive MJG   -mi

A simple genitive form must, in NWM, be augmented by 'linker' *-njin* before a non-zero case inflection; for example *yara-ŋu-njin-du* 'man-SIMPLE.GEN-LINK-ERG'. G substitutes *-ŋiñ* for *-ŋu-njin*; thus *yara-ŋiñ-ju* 'man-SIMPLE.GEN-ERG'.

A general genitive takes case inflections directly, as in *yara-mi-gu* 'man-GENERAL.GEN-ERG'.

Put briefly, the simple genitive indicates that some object is, or is about to be, actually in a person's possession. General genitive—which occurs much less frequently—indicates that the person used to own the object, or that they still own it but do not actually have it in their possession at the present time. There is further discussion of the meanings and functions of the two genitives on pp. 42–3, 105–10 of *DDL*.

Note that general genitive is only found with nominals, not with noun markers, pronouns, or interrogative/indefinites.

11.1.3 Nominal reduplication

In WMJG, a noun or adjective is marked for plurality by full reduplication (*DDL*: 242–3); for example *mularri-mularri* 'lots of initiated men'.

N differs in reduplicating just the first two syllables: *mula-mularri*. In this it is like Yidiñ (Dixon 1977a: 156–7).

11.1.4 Plurals

Plural forms are known for a handful of nouns referring to humans (*DDL*: 241–2);

(a)	'man'	MJG	yara	plural yara-rrji
(b)	'child'	MG	ñalŋga	plural ñalŋga-ymbaru
(c)	'youth before initiation'	N	baRŋan	plural baRŋan-ba
		MJG	barrŋan	plural barrŋan-mi
(d)	'youth after initiation'	N	wugun	plural wugun-mi
		MJG	rugun	plural rugun-mi
(e)	'girl before puberty'	MJG	gajiya	plural gajiya-mi
(f)	'pubescent girl'	NMJ	nayi	plural nayi-nba
		G	nayi	plural nayi-li

The N term for 'girl before puberty' (corresponding to *gajiya* in MJG) is *yabuRu*. This does not have any special plural form, showing plural simply in the regular manner, by reduplication: *yabu-yaburu*.

There is also a plural form for two adjectives:

(g)	'big'	MJ	bulgan	plural	bulgan-gay
		G	jagiñ	plural	jagiñ-gay
(h)	'very big, huge'	JG	jugi	plural	jugi-gay

The adjectives 'big' in N, *baɲan*, and in W, *dugi:*, form plurals in the regular manner, by reduplication: *baɲan-baɲan* and *dugi:-dugi:*.

When I enquired whether *midi* 'small' had a plural form *midi-gay*, I was told that one could say *midi-gay* just as a joke. Its plural is, in fact, *midi-midi*, by reduplication.

11.1.5 Suffixes to kin terms

A number of suffixes can be added to kin terms (*DDL*: 318). First, in MJG we have:

- 'mother, mother's younger sister' can be called *yabu* or *yabu-ndi*
- 'father, father's younger brother' can be called *ŋuma* or *ŋuma-ndi*

I was given an analogy to English: *yabu* and *ŋuma* are like 'mother' and 'father', whereas *yabu-ndi* and *ŋuma-ndi* are like 'mum' and 'dad'. Similarly, 'mother's younger brother' can be *gaya* or *gaya-ndi*. It seems that *-ndi* adds a note of affection.

There is a suffix *-rrin* which can be added to terms for grandparents and parent's siblings—see section 4.1. It appears to have a similar role to *-ndi* on terms for parents; for example, 'mother's father' can be *ŋagi* or *ŋagi-rrin*, 'mother's elder brother' can be *mugu* or *mugu-rrin*.

A further suffix, *-(n)ja*, may be added in MJG to terms for grandparents and parent's siblings. It indicates 'a place associated with that person', as in the following from a text in G. (There may be other meanings in addition.)

(6) ŋa-gu-l-daya   bulu-nja-gu
     NOT.VISIBLE-DAT-I-MEDIUM.DISTANCE.UPHILL father's.father-PLACE-DAT
     añja ŋayba$_S$ banagay-gu
     NEW 1sg.S   go.back-PURP
     And I have to go back to my father's father's remembered place a medium
         distance uphill

Table 4.2, in chapter 4, lists terms for people in a reciprocal kinship relation, some of which involve suffixation to a kin term.

11.1.6 Nominal inflection

We now deal with the system of case inflection on nominals (*DDL*: 42–4, 236–9). First note that **absolute** case (called 'nominative' in *DDL*), which marks S and O functions, is always zero.

(a) Ergative-instrumental and (b) Locative

Ergative and instrumental have exactly the same form but can be distinguished as separate cases on syntactic grounds; see *DDL*: 93–5. All allomorphs end in *-u*. Locative has identical form to ergative-instrumental, save that all allomorphs end in *-a*. In view of this, it is convenient to consider these suffixes together, quoting ergative-instrumental/locative.

(i)	NWMAJG	-ŋgu/-ŋga	after a disyllabic stem ending in a short vowel
	NWMAJG	-gu/-ga	after a trisyllabic or longer stem ending in a short vowel
	NWMAJG	-Hu/-Ha	after a nasal, where H is a stop homorganic with the nasal; i.e. *-bu* after *-m*, *-du* after *-n*, *-ju* after *-ñ*
(ii)	WMAJG	-ju/-ja	after *-y*
	N	-u/-a	after *-y* [In N, most *y*-final forms have developed a long vowel, *ay* > *a:* and *uy* > *i:*. Those which retain the *y* just take *-u/-a*.]
(iii)	MAJG	-ru/-ra	after a stem ending in *l*, *r*, or *rr*, with deletion of the stem-final *l*, *r*, or *rr*
	NW	-u/-a	after a stem ending in *l* [In NW most final *Vl* have become *V:*. Those that remain take *-u/-a*.]
	W	-ru/-ra	after a stem ending in *rr*, replacing the *rr*
	W	-u/-a	after a stem ending in *r*, where this is retained
	N	-u/-a	after a stem ending in *R*. Most of these relate to an original *rr*, some to *r*, where this is retained.
(iv)	W	-ru/-ra	after a stem ending in a long vowel, with length omitted
	N	-Ru/-Ra	after a stem ending in a long vowel, with length retained, when the long vowel comes from final *Vl* or *Vr*, or *uy* (giving *i:*)
	N	-ju/-ja or -Ru/-Ra	after a stem ending in a long vowel, with length retained, when the long vowel comes from final *ay*

Allomorphs (i) are the same in all dialects. Those in (ii)–(iv) show differences in N and W, as a consequence of the long-vowel-creating changes set out in (1) above. Table 11.1 exemplifies these differences, first quoting forms in M, which has no long vowels, and then corresponding forms in W and N. Locative is given for some roots, and ergative-instrumental for others, according to the examples available in the corpus.

The most interesting point concerns allomorphs after a long vowel in N. Rows (a) and (c) of the table show *-Ru/-Ra* after a long vowel which evolved from *Vl* or *Vr*, corresponding to forms in M and W. But final *Vy* also developed into a long vowel in N (not in W). All examples in the corpus of roots showing the change *uy* > *i:* take *-Ru/-Ra*, as in row (i). But some roots which undertook the change *ay* > *a:* take *-ju/-ja*, as in row (f), some take, *-Ru/-Ra*, as in row (g), and for others both allomorphs have been recorded (at different times), as in row (h).

TABLE 11.1. Examples of ergative/instrumental and locative inflections in M, W, and N

		M root	+LOC or -ERG	W root	+LOC or -ERG	N root	+LOC or -ERG
(a)	'cheek'	jagal	jaga-ra	jaga:	jaga-ra	jaga:	jaga:-Ra
(b)*	'lizard sp'	wurambal	wuramba-ru	wurambal	wurambal-u	wurambal	wurambal-u
(c)	'wallaby sp'	gubar	guba-ru	guba:	guba-ru	guba:	guba:-Ru
(d)*	'sword'	bagur	bagu-ru	bagur	bagur-u	baguR	baguR-u
(e)	'basket'	yingarr	yinga-ra	yingarr	yinga-ra	yingaR	yingaR-a
(f)	'road'	yalgay	yalgay-ja	ya:gay	ya:gay-ja	ya:ga:	ya:ga:-ja
(g)	'possum sp'	bunay	bunay-ju	bunay	bunay-ju	buna:	buna:-Ru
(h)	'spear'	bangay	bangay-ju	bangay	bangay-ju	banga:	banga:-ju/-Ru
(i)	'sand'	waguy	waguy-ja	waguy	waguy-ja	wagi:	wagi:-Ra
(j)*	'snake sp'	walguy	walguy-ju	walguy	walguy-ju	walguy	walguy-u

* The long-vowel-creating changes, set out in (1), have not been applied here.

The *-ju/-ja* forms are a natural historical development; by change (1)—*yalgay-ja* in M gives *ya:ga:-ja* in N, as in row (f). It is clear that allomorphs *-Ru/-Ra*, used after long vowels which emanate from *Vl* and *Vr*, are being generalised to apply after all long vowels, including those which come from *Vy*. It appears that *-ju/-ja* has been fully replaced by *-Ru/-Ra* after roots ending in *i:*, but the change is still in progress for roots ending in an *a:* which comes from *ay*.

There is further discussion of ergative/instrumental and locative allomorphy within the account of long vowel evolution, in section 13.3.

The other case inflections are more straightforward.

NWMAJG -gu   (c) **dative** and (d) **allative**, which have the same form but
                   are distinguished syntactically (*DDL*: 236).
NWMAJG -ŋunu (e) **ablative**, which is identical to derivational suffix
                   (e) in section 11.1.1.
NWMJG   -ña   (f) **accusative**, marking O function with proper names and
                   some kin nouns. Note that nouns which take *-ña* may have
                   dative *-ñangu* and locative *-ñaŋga*, based on this.
                   (See *DDL*: 43–4, 221.)

Post-case increment *-rru* in WMJG, *-Ru* in N, can be added after allative or locative suffixes with a meaning 'through' or 'along' (*DDL*: 57).

11.1.7 Verbalising suffixes

Verbs can be derived from nouns and adjectives by adding suffixes:

(a) **Inchoative**, forming an intransitive verb stem:
     WMAJG   -bi-l
     N   -bi-y [Inchoatives have here been shifted to the -y
              conjugation, to which most intransitive verbs belong.]

(b) **Causative**, forming a transitive verb stem:
     NWMAJG -ma-l   after a disyllabic root
             -(m)ba-l after a longer forms

(c) **Delocutive**, forming intransitive verb stems (indicating 'saying a locution'):
     NMJ-   -mba-y

Note that inchoative and causative verbalisers may also be applied to verb markers, locational nominals, time qualifiers, and some particles; see *DDL*: 85–9.

The delocutive suffix is not in *DDL* but is described in Dixon (1977d).

11.2 Noun and verb markers, and demonstratives

We can repeat the basic noun marker paradigm from (5) of chapter 2 (and see *DDL*: 44–7, 254–9):

(7)	Gender	Absolute (S and O functions)	Ergative (A function) and Instrumental	Dative	(Simple) Genitive
	I	bayi	ba-ŋgu-l	ba-gu-l	ba-ŋu-l
	II	bala-n ~ ba-n	ba-ŋgu-n	ba-gu-n	ba-ŋu-n
	III	bala-m ~ ba-m	ba-ŋgu-m	ba-gu-m	—
	IV	bala	ba-ŋgu	ba-gu	ba-ŋu

This applies in MAJG. Dialects N and W differ only in that the long vowel rule *Vl > V:* has applied for the non-absolutive forms in gender I, giving *baŋgu:*, *bagu:*, and *baŋu:*.

All six dialects can substitute *ya(la)-* 'here and visible' and *ŋa(la)-* 'not visible (audible, or remembered from the past)' for the initial *ba(la)-*, which is 'there and visible' and also the default term in the system.

In all dialects, absolutive forms commencing with *ya(la)-* only occur in complex combinations. In their place are demonstratives, which only occur in absolutive case except in G where there is also a locative (*DDL*: 258):

(8)	gender		I	II	III	IV
	NWMAJ	absolutive	giyi	giña-n	giña-m	giña
	G	absolutive	ŋiyi	ŋiña-n	ŋiña-m	ŋiña
	G	locative	ŋiyi-ŋga	ŋiña-n-ga	ŋiña-m-ga	ŋiña-ga

Just in G (*DDL*: 258–9), noun markers can be suffixed with -*(ŋ)ga*, corresponding to *gila-* forms in other dialects; see (11–12) below.

The paradigm for verb markers can be repeated from (15) of chapter 2 (and see *DDL*: 56–7, 254–7):

(9)		THERE	HERE	NOT VISIBLE
	locative 'at'	bala-y	yala-y	ŋala-y
	allative 'to place'	ba-lu	ya-lu	ŋa-lu
	allative 'to direction'	ba-li	ya-li	—
	ablative 'from'	ba-ŋum	ya-ŋum	ŋa-ŋum

This applies for MAJG. The two northern dialects have a single allative form, and we get final *ay > a:* in N:

(10)			THERE	HERE
	locative 'at'	N	bala-:	yala-:
		W	bala-y	yala-y
	allative 'to'	NW	ba-li	ya-li
	ablative 'from'	NW	ba-ŋum	ya-ŋum

Verb markers commencing with *ŋa(la)-* (which are rare in MAJG) have not been recorded for N or W, but are likely to have occurred there.

In NWMJ, there is another variety of noun and verb markers commencing with *gila-* 'somewhere' (*DDL*: 256–7). The paradigm for noun markers is:

(11)	Gender	Absolutive	Ergative and Instrumental	Dative		(Simple) Genitive
	I	gila	gila-ŋgu-l		gila-gu-l	gila-ŋu-l
	II	gila	gila-ŋgu-n		gila-gu-n	gila-ŋu-n
	III	gila	gila-ŋgu-m		gila-gu-m	—
	IV	gila	gila-ŋgu		gila-gu	gila-ŋu

Note that no gender distinction is made in the absolutive. As in (7), the final $Vl > V$: change has applied for the non-absolutive forms of gender I in N and W, giving *gilaŋgu:, gilagu:,* and *gilaŋu:*.

There are also verb markers based on *gila-* (note that locative is just *gila*):

(12)	locative	NWMJ	gila
	allative of place	MJ	gila-rru
	allative of direction	MJ	gila-rri
	allative	N	gila-Ri
		W	gila-rri
	ablative	NWMJ	gila-ŋum

Gila- markers do not occur in G. Consultants translated J forms into G using demonstratives and other noun markers; for instance, J *gila* as G *ŋiyi-ŋga*, J *gilagul* as G *yagulga*, J *gilagu* as G *yagu-ga* (see also *DDL*: 259).

11.2.1 'Up' and 'down' suffixes

Every kind of noun and verb marker (including those based on *gila-*), plus demonstratives, may optionally be followed by a suffix from either of two paradigms. Paradigm (16) from chapter 2 applies for MJG (*DDL*: 48):

(13)	-bayji	'short distance downhill'	-dayi	'short distance uphill'
	-bayja	'medium distance downhill'	-daya	'medium distance uphill'
	-bayju	'long distance downhill'	-dayu	'long distance uphill'
	-balba(la)	'medium distance downriver'	-dawa(la)	'medium distance upriver'
	-balbu(lu)	'long distance downriver'	-dawu(lu)	'long distance upriver'
		-guya 'across the river'		
		-bawal 'long way (in any direction)'		

There is a dialect variation; the 'medium distance river' forms are -*balbara* and -*dawara* in G, in place of -*balba(la)* and -*dawa(la)*. The final *la/rra* and *lu* of 'river' suffixes are always included in J and G but optionally omitted in M (*DDL*: 263).

The two northern dialects, N and W, employ a smaller paradigm:

(14) -baːji 'downhill'	-dayi 'uphill'	
-baːbu 'downriver'	-dawu 'upriver'	
	-guya 'across the river'	
-baːndu 'long way (in any direction)'		

Interestingly, in MAJG, of the three 'downhill' and three 'uphill' forms, the 'short distance' terms are by far the most common (making up 75 per cent of occurrences). In contrast, of the two 'downriver' and two 'upriver' forms, the 'long distance' forms are by far the most common (making up 80 per cent of occurrences). This correlates with the fact that N and W have just retained what were originally the 'short distance' forms for 'hill' and the 'long distance' ones for 'river'.

The second paradigm applies in NWMAJG. Repeating (18) from chapter 2, it is (*DDL*: 48):

(15)   -gala 'up (vertically)'
        -gali 'down (vertically)'
        -galu 'out in front'

Just in J and G (*DDL*: 48), a suffix from (13) may be followed by one from (15).

There are two further suffixes which can be added to noun and verb markers and demonstratives:

- 'behind' (*DDL*: 48), N -ŋaRu, WM -ŋarru
- 'somewhere' (*DDL*: 261), NMJ -ŋunda (this was not recognised by W consultants)

11.3 Pronouns and interrogatives/indefinites

11.3.1 1st and 2nd person pronouns

We can first consider the forms and functions of singular 1st and 2nd person pronouns:

(16)		S function	A function	O function (accusative)	genitive	dative
1sg	NWMJ		ŋaja	ŋaygu-na	ŋaygu	ŋaygu-ngu
	G	ŋayba	ŋaja	ŋaña	ŋaygu	ŋaygu-ngu
2sg	NWMJ		ŋinda	ŋinu-na	ŋinu	ŋinu-ngu
	G	ŋinba	ŋinda	ŋina	ŋinu	ŋinu-ngu

As mentioned in section 1.5, just the singular pronouns in G have separate forms for S (intransitive subject) and A (transitive subject) functions. Other pronouns in G, and all pronouns in other dialects, have a single form (nominative) covering both S and A. An interesting feature in NWMJ is that, for both 1sg and 2sg, the accusative form (for O function) involves the addition of *-na* to the genitive. In contrast, duals and plurals form accusative by adding *-na* (or *-ña*) to the nominative.

The 1sg and 2sg paradigm in G is identical to that in G's southerly neighbour Warrgamay (Dixon 1981a: 40) and also to that in Warrgamay's southerly neighbour Nyawaygi (Dixon 1983: 464). There are also similarities for 1st and 2nd person duals and plurals. However, other aspects of the grammars are quite different, such that it is not feasible to posit a close genetic relationship between any of the three languages.

Dual and plural pronouns, across five dialects, are set out in table 11.2. We can first comment on the forms:

- ` As described in section 4.3, the N, W, and M dialects make a distinction between two 1du pronouns. Harmonic *ŋali* is used when the two people involved are in the same generation or two generations apart, while disharmonic *ŋanaymba/ ŋana:mba* is used when they are one or three generations apart. J and G have a single 1du pronoun, with the same form as the harmonic member in northern dialects.
- All non-singular pronouns in J, and 2du in G, have *ji* added. In the materials I recorded from a mixed J and G community there was a good deal of variation concerning the inclusion or omission of *ji*.
- 2du *ñubala* is the only pronoun with more than two syllables (leaving aside disharmonic 1du, and those with final *ji*). In N it appears to have been shortened to disyllabic *ñubal*, with the long-vowel change then creating *ñuba:*. (Note that for 1du in W, forms identical to those in N, and to those in M, were heard.)
- The second vowel in 2du varies. Compare base form *ñubala* in NWMJ with *ñubila* in G. (2du is *ñubula* in both Warrgamay and Nyawaygi.)
- In M, 2pl is *ñurray* for nominative and genitive, but just *ñurra* for accusative and dative. In N, *ñurray* has become *ñuRa:* and the long vowel is retained in all columns.

We can now examine the case and genitive suffixes.

- As described in section 11.1.6, proper names and some kin terms may take accusative suffix *-ña*. The same form, *-ña*, is found on 1du disharmonic in N, and on 1du, 1pl, 2pl (not on 2du) in G. Elsewhere, the accusative suffix is *-na*.
- Genitive is basically *-ŋu* after a disyllabic and *-nu* after a longer form (except that we get *ñuba:-nu* and *ñuRa:nu* in N).

TABLE 11.2. Paradigm of 1st and 2nd person dual and plural pronouns

		SA functions (nominative)	O function (accusative)	genitive	dative
1du harm	NWM	ŋali	ŋali-na	ŋali-ŋu	ŋali-ngu
1du dis- harm	N	ŋana:mba	ŋana:mba-ña	ŋana:mba-nu	ŋana:mba-ña-ngu
	W	ŋanaymba	ŋanaymba-na	ŋanaymba-nu	ŋanaymba-gu
	M	ŋanaymba	ŋanaymba-na	ŋanaymba-nu	ŋanaymba-na-ngu
1du	J	ŋaliji	ŋaliji-na	ŋaliji-nu	ŋaliji-ngu
	G	ŋali	ŋali-ña	ŋali-ŋu	ŋali-ña-ngu
1pl	NWM	ŋana	ŋana-na	ŋana-ŋu	ŋana-ngu
	J	ŋanaji	ŋanaji-na	ŋanaji-nu	ŋanaji-ngu
	G	ŋana	ŋana-ña	ŋana-ŋu	ŋana-ña-ngu
2du	NW	ñuba:	ñuba:-na	ñuba:-nu	ñuba:-ngu
	WM	ñubala	ñubala-na	ñubala-nu	ñubala-ngu
	J	ñubalaji	ñubalaji-na	ñubalaji-nu	ñubalaji-ngu
	G	ñubilaji	ñubilaji-na	ñubilaji-nu	ñubilaji-ngu
2pl	N	ñuRa:	ñuRa:-na	ñuRa:-nu	ñuRa:-ngu
	WM	ñurray	ñurra-na	ñurray-ŋu	ñurra-ngu
	J	ñurraji	ñurraji-na	ñurraji-nu	ñurraji-ngu
	G	ñurra	ñurra-ña	ñurra-ŋu	ñurra-ña-ngu

- Dative adds *-ngu* to the accusative for 1du disharmonic in N and M, and for 1du, 1pl, and 2pl in G. Elsewhere, *-ngu* is added to the nominative (in W, it is just *-gu* for 1du disharmonic).

1st and 2nd person pronouns are discussed on pp. 49–51 and 243–6 of *DDL*.

11.3.2 3rd person pronouns

Warrgamay and Nyawaygi, to the south of Dyirbal, have a full array of 3rd person pronouns, in three numbers. Yidiñ, to the north, has none. Dyirbal lacks 3sg, with noun markers and demonstratives taking on some of the functional load covered by 3sg in other languages.

However, there are 3du and 3pl pronouns, and these differ between dialects; like 1st and 2nd person pronouns, they are restricted to human reference.

G has 3du *bulajin*, which can be shortened to *bulaji* or just *bula* in S function, and 3pl *jana*. Like 1sg and 2sg in G, there are separate forms for the three core syntactic functions, S, A, and O. The paradigm is:

(17)		S function	A function	O function	genitive	dative
	3du	bula, bulaji, bulajin	bulajin-du	bulajin-a	bulajin-u	bulajin-a-ngu, bulajin-gu
	3pl	jana	jana-ŋgu	jana-ña	jana-ŋu	jana-ña-ngu

These non-singular 3rd person pronouns in G are similar to those in Warrgamay and Nyawaygi.

A quite different situation prevails in NWMJ. Here we have complex forms *bala-garra* (*bala-gaRa* in N) for 3du, and *bala-maŋgan* for 3pl. They involve the 3sg absolutive gender IV noun marker *bala*—see (7)—plus two of the nominal derivational suffixes discussed in section 11.1.1: *-garra/-gaRa* 'one of a pair', and *-maŋgan* 'one of a group of more than two'. These inflect on an absolutive-ergative basis, like noun markers and nominals (and unlike 1st and 2nd person pronouns in all dialects, and 3rd person forms in G). The paradigm for *bala-garra* is:

(18)		Absolutive	Ergative	Dative	Genitive
	(a)	bala-garra	baŋgu-garra	bagu-garra	baŋu-garra
	(b)		bala-garra-gu	bala-garra-gu	bala-garra-ŋu
	(c)		baŋgu-garra-gu	bagu-garra-gu	baŋu-garra-ŋu

That for *bala-maŋgan* is similar.

The fascinating feature is that just the *bala* component may inflect for case, as in row (a), or the whole form, as in row (b), or both at once, as in (c). The possibilities in each column alternate freely in texts.

In rows (b) and (c), ergative is *-gu*, the allomorph used on a stem of more than two syllables, showing that *-garra/-gaRa* and *-maŋgan* do here have the status of suffixes.

Note that these hybrid 3du and 3pl forms do not show gender. They are typically accompanied by a noun marker or demonstrative such as *balan* or *giyi* which indicates the sex of the participants.

In the two northern dialects, accusative *-(ñ)a* can be added for O function and also be the base for dative. For example, I have heard accusative *bala-maŋgan-a* in N, and dative *bala-garra-ña-ngu* in W.

Similar dual and plural forms are formed on *giña-/yala/-ŋala-* and also *waña* 'who'; for example genitive *yaŋu-maŋgan-u* 'belonging to two people here' in N. There is further discussion of 3du and 3pl pronouns in *DDL*: 51–3.

11.3.3 Interrogative/indefinites

As in many Australian languages, a single form can cover both interrogative and indefinite meanings—'who' and 'someone', 'what' and 'something', and so on. For ease of exposition, just the interrogative glosses are used here.

There is a set of interrogative/indefinite noun markers, indicating 'where' (or 'somewhere'). The basic paradigm for NWMAJG is:

(19)	Gender	Absolutive	Ergative and Instrumental	Dative	Genitive
	I	wuñjiñ	wuñja-ŋgu-l	wuñja-gu-l	wuñja-ŋu-l
	II	wuñja-n	wuñja-ŋgu-n	wuñja-gu-n	wuñja-ŋu-n
	III	wuñja-m	wuñja-ŋgu-m	wuñja-gu-m	—
	IV	wuñja	wuñja-ŋgu	wuñja-gu	wuñja-ŋu

There are two variations:

- As in paradigm (7), final *ul* > *u*: in N and W, so that the non-absolutive gender I forms are *wuñjaŋgu:*, *wuñjagu:*, and *wuñjaŋu:*.
- In N, W, and A, gender I absolutive is just *wuñji*. (Interestingly, in recent times the last semi-speakers of the mixed J/G variety at Murray Upper appear to have replaced *wuñjiñ* by *wuñji*—see the appendix to chapter 16.)

Looking now at other interrogative/indefinites, 'what' inflects like a noun, 'how many' like an adjective—both on an absolutive-ergative basis—and 'when' like a time word (*DDL*: 58, 252–3). The cross-dialectal forms are:

(20)		'what'		'how many'		'when'
	NWMJ	miña	NWMJG	miñañ	N	miña:
	G	waña			WMJ	miñay
					G	miñi

In contrast, 'who' has separate forms for S, O, and A functions in NWMJ. However, S and O fall together in G:

(21) 'who'	S function	O function	A function	genitive	dative
NWMJ	waña	wañuna	wañju	wañuŋu	wañungu
G		wañuña	wañju	wañuŋu	wañungu

The following historical scenario can be suggested:

- G originally had *miña* for 'what', like all other dialects.
- G originally had 'who' forms like other dialects, save that the O form ended in *ña* instead of the *na* in NWMJ. That is: S *waña*, O *wañuña*, A *wañju*. This

is consistent with G's accusative suffix *-ña* on 1st and 2nd person pronouns, in table 11.2.

- G tabooed *miña*, and replaced it with *waña*, moving this from S function for 'who' to become 'what'.
- The S slot in the 'who' paradigm was filled by *wañuña*, which was extended to cover both O and S functions.

11.4 Verbals

The suffixes now to be described apply equally to verbs and to adverbals. For each suffix, we quote its form when applied to a stem of the -l conjugation, and then to stems of the -y conjugation which end in *a* or in *i*. (The latter two could be combined, with a rule *iy > i* before a consonant.) Note that no verb in the -y conjugation ends in *u*; however, verbs in the -l conjugation end in all three vowels, *i, a,* and *u*.

Section 13.4 discusses the details of verbal morphology within the context of the long-vowel-creating changes in N and W.

11.4.1 Verbal derivations which affect transitivity

There are three suffixes which apply to transitive stems and derive intransitives: (a) antipassive (just called 'the *-ŋay* construction' in *DDL*: 65–7); (b) reflexive, which can also be a second antipassive and a general intransitiviser (*DDL*: 89–92); and (c) reciprocal (*DDL*: 92–3).

Suffix (d), applicative, can apply to an intransitive stem and derives a transitive one (this is called 'comitative' in *DDL*: 96–9), or it can apply to a transitive verb, rearranging its arguments ('instrumentive' in *DDL*: 95–6).

	a-y	-i-y	-i	
(a) NW	-na-y	-na-y	-:na-y	antipassive
MAJYG	-na-y	-na-y	-l(ŋ)a-y	

The *ŋ* in the -l conjugation column is included in M, optional in J, and omitted in G—see (30) in section 10.3.

(b) N	-:máRi-y	-máRi-y	-(:)Rí-y	reflexive
WMYG	-ymárri-y	-márri-y	-rrí-y	
AJ	-ymárri-y	-márri-y	-(yi)rrí-y	

Reflexive on the -l conjugation in AJ is *-yirrí-y* when next but one after a stressed syllable and *-rrí-y* elsewhere (that is, when following a stressed syllable, or after two or more unstressed syllables). In N it is *-:Rí-y* next but one after a stressed syllable and *-Rí-y* elsewhere. Note that *-yirrí-y* is the only suffix in the language which is stressed on the second syllable. It is likely that the original form was as in AJ, with the unstressed initial *-yi-* being replaced by vowel length in N and simply omitted in WMYG.

For a verb from the -y conjugation, the forms quoted are those after a disyllabic stem. Following a longer stem, the *-má-* is replaced by *-(m)bá-*.

(c)	N	-:baRi-y	-baRi-y	-:baRi-y	reciprocal
	W	-ybarri-y	-barri-y	-:barri-y	
	MJG	-ybarri-y	-barri-y	-l(n)barri-y	

Reciprocal also involves reduplication of the verb.

(d)	N	-:m(b)a-l	-m(b)a-l	-:m(b)a-l	applicative
	W	-ym(b)a-l	-m(b)a-l	-:m(b)a-l	
	MAJYG	-ym(b)a-l	-m(b)a-l	-lm(b)a-l	

The basic form is *-ma-l* next but one after a stressed syllable, and *-mba-l* otherwise. Applicative forms of the irregular verb *yanu(-l)* are: *yanu:ma-l* in N, *yanuma-l* in WM, *yanuma-l* or *yanulma-l* in J, and *yanulma-l* in G.

11.4.2 Verbal derivations which do not affect transitivity, and reduplication

These four suffixes can be added to a verb of either transitivity value, and do not affect this. Full details of meanings are in *DDL*: 248–50.

		-a-y	-i-y	-l	
(a)	N	-yaRa-y	-yaRa-y	-yaRa-y	'start, continue'
	WMAJYG	-yarra-y	-yarra-y	-yarra-y	
(b)	MG	-ngani-y	-ngani-y	-lgani-y	'do repeatedly'
	J	-ngani-y	-ngani-y	-gani-y	
(c)	NW	-nja-y	-nja-y	-:ja-y	'many S or O, etc.'
	MAJG	-nja-y	-nja-y	-lja-y	
(d)	MAJG	-gali-y	-gali-y	-gali-y/-nba-l	'go quickly'

In the -l conjugation, *-gali-y* is used with intransitive and *-nba-l* with transitive stems.

In NWMJG, reduplication involves just the first two syllables of a verb, and indicates 'done to excess' (*DDL*: 251–2).

11.4.3 Verbal inflection

We again give forms in the -y conjugation (for final *a* and *i*) and in the -l conjugation, with a column added for the only irregular verb, *yanu(-l)* 'go' (see *DDL*: 246–7, 251).

		-a-y	-i-y	-l	yanu(-l)	
(a)	NMJYG	-ñu	-ñu	-n	yanu	past tense
(b)	N	-ñ	-ñ	-:ñ	yanu-ñ	future tense
	WMJY	-ñ	-ñ	-ñ	yanu-ñ	
	G	-njay	-njay	-ljay	yanu-ljay	

In NWM, future also covers present tense; in JG past also covers present (the situation in Y is unknown).

| (c) | M | -ñu-ga | -ñu-ga | -n-uga | — | done irretrievably |

This suffix, only found in M, involves *-(u)ga* added to past tense forms (*DDL*: 114).

(d)	N	-:gu	-gu	-li	yanu-li	purposive
	WMAJYG	-ygu	-gu	-li	yanu-li	
(e)	NWMAJYG	-ø	-ø	-ø	yana	positive imperative
(f)	NW	-m	-m	-m	yana-m	negative imperative
	MAJ	-m	-m	-m	yanu-m	
	G	-mu	-mu	-lmu	yanu-lmu	
(g)	N	-guRa	-guRa	-guRa	yanu-guRa	A = S/O, etc.
	W	-gurra	-gurra	-gurra	yanu-gurra	
	MJ	-ŋurra	-ŋurra	-ŋurra	yanu-ŋurra	
	G	-ŋarra	-ŋarra	-ŋarra	yanu-ŋarra	

This suffix on the verb of a clause indicates (1) that the S or O argument of the clause is identical to the A argument of the preceding clause; and (2) that the activity described by the clause follows immediately after that of the preceding clause (*DDL*: 77–9).

(h)	N	-mba:	-mba:	-:ba	yanu-:ba	apprehensive
	W	-mba	-mba	-:ba	yanu-:ba	
	MY	-mba	-mba	-lba	yanu-lba	
	AJ	-mbila	-mbila	-lbila	yanu-lbila	
	G	-nbila	-nbila	-lbila	yanu-lbila	

A recent development in the mixed J/G community at Murray Upper is that when apprehensive follows inchoative verbaliser *-bi-l* (see section 11.1.7), *-bila* can be reduced to *-ba*; that is, *-bi-lba* in place of the older *-bi-lbila* (this is presumably to avoid consecutive *-bil*'s). See also section 16.4.

(i)	MJG	-ymuŋa	-muŋa	-lmuŋa	—	agentive participle
	MU	-yginay	-ginay	-lginay	—	

(j)	N	-:	?	-:	—	agentive participle
	W	-y	?	?	—	
	MJ	-y	-ø	-l	—	

Participle (j) refers to someone doing something habitually, and (i) to them doing something habitually a lot. It appears that *-ginay* is a variant of (i) found mostly in the U dialect (related to nominal derivational suffix *-ginay* 'covered with, full of', (d) in section 11.1.1). Participles are derived nouns and take nominal morphology (*DDL*: 91–5).

| (k) | WMAJYG | -ŋu | -ŋu | -ŋu | yanu-ŋu | relative clause |
| (l) | NWMY | -ñu-mi | -ñu-mi | -n-mi | yanu-mi | relative clause |

Most dialects (N and AJG) have just one relative clause marker. There are two in WMY: (l) refers to an action which is completed and (k) to one that is continuing (*DDL*: 99–105). Note that (l) involves the addition of *-mi* to past tense forms, similar to (c). Each relative clause marker is followed by a case suffix indicating the function of its NP within the main clause (S and O functions are shown, as usual, by ø); see section 7.1.2.

It is interesting that two genitive suffixes (section 11.1.2) have the same forms as the two relative clause markers: *-ŋu* and *-mi*. It is instructive to compare their dialect distribution (reliable information is not available for genitive in A and Y).

	as genitive	as/within relative clause marker
-ŋu	NWMJG	WMAJYG
-mi	MJG	NWMY

Note that *-mi* is the only relative clause marker in N, but is not attested as a genitive in that language. (An early discussion of this topic is in Dixon 1969.)

11.5 Particles

We can first describe the cross-dialectal distribution of the particles discussed in *DDL*: 116–22.

(a)	G	gawu	'come on!'
(b)	MJG	gaji	'try (to do it)!'
(c)	NWMJYG	añja	'new topic/action/quality'
(d)	NWMAJYG	gulu	'not'

(e)	N	ŋaRu	'don't'
	WMG	ŋarru	
	AJ	galga	

(f)	N	waRa	'inappropriate S or O'
	WMAJG	warra	

(g)	NWMJYG	mugu	'couldn't help doing it'

(h)	N	balu	'maybe'
	MJ	yamba	
	G	marri	

(i)	N	yuwuR	'always happening'
	M	yuwurr	
	JG	banjul	

(j)	NWMJG	gana	'to a partial extent'
(k)	NWMAJG	yanda	'tried and failed'

(l)	N	ŋa:Ra	'couldn't do it'
	WMAJG	ŋara	

(m)	N	ŋurma	'had intended to do it, or had tried to do it'
	MJG	ŋurrma	

(n)	N	biRi	'might well have happened'
	MG	birri	
	J	biya	

(o)	N	yuRmu	'just'
	WM	yurrmu	
	JG	jamu	

(p)	N	ŋuRi	'in turn'
	WMAJYG	ŋurri	

The following additional particles have come to light since *DDL*:

(q)	J	ŋunman	'supposed to be'
	G	ŋuna(n)	

This particle indicates that something was supposed to be the case but wasn't, or that something was supposed to happen, but didn't. In Chloe Grant's autobiographical text, she tells how she had thought that her foster-mother was her real mother:

(22) ŋunman   ŋaja   bala-n   ŋaygu   yabu
     SUPPOSED   1sg.NOM   THERE.ABS-II   1sg.GEN   mother
     I supposed she was my mother (but I was mistaken)

Other examples include:

(23) ŋuna   bayi$_S$ ŋulga-gu-bi-li
      SUPPOSED THERE.ABS.I tomorrow-UNTIL-INCH-PURP
      He was supposed to (stay there) until the next morning (but instead went
         on, travelling through the night)

(24) ŋaja$_S$ ŋuna   bani-gu/   maya ŋaja$_S$ ñina-ñu
      1sg.NOM SUPPOSED come-PURP NO   1sg.NOM stay-PAST
      I was supposed to come, (but) no, I (changed my mind and) stayed

(r)   NM gaba 'do on one's own'
      G   gala

This particle indicates that a person acts on their own, independently of anyone
else.

(25) gaba   yana/ ŋana$_A$ banja-li
      ON.ONE'S.OWN go.IMP 1pl.NOM follow-PURP
      Let (him) go (ahead) on his own, for us to follow (him later)

(26) gala   ŋinda$_A$ balga
      ON.ONE'S.OWN 2sg.NOM hit.IMP
      You hit (him) on your own (I'm not going to be any part of it)

One day, when I was working with Bessie Jerry playing back a text she had recorded,
visitors arrived. I stopped. Bessie told me to continue by saying just '*Gala!*', meaning
'Carry on regardless of them!'

(s)   JG   gila   'look out! (e.g. get out of the way of something coming)'

(t)   M   galaguy   'hurry up!'
      J   yurrgi

One item which was said to be a particle in *DDL*: 121 is now analysed as an adjective,
since it takes nominal inflections (which particles never do). This is NWJ *yama*, MG
yaja 'do gently, slackly, just a bit, quietly'.

11.6 Clitics, universal affixes, and interjections

11.6.1 Clitics

These enclitics attach to the first word of a sentence (*DDL*: 122–3).

(a)	WMJG	=ma	interrogative
(b)	M	=rriga	'definitely the case'
	JG	=girra	
(c)	N	=giRa	'should be the case (but there is an element of doubt)'
	M	=girra	

One more clitic has come to light since *DDL*:

(d)	JG	=ŋana	focus marker, 'this is the one'

For example:

(27) [bayi=ŋana   yabuju]ₛ   ŋaliji-ngu marri-n
      THERE.ABS.I=FOCUS younger.brother 1pl-DAT   follow-PAST
      He's the one, it's younger brother who followed us

(28) yimba=ŋana jigil
      NO=FOCUS   good
      No, it's not this (foodstuff which is emitting a rotten smell; this is) good

11.6.2 Universal affixes

These can be added after almost any type of word (*DDL*: 266–8, 239–40).

(a)	WMJG	-(a)rru	'another'
(b)	AJG	-bu	'only'
(c)	WMAJG	-bi	'as well, too'
(d)	NWMJG	-jan(a)	emphasis
	NW	-ba	
	MJG	-ban	

11.6.3 Interjections

There is a list of interjections in *DDL*: 124. Dialect distribution of the two main ones is:

(a)	NWMJG	ŋa	'yes'
(b)	NWMJY	yimba	'no, nothing, no more'
	G	maya	

Having in this chapter surveyed grammatical variation across Dyirbal dialects, in the next chapter attention is directed towards the lexicon.

12

Dyirbal dialectology: Lexical variation

As a partial complement to the survey of grammatical forms in the previous chapter, this chapter examines a corpus of 360 nouns in Dyirbal. We investigate whether, for a given meaning, there is a single form across all dialects, or two, or more, and also whether there are cognates in neighbouring languages. The final section of the chapter focuses on the varying meanings of a number of lexical forms.

The ten dialects of Dyirbal were listed in section 1.3.1, and are here identified by the code letters introduced there—from N in the north to L in the south. To the north of Dyirbal there is Yidiñ (Dixon 1977a, 1991a), to the south Warrgamay (Dixon 1981a), and beyond that Nyawaygi (Dixon 1983). Cognates were also looked for in the limited materials available for Warungu—spoken to the west of Dyirbal and Warrgamay—based on my field notes and (used with caution) on Tsunoda (2003).

All of these languages have the same system of consonants, set out in section 1.4, save that in the N dialect of Dyirbal there is a single rhotic, written as *R*. All the languages have three vowels. The contrastive length in initial syllables for Warrgamay and Nyawaygi is an archaic feature, which has been lost in the other languages; compare, for example, the verb *ba:lba-* 'roll' in Warrgamay with *balba-* in Dyirbal and Warungu. Recent changes, of quite different kinds, have led to the introduction of a length contrast in the N and W (and P) dialects of Dyirbal and in Yidiñ; full details are in chapters 13 and 14.

A little information is available on Mbabaram, spoken to the north-west of Dyirbal (Dixon 1991b). This language had undergone profound changes. For example an initial syllable with a short vowel had been lost from many words; corresponding to *bamba* 'stomach' in Dyirbal and Warungu, there is *mba* in Mbabaram. And an initial syllable with a long vowel was replaced by *a*; corresponding to Warrgamay *ba:di-* 'cry weep'. Mbabaram has *adi-*. (This verb is *badi-* in Yidiñ.)

12.1 Lexical variation across the dialects of Dyirbal

For this pilot lexical survey I chose 360 nouns. All items are attested for at least three dialects (M, J, and either N or G); the great majority are known for four, five, six, or more dialects. Words that have fairly specialised meaning were as a rule excluded (for instance, *malga* 'water lying on branches or leaves after rain', and *gurgarri/yirrgun* 'cassowary neck'). For most, but not quite all, of the items chosen the equivalents in surrounding languages are known; it must be borne in mind that the material on surrounding languages is less rich than that available for Dyirbal.

All 360 items are attested in M and J, about 340 in G, 310 in N, 250 in A, 200 in W, 120 in each of Y and U, 80 in L, and 45 in P.

The lexemes fall into three groups: (a) with the same form in all dialects; (b) with two forms; and (c) with three (or more) forms.

(a) Identical form in all dialects (for which material is available). There are 190 of these, slightly more than half the corpus. About three-quarters also occur in one or more of the surrounding languages.

About 35 per cent occur in a language in just one direction. Thus *ŋayi* 'voice, glottis' is also found in Warrgamay, and *ñumba* 'spittle' in Yidiñ.

About 30 per cent are found in languages from two directions e.g. *biguñ* 'finger/toe-nail' is also in Yidiñ, and in Warungu; *marbu* 'louse' is in Warungu, and in Warrgamay; *waymin* 'mother-in-law' is in Yidiñ and in Warrgamay.

A tenth of the 190 forms occur in languages from all three directions. They include *jagal* 'cheek/jaw', *ŋamun* 'breast', *jarra* 'thigh', *buŋgu* 'knee', *jambun* 'grub', *warrjan* 'raft', *gambi* 'clothing', and *guyŋgan* 'spirit of a dead woman'.

(b) Two forms. There are 120 examples of this. Almost all of them have one form in a northern and another in a southern part of the region in which the language is spoken. The isoglosses cover virtually all possible combinations of dialect boundary, as the following examples indicate:

N	waju	WMPAJUG	dara	'nape'
NW	jawa	MPAJUYG	ŋangu	'mouth'
NWP	wuja:	MAJUYGL	buyin	'eyebrow'
N WM	ŋiRma ŋirrma	AJUYG	guwal	'language'
N WMAUYL	muŋaRa muŋarra	JG	guyjarri	'scrub turkey'
NWMPAJUY	bana	GL	gamu	'water'
N WMPAJY	gaRan garran	UG	bunu	'smoke'
NWMPAJUYL	guwu	G	wudu	'nose'

About 60 per cent of the forms that occur in a northern area (exemplified in the left-hand column above) and about 70 per cent of the southern forms (corresponding to the right-hand column) have cognates in one or more neighbouring languages.

There are about the same number of isoglosses along each dialect boundary within Dyirbal (taking into account the limited data available for some dialects) except that slightly more isoglosses set off N from the other dialects, and also G from the other dialects. N and G probably have a bit less than 90 per cent vocabulary in common with their neighbours, while most other pairs of dialects appear to have 90 per cent or more shared vocabulary.

There are less than ten examples of one form occurring in just one central dialect (that is, not in N or G) and a second form in all other dialects. They include:

J	garrin	N		jamaRa	'spider web'
		MYG		jamarra	
W	gu:guli	NMAJUGL	miju		'brain'

In a handful of cases one form occurs in both a northern and a southern region and another in a number of central dialects. Consider:

'black bean'			'stone'		
NW	gañju:	N		naŋga:	
MAJU	mirrañ	WMYUAJ	diban		
G	gañjur	G		naŋgay	

The fact that *gañjur/gañju:* 'black bean (*Castanospermum australe*)' is found at both extremes of the language area might be taken to suggest that this was the original form, and that *mirrañ* has replaced it in a central region. Unfortunately, we have no idea where the form *mirrañ* could have come from (neither *gañjur* nor *mirrañ* occurs in any neighbouring language). The question of which was the original name for this important foodstuff must remain open. (It is interesting that the Jalnguy term is *dirraba* for M and J, and *miRañ* for N, taking over the everyday style form from neighbouring dialects; see chapter 6.)

We can, however, draw an historical inference in the case of 'stone'. Note that *naŋgay* occurs only in G and in N (where it has become *naŋga:*, by regular change); and *diban* is found in all the intervening dialects (information is lacking only for P and L). This suggests rather strongly that the proto-Dyirbal form was *naŋgay*, that it was originally replaced in one central dialect by *diban*, and that this form has now spread so that it covers almost the whole language area. *Naŋgay* is not known to occur in any other language, but *diban* is used for 'rocky summit of a mountain' (extended to 'bald head') in Yidiñ. Although it is always difficult to be certain of the direction of a borrowing, it seems rather likely that *diban* could have been borrowed from Yidiñ into Dyirbal with the meaning 'stone'.

We should note that, like peoples in many other parts of the world, Aboriginal Australians commonly tabooed the name of any dead person, and also proscribed any lexeme that was phonologically similar to this name. Tabooed forms would be replaced by borrowing from a nearby language, or by the shift in meaning of an already existing lexeme in that language, or—occasionally—by the formation of a new compound. This practice is certainly the major cause of lexical replacement in Australian languages; since many people were multilingual, there was no difficulty in borrowing a word from the language of a neighbouring tribe.

(c) **Three (or more) forms.** About fifty of the 360-item corpus show three different forms across the dialects of Dyirbal. (One item in the corpus, 'toothache', has four distinct forms: N *junguñ*, WMA *murru*, JU *ñamay*, G *muju*.)

For just a few of these, none of the three forms occurs with the same meaning in any nearby language. This applies to 'woman', which is *yibi* in NWMPY and northern A, *jugumbil* in southern A and UJ, and *gumbul* in G (it is *buña* in Yidiñ, *ŋulmburu* in Warrgamay and *warrŋu* in Warungu). It is in fact a common feature of the Australian language area that there is a different word for 'woman' in each language, and often in each dialect within a language. In contrast, a number of contiguous or related languages will often share a form for 'man'. (The form *yibi* does occur in Warrgamay, but with a different meaning, 'child'; it is found most frequently in reduplicated form, indicating plurality, *yibiyibi* 'children'.)

For forty of the fifty items at least one of the three forms is also found in a nearby language. Mostly it is just one form, but a handful have two or even all three forms occurring elsewhere. For example, 'mud' is *waja* in the G dialect and in Warrgamay, *maru* in WMAJU and in Warungu, and *ja:mbu:* in N, presumably cognate with *jalmbul* in Yidiñ.

In some cases it is tempting to attempt hypotheses concerning which of the three forms for a certain noun is likely to have occurred in proto-Dyirbal. Consider:

'boomerang'	N and northern A	maŋañ
	W	warrgiñ
	southern A and MJUY	waŋal
	G	warrgiñ

(The Jalnguy terms are *muyu:* in N, *muyur* in M, and *warrgiñ* in J.)

Note that *warrgiñ* is found in W and then, several dialects distant, in G; it also occurs in Warrgamay. *Waŋal* is the word for 'boomerang' in Yidiñ and Warungu. It is interesting to note that Nyawaygi, to the south of Warrgamay, has *wa:ŋal*. In Mbabaram, to the north-west of Dyirbal, the form *aŋal* is likely to reflect an original long vowel in the initial syllable, as in *wa:ŋal*. The form *maŋañ* is not known to occur elsewhere.

The simplest hypothesis here would be that *maŋañ* was the original Dyirbal form with *waŋal* and *warrgiñ* being borrowed from neighbouring languages. The forms in Nyawaygi and Mbabaram indicate that these languages could not have borrowed this word from Dyirbal, at least not since Dyirbal lost the original length contrast in initial syllables (which probably happened a considerable time ago), whereas there would be no impedance to some Dyirbal dialects borrowing *waŋal* from a neighbour to the north, west, or south. An original Dyirbal *maŋañ* does seem the most likely solution, but only by a small margin; the various other possibilities cannot be eliminated.

12.2 Semantic variation

It can be instructive to compare the meanings of a single lexeme across the dialects of Dyirbal, and in surrounding languages. Consider, for example, the various meanings of *malan* set out in table 12.1.

The factor common to all these occurrences of *malan* is a reference to river. In Yidiñ, *malan* refers to large flat rocks found along the middle reaches of a river, worn smooth by the passage of water. There was in fact a Yidiñji local group called Malan-barra, living along the rocky parts of the Mulgrave River. The Dyirbal group speaking Gulngay (U) was also called Malan-barra, because they lived along the lower part of the Tully River where it flows between sand-banks, downstream from the flat-rock portion of

---

TABLE 12.1. The meanings of *malan*

In Yidiñ: *malan* 'flat rock' (equivalent to Dyirbal *bala bajala*)

In Dyirbal:

    NWM   *balan malan* 'main river (which flows during all seasons of the year)' (the corresponding form in AJUYG is *balan yuramu*)

    A   *bala malan* 'coast country' (equivalent to *bala jabun* in MJG)

    JU   *bala malan* 'sand-bank of a river'

In Warrgamay and Warungu:

    malan 'creek (i.e. river that flows during just part of the year)' (equivalent to *balan wiñju/garrgal* in Dyirbal)

Consultants for G in the 1960s and 1970s consistently stated that *malan* was not in that dialect; but G vocabularies gathered by John Mathew in 1926 and by N. B. Tindale in 1938 include *malan* 'creek, river', suggesting that the form may possibly have been proscribed in G during recent years.

the river. (For *-barra* 'belonging to, associated with' see section 11.1.1, and Dixon 1972: 224–5.) What we are not able to do is decide on the original sense of *malan*, and determine how its meaning changed.

The modern town of Malanda, in N-speaking territory, was undoubtedly named by adding locative suffix *-da* to *malan* 'main river'; that is 'at the main river'.

There are examples of one form extending down from the north and a second form extending up from the south, and of both forms being found in a central dialect, but with slightly different significations. Consider the words for 'ribs':

(1) At the northern extreme, N and W have *waŋgirr* 'ribs' (which is also found in Yidiñ). These dialects do not have any form *ɲiyar*.

(2) At the southern extreme, G has *ɲiyar* 'ribs'. (Warrgamay has *ɲiyara*.) G does not have any form *waŋgirr*.

(3) The central dialects M, A, and J have both *waŋgirr* and *ɲiyar*:
- M follows its neighbours to the north in having *waŋgirr* as the main term, describing 'true ribs' and also for referring to the complete 'rib cage'; *ɲiyar* in M refers to 'false ribs, floating ribs'.
- J follows G in using *ɲiyar* for 'rib cage'; *waŋgirr* in J is 'side of body at ribs, flank', also extended to 'side of hill'. (I have no sure information on the exact meanings of *waŋgirr* and *ɲiyar* in A.)

A number of nouns whose primary reference is to body parts are also used to describe parts of plants or parts of the environment. Thus *bala yumal* 'body' is also 'trunk of a tree', *bala guga* 'skin' is also 'bark'; these senses apply over all dialects. Some other meaning extensions of body-part lexemes are dialect-specific. Thus all dialects use *bala garrgal* (gender IV) relating to 'arm' (it is 'upper arm just above elbow' over most of the area, and 'whole upper arm' in G), but only J and G also have *balan garrgal* (gender II) for 'creek' or 'small river' (a creek flowing into a larger river is compared to the arm joining the body). Other dialects (NWMAUL) have *balan wiñju* 'creek'. We find *bala jarra* 'thigh' in all dialects; it is also 'pocket (clearing) in the scrub' just in MJ.

Another example of this type, but in the opposite direction, is that all dialects have *balan binda* (gender II) 'waterfall', while NWM and northern A have *bala binda* (gender IV) 'shoulder'. ('Shoulder' is *bala baŋgal* in AJ, *bala burru* in UY, and *bala bigil* in G.) *Binda* also occurs as both 'shoulder' and 'top of waterfall' in Yidiñ, and as 'shoulder' in Warrgamay ('waterfall' is here *jinda*). It is by no means obvious what the original meaning of *binda* was, what the metaphorical extension was, and what changes have occurred.

Other dialect-specific extensions of body-part nouns include *bala dirra* 'tooth' (in all dialects) being used for 'hailstone' in N (other dialects have *bala balbay*). Alongside *bala ŋuwun* 'forehead', in all dialects except N and P, we find *balan ŋuwun* for 'headwaters of a river' just in G (the correspondent in J is *balan gumun*).

There are a number of instances where northern dialects of Dyirbal behave like languages to the north and southern dialects like languages to the south, with respect to some semantic 'lumping' or 'splitting'. Thus NWMPAJUY are like Yidiñ in having two distinct words *bala yugu* 'wood' and *balan buni* 'fire', while G has just *yugu* 'wood, fire'—*bala* when referring to 'wood' and *balan* for 'fire'—following the pattern of Warrgamay and Nyawaygi. (Note though that the actual forms are quite different in the neighbouring languages: Yidiñ *jugi* 'wood', *buri* 'fire'; Warrgamay *wagun* 'wood, fire'; Nyawaygi *janu* 'wood, fire'.)

A geographical pattern is also found with terms for 'cloud', 'sky', and 'rain', as set out in table 12.2. Note that, across all dialects of Dyirbal, 'cloud' and sky' are gender IV, shown by noun marker *bala*, while 'rain' is gender II, shown by *balan*.

We see that *jurra* is 'cloud, sky' in JG (and in Warrgamay) but just 'cloud' in MU; in addition, Y *ŋunara* 'cloud, sky' is surely cognate with W *ŋuna:* 'cloud'. The form for 'sky' in NWM, *yugan* (presumably cognate with Yidiñ *yigan*, the first vowel having assimilated to the preceding semi-vowel), occurs as 'rain' in G and in Warrgamay and Nyawaygi. Note that *yugan* does not occur, with either meaning, in the intermediate area, consisting of U, Y, and J. In Nyawaygi there are again separate forms for 'cloud' and 'sky' (and Nyawaygi *magurr* 'cloud' is presumably related to *magurr* 'fog' in M).

Another interesting cross-dialectal distribution concerns terms for 'star (generic)', 'morning star', and 'evening star', as set out in table 12.3. (These are all gender II, *balan*,

TABLE 12.2. Terms for 'cloud', 'sky', and 'rain'

	'cloud'	'sky'	'rain'
Yidiñ	marun	yigan	gaba:n
Dyirbal			
N	ŋulban	yugan	wuRuñ
W	ŋuna:	yugan	gamba:
M	jurra	yugan	gambal
U	jurra	ŋuruy	gambal
Y	ŋunara		gambal
J	jurra		gambal
G	jurra		yugan
Warrgamay	jurra		yugan
Nyawaygi	magurr	ŋurul	yugan

TABLE 12.3. Terms for stars

	'star (generic)'	'morning star'	'evening star'
Yidiñ	bijugan	bunu	jinagambil
Dyirbal			
N	dulubu	bunu	
W	dulubu	gayira	
M	giñja	dulubu	yabulga
AJ	giñja	yabulga	
U	giñja	gayira	yabulga
G	yirrginjarra	yabulga	
Warrgamay	yirrginjara	yabulga	?

in Dyirbal.) It can be seen that there are separate terms for 'morning star' and evening star' just in the M and U dialects of Dyirbal, and in Yidiñ. The varied meanings of some of the forms is interesting:

- *dulubu* is used for 'all the stars' in NW, and for 'morning star' in M
- *gayira* covers both 'morning star' and 'evening star' in W, but is just 'morning star' in U
- *yabulga* covers both 'morning star' and 'evening star' in AJG, but is just 'evening star' in MU. (*Yabulga* was given for 'morning star' in Warrgamay; the term for 'evening star' was not obtained.)

The final example of semantic variation is in table 12.4. Note that terms for 'fish (generic)' and 'black bream (or sooty grunter, *Hephaestus fuliginosus*)' are gender I, *bayi*, in Dyirbal, while 'ground' is gender IV, *bala*. Mollie Raymond, major consultant for N, volunteered that black bream only appeared in N territory quite recently, which is why in N it is only referred to by the general label.

Guya is the generic term for 'fish' in many Australian languages (see Dixon 2002a: 103). It occurs in northern (NWM) and southern (G) dialects of Dyirbal, but not in A or J. There could possibly have been taboo replacement here, with *jabu*, the term for 'black bream' in M, being used instead of *guya* in J and southern A. However, Warrgamay has *ja:bu* for 'fish (generic)'. The long vowel shows that this is an old form. *Jabu* in Dyirbal might have been borrowed from *ja:bu* in Warrgamay, but not vice versa (or there might have been no borrowing here).

Guyu, in northern A and Warungu, plainly developed from *guya* by vowel assimilation; and *yu* in Mbabaram is likely to be a reduction from *guyu*.

TABLE 12.4. Terms for 'fish (generic)', 'black bream', and 'ground'

	'fish (generic)'	'black bream'	'ground'
Yidiñ	\<no term>	gulugulu	jabu
Dyirbal			
N	guya	guya	jabu
W	guya	malaguma	jabu
M	guya	jabu	jigay
northern A	guyu	bugal	jigay
southern A	jabu	bugal	jigay
J	jabu	bugal	jigay
G	guya	mugil	jigay
Warrgamay	ja:bu	mu:gil	gayi
Warungu	guyu	mugil	ñani
Mbabaram	yu	—	abu

The fascinating feature of table 12.4 is that *bayi jabu* occurs in both the 'fish (generic)' and 'black bream' columns while *bala jabu* is 'ground' for NW; in addition, *jabu* is 'ground' in Yidiñ. And Mbabaram has *abu* 'ground', the initial *a* showing that it evolved from a disyllabic form with a long vowel in the first syllable; this could well have been *ja:bu*.

We have *jabu/ja:bu* for terms describing fishes, and *jabu(/ja:bu?)* for 'ground'. The difference in meaning is so great that we should perhaps regard this as an accidental resemblance. There is, however, a further occurrence of *jabu*, which might be relevant.

All Dyirbal dialects have *bala bilmba* 'hole in the ground', but J also has *bala jabu*, which is usually given the same gloss. (This has a different gender from *bayi jabu* 'fish (generic)' in J.) Some fish do hide in holes in the ground, at the bottom of a river or under submerged roots. Maybe this is a link?

On detailed investigation I was told that the two nouns in J have a degree of substitutability but that *bala bilmba* is preferred to describe a natural hole, or one that has been there for a long time (the sort of hole which fish might hide in), while *bala jabu* would be used for a newly-dug hole (including a grave). So this is no help at all in resolving the question of whether *ja(:)bu* as 'fish' and *ja(:)bu* as 'ground' are related, or are simply homonyms.

Having discussed grammatical variation in the last chapter, and lexical variation in this one, we focus on phonology in the following chapter.

This chapter is a greatly shortened and revised version of a 1982 paper 'Problems in Dyirbal dialectology'.

13

Compensatory phonological changes

13.1 Introduction

The Ngajan (N) dialect of Dyirbal has gained one contrast in its phonology and lost another. This chapter describes the series of changes through which N developed a distinction between short and long vowels, and those through which it neutralised the opposition between two rhotic phonemes. These changes are related and, in a sense, complementary. It is interesting to compare N with the adjoining Waribarra Mamu (Wari, or W) dialect which has also innovated long vowels—although not so many as N—but has retained the rhotic contrast.

It will be suggested that the continuant rhotic naturally engendered length on a preceding vowel and that this length then became the contrastive feature, with the continuant and trill rhotics falling together as a single phoneme. Vowel length then spread both (i) within Ngajan, through the replacement of syllable-final *l* and *y* by length on the preceding vowel; and (ii) by diffusion of some of the Ngajan changes into the Wari dialect.

Yidiñ, to the north of N, has a length distinction in vowels. This is also a recent innovation, but by a completely different set of changes from those in N. Section 14.6 surveys vowel length as an areal phenomenon in the Cairns Rainforest region, and considers whether this contrast developed first in N or in Yidiñ.

The present chapter focuses on changes which have taken place in N and in W. For Ngajan we take account of vocabulary in both the everyday style (N) and the Jalnguy avoidance style (Nja). It was not possible to gather any Jalnguy forms for Wari, so here we only have everyday style lexemes (W).

We can first introduce the changes which have taken place:

(I) **N shows a length contrast for all three vowels, *a*, *i*, and *u*.** Illustrating this with cognates from dialects which have not undergone change:

	N	other dialects	
(1)	jaja:	jajar	'bird nest/roost'
(2)	jaja	jaja	'baby'
(3)	ba:ga-	balga-	'hit'
(4)	baga-	baga-	'spear'
(5)	bana-:ñ	bana-ñ	'break off-FUTURE'
(6)	jana-ñ	jana-ñ	'stand-FUTURE'

(II) N lacks a rhotic contrast. Other Dyirbal dialects have two rhotic or grooved-tongue phonemes: /rr/, which is generally pronounced as an apico-alveolar tap or trill, and /r/, which is a semi-retroflex continuant, with the tongue tip turned back to touch the hard palate. Ngajan has neutralised this distinction and has a single rhotic phoneme, pronounced as an apico-alveolar tap or continuant, which I write as /R/ (to avoid confusion with /rr/ and /r/ in other dialects). Compare:

	N	other dialects	
(7)	mugaRu	mugarru	'fish net'
(8)	magaRa	magara	'skin off dead person'
(9)	maguRa	magurra	'*Ficus variegata* tree'
(10)	damaRi	damarri	'centipede'
	Nja	Mja, Jja	
(11)	gumaRi	gumari	'blood'

These two changes—the gain of a length contrast in vowels, and the loss of a rhotic contrast—are intertwined. There is a real sense in which one change compensates for the other. However, the interrelation between the two changes is not simple. Note that W, the next dialect south of N, has also gained a length contrast for all three vowels, but it has not lost the rhotic contrast. Thus:

	N and W	other dialects	
(3)	ba:ga-	balga-	'hit'
(4)	baga-	baga-	'spear'

but

	N	Wari and other dialects	
(12)	ju:Ra-	jura-	'crawl'
(13)	juRa-	jurra-	'rub'

The remainder of this chapter examines in detail the phonological changes that have occurred in N and W, and looks at their possible origin and diffusion. (Note that, so as not to clutter the presentation, cognates are generally quoted just for the five dialects for which most information is available: N, W, M, J, and G.)

13.2 Changes in root forms

13.2.1 Ngajan

Long vowels in Ngajan have two main sources (one further, minor, source will be described in section 13.4.1, on the reflexive derivational affix).

(a) **Length associated with the loss of** *r, l,* **or** *y* **at the end of a syllable.** For example:

(14) *r*   MJG marbu   N ma:bu   'louse'
(15)   MJ ŋamir   N ŋami: 'hungry'
(16) *l*   MJG gulgu   N gu:gu   'brought together'
(17)   MJG bulal   N bula: 'firefly'
(18) *y*   MJG wayñji-   N wa:ñji-   'move up'
(19)   MJG buybu-   N bi:bu-   'spit at'
(20)   MJG burrubay   N buRuba: 'a boil'
(21)   M   ñurruy   N ñuRi: 'snot, nasal mucus'

For a syllable that ended in *r* or *l* the vowel retains its quality and is lengthened when the *r* or *l* is dropped. With *y* the situation is slightly different: here *ay* becomes *a:*, as in (18) and (20), but *uy* becomes *i:*, as in (19) and (21). That is, in development from *uy*, the quality of the resulting vowel is determined by the quality of the semi-vowel *y*, not of the original syllabic nucleus, *u*. (No words in Dyirbal contain *i* followed by a syllable-closing *y*.)

That is, we get, in N:

Vl > V: / –C, –#
Vr > V: / –C, –#
ay > a: / –C, –#
uy > i: / –C, –#

The change takes place at the end of a syllable, that is, before C, the initial consonant of the following syllable, or #, a word boundary.

The examples given have all involved change (a) in the first or last syllable of a word. The majority of Dyirbal roots do consist of just two syllables (there are no monosyllables, except for two interjections, ŋa 'yes', ŋu 'alright' and four reduced forms of noun markers—see (5) in chapter 2). Some roots do consist of three or more syllables, but whereas consonant clusters are common between the first and second vowels of a root, they are quite rare between second and third (or third and fourth) vowels. I know of a handful of forms in M, J, or G that have a cluster beginning with *r*, *l*, or *y* between second and third vowels, but for only two of these is an N cognate attested. In each case change (a) has applied: Mja *mugilbarram*, Nja *mugi:baRam* 'bee' and M *burraymbun*, N *buRa:mbun* 'moss (Usnea)'.

Change (a) can apply twice in a single word, in both initial and final syllables. For example:

(22) MJ   jalgur   N   ja:gu: 'meat'
(23) MJG   yalgay   N   ya:ga: 'road, track, path'
(24) MJG   jurgay   N   ju:ga: 'sibling'
(25) Mja, Jja galgul   Nja ga:gu: 'vine'
(26) MJ   milgir   Nja mi:gi: 'brand new'

Note that the apico-alveolar rhotic, *rr* (which is a trill or a tap) behaves differently from the semi-retroflex continuant *r*. Rhotic *rr* is not lost in N, and the preceding vowel is not lengthened. For example:

(27) WMJ gurrga   N guRga   'neck'
(28) MJG digirr   N digiR   'headache'

(b) Lengthening of the vowel in the first syllable of a word, when followed by syllable-initial r; the rhotic is retained. Compare:

(12) WM   jura-   N   ju:Ra-   'crawl'
(13) MJG   jurra- N   juRa-   'rub'

(29) WMJG buru   N   bu:Ru   'ground grub'
(30) WMJG burru   N   buRu   'elbow'

(31) WMJG yara   N   ya:Ra   'man'
(32) MJG yarra   Nja yaRa   'fishing line'

Note that no vowel lengthening takes place before syllable-initial *l*, *y* (or *rr*). N is like other dialects in the forms *mala* 'hand', *baya-* 'sing', etc. (see also (17) and (21) above).

Change (b) applies only in the initial syllable of a word, and can be stated:

Vr > V:R / #C–V

Examples (8) and (11) above illustrate words with a vowel in the second syllable, followed by a syllable-initial *r*, which have not been lengthened in N (there are several dozen other examples of this type).

Pairs (12)/(13), (29)/(30), and (31)/(32) illustrate minimal pairs in M, J, and G distinguished only by *r/rr* at the beginning of the second syllable; corresponding to this, N has a length contrast in the first syllable. If there were any minimal pairs in M, J, or G distinguished only by *r/rr* at the beginning of the third (or fourth) syllable then these should fall together in N; (7–9) illustrate forms with close similarities, but there is in each case a vowel difference. I do know of one such pair in southern dialects: J and G have *gaburra* 'candlenut tree (*Aleurites moluccana*)' and *gabura* 'bolly wood tree (*Litsea leefeana*)'. N retains *gabuRa* 'bolly wood tree' but has a different lexeme *ŋabala* 'candlenut tree'.

A productively reduplicated form is made up of two phonological words, and here change (b) can operate in the first syllable of each part. For example, WMJG *bara-*, N *ba:Ra-* 'to punch' becomes, when reduplicated, WMJG *bara-bara-*, N *ba:Ra-ba:Ra-*. (Compare this with forms involving what is called 'inherent reduplication'. These constitute one phonological word, and change (b) applies only in the first syllable; for example M *buruburuŋgurr*, N *bu:RubuRuŋguR* 'wart', and M *wiriwiri*, N *wi:RiwiRi* 'wrinkle'.)

Changes (a) and (b) can both apply to the same word. For example:

(33) MJG burujingal   N bu:Rujinga: 'rufus fantail bird'
(34) MJG giray   N gi:Ra: 'mother of new-born child'

The change under (a), as it concerns *r*, clearly interrelates with change (b), suggesting a sequence of simple phonological changes in N:

(i)   a vowel in an initial or final syllable was lengthened before *r*;
(ii) *r* was lost when it both followed a long vowel and came at the end of a syllable (that is, when it was followed by another consonant, or by a word boundary, but not when it was followed by a vowel);
(iii) *r* and *rr* then fell together as a single rhotic *R*.

Thus:

original form, as in other dialects	Change (i)	Change (ii)	Change (iii)
(14) marbu	ma:rbu	ma:bu	—
(15) ŋamir	ŋami:r	ŋami:	—
(12) jura-	ju:ra	—	ju:Ra-
(13) jurra-	—	—	juRa-
(27) gurrga	—	—	guRga
(28) digirr	—	—	digiR
(9) magurra	—	—	maguRa

This is a plausible scenario. Vowels often do have a phonetically long variety before a rhotic continuant (see Dixon 1981a: 18 on Warrgamay). In fact, (i) could have been an allophonic statement, conditioned by the presence of a following *r*, which only became phonologically significant when *r* was lost, under (ii). Change (iii) is itself fairly natural, since after (i) and (ii) had applied *r* and *rr* were in almost complementary distribution: *rr* would have occurred immediately follow-ing a short vowel in an initial syllable, as in (27) and (13), or at the end of a word, as in (28), while *r* would have occurred after a long vowel in an initial syllable, as in (12). The only environment in which both *r* and *rr* could have occurred is after the (short) vowel in a non-initial syllable, as in (8) and (9), and—as already mentioned—there appear to have been very few minimal pairs distinguished only by *r/rr* in this environment. The functional load of the *r/rr* contrast would—after changes (i) and (ii)—have been very low, and it is natural that the contrast should have been lost in N.

The critical phonetic distinction between the two rhotics in dialects other than N is that *rr* is pronounced further forward, on the alveolar ridge, while for *r* the tongue makes contact with the hard palate, at the back of the alveolar ridge. A concomitant feature is that *rr* is usually a tap or a flap, while *r* is a rhotic continuant. The single rho-tic *r* in Ngajan is articulated at the alveolar ridge, like *rr* in other dialects; it may be a continuant or a tap.

It is also interesting to note that in N (but in no other dialect) the phoneme /l/ can have a semi-retroflex rhotic continuant allophone [ɽ] in the environment /u/–/u/. For example, /dulubu/ 'star' can be [dulubu] or [duɽubu]. That is, /l/ can in this environment sound like /r/ in other dialects. It appears that the pro-nunciation of /l/ has moved to 'fill' the phonetic gap left by the disappearance of /r/ from N.

The putative diachronic changes (i), (ii), and (iii) provide a plausible explanation for the evolution of vowel length as it relates to an original *r*, in change (a). But, besides *Vr* > *V:* / –C, –#, we also get *Vl* > *V:* / –C, –# and *Vy* > *V:* / –C, –#, and there is no lengthening of any vowel before a syllable-initial *l* or *y*, as there is before syllable-initial *r*. We return to this in section 13.6.

13.2.2 Wari

The length distinction is well attested in W, but it has a slightly lower functional load than in N. All long vowels in the W dialect come from:

(a′) **Length associated with the loss of r or l from the end of any syllable, or the loss of y from the end of a non-final syllable.** That is:

Vl > V: / –C, –#
Vr > V: / –C, –#
ay > a: / –C
uy > i: / –C

The W forms corresponding to (14)–(16) and (18)–(19) are thus identical with those in N; that is, *ma:bu, ŋami:, gu:gu, wa:ñji-, bi:bu-.* (However, (17) 'firefly' is *bulal* in W, an exception to the rule.)

W differs from N in retaining *y* at the end of a word, as in

(20′) WMJG burrubay   N buRuba: 'a boil'
(21′) WM   ñurruy   N ñuRi: 'snot'

and

(23′) MJG yalgay   W ya:gay N ya:ga: 'road, track, path'
(24′) MJG jurgay   W ju:gay N ju:ga: 'sibling'

W retains the rhotic contrast and does not have a long vowel before syllable-initial *r*, as N does through change (b). For (12)/(13) and (29)/(30), W has *jura-/jurra-* and *buru/burru*, again the same as M and different from N. (No W cognate is known for 'fishing line' in (32).)

We suggested that in N the change *Vr > V: / –C, –#* could be explained in terms of (i) *V > V: / –r*, and (ii) *r > ø / V:–C, V:–#*. This seemed plausible since (i) occurs independently in N. But (i) does not apply in W, and this explanation is thus not appropriate for that dialect.

We return to this below. But first, it is appropriate to investigate how the phonological changes relate to morphological processes in Dyirbal.

As stated in section 1.3.1, the dialect referred to as 'P' (probably Jirri-barra Mamu) is known only from a list of 137 words headed 'the Mourilyan language' in an 1884 letter from 'Christy Palmerston, explorer' to anthropologist A. W. Howitt. Ten of these words appear to show long vowels. Some have the same form as in W and N. For instance, 'large cuts about the body, meinkah' is likely to be *mi:nga*, the word for cicatrices in NW (MJG have *muynga*). And 'angry, ahmee' is probably in fact *ŋami:* 'hungry' in NW (MJ have *ŋamir*). Interestingly, P appears to be like N, and unlike W, in showing *ay > a:* at the end of a word; there is 'hair, moorah', presumably *murra:* like N (WM have *murray*), and 'road, yackah' is likely to be *ya:ga:*, as in N (whereas W has *ya:gay* and M *yalgay*, as in (23′)). This suggests that P territory may have adjoined that of N (perhaps north of the present town of Innisfail).

13.3 Changes relating to nominal morphology

Within the inventory of derivational and inflectional suffixes to nouns and adjectives which are attested for N and/or W (see section 11.1) we find MAJY *-ŋaŋgay* 'without'. This behaves in a regular fashion, becoming *-ŋaŋga:* in N but remaining *-ŋaŋgay* in W. (No other suffix, for N or W, ends in *r*, *l*, or *y*.)

Generally, nominal derivational (including genitive) and inflectional suffixes are simply added to base forms, including those ending in a long vowel. For instance: the absolute form of 'pademelon wallaby (*Thylogale stigmatica*)' is *gubar* in M and *guba:* in NW; the dative-allative forms are *gubar-gu* and *guba:-gu* respectively.

The only complication arises with ergative/instrumental or locative inflection onto a root which originally ended in *r*, *l*, or *y*. This was fully described in section 11.1.6, and exemplified in table 11.1 there. Final-*r* and final-*l* forms can be illustrated with *gubar/guba:* 'pademelon wallaby' and *jagal/jaga:* 'cheek':

(35)

	absolutive	ergative	absolutive	locative
M	gubar	gubaru	jagal	jagara
W	guba:	gubaru	jaga:	jagara
N	guba:	guba:-Ru	jaga:	jaga:-Ra

In W, we get *Vr/Vl > V:* in absolutive form but the ergative/locative remains unchanged (the same as in MJG), without any long vowel. N has a long vowel in ergative/locative forms. Note that this is not an instance of a vowel being lengthened before syllable-initial *r*—change (b)—since this only applies in the first syllable of a word; see (8) and (11). What is happening here is that N is simply adding ergative/instrumental *-Ru* and locative *-Ra* to the absolutive form of the word, after the long vowel, just as happens for dative-allative *-gu* and all other nominal suffixes.

It can be seen that, through this change, N has a maximally simple process of ergative/locative inflection for a stem ending in a long vowel (which descends from an original *r* or *l*): simply add *-Ru/-Ra*. In other dialects, the inflection involves the addition of *-ru/-ra* and also a deletion (of stem final *l* or *r* in M, J, and G, and of vowel length in W).

Forms ending in rhotic *rr* did not give rise to long vowels. 'Eel-catching basket' is absolutive *yiŋgarr* in MW, *yiŋgaR* in N, and locative *yiŋgara* in MW, *yiŋgaRa* in N.

In dialects other than N, two roots that differed only in final *rr/r* would be indistinguishable in ergative and locative inflections. Suppose we had *babar* and *babarr* in M, both would have locative *babara*. In W the root forms would be *baba:* and *babarr*, and again both locatives would be *babara*. But in N *baba:* (from *babar*) would have locative *baba:Ra*, while *babaR* (from *babarr*) would have a different locative, *babaRa*. (I know of no such minimal pair, but the theoretical possibility is still of interest.)

In M, J, and G, forms differing only in final *l/r* (for example, *babal*, *babar*) would also have the same locative, *babara*. For these words, both root form and also locative/ergative would fall together in N and in W: root *baba:*, locative *babara* in W, *baba:Ra* in N.

In section 11.1.6 there was illustration of nominals in N ending in a long vowel which comes from *Vy*. For instance, with 'spear' we find:

(36)

	absolutive	ergative/instrumental
WMMJG	baŋgay	baŋgay-ju
N	baŋga:	*both* baŋga:-ju *and* baŋga:-Ru *have been heard*

As described in section 11.1.6—and shown in table 11.1—within the collected corpus, nominals in N with a final *-i:* from an original *-uy* all take *-Ru/-Ra*. For those with a final *-a:* from an original *-ay*, some were given with *-ju/-ju*, some with *-Ru/-Ra*, and some—like 'spear'—were given at different times with both.

It appears that the original *-ju/-ja* inflection on these forms is in the process of being replaced by *-Ru/-Ra*, an analogic change. If *-ju/-ja* were maintained, a speaker of N would have to memorise, for each root that ended in a long vowel, which of *-ju/-ja* and *-Ru/-Ra* it takes. (This relates to whether the long vowel developed from *y* or from *l* or *r*. But speakers are generally not aware of the diachronic changes which led up to the present-day state of their language.)

If *-ju/-ja* were fully replaced by *-Ru/-Ra*, N would have the straightforward rule: for all roots ending in a long vowel, simply add ergative/instrumental *-Ru* and locative *-Ra*. The analogic replacement of *-ju/-ja* by *-Ru/-Ra* is well advanced. Most roots with a final long vowel derived from vowel-plus-*y* take *-Ru/-Ra*. Within the corpus, just some of the most common roots, such as *ya:ga:* 'road', *banga:* 'spear', and also *nanga:* 'stone', take *-ju/-ja,* or alternate *-ju/-ja* with *-Ru/-Ra*.

As will be discussed in section 13.5 below, there are exceptions to the rules—a number of nominal roots in N and W which end in *r* or *l*, and some in N which end in *y*. Their inflections were dealt with in section 11.1.6.

13.4 Changes relating to verbal morphology

The different dialectal forms of verbal suffixes are generally explainable in terms of change (a). We can repeat relevant parts of paradigms for applicative and reciprocal derivations, from section 11.4:

(37)	applicative		reciprocal	
	<u>-a-y</u>	<u>-l</u>	<u>-a-y</u>	<u>-l</u>
N	-:m(b)a-l	-:m(b)a-l	-:baRi-y	-:baRi-y
W	-ym(b)a-l	-:m(b)a-l	-ybarri-y	-:barri-y
MJG	-ym(b)a-l	-lm(b)a-l	-ybarri-y	-l(n)barri-y

For both of these suffixes, the conjugation marker *l,* as a syllable closing segment, is replaced by vowel length in N and W. The conjugation marker *y* (where it occurred, on *-y* conjugation stems ending in *a*) is also replaced by vowel length in N, but not in W. Recall that N has *ay > a:* and *uy > i:* applying both medially and finally, whereas W shows the change only medially. Here the *y* in, say, *jana-y-ma-l* ('stand-APPLICATIVE') is word-medial but not morpheme-medial. We can perhaps more accurately specify that the changes *ay > a:* and *uy > i:* apply in W only morpheme medially. This also explains why purposive verbal inflection, in the *-y* conjugation, is *-:gu* in N but *-ygu* in W, as it is in MAJYG.

The change *Vl → V:* applies at the end of any syllable in both N and W. It replaces conjugation marker *l* by vowel length for the derivational suffix 'many S or O, in many directions', whose -l conjugation form is *-:ja-y* in NW as against *-lja-y* in MAJG. A similar change applies for antipassive in the -l conjugation, but here the picture is more complex:

(38)   antipassive   -y   -l
        NW   -na-y   -:na-y
        M   -na-y   -lŋa-y
        J   -na-y   -(l)ŋa-y
        G   -na-y   -la-y

If only NW and G forms were attested, for the –l conjugation, it would be difficult to relate them. But the allomorphs in intermediate dialects indicate that the original form was *-lŋa-y*, with the *ŋ* dropping from G (and optionally from J) and *Vl > V:* in NW. Finally, there was analogic change *-:ŋa-y > -:na-y*, with the -l conjugation suffix becoming more similar to that in the -y conjugation for NW. (This shows the value of gathering information on as many dialects as possible, when documenting a language.)

Let us now consider future tense inflection (which also covers present in NWM):

(39)   future   -y   -l
        G   -n-jay   -l-jay
        WMJ   -ñ   -ñ
        N   -ñ   -:ñ

Future in G accords to the regular Dyirbal (and, indeed, pan-Australian) pattern of conjugation marker (*n* or *l*) plus inflection (*-jay*):, this can be taken as the original form. In all dialects north of G the final *-ay* has been lost. But a word in Dyirbal cannot end in a consonant cluster, nor in a stop. The cluster of apico-alveolar nasal *n* plus lamino-palatal stop *j* in the -y column naturally contracted to a lamino-palatal nasal *ñ*, which combines features of both sounds from the original cluster. The -l class inflection *-l-jay* has also contracted to *-ñ*, perhaps by analogy.

Support for this hypothesis of change is provided by the name *guguwuñ* for the brown pigeon (*Macropygia amboinensis*) whose call is imitated as [guguwuj]. Here *ñ* is substituted for a word-final [j]. Stops are used by Dyirbal speakers word-finally in imitations of bird calls, but not in lexemes.

The question now arises why N has *-:ñ* in the -l column and *-ñ* for the -y conjugation, whereas W, M, and J have *-ñ* with all verbs. This vowel length in N is surely linked to the original conjugation marker *l* in *-l-jay*. It implies that the replacement of *l* by length predated the reduction of future to *-ñ*. That is:

(40)

	-y̱	-ḻ
original forms	-n-jay	-l-jay
change (a) in N	—	-:jay
reduction	-ñ	-:ñ

It is significant that although this part of change (a) appears to apply in both N and W (as far as roots are concerned), the future inflection in W is everywhere -*ñ*, with no trace of vowel length.

The reduction of future inflection to -*ñ* would have begun in one dialect and then diffused across the language area. It looks as if this happened after *Vl > V: / –C* applied in N, but before this change extended into W. (See the discussion in section 13.6 below.)

In contrast, negative imperative for the -l conjugation is -*l-mu* in G but just -*m* in all other dialects. That is, it is not -:*m* in N or W. We infer that the reduction -*lmu* > -*m* must have taken place earlier than the creation of long vowels in N and W. (Thus, negative imperative reduction must have preceded future tense reduction.)

Past tense is the same in all dialects: -*ñu* for the -y and -*n* for the -l conjugation. It may be that the original -l conjugation form was -*l-ñu*, as it is for the corresponding conjugation in Yidiñ. This would then have dropped its final *u*, and the cluster of apico-alveolar lateral *l* plus lamino-palatal nasal *ñ* fused to become apico-alveolar nasal *n*. The reason why the final *u* was not also dropped from the -y conjugation form -*ñu* would be to avoid it falling together with the future tense suffix -*ñ*. This explanation presupposes that future reduction -*n-jay/-l-jay* > -*ñ* happened before the putative past tense reduction.

Finally, consider the apprehensive or 'lest' inflection, which is used on the second verb in a sentence such as 'you hide, lest he see you!'. Its forms are set out in the left-hand portion of (41).

(41)

	apprehensive inflection on verbals		2 dual pronoun	'with' derivation on nominals
	-y̱	-ḻ		
G	-nbila	-lbila	ñubila	-bila
J	-mbila	-lbila	ñubala	-bila
M	-mba	-lba	ñubala	-ba
W	-mba	-:ba	ñuba:	-ba
N	-mba:	-:ba	ñuba:	-ba

Once more, the forms for apprehensive in the conservative G dialect can be taken as original. In other dialects, the conjugation marker *n* has become *m*, assimilating in place of articulation to the following *b*. In N and W, conjugation marker *l* has been replaced by vowel length, by the natural application of change (a).

A number of suffixes do have shorter forms in northern than in southern dialects. The intensifier was described in section 11.1.1. An original form -*jilu* (retained in JG), became *-julu* (in A), by assimilation, and was then shortened to *-ju* (in NWM). Unfortunately, there is no intermediate form *-bala* to mediate a similar development for apprehensive.

The fourth column of (41) shows the forms of the 2nd person dual pronoun (omitting the ubiquitous final *-ji*), from table 11.2. Assuming once again that G retained the original form, *ñubila*, we then get vowel assimilation giving *ñubala* in JM. The final vowel would have been lost in NW and then the long-vowel change applied: *ñubala > ñubal > ñuba:*. (Note that M has the longer pronoun form, *ñubala*, but the shorter apprehensive, *–mba/–lba*. The changes have applied in varying ways for different dialects.)

Length on the vowel for the -y conjugation apprehensive in N might have evolved in the same way as for 2 dual: *-mbila > -mbala > -mbal > -mba:*. Note that W just has *-mba* here, perhaps under the influence of M. (W consultants gave 2 dual sometimes as *ñuba:*, like N, and sometimes as *ñubala*, like M.)

Why then, if N has *-mba:* apprehensive on verbs from the -y conjugation, does it not have *-:ba:*, also with a final long vowel, for the -l conjugation? This dialect does permit long vowels in successive syllables, as exemplified in (22–26) and (34)—*ja:gu:* 'meat', *ya:ga:* 'road', and so on. But here the first syllable is stressed and the second unstressed. A typical apprehensive, onto a disyllabic verb, would be *bana:lba* 'lest it break', with the second and third syllables unstressed. Perhaps there is a preference not to have a form like **bana:ba:*, where a long vowel occurs in successive unstressed syllables. This is speculative, but it is an interesting speculation.

The right-hand column of (41) shows the nominal suffix 'with'. It has the same form as apprehensive, but this is likely to be coincidental (not evidence of any grammatical relationship). The point of interest is that the longer form is found in JG, and the shorter one in MWN, just like apprehensive, another instance of the tendency to shorten suffixes in northern dialects.

13.4.1 Reflexive derivation

At the beginning of section 13.2.1, a third source for long vowels in N was mentioned. This involves the reflexive verbal derivation. Its forms can be repeated from section 11.4.1:

(42)

	-y conjugation	-l conjugation	
		next but one after	elsewhere
		a stressed syllable	
N	-:máRi-y	-:Rí-y	-Rí-y
WMG	-ymárri-y	-rrí-y	-rrí-y
AJ	-ymárri-y	-yirrí-y	-rrí-y

We can take the original allomorph for reflexive on an -l conjugation verb, when next but one after a stressed syllable, to be *-yirrí-y*, as in dialects A and J. This is the only suffix in Dyirbal which is stressed on the second syllable.

It appears that the unstressed first syllable was simply omitted for G, M, and W. In N, the unstressed syllable *-yi-* was replaced by vowel length:

-yirrí-y > -:rrí-y

13.5 Exceptions to the rules

Change (a), as it concerns *r* and *l*, has applied widely but not universally in N and W. Besides examples like (14–16), where the change has applied, we also get forms where it has not applied, such as:

(43)   N buRŋgan, WMJG burŋgan 'termite sp.'
(44)   N banjaR, WMJG banjar   'simple, half-witted'
(45)   NWMJG bulbu   'grey hair'
(46)   NMJ dandal   'collar bone'

Table 13.1 indicates the extent of application of the changes. (Note that the W corpus is less extensive than that for N, and also there is no information on the Jalnguy avoidance style in W.)

It will be seen that word-finally the percentages of possible instances in which the change has applied range from 74 per cent to 87 per cent (the overall figure is

TABLE 13.1. Change (a) relating to *l* and *r*

	N and Nja			W		
	change applied	not applied	% of cases applied	change applied	not applied	% of cases applied
l at end of initial syllable	81	36	69%	37	13	74%
l at end of final syllable	54	8	87%	25	9	74%
r at end of initial syllable	14	5	74%	6	4	60%
r at end of final syllable	33	6	85%	20	3	87%

TABLE 13.2. Change (a) relating to *y*

	N and Nja			W		
	change applied	not applied	% of cases applied	change applied	applied	% of cases applied
y at end of initial syllable	17	31	35%	8	13	38%
y at end of final syllable	59	19	76%	1	37	3%

84 per cent). The figures are slightly lower for the initial syllable of a word, ranging from 60 per cent to 74 per cent (with an overall figure of 70 per cent).

When we now examine how change (a) applies for syllable-final *y*, a quite different picture emerges, as seen in table 13.2. At the end of a word the change has applied in N for 76 per cent of possible cases, a figure close to that for *l* and *r* in that position. In W there is just one word ending in a long vowel that reflects an original *y*: 'shadow, reflection' is *mali:* in N and W. (Yidiñ has *maluy* 'shadow' which is presumably the origin for the NW forms. N would have borrowed *maluy* from Yidiñ with the long-vowel change producing *mali:*, which lexeme was then borrowed into W. Note that MJG have *mulgal* 'shadow, reflection'.)

We said before that change (a) applied to *y* at the end of an initial syllable in both N and W. But it has only operated in 35 per cent (N) or 38 per cent (W) of possible instances. (Note that the W figure is based on a smaller corpus, and should not be taken to imply that this change has applied more frequently in W than in N. I know of one instance where it has applied in N and not in W—we find *gi:ŋgan* in N and *guyŋgan* in W for 'spirit of a dead woman'—and none the other way around.)

The long-vowel-creating rules have applied in regular fashion to grammatical words, with just a couple of exceptions. We can first list the regularities:

- Particle 'couldn't do it' is *ŋa:Ra* in N, *ŋara* in WMAG.
- For non-absolutive forms of gender I noun markers in NW, final *ul > u:*. For example, ergative *baŋgu:* in NW, *baŋgul* in MAJG.
- For locative verb marker, final *ay > a:* just in N. For instance, *bala:* in N, *balay* in WMAJG.
- Suffixes to noun and verb markers include *-bayji* 'downhill' and *-balbu* 'downriver' in MJG. These are *-ba:ji* and *ba:bu* in both N and W.
- The 2nd person plural is *ñurray* in M and W, *ñuRa:* in N.
- The interrogative/indefinite 'when, some time' is *miñay* in WMJ, *miña:* in N.

We have inferred that the changes *ay > a:* and *uy > i:* applied only within a morpheme in W, not at the end of a word or before a morpheme boundary. The 1st person dual disharmonic pronoun (used when the two people are one or three generations apart) is *ŋanaymba* in M and, as expected, *ŋana:mba* in N. The form in W is *ŋanaymba*. We can suggest that, a short time in the past, this pronoun was constructed from *ŋanay* (which is likely to be related to 1pl *ŋana*) plus suffix *-mba* (which is probably related to nominal suffix *-ba* 'with'). The sequence *ay* would have come before a morpheme boundary and this would explain why, in W, it was not replaced by a long vowel.

One of the most frequent words in the language is 1st person singular genitive *ŋaygu* 'my', which occurs in all dialects. This might have been expected to become *ŋa:gu* in N and W, but it remains *ŋaygu*. The most common words are typically exceptions to rules of diachronic change.

13.5.1 Some reasons for the exceptions

One possible explanation for why a putative phonological change has not applied to a certain word is that the word was borrowed into the language after the change had taken place in that part of the vocabulary. This undoubtedly explains some of the exceptions.

There are a fair number of words for which N agrees with Yidiñ, and differs from other Dyirbal dialects. For some of them, change (a) has applied in N, and they are likely to be loans to N from Yidiñ before long vowels evolved in N. These include (note that (49) and (50) are Jalnguy lexemes, in Yidiñ, N, and M):

	Yidiñ	N			
(47)	gujal	guja:	WMJ	muygam	'pregnant'
(48)	jalmbul	ja:mbu:	WMJ	maru	'mud'
(49)	mulñarri	mu:ñaRi	M	muyñarri	'bark blanket'
(50)	ŋalbu	ŋa:bu	M	ŋarmbu	'mother'

(For (49) and (50), I at first thought that N had undergone an irregular shift, since if change (a) applied to the M forms we would get *mi:ñari* and *ŋa:mbu*. But the N forms do, of course, relate to Yidiñ cognates in this case, and not to M.)

There are also a number of cognates for which change (a) has not applied in N. These may be loans from Yidiñ into N after the time at which syllable-final *r*, *l*, or *y* were replaced by vowel length in N. For example (note that (55) are Jalnguy lexemes, in Yidiñ, N, M, and J):

(51)	Yidiñ, N milga	MJG gubaguba	'pearl shell'
(52)	Yidiñ, N malgumalgu	MJ ralu	'sound of a bell'
(53)	Yidiñ gambur, N gambuR	M majila	'white clay'
(54)	Yidiñ wujar, N wujaR	W wujarr, M magurr	'fog'
(55)	Yidiñ murjañ, N muRjañ	M murjañ, J yurigan	'clothing'

For (54) it is likely that the form was borrowed by N from Yidiñ *(r* becoming *R),* and then by W from N (the rhotic *R* in N is phonetically closer to *rr* than to *r* in W, and so becomes *rr* in W). For (55), the form may have been borrowed from the Jalnguy style of Yidiñ into Nja, and thence into Mja (here the M rhotic does correspond to the Yidiñ rhotic, *r*).

Recent loans from English—which were not counted in the figures for tables 13.1 and 13.2—do not contain long vowels, but do involve some instances of syllable-final *y* and *l*; for example, *baybu* 'pipe', *mayŋgu* 'mango', *milgi* 'milk', and *jalgi* 'sulky (two-wheel, one-horse vehicle)'. Borrowings from English plainly took place after operation of the long-vowel-creating rules.

Some apparent exceptions can be explained in terms of contractions:

- 'Head hair' is *jilmurray* in Mja and *jilmuRa:* in Nja, with the long-vowel change having applied to the final *ay* but not to the medial *il*. In section 6.4, we speculated that this word may have been a shortening of *jili-murray*, with the contraction having followed application of the long-vowel rule.
- A similar example concerns 'tongue', which is *jalŋgulay* in WMAJG and *jalŋgula:* in N; again, the long vowel change has applied finally but not medially. This word is likely to be a reduction of *jalañ-gulay* (*jalañ* is 'tongue' in Warrgamay; *gulay* is of unknown origin). Once more, the reduction must have followed application of the long-vowel rule.

However, only a portion of the 'exceptions' to change (a) in N are explainable as post-change-(a) borrowings, or as recent contractions. Some may be recent borrowings from other Dyirbal dialects, but it is unlikely that all can be accounted for in this way. Nevertheless, change (a) as it affects *l* and *r* in both N and W, and as it affects word-final *y* in N, has applied in the great majority of possible forms.

The change which affected syllable-final *y* in medial position in N and W has applied to less than half the possible forms, suggesting that it may have begun rather recently, and not yet spread through the total vocabularies of these dialects.

If a word has two positions in which changes (a) and (b) could have applied, we would expect the changes to have operated in both places, or in neither. Most examples conform to this expectation. There are two long vowels in each of (22–26) and (33–34), and none in, for instance:

(56) N waymaR WMJG waymar 'restless, unsettled'

However, we also find:

(57)   N bayga: MJG baygay   'without company'
(58)   N mayŋgu: M   mayŋgur   'lignum tree (*Austromyrtus dallachyanum*)'

Here word-final *y* and *r* have been replaced by vowel length but the *y* at the end of the first syllable has been retained. This provides further support for the hypothesis that change (a), as it affected *y* in a medial syllable, took place later than the other parts of change (a), and did not penetrate right through the vocabulary.

13.6 Genesis and diffusion

I suggest the following as the most likely sequence of events to explain these facts about the evolution of long vowels in N and W, and the loss of a rhotic contrast in N.

(i) In the N dialect, vowels tended to be lengthened before *r* (a natural phonetic phenomenon) in an initial, stressed syllable, or in a final syllable:

$$V > V: / \#C- r, -r\#$$

At first, length on the preceding vowel would have been a concomitant phonetic feature, accompanying these occurrences of *r*. Gradually, the vowel length would have become the major factor, and the fact that every long vowel was followed by *r* would then have been the concomitant factor. It was natural that this (predictable) *r* should be lost from syllable-final position, where an allowed phonological word shape would result; it could not be lost from syllable-initial position, since a sequence of vowels is not permissible in Dyirbal. Thus:

(ii) Syllable-final r was lost:

$$r > ø / -C, -\#$$

Combination of change (i), in the environments $\#C-rC$ and $-r\#$, and (ii) yielded:

(a_1) $Vr > V: / -C, -\#$

And:

(b) $V > V: / \#C- rV$

The two rhotics *r* and *rr* were now almost in complementary distribution: they contrasted only between the second and third, or third and fourth, vowels of a word (recall that most words in Dyirbal are disyllabic).

(iii) It was thus natural that the rhotic distinction should be neutralised:

$$r > R, rr > R$$

Change (b) can now be restated, taking (iii) into account:

(b') Vr > V:R / #C–V

At this stage N had undergone two phonological changes—vowel lengthening and rhotic neutralisation—which almost compensated for each other. Minimal pairs such as (12)/(13) *jura-/jurra-* became *ju:Ra-/juRa-*, and (1)/(2) *jajar/jaja* became *jaja:/jaja*.

(iv) Change (a$_1$) was now extended, first to *l*, a sonorant that is phonetically very close to *r*. (It did *not* extend to *rr*, which is normally pronounced as a trill or tap in Dyirbal.) Thus:

(a$_2$) Vl > V: / –C, –#

It also extended to *y*, but at this stage only to *y* in word-final position or at a morpheme boundary (shown as M):

(a$_3$) ay > a: / –#, –M; uy > i: / –#, –M

This change affected a *Vy* sequence at the end of nominals, which are free forms (as in *baŋgay > baŋga:* 'spear') and at the end of a nominal suffix (*-ŋaŋgay > -ŋaŋga:* 'without'). Verbals are bound forms, and conjugation marker *y* triggered change (a$_3$) across a root-suffix boundary (for example, *jaŋgay-gu > jaŋga:gu* 'eat-PURPOSIVE'). Further examples of *ay > a:* across a morpheme boundary in N include applicative and reciprocal in (37), and reflexive in (42). (Note that change (a$_3$) has not diffused into W.)

(v) At this stage—when N alone among Dyirbal dialects had contrastive vowel length—a reflexive allomorph on -l conjugation stems was reduced from *-yirrí-y* to *-rrí-y* in G, M, and W. It was natural that in N the loss of unstressed *-yi-* should be compensated for by lengthening of the preceding stem-final vowel:

   -yirrí-y > -:Rí-y

Reflexive allomorph *-yirri-y* reduced just to *-rri-y* (not *-rri-y)* in W, perhaps because at this stage W did not have any long vowels.

(vi) The next step would have been for changes (a$_1$) and (a$_2$) to diffuse from N into the neighbouring dialect, W. Note that neither (a$_3$) nor (b) was borrowed by W. Thus, W maintained the original rhotic distinction, as in (12)/(13) *jura-/ jurra-*.

Change (b) applied in N only in the initial syllable of a word. Thus, alongside *buru > bu:Ru*, in (29), we have *gumari > gumaRi*, in (11). A root ending in *r* such as *gubar* would originally have had ergative *gubaru*. Change (a) derived *gubar > guba:* but change (b) would not have affected the vowels in *gubaRu*.

(vii) Now, N simplified its rule for locative and ergative inflections, by simply adding -*Ru*/-*Ra* to a root ending in a long vowel, without shortening the vowel; that is, *guba:*, ergative *guba:-Ru*. (This change has not diffused into W.)

(viii) Finally, change (a) was extended, in both N and W, to apply to *y* at the end of a morpheme-medial syllable:

(a$_4$) ay > a: / –C; uy > i: / –C

That this change was relatively recent is shown by the fact that it has spread to less than half the possible lexemes, in both dialects.

   Change (a$_4$) could have first arisen in either N or W, and then spread to the other dialect. For two reasons it is perhaps most likely to have begun in N. First, N already had undergone change (a$_3$), replacing syllable-final *y* by vowel length at the end of a morpheme; this has not diffused into W. Secondly, the only example I have of a word where (a$_4$) has applied in one dialect only is N *gi:ŋgan*, WMJG *guyŋgan* 'spirit of a dead woman'.

Some of the reductions of verbal inflections, etc., discussed in section 13.4, can be dated with respect to this putative historical sequence:

(1) The reduction of negative imperative allomorph -*lmu* > -*mu* would have preceded (iv), since N did not extract a long vowel here (that is, we did not get -*lmu* > -*:mu* in N). It may well have preceded (i).

(2) The reduction of future tense allomorph -*ljay* > -*:ñ* in N would have followed (iv), since here the conjugation marker *l* did give rise to length. But it is likely to have preceded (vi), the diffusion of changes (a$_1$) and (a$_2$) into W. (Note that for other verbal affixes, conjugation marker *l* has given rise to vowel length in both N and W, as in applicative -*l-ma-l* > -*:-ma-l*.)

(3) The apprehensive inflection is likely to have reduced—in dialects north of J—by two stages: (I) -*bala* > -*bal*, (II) -*bal* > -*ba* (MW), -*ba:* ~ -*ba* (N). Stage (II) must also have followed (iv), the change *Vl* > *V:* in N, and preceded (vi), the diffusion of this change into W.

(4) The reduction of *jalañ* plus *gulay* 'tongue' to WMJG *jalŋgulay*, N *jalŋgula:*, and of *jili* plus *murray* 'head hair' to Mja *jilmurray*, Nja *jilmuRa:*, must have been very recent. That is, the *l* must have been brought into syllable-final position after completion of the changes that replaced syllable-final *l* by vowel length, in both N and W.

Of the changes discussed in this section, (i)–(vi) are likely to have applied in this order; (vii) could have applied at any stage after (iv). By the evidence of such N forms as (57) *bayga:* and (58) *mayŋgu:* (for which W cognates are not known), where rules (a_1) and (a_3) have applied, but not (a_4), (viii) must have followed (iv). The fact that it has applied to such a small fraction of the lexicon is further evidence that it was a recent change.

13.7 Conclusion

Ngajan—the most northerly Dyirbal dialect—developed a contrast between long and short vowels. It also neutralised the contrast between two rhotic phonemes. The functional gain in one case almost compensated for the functional loss in the other; only words originally distinguished by different rhotics at the beginning of a third or later syllable would fall together, and such minimal pairs are very rare (I know of only one such pair, and that is only in southern dialects.)

The occurrence of long vowels was then extended by other changes, involving *l* and *y*, and at a later stage diffused in part into the contiguous Wari dialect of Dyirbal. The genesis of the length contrast, and its extension and diffusion, can be reconstructed with a fair degree of confidence by close comparison of lexical forms and of grammatical paradigms between the various dialects of Dyirbal.

There are two main reasons for language change. It may be internally motivated, following a natural drift in the development of a language—as when vowels were lengthened before a continuant rhotic but not before a trilled rhotic in Ngajan, and the contrast of vowel length took over as the phonologically contrastive parameter, with the rhotic contrast becoming neutralised. Or the change may be due to diffusional pressure from neighbouring dialects and languages, relating to the tendency of languages spoken in a given geographical region, whose speakers have strong social contact, to become more like each other.

The next chapter examines the Cairns rainforest region as a small linguistic area, discussing how the languages spoken there have influenced each other with respect to five linguistic parameters. One of these is contrastive vowel length. We shall investigate, among other things, the relative chronology for evolution of vowel length in Ngajan and in Yidiñ.

This chapter is the revision of a 1990 paper 'Compensating phonological changes: an example from the northern dialects of Dyirbal'.

14

A study of language contact

In this chapter we look at how languages in the Cairns rainforest region have exerted structural influence on each other, examining Dyirbal, Yidiñ, Warrgamay, and also Yidiñ's northerly neighbour Ja:bugay. Five topics are studied: demonstratives and related items, in section 14.2; tense systems, in section 14.3; pronoun systems, in section 14.4; initial rhotics, in section 14.5; and contrastive vowel length, in section 14.6. In each instance, the likely direction of diffusion is examined.

But first, it will be useful to step back and examine the wider picture.

14.1 Introduction

From about 125,000 BP, Australia, Tasmania, and New Guinea formed one land mass. Archaeologists are agreed that the first humans arrived around 40,000 BP (some prefer an earlier date). It would have taken only a few thousand years for people to spread out over all habitable regions of the land mass. Rising sea levels cut off Tasmania from mainland Australia about 14,000 years ago, and the last land bridge between Australia and New Guinea (at Torres Strait) was inundated about 7,000 BP. (For fuller information and map see Dixon 1997: 87–93; 2002a: 7–12, and Lambeck and Chappell 2001.)

Australia/New Guinea divides into two geographic areas. There is mountainous territory covered with rainforest over a good deal of New Guinea, with a finger extending down the north-east coast of Australia to just beyond Cairns. The remainder of Australia is fairly flat country, with sparse forest, grasslands, or desert. As is the situation elsewhere in the world (for example, South America) we find different kinds of language, and different language contact situations, in the two geographic areas.

The earliest arrivals in Australia may have spoken one language or more than one. As people spread across the continent, languages would have split. For a few thousand years, it should have been possible to map the genetic relationships between languages using a 'family tree' model. But that time is now far in the past. For the last few tens of millennia, Australia has comprised a gigantic linguistic area, with all kinds of linguistic traits diffusing from language to neighbouring language.

Detailed examination of the approximately 250 languages spoken across Australia at the time of the European invasion (which commenced in 1788) allows us to recognise about three dozen small genetic groups (most with just two, three, or four members), probably due to language splits as people moved—in relatively recent times—into new areas in which water resources had become more abundant. There are also many isolate languages, for which no genetic sibling can with confidence be recognised. No high-level family tree can be justified.

The 'Pama-Nyungan' idea, suggesting that it is possible to relate together all or almost all Australian languages in a family tree, has been widely propagated but lacks credence. For detailed discussion see Dixon (2001: 89–98, 2002a: 44–54, 2006d).

There is evidence that—at some time in the past—there may have been living, in the Cairns rainforest region, people of a different physical type from those in the rest of Australia. (See Tindale and Birdsell 1941 and Dixon 1977a: 15–16.) Nothing is known about their languages. This rainforest region was then invaded by people of typical Australian physical type. People who speak Yidiñ have legends which say that they came from the north; this is corroborated by linguistic similarities with northerly languages. Speakers of Dyirbal have legends which specify a southerly origin; this is again supported by linguistic similarities. These two incursions met in the middle of the Cairns rainforest region. It is the aim of the present chapter to investigate some significant similarities between these languages, and—where possible—to examine the directions of diffusion. Attention is also paid to Ja:bugay, Yidiñ's northerly neighbour and close genetic relation, and to Warrgamay, spoken to the south of Dyirbal (no close genetic relationship can be shown in this case).

Details of the languages, their dialects (plus code letters used for them), and territories, are in section 1.3; see also the map.

The Ja:bugay and Yidiñ languages make up one small genetic group; they share just over 50 per cent general vocabulary (closer to 60 per cent for verbs) and have very similar grammatical systems with many cognate forms (see Dixon 1977a, 2002a: 660). No other genetic link can be established between the languages in this region; that is, they are all isolates.

As mentioned before, it is likely that the Dyirbal language was originally spoken in the southern part of its present-day territory, next to Warrgamay, and that it expanded north fairly recently. It is also likely that speakers of Yidiñ came from the north into their present-day territory rather recently. That is, Dyirbal and Yidiñ have been in contact for a relatively short time.

The similar phonological systems of the languages were summarised in section 1.4.

14.2 Demonstratives and related items

There are quite different forms for demonstratives and related items across the languages. (This is one of the few grammatical features in which Ja:bugay and Yidiñ differ.) Basic roots are:

Ja:bugay   gulu 'this', guji 'that' (and see Patz 1991: 273–5)
Yidiñ   yi-, ŋu-, yu-
Dyirbal   giña-/ŋiña-; ya(la)-, ba(la)-, ŋa(la)-
Warrgamay ñuŋga 'this', ñuŋgaji 'that' (and see Dixon 1981a: 43–5)

We focus here on the two central languages.

As described in sections 2.1 and 11.2, Dyirbal has a set of demonstratives 'here', based on *ŋiña-* in G and *giña-* in other dialects, which are used only in S and O functions. It also has paradigms of noun markers and verb markers (which cover all syntactic functions), whose initial element is one of:

(1)   ya(la)- here and visible
      ba(la)- there and visible
      ŋa(la)- not visible (may be audible, or remembered from the past)

All dialects of Yidiñ have the same three roots for demonstratives, but the meanings differ between dialects:

(2)   <u>root</u>   <u>coastal (c) dialect</u>   <u>tablelands (t) dialect</u>
      yi-   'near speaker and visible'   'visible and near speaker'
      ŋu-   'at a distance from speaker and   'visible and not near speaker'
              visible'
      yu-   'at a considerable distance from   'not visible (may be audible or
              speaker but still visible'   remembered from the past)'

That is, the c dialect codes three degrees of distance, with no contrast concerning visibility. But the t dialect of Yidiñ, which is in contiguity with the northernmost dialect of Dyirbal, has the same forms as the coastal dialect of Yidiñ but the same meanings as in Dyirbal.

This appears to be an instance of the meaning system being borrowed from Dyirbal into the adjoining dialect of Yidiñ.

14.3 Tense systems

Ja:bugay has two verbal conjugations, whose roots end in -*n* and -*l*. Yidiñ has the same two conjugations and also a third, minor, conjugation, whose roots end in -*r*. We can

TABLE 14.1. Tense systems in Ja:bugay and Yidiñ

	Ja:bugay				Yidiñ	
-n class	-l class				-n class	-l class
-n	ø	imperative			-n	ø
-ñ	-ñ	past			-ñu	-lñu
-ŋ	-l	present	}	-ŋ		-l
-na	-lna	future				
-yŋgu	-luŋ	purposive			-na	-lna

compare, in table 14.1, the inflectional systems and their forms in the corresponding conjugations for these two closely-related languages.

It is most plausible to suggest that the actual system in proto-Ja:bugay-Yidiñ was similar to that in modern Ja:bugay:

- Imperative suffixes have the same form in both modern languages and can be assumed for the proto-language.
- Past tense suffix probably had the same form as in Yidiñ, *-ñu ~ -lñu.* In Ja:bugay it has contracted to be just *-ñ* in both conjugations. That is, final *-u* has been dropped and then *-lñ* simplified to *-ñ* (there are no final consonant clusters in Ja:bugay or Yidiñ, as there are not in Dyirbal or Warrgamay).
- It is likely that *-na ~ -lna* originally marked future. In Yidiñ it has shifted its meaning to purposive (replacing the original purposive *-yŋgu ~ -luŋ*).
- Following this shift in Yidiñ, the original present tense forms, *-ŋ ~ -l,* expanded their reference to cover future as well as present tense.

Dyirbal has two verbal conjugations, the -y and -l classes. A full statement of inflections, across the dialects for which information is available, was presented in section 11.4.3. Each dialect has a two-term tense system, but in the north (dialects N, M, and W) it is past versus non-past (present/future) whereas in the south (dialects J and G) it is future versus non-future (present/past).

(3)   G | J   M, W | N

	G		J				M, W		N	
	-y	-l	-y	-l			-y	-l	-y	-l
	-ñu	-n	-ñu	-n	{	past	-ñu	-n	-ñu	-n
						present				
	-njay	-ljay	-ñ	-ñ	}	future	-ñ	-ñ	-ñ	-ñ

TABLE 14.2. Summary of tense systems in Ja:bugay, Yidiñ, and dialects of Dyirbal

	Ja:bugay	Yidiñ	Dyirbal: N, W, M dialects	Dyirbal: J, G dialects
past	-ñ	-ñu ~ -lñu	-ñu ~ -n	-ñu ~ -n
present	-ŋ ~ -l	-ŋ ~ -l	-ñ ~ (:)ñu	
future	-na ~ -lna			-ñ/-njay ~-ljay

The point of particular interest is that the northern dialects of Dyirbal have exactly the same tense system as their neighbour, Yidiñ. This is summarised in table 14.2.

One cannot be certain of whether the northern dialects of Dyirbal changed their tense system so that it became more like that in the adjacent Yidiñ language, or vice versa. All we can say for certain is that there has been change so that these neighbours came to have the same tense system. Speculatively, it is perhaps most likely that the northern dialects of Dyirbal changed to become more like Yidiñ. (Girramay has the most conservative forms. This does not automatically mean that it has the original system, although this is rather likely.)

It should be noted that the system of verbal inflections in Warrgamay is totally different. This language has no tenses at all, just a system of aspects (plus positive and negative imperative, and purposive); see Dixon (1981a: 45–7).

14.4 Pronoun systems

All dialects of Dyirbal (and Warrgamay also) have singular, dual, and plural forms of 1st and 2nd person pronouns. Full details were given in section 11.3.1.

The relative frequencies of pronouns are interesting. The number of S/A pronouns in a selection of texts from the M, J, and G dialects is:

(4)   1sg ŋaja/ŋayba—120   2sg ŋinda/ŋinba—98
      1du ŋali—57   2du ñubala/ñubila—13
      1pl ŋana—17   2pl ñurra/ñurray—6

TABLE 14.3. Subject forms of pronouns in proto-Ja:bugay-Yidiñ, in Ja:bugay and in Yidiñ

	proto-Ja:bugay-Yidiñ		Ja:bugay		Yidiñ	
PERSON	SG	NON-SG	SG	NON-SG	SG	NON-SG
1st	*ŋayu	*ŋañji	ŋawu	ŋañji	ŋayu	ŋañji
2nd	*ñundu	*ñurra	ñurra	ñurra-mba	ñundu	ñundu-ba

What is of particular significance here is that *ŋali* is by far the most common of the non-singular pronouns. In southern dialects *ŋali* is the only 1du pronoun, 'us two', while in M, W, and N it is 1du harmonic 'I and someone else from the same generation, or two generations apart'; see section 4.3.

Ja:bugay and Yidiñ have a simpler system—basically just singular/non-singular—with quite different forms from those in Dyirbal (and Warrgamay). The forms of the main four pronouns, and a reconstruction for the ancestor language proto-Ja:bugay/Yidiñ, are in table 14.3.

We can now comment on table 14.3:

- Original 1 sg *ŋayu has become ŋawu in Ja:bugay through *y* assimilating to the following *u*.
- 1 non-sg is *ŋañji* in both modern languages.
- For 2nd person, we reconstruct (by comparison with forms in other Australian languages) sg *ñundu and non-sg *ñurra for the proto-language. In Yidiñ, the original 2 non-sg form *ñurra* has been replaced by *ñundu-ba*, made up of 1 sg *ñundu* plus -*ba*, which is a nominal suffix meaning 'one of a group'; that is, 'you (singular) plus one or more others'. In Ja:bugay, *ñurra* has shifted its reference from 2 non-sg to 2 sg (a similar change to that which has applied to *you* in English). A new 2 non-sg has been created through the addition of -*mba*. This is plainly cognate with Yidiñ -*ba*. Attached to a nominal in present-day Ja:bugay -*ba* indicates 'one of a pair', but in the 2 non-sg pronoun the meaning is 'one of a group'.

Ja:bugay just has the four 1st and 2nd person pronouns shown in table 14.3. But Yidin has a fifth, 1 dual *ŋali*, for referring to 'two people, one of whom is the speaker'. Now *ŋali* is not mutually exclusive with 1 non-sg *ŋañji*, which refers to 'two or more people one of whom is the speaker'. What we find is that *ŋañji* is the unmarked non-singular 1st person form, exactly corresponding to 2 non-sg *ñunduba*. The fifth pronoun, *ŋali*, is a marked dual form, making a further optional distinction within non-singular. In diagrammatic form:

(5) 1st PERSON   2nd PERSON

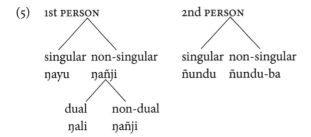

singular non-singular   singular non-singular
ŋayu   ŋañji   ñundu   ñundu-ba

      dual   non-dual
      ŋali   ŋañji

We find that *ŋali* is used much less frequently than any other pronoun. The first nine texts collected in Yidiñ showed the following instances:

(6) 1sg ŋayu forms—255   2sg ñundu forms—44
     1non-sg ŋañji forms—131   2non-sg ñunduba forms—18
     1du ŋali forms—1

Compare this with the frequency of *ŋali* forms within Dyirbal texts, shown in (4).

In Yidiñ, pronoun *ŋali* is used when it is desired to emphasise that just two people (rather than three or more) are being referred to. It is often used in a text for first reference to a pair (establishing that there are just two people involved), with *ŋañji* being used for later reference to them (see Dixon 1977a: 166; 1991a: 33).

The point of particular interest is that Yidiñ, but not Ja:bugay, has this fifth pronoun, which is used so sparingly. It is not an integral part of the pronoun system but a sort of optional extra, pretty certainly introduced into the language rather recently. (In the fullness of time, *ŋali* would be likely to become a part of the system, always used for referring to 'two' with *ŋañji* then used only for 'three or more'; see Dixon 2002a: 285–99.)

Where did it come from? Without doubt, Yidiñ borrowed *ŋali* from its southerly neighbour Dyirbal.

14.5 Initial rhotic

All the languages and dialects discussed here allow a word to begin with a stop, nasal, or semi-vowel. There are virtually no words (save onomatopoeia) commencing with the lateral.

Out of a vocabulary of *c*2,400 Yidiñ words, I recorded just one item with initial *l*, the verb *lululumba-* 'rock a baby to sleep, singing "*lu-lu-lu-lu . . .*"'. This also occurs in N; other dialects of Dyirbal use the form *yululumba-*. I know of one noun commencing with *l* in the G dialect of Dyirbal; see section 16.4.

Concerning initial rhotics, the situation varies. We can first describe the rhotic phonemes:

- Warrgamay, Yidiñ, Ja:bugay, and all dialects of Dyirbal except Ngajan, each have two rhotic phonemes:

/rr/ normally an apico-alveolar trill (sometimes a single tap)

/r/   generally an apico-post-alveolar continuant, with the tongue tip turned back to touch the anterior part of the hard palate (semi-retroflex sound)

There is some variation. In Warrgamay and Yidiñ /r/ can be a short post-alveolar trill, and in Ja:bugay it can be a post-alveolar flap. When this occurs, the two rhotics are distinguished more in terms of place than of manner of articulation.

- The Ngajan dialect of Dyirbal has a single rhotic, /R/, which is generally an apico-alveolar continuant or tap.

The possibilities for words commencing in a rhotic are shown in table 14.4.

We can ask what has happened in the N and W dialects to words that originally began with /r/ and are maintained as such in other dialects. Many such lexemes have rather specialised meanings and no N or W cognates are known; for example *riyin* 'corner of eye', *rañjarañja* 'harsh voice', *ralirali* 'be shaky on feet'. Others have non-cognate correspondences; for example MAJU *riji*, N *muyŋiRiñ*, W *muyŋiriñ* 'mosquito' (G has *diyu*); MJG *rawurray*, N *mayŋiR*, W *mayŋirr* 'lazy'.

There are however, just a few cognates between N and W and southern dialects:

(7) (a) 'bird's wing'   MJG rigul   N   yigu   r > y /–i
     (b) 'forked stick'   MJG raba   NW daba   r > d /–a
     (c) 'ankle bone'   MJG ragul   N   dagul   r > d /–a
     (d) 'heart'   MJG rulgu   NW dulgu   r > d /–u
     (e) 'youth'   MJG rugun   N   wugun   r > w /–u

TABLE 14.4. **Possibilities for words commencing in a rhotic**

	INITIAL /rr/	INITIAL /R/	INITIAL /r/
Ja:bugay	none		none
Yidiñ	none		none
Dyirbal dialects			
N		none	
W	none		none
M, A, J, U, G	none		a few (*c*3% of lexicon)
Warrgamay	none		a few (*c*1% of lexicon)

It can be seen that in (a) initial *r* was replaced by *y* before *i*, and in (b) and (c) initial *r* was replaced by *d* before *a*. When followed by *u*, there is one example of *r* being replaced by *d*, in (d), and one of it being replaced by *w*, in (e).

It is clear that the N and W dialects of Dyirbal eliminated rhotics from word-initial position so that their phonotactics would accord with that of their northerly neighbour Yidiñ.

14.6 Contrastive vowel length

The preceding chapter provided a detailed account of the development of contrastive vowel length in the N and W dialects of Dyirbal. Recent changes—of a totally different nature—have led to the development of a length contrast in Yidiñ, and in Jaːbugay. Warrgamay retains an archaic length distinction. The remaining dialects of Dyirbal do have long vowels, but only at the phonetic level.

The status of long vowels across the languages and dialects of our region of study is summarised in table 14.5. Each language and set of dialects is then provided with a characterisation.

14.6.1 Warrgamay

There is a contrast between short and long vowels just in the initial syllable of a phonological word. Minimal pairs include:

(8) badi- 'to hook a fish'   baːdi- 'to cry, weep'
     jurra 'cloud, sky'   juːrra 'to rub, wipe'
     giba 'liver'   giːba- 'to scratch'

About 10 per cent of the roots in my 920-item lexicon involve a long vowel. And on a text count, about 10 per cent of words include a long vowel.

If there is no long vowel in a word, stress goes onto the first syllable of a word with two or four syllables and onto the second syllable of a word of three or five syllables. But if there is a long vowel, this always takes stress. Compare:

(9) gagárra 'woven cane bag'   gíːbara 'large fig tree'

In a monosyllable, /uː/ can be realised as [uː] or [uwu], /iː/ as [iː] or [iyi] and /aː/ as [aː] or [aʔa]. Thus we have [guːñ] alternating with [guwuñ] 'spirit of a dead man', [yiyil] with [yiːl] 'name', [maːl] with [maʔal] 'man', etc.

The question arises of whether these 'long vowels' should be treated as phonological long vowels (a single syllable) or as being underlyingly a sequence of two phonological syllables; that is, whether as /yiːl/ or as /yiyil/. The question can be resolved by reference to the grammar.

TABLE 14.5. **Status of long vowels between languages and dialects**

Ja:bugay	phonologically contrastive (recent innovation) • mostly in open final syllable • low functional load • long vowel is not always stressed
Yidiñ t and c dialects	phonologically contrastive (recent innovation) • never in initial syllable, mostly in closed final syllable • high functional load • long vowel is always stressed
Dyirbal dialects N, W	phonologically contrastive (recent innovation) • typically in initial syllable and open final syllable • functional load medium in N, low in W • independent of stress (which is always on the initial syllable)
M, A, J, U	not phonologically contrastive • occasional phonetic realisation of vowel-plus-semivowel-plus-vowel in disyllabic word
G	not phonologically contrastive • common phonetic realisation of vowel-plus-semivowel-plus-vowel in initial syllable of a word
Warrgamay	phonologically contrastive (archaic retention) • only in initial syllable • low functional load • long vowel is always stressed

Positive imperative inflection on verbs has two allomorphs (note that verb roots end in *a* or *i*, never *u*):

- *-ya* after a disyllabic stem ending in *i*
- ø (zero) elsewhere; that is, after any stem ending in *a* or after a trisyllabic stem ending in *i*.

Now consider the positive imperative inflection of four verbs:

(10)   stem wugi-   positive imperative wugi-ya   'give'
           baba-   baba-ø   'spear'
           gungarri-   gungarri-ø 'cut'
           bu:di-   bu:di-ya   'take'

It will be seen that *bu:di-* takes allomorph *-ya*, being treated as a disyllabic form. This confirms our analysis of a long vowel as a single phonological unit.

Vowel length in the first syllable of a word is undoubtedly an ancient feature, which is retained in Warrgamay as it is in its southern neighbour Nyawaygi. There are cognate verb roots, with an initial long vowel, in a scattering of languages from the periphery of the continent, ranging from eastern Arnhem Land, in the Northern Territory, down the Queensland and New South Wales coasts from Cooktown to Sydney (see Dixon 2002a: 595, 124).

The actual phonetic length of a vowel in Warrgamay appears to depend on the following consonant (Lehiste 1970: 27)—the shortest variety is before a stop, with a slightly longer variety before a nasal, and the longest variety before the apico-post-alveolar rhotic /r/.

14.6.2 Dyirbal—N and W dialects

As described in the last chapter, N has innovated a length contrast for vowels in all syllables, and—in a related change—lost the contrast between two rhotic phonemes. Only some of the changes which have taken place in N have also applied in W. On a dictionary count, about 20 per cent of N entries include at least one long vowel, and about 12 per cent of W entries.

14.6.3 Dyirbal—J, A, U, and M dialects

There is no phonologically contrastive vowel length in these central dialects of Dyirbal. The original length in the initial syllable of a word (retained in Warrgamay) has simply been lost. Compare:

(11)	Warrgamay	jurra 'cloud, sky'	juːrra 'to rub, wipe'
	Dyirbal	jurra 'cloud'	jurra 'to rub, wipe'

These dialects do show some phonetic long vowels. Certain stressed-vowel-plus-semi-vowel-plus-identical-vowel sequences in a disyllabic word can be pronounced as a long vowel. For example:

(12)	/guwu/	[guwu] or [guː]	'nose'
	/mawa/	[mawa] or [maː]	'shrimp'
	/giyi/	[giyi] or [giː]	'this (gender I)'

The pronunciation with a long vowel is only occasionally heard. In elicitation, when a word is being cited, it is always accorded a disyllabic pronunciation. Furthermore, when a word is made longer, by the addition of a suffix, the long vowel alternative is not available. Thus /guwu-ŋga/ (nose-LOCATIVE) 'on the nose' is always [guwuŋga], never [guːŋga]. It is clear that long vowels in these dialects are purely phonetic, an infrequent realisation of *uwu*, *awa*, or *iyi* under restricted conditions.

14.6.4 Dyirbal—G dialect

Long vowels are heard more often in the G dialect. The circumstances just described for central dialects apply save that the long vowel pronunciation of a word such as /mawa/ is more common. And a long vowel may also be heard in the first syllable of a longish word. For example, the name for the northern white quandong tree (*Elaeocarpus foveolatus*) is pronounced as follows:

(13)   [juwumba] in the N, W, M, and J dialects
        generally [juːmba], sometimes [juwumba] in the G dialect

We need to ask whether the underlying form of this word in G should be /juwumba/, as in the other dialects, or /juːmba/, similar to the situation in neighbouring Warrgamay. Once again, grammatical data help us decide.

In all dialects of Dyirbal, locative inflection is *-ŋga* on a disyllabic stem ending in a vowel, and *-ga* on a longer stem ending in a vowel. For example, across all dialects the locative form of *banba* 'Moreton Bay fig tree (*Ficus watkinsiana*)' is *banba-ŋga*, and that of *bangula* 'wild cucumber' (*Trichosanthes sp.*) is *bangula-ga*. The locative allomorph used with 'northern white quandong' is, in all dialects, *-ga*. This indicates that the phonological form is consistently /juwumba/, with three syllables.

The long [uː] in G pronunciation is a phonetic realisation of /uwu/. That is, exactly the same comments apply to G as to the central dialects. The difference is that pronunciation of a phonological stressed-vowel-plus-semi-vowel-plus-identical-vowel sequence as a phonetic long vowel is more common in G than in J, A, U, and M. It is highly likely that this is due to contact with neighbouring language Warrgamay. While G retains the same phonological system as central dialects, its pronunciation involves a fair number of phonetic long vowels, making it sound more like Warrgamay.

14.6.5 Yidiñ

In all dialects of Dyirbal, primary stress goes on the first syllable of a word. This applies in N and W even though there may be a long vowel in a non-initial syllable; thus *máːbu* 'louse' and *jágaː* 'cheek'. Secondary stress goes on alternate syllables of a word (third, fifth, etc.) except that a final syllable is never stressed. A trisyllabic word thus has an initial stressed syllable followed by two unstressed syllables, e.g. JMW *mágara*, N *mágaRa* 'top layer of skin on dead human'.

In Yidiñ, if a word has no long vowels, then stress goes on the first syllable and on alternate syllables after that. But, similar to Dyirbal, stress does not go on to a final syllable which has a short vowel. Yidiñ differs from Dyirbal in that it *never* allows a sequence of two unstressed syllables in a word. To avoid this, it has a number of synchronic phonological rules which create long vowels.

Stress is assigned to the first syllable containing a long vowel. If there is no long vowel, it is assigned to the first syllable of the word. Further stresses are then assigned (recursively) to the syllable next but one before, and the next but one after, a stressed vowel. In every Yidiñ word there is alternation of stressed (S) and unstressed syllables: US(US) or SU(SU) or USU(SU) and so on. Just as there is never a sequence of two unstressed syllables, so there is never a sequence of two stressed syllables. The morphological and phonological principles of the language combine to ensure that if there are two long vowels in a word, they are separated by an odd number of syllables.

Long vowels are pervasive in Yidiñ. On a text count, about 40 per cent of words include at least one long vowel; that is, the length distinction has a high functional load. However, Yidiñ differs from Warrgamay, Ja:bugay, and the N and W dialects of Dyirbal in one very important respect—it is not appropriate to recognise long vowels in underlying forms (save for three derivational affixes and no more than a dozen lexemes). Length is introduced by one phonological rule, and then made contrastive by another rule. Basically, we have:

RULE 1. PENULTIMATE LENGTHENING
> In any word with an odd number of syllables, the penultimate vowel is
> lengthened.

For example:

(14) ROOT   mujam 'mother'   jinjalam 'grasshopper'
      ABSOLUTIVE (ø suffix)   mujam   jinja:lam
      ERGATIVE (-bu suffix)   muja:m-bu   jinjalam-bu

The trisyllabic forms *muja:mbu* and *jinja:lam* have their penultimate vowel lengthened. There is no lengthening in a disyllabic word such as *mujam* or a quadrisyllabic form like *jinjalambu*.

RULE 2. FINAL SYLLABLE DELETION
> The final syllable is deleted from a word with an odd number of syllables,
> under certain phonological and morphological conditions.

There are, basically, two circumstances in which Rule 2 applies.

(a) AFFIX REDUCTION
The preliminary statement of Rule 2 is:

$XV_1:C_1(C_2)V_2\# \rightarrow XV_{1:}C_1\#$
If (i) $XV_1C_1(C_2)V_2\#$ is an odd-syllabled word (its penultimate
     vowel will then have been lengthened by application of Rule 1);
and (ii) C_1 is one of the set of allowable word-final consonants (a
     nasal, lateral, rhotic, or *y*, not a stop or *w*);
and (iii) there is a morpheme boundary between V_1 and C_1.

We can exemplify operation of the rule from verb forms (see the paradigm in table 14.1 of section 14.3). Consider the verb *guji-* 'smell', which belongs to the -l conjugation:

(15a)   verb root   guji-
         non-past form guji-l disyllabic form; Rules 1 and 2 do not apply
         surface form   gujil

(15b)   past form   guji-lñu trisyllabic form; Rules 1 and 2 apply
         • Rule 1 applies guji:-lñu
         • Rule 2 applies guji:-l
         surface form   guji:l

Rule 1 by itself is simply a phonetic specification of vowel length. The addition of Rule 2 makes the vowel length contrastive, as shown by the minimal pair *gujil/guji:l* for the non-past/past forms of *guji-* 'to smell'.

(b) ROOT REDUCTION
Of the 1,300 or so nominal roots in my corpus of Yidiñ, the great majority decline regularly, on a simple agglutinative pattern. There are around 80 items which inflect in a special way. These can best be described by assigning to each a root whose final segment is a morphophoneme, *A*, *I*, or *U*. Compare the forms in table 14.6: 'red water' and 'black goanna' with regular roots, and 'youth', which requires the use of a morphophoneme.

Although 'youth' and 'black goanna' both have absolutive forms ending in *r*, they decline quite differently. For ergative case *gugar* drops the final *r* and adds -*du*, like other consonant-final roots, and for ablative it simply adds -*mu* to the absolutive form. In contrast, 'youth' shows a trisyllabic root before a monosyllabic affix, just like 'red water', in each case yielding a quadrisyllabic word—*gumari-ŋgu*, *gumari-mu* and *waŋari-ŋgu*, *waŋari-mu*.

TABLE 14.6. **Roots and case inflections of nouns in Yidiñ**

	'red water'	'youth'	'black goanna'
root	gumari	waŋarI	gugar
absolutive case	guma:ri	waŋa:r	gugar
ergative case	gumari-ŋgu	waŋari-ŋgu	guga:-du
ablative case	gumari-mu	waŋari-mu	guga:r-mu

But whereas 'red water' keeps the trisyllabic root in absolute form (simply lengthening the penultimate vowel to give a USU stress pattern, *guma:ri*), 'youth' drops the final vowel, producing a disyllabic absolute form, *waŋa:r*. To deal with this, 'youth' is assigned a trisyllabic root ending in morphophoneme *I*. This triggers the application of the final syllable deletion rule. We can now refine the statement of Rule 2 by expanding condition (iii) to read:

(iii') EITHER there is a morpheme boundary between V_1 and C_1

  OR V_2 is a morphophoneme, *A*, *I*, or *U*.

We then need to specify that if a morphophoneme is not deleted by Rule 2, then it is realised by the corresponding vowel; that is, *waŋarI-ŋgu* becomes *waŋari-ŋgu*, and so on.

This has provided a basic overview of how long vowels are created in Yidiñ. There are some other minor sources—(i) three derivational suffixes to verbs have allomorphs with an inherently long vowel, (ii) a syllable-final yotic deletion rule, *iy → i:* and (iii) a dozen nominals whose roots end in *a:* or *u:*. (Full details are in Dixon 1977a: 42–98; 1977b.)

It has been shown that the long vowels which occur in Yidiñ, and in the adjacent N and W dialects of Dyirbal, have quite different possibilities (see table 14.5):

- A long vowel is always stressed in Yidiñ, whereas in Dyirbal stress goes on the first syllable of a word, irrespective of whether there is a long vowel or where it is located.
- Long vowels may occur in consecutive syllables in N and W, never in Yidiñ (to avoid having consecutive stressed syllables).
- In Yidiñ, long vowels never occur in an initial syllable and are mostly found in a closed final syllable, while in N and W they occur in an initial syllable and an open final syllable (never in a closed final syllable). (Bringing Warrgamay into the picture—there can only be one long vowel in each phonological word, and it is always in the first, stressed, syllable.)
- Long vowels in N and W—as in Warrgamay and Ja:bugay—occur in the forms of roots. In N and W (and to at least some extent in Ja:bugay) it is due to recent historical changes, whereas in Warrgamay it is an ancient retention. In Yidiñ (save for three suffixes and a dozen roots with an inherent long vowel), length is generated by synchronic rules, operating on underlying forms which do not involve long vowels.

14.6.6 Ja:bugay

Ja:bugay has been less intensively studied than Yidiñ and Dyirbal, but it is clear from Patz (1991) that it shows contrastive vowel length. In Patz's vocabulary of c1,100 words, a little less than fifty involve a long vowel. On a text count, about 10 per cent of words include a long vowel.

The majority of roots with a long vowel have the form CVCV:. A few have cognates in Yidiñ.

(16) Ja:bugay wúru: Yidiñ wurú: 'river'
            dúrgu: durgú: 'mopoke owl'
            gúri: gúrriñ   'good'
            jágu: jáguy   'left hand'
            gúrra: gudá:ga   'dog'
            búru   burú:gu   'black duck'

The first two rows relate to two of the dozen roots in Yidiñ which end in a long vowel. The remainder appear to have replaced a final C or CV by vowel length, but in an ad hoc manner.

Some other roots with a long vowel in Ja:bugay relate to a form in Yidiñ without any vowel length. For example *jina:* as against *jina* 'foot' and *biri:* as against *biri* 'again'.

Stress generally goes onto the first syllable of a word in Ja:bugay, and this is maintained in a disyllabic word with a final long vowel, such as *jína:*. However, if the second syllable is closed, a long vowel there does bear stress—*gulá:y* 'these' and *gujá:y* 'those'. A long vowel in the second syllable of a trisyllabic word takes stress, as in *bundá:rra* 'cassowary'. In keeping with this, when *jína:* 'foot' takes locative suffix *-la*, stress shifts to the second syllable, *jiná:la*.

Unlike Yidiñ, Ja:bugay does have nine monosyllabic roots, for five of which longer cognates are available:

(17) Ja:bugay ju: Yidiñ   wáñju   'who'
            ñi: wáñi   'what'
            ja: wáñja   'where'
            ma: máyi   'vegetable food'
            gu: Dyirbal gúwu   'nose'

Note that for the three interrogatives the initial syllable has been lost, while for the other two final *-yi* and *-wu* have been replaced by vowel length. The other four monosyllabic roots are verbs. It appears that every word must include at least two moras. Since—as seen in table 14.1 from section 14.3—some verbal inflections just involve a syllable-closing consonant (or zero), if a verb root is monosyllabic it must involve a long vowel.

14.6.7 Chronology

The preceding chapter demonstrated how the N and W dialects of Dyirbal developed long vowels by regular changes, which must have been relatively recent. Examining the roots in Yidiñ requiring a final morphophoneme (which triggers final syllable omission), there are in most cases cognates in a neighbouring language with a regular trisyllabic root. For example:

(18)   Yidiñ waŋarI   Ja:bugay waŋari   'youth'
       gangulA   gangula   'grey wallaby'
       dumbunU   dumbunum 'scorpion'

This indicates that the changes in Yidiñ must—like those in N and W—have been fairly recent.

Yidiñ and the N dialect of Dyirbal are similar to each other in that each has created a long vowel contrast which has a significant functional load, although they have done so in completely different ways. Can we tell which set of changes came first? One possible source of information might be the forms of loans. Each borrowing took place at some point in time; this may have been before or after the application of rules which created long vowels. As described in section 13.5.1, all loan words from English into Dyirbal were very recent, after the application of long-vowel-creating rules. This also applies for Yidiñ; for example, 'necklace' is *nigi:li* (rather than **nigi:l*).

If there is a form in N which differs from the forms of this lexeme in other dialects of Dyirbal but is the same as that in Yidiñ, then it is likely to be a loan from Yidiñ. A sample is in table 14.7 (quoting absolute forms).

TABLE 14.7. **Similarities between forms in the N dialect of Dyirbal and in Yidiñ**

		From Yidiñ	Into N		Forms in adjacent dialects of Dyirbal	
1. 'bone'	tc	baba:l	N	babala	WMJUG	wurrmburr
2. 'kidney'	tc	wanga:m	N	waŋgamu	M	jibanjiban
3. 'pregnant'	tc	gujal	N	guja:	WMJU	muygam
4. 'mud'	tc	jalmbul	N	ja:mbu:	WMUAJ	maru
5. 'white clay'	tc	gambur	N	gambuR	WMU	majila
6. 'pearl shell'	tc	milga	N	milga	MUJG	gubaguba

Note that rows (3–6) are repeated from examples (47), (48), (53), and (51) from section 13.5.1. Note also that in 2 'kidney', the form in Yidiñ involves a heterorganic sequence *-ng-* while that in N has a homorganic sequence *-ŋg-*.

As exemplified by rows 1–2 in table 14.7, all borrowings from Yidiñ into N which relate to long vowels in Yidiñ appear to have taken place before the application of long-vowel-creating changes in Yidiñ.

Cognate sets 3–6 show loans into N which had an appropriate form to undergo long-vowel-creating rules in N. We see that 3–4 do have long vowels, and must have been borrowed before these rules applied, whereas 5–6 must have been borrowed after the rules applied (otherwise N would have *gambu: and *mi:ga).

A number of lexemes have the same form in Dyirbal and in the t dialect of Yidiñ, but differ in the c dialect, suggesting that they were borrowed from Dyirbal into the t dialect. For example:

(19) Dyirbal   loan into t   form in c
      ñamu   ñamu   muyŋgin   'cooked'
      burrubay   burrubay   junga   'a boil'
      (buRuba: in N)

Unfortunately, none of these would be candidates for application of the long-vowel-creating rules in Yidiñ.

Having examined loans from Yidiñ into the Ngajan dialect of Dyirbal we saw that:

- All loans which might have undergone the long-vowel-creating changes in Yidiñ appear to have been borrowed before the operation of these changes (exemplified by 1–2 in table 14.7).
- Of the loans which would be candidates for the long-vowel-creating changes in the Ngajan dialect, some (exemplified by 3–4) appear to have been borrowed before these changes applied and others (exemplified by 5–6) after.

This suggests that the long-vowel-creating changes in Ngajan are likely to have preceded those in Yidiñ (but there is no absolute certainty about this).

14.6.8 Summary

Ja:bugay, Yidiñ, and the N and W dialects of Dyirbal form a small linguistic area in which vowel length is contrastive. To the north and west of Ja:bugay was spoken Gugu-Yalanji and to the west of Dyirbal and Warrgamay was spoken Warungu (not genetically related to any of the languages discussed above). Neither of these languages has any contrastive vowel length. On the seaside, to the east of the c dialect, were spoken further dialects of Yidiñ—Guŋgay and Wañurr. These are known only from old word lists, but it does appear that they lacked long vowels. For instance, in the t and c dialects 'two' has root *jambulA*, giving absolutive (and citation) form *jambu:l*; the form was given as *jambula* in both Guŋgay and Wañurr.

Contrastive vowel length has its highest functional load in the Ngajan dialect of Dyirbal and in the t and c dialects of Yidiñ. The contrast plays a lesser role in Jaːbugay, to the north of Yidiñ, and in W, to the south of Ngajan. (We saw in the last chapter that within Dyirbal the contrast must have evolved in N and then diffused in part into W.) That is, it gradually fades off, being absent from Jaːbugay's neighbour, Gugu-Yalanji, and from dialects of Dyirbal south of W.

Where did it start? First in Yidiñ? Or first in Ngajan? Or in both at the same time? It is hard to provide a firm answer to this question. But evidence from loans, summarised in section 14.6.7, suggests Ngajan as the original source. Yidiñ would then have evolved a vowel length contrast, almost entirely by the innovation of synchronic Rules 1 and 2, set out in section 14.6.5, in order to make its surface phonology and phonetics more similar to that of Ngajan. Note, though, that the similarity is pretty superficial. For example, long vowels are always stressed in Yidiñ, not so in Ngajan. And they typically occur in a closed final syllable (never an initial syllable) in Yidiñ whereas in Ngajan long vowels are typically found in an initial syllable or in an open final syllable—see table 14.5.

The central dialects of Dyirbal, south of N and W, do not have contrastive vowel length but allow a phonetic long vowel as the occasional and restricted realisation of /uwu/, /awa/, and /iyi/. Girramay, the southernmost dialect, has—as described in section 14.6.4—a more frequently occurring phonetic long vowel, but it again relates to two initial syllables at the phonological level. This enables Girramay to sound more similar than central dialects to its southern neighbour Warrgamay, which has phonological long vowels just in the first syllable of a word.

14.7 Conclusion

We have examined the linguistic situation in an area of mountainous rainforest in north-east Queensland. There are eight rivers which rise on the eastern side of the Great Dividing Range and meander their way down to the sea. Each language or dialect is associated with one river, or with a part of a river. The major focus has been on the Yidiñ language, spoken around the Mulgrave River, and the Ngajan dialect of Dyirbal, spoken around the Russell River. There was considerable contact between nearby groups—marriage exchange, and meetings for song and dance and for fighting contests. Five results of language contact have been examined.

- **Demonstratives and related items** (section 14.2). We saw here that there was borrowing from Dyirbal into the adjacent t dialect of Yidiñ of the meaning system (forms being unaffected). Generally, languages show a tendency not to borrow closed classes, but rather to re-structure them.
- **Tense systems** (section 14.3). We saw that Yidiñ and the northern dialects of Dyirbal have the same past/non-past system, different from the tense system

in Yidiñ's close relative Ja:bugay, and from that in southern dialects of Dyirbal. It is hard to say for certain here which language copied which, although it does seem most likely that the northern dialects of Dyirbal changed to become more like Yidiñ.

- **Pronoun systems** (section 14.4). It is clear that Yidiñ borrowed the 1 dual pronoun *ŋali* from Dyirbal.

Carlin (2006: 320–2) discusses a similar instance of pronoun borrowing, from Carib into Mawayana, an Arawak language spoken in Brazil, Guyana, and Suriname.

- **Initial rhotic** (section 14.5). It is clear that the N and W dialects of Dyirbal eliminated word-initial rhotics, to accord with the phonotactics of their northerly neighbour Yidiñ.
- **Contrastive vowel length** (section 14.6). We have examined a small area in which all languages/dialects show contrastive vowel length, but their neighbours lack it. The contrast certainly evolved in the central portion of this area—where it has a high functional load—involving the t and c dialects of Yidiñ and the Ngajan dialect of Dyirbal. However, it evolved in two completely different ways. It is hard to be absolutely certain where it started—it is most likely to have been in Ngajan, with the Yidiñ dialects then changing to achieve a degree of phonological and phonetic similarity.

  Ja:bugay, to the north of Yidiñ, then developed a length contrast but on a much more modest scale than Yidiñ. Just some of the changes in Ngajan which had produced long vowels then diffused into its southern neighbour, the Waribarra Mamu dialect. (The changes were not pervasive enough to lead to the loss of the rhotic contrast, as happened in Ngajan.)

  More southerly dialects of Dyirbal lack any length contrast. Central dialects have a whiff of a phonetic long vowel. This is more developed in the most southerly dialect, Girramay, to make it sound more like the language to the south, Warrgamay, which has a length contrast just in initial, stressed syllables, this being an ancient retention.

In summary, contact across the Yidiñ/Dyirbal language boundary has led to:

YIDIÑ CHANGED TO BE MORE LIKE DYIRBAL	DYIRBAL CHANGED TO BE MORE LIKE YIDIÑ
Demonstrative system (definitely)	Loss of initial rhotic (definitely)
Pronoun system (definitely)	
Length contrast (probably)	Tense system (possibly)

Overall, we see that in this contact situation, languages have influenced each other back and forth, as is always likely to happen. This applies especially in Australia, which constitutes the longest-lasting diffusion area in the world.

The fourteen chapters thus far have described languages when they were in full flower. But all that is now gone. As a final adieu, we need to say a little about the way in which the languages have declined and disappeared.

This chapter is the revision of a 2008 paper 'Language contact in the Cairns rainforest region'.

Part V

Languages Fading Away

The lives of the indigenous peoples of the Cairns rainforest region were cataclysmically disturbed upon invasion of their lands by European 'settlers', commencing in the 1860s and 1870s. Cultural practices contracted, together with language use. There are today no fluent speakers remaining for any of the languages.

As a language, L, moves towards extinction, we can recognise the following stages:

generation T	fluent speakers, who spoke the traditional form of L as first language during their younger years
generation(s) S	semi-speakers, who only partly learned the language; can use it, to some extent, in limited circumstances; have a smallish vocabulary and simplified grammar (and sometimes also simplified phonology)
generation N	although identifying—at some level—with the ethnic group which spoke the language, have no real knowledge of it (besides perhaps a few isolated words and a couple of formulaic phrases)

I have worked almost exclusively with generation T. All of the data, results, and generalisation of the preceding fourteen chapters, are based on consultation with fluent speakers.

In some instances that was all there was. Information on Warrgamay comes predominantly from three members of generation T. These were John Tooth and Lambert Cocky (both born in the 1890s) and Nora Boyd (born in the early 1880s); the last of them passed away in 1984. All three spoke Warrgamay as first language during their early years. Description of Warrgamay in chapter 10 and other chapters is thus of the language when it was still in full bloom, around 1900. The information provided by the three speakers was clear and consistent.

For Warrgamay I know of no one who could be identified as generation S; that is, I encountered no semi-speakers (although there may have been some in the past). However, there is today a generation N, people from around Ingham who identify—by blood—as Warrgamaygan, and are claiming 'land rights' on that basis. It appears that nothing of the language has been handed down to them. My 1981 grammar and vocabulary are eagerly consulted, and I am asked how the last part of the language name should be pronounced. Is it as in English *may*, or as in *my*? (The latter is correct.)

Similar remarks apply for Nyawaygi, to the south of Warrgamay. My 1983 grammar and vocabulary were based on information from two members of generation T: Long Heron, born in the early 1870s and died in 1971, and Willie Seaton, born in the 1890s and died about 1988. (I encountered one semi-speaker, Roy Heron, who died in the late 1960s.) In 2002, a man from generation N, who identifies with this ethnic group, told me that he was *Nyá-wey-ji*, when it should be *Nya-wáy-gi*, with stress on the second syllable and a hard *g* sound. The language name was an English-style pronunciation of a written form, rather than something which had been passed down from parents or grandparents.

The grammar of Yidiñ (published in 1977) was based on work with three members of generation T. When I returned to do further work on a thesaurus/dictionary (published in 1991), two of the fluent speakers had passed on and the third was no longer mentally agile. I did then receive invaluable assistance from three good semi-speakers. It was fascinating to observe the alterations they had wrought in the traditional grammar; these are described in chapter 15. (There are today no semi-speakers remaining for Yidiñ. Some from generation N are engaged in re-assertion of the language, based largely on materials I published.)

For five dialects of Dyirbal, I worked almost exclusively with members of generation T. Peoples speaking southern dialects had been impacted by the European invasion a couple of decades later than others of the region. Those born up to around 1930 were, as a rule, fluent speakers, and there were several dozen people using the language on a daily basis when I commenced fieldwork in 1963. Over the next thirty years they gradually decreased in number so that there were only a couple remaining when I completed work on a thesaurus/dictionary in 1992; this is now being prepared for publication. (The last member of generation T died in March 2011.) Chapter 16 documents how, over three decades, I worked on a variety of topics with fluent speakers. As the major consultant for a dialect passed away, I was able to turn to another, and so on, until I was working with the last members of that generation T.

This language does have a vibrant—but ageing—generation S; the appendix to chapter 16 briefly comments on the language of semi-speakers, based on the fine account in Schmidt (1985).

15

The last change in Yidiñ

15.1 Introduction

On commencing fieldwork in 1963, I undertook a linguistic survey of the whole Cairns rainforest region before deciding to focus, for the time being, on Dyirbal. Several hundred lexemes in Yidiñ were recorded from Jack and Nellie Stewart and some from other elderly members of Generation T, all of whom passed away before the end of the 1960s.

Between 1970 and 1975, I worked intensively on a comprehensive grammar of Yidiñ with the three remaining members of generation T:

Dick Moses, c1898–1977
Tilly Fuller, c1903–1974
Pompey Langdon, c1898–1991

Dick Moses and Tilly Fuller could each give fluent texts and were able to answer every type of lexical and grammatical query. A simple question would often set them off dictating a long 'conversation' in Yidiñ, sometimes two or three pages in length. Pompey Langdon would not give texts but his Yidiñ was full and consistent. As described in chapter 6, both Tilly Fuller and Pompey Langdon were able to remember a fair amount of the avoidance style, Jalnguy.

By 1975 I had a good-sized lexicon on the basis of texts and elicitation with members of generation T, but there were entries in need of clarifying and more that should be added. Between 1979 and 1989 I worked on this, mainly with the assistance of three knowledgeable and intelligent semi-speakers:

George Davis, c1919–2002
Ranji Fuller, c1908–1988
Katie Mays, c1916–early 1990s

Pompey Langdon, the last member of generation T, was able to provide a little help, but he was now slipping into senility.

15.2 Semi-speakers

Dorian (1981: 107) characterises 'semi-speakers' of East Sutherland Gaelic in the following terms:

Unlike the older Gaelic-dominated bilinguals, the semi-speakers are not fully proficient in Gaelic. They speak it with varying degrees of less than full fluency, and their grammar (and usually also their phonology) is markedly aberrant in terms of the fluent-speaker norm. Semi-speakers may be distinguished from fully fluent speakers of any age by the presence of deviations in their Gaelic which are explicitly labeled 'mistakes' by the fully fluent speakers. That is, the speech community is aware of many (though not all) of the deficiencies in semi-speaker speech performance. Most semi-speakers are also relatively halting in delivery, or speak Gaelic in rather short bursts, or both; but it is not manner of delivery which distinguishes them, since semi-speakers of comparable grammatical ability may speak with very different degrees of confidence and 'fluency'.

The three semi-speakers of Yidiñ with whom I worked all showed characteristics of semi-speakers.

(a) Lexical interference from English. The older speakers of traditional Yidiñ mingled very little English into their Yidiñ. I recorded seventeen texts from Dick Moses and these included just two English interpolations: 'find him' in one text and 'dinner time now' in another. In four texts from Tilly Fuller there were odd occurrences of 'and', 'that', 'now', 'like', 'from', 'no more', 'standing there today', and 'all the way'; most of these bits of English stood outside the structure of Yidiñ sentences.

A text from Katie Mays, although still a fair sample of Yidiñ, showed more English elements, and of a more fundamental type, than texts given by Dick Moses and Tilly Fuller. For example (with English items underlined):

(1) [young fellow]$_S$ waŋga:ji-ñu
                         get.up-PAST
     The young fellow got up

(2) gunda-gunda-:l   miña$_O$ an' then [waymin an' all them]$_A$
     REDUPLICATED-cut-PAST meat   cousin
         budi-:l   ŋuŋgu
         put.down-PAST THERE
     The meat was cut up and then waymin and all of them put it down there (to be cooked)

(3) ŋañji   miña-gimbal,   only baba:l
     1non.sg meat-WITHOUT   bone
     We haven't any meat, only bones

(4) ŋañji$_A$ f̱ind̲i-mal-ñu   baba:l$_O$ <u>can't</u> buga-ŋ
     1non.sg find-VERBALISER-PAST bone   eat-PRESENT
     We only found bones, and can't eat them

Note here an English noun phrase as subject of a Yidiñ verb in (1); an English addition to a Yidiñ head noun in (2); and in (4) the transitive verbalising suffix *-ma-l* added to the nonce loan *find̲i* (the final *i* is necessary to satisfy the constraint that all roots in Yidiñ should have at least two syllables). There is also the fact that *waymin*, although the subject of the transitive verb *budi-l* 'put down' in (2), does not bear ergative case inflection (this is at least partly due to the occurrence in the same noun phrase of *an' all them*). None of these features is found in any of the texts of Dick Moses or Tilly Fuller.

(b) Occasional omission of case endings. In traditional Yidiñ, every word in a noun phrase had to show an appropriate case inflection. In most sentences given by the semi-speakers this still held, but there were occasional instances of, say, an ergative affix being omitted. (And this did happen where there was no English element in the sentence, as there was in (2).)

(c) Variation in allomorphs used. The three speakers of generation T would always give a single form for each case inflection of a given word and were almost totally consistent in this. In contrast, the semi-speakers did—in direct elicitation—sometimes hesitate between two variant forms, and often said that both were acceptable. Usually, one was the traditional Yidiñ form with the other being based on a 'new' root that is identical to the absolutive form. This is discussed in section 15.4 below.

(d) Limited knowledge of lexemes. I have always tried to check each lexeme with at least two speakers. While the semi-speakers had a fair-sized Yidiñ vocabulary (many hundreds of lexemes), they drew a blank at some uncommon words, from all the open word classes, which had been given by fluent speakers.

I have also done exhaustive botanical identification in the rainforest with speakers of both Dyirbal and Yidiñ. Fluent speakers of Dyirbal (aged 50–90) could give a name for every tree and plant in the forest, as could Dick Moses. But Ranji Fuller and George Davis were only able to name the more important flora and fauna. There are a number of trees (those that are of little general use or interest), and some animals, the names for which they never learnt.

Note that degree of competence does not necessarily correlate with age. George Davis, although the youngest of the semi-speakers, was also the most fluent of them; he was brought up by his grandfather and used Yidiñ a great deal until he was about fifteen. (Dorian 1980 mentions the beneficial effect of grandparent contact on language retention.) The one text that George Davis gave (see Dixon 1991a: 103–6) had no English interpolations and no grammatical errors or omissions. However, he did reassign some absolutive forms as roots for oblique cases, although less frequently than Katie Mays or Ranji Fuller.

Ranji Fuller had a white father, by whom he was largely brought up, and thus enjoyed less contact with 'the old people' of the tribe than did George Davis. Katie Mays was also brought up in more contact with whites than her elder half-sister, Tilly Fuller. (Tilly Fuller was Ranji's step-mother; she was the second wife of his white father.)

The next section discusses nominal inflection in traditional Yidiñ as a preliminary to the description of root re-assignment by semi-speakers, in section 15.4.

The development of contrastive vowel length in Yidiñ was described in section 14.6.5, and is relevant for the discussion which follows here. Recall that, by Rule 1, a word with an odd number of syllables has the vowel in its penultimate syllable lengthened, as in *wagu:ja* 'man'. And then Rule 2 specifies that, under certain conditions, a final *(C)V* may be omitted: *buña-ŋgu* 'woman-ERGATIVE' becomes *buña:ŋgu* by Rule 1, and then reduces to *buña:ŋ* by Rule 2.

15.3 Nominal inflection

There are seven distinct case forms for each noun in Yidiñ. It will be sufficient to illustrate here with four cases (full details are in Dixon 1977a: 124–42).

(a) ABSolutive, marking intransitive subject (S) and transitive object (O), has zero realisation.

(b) ERGative, marking transitive subject (A), is:

> -*ŋgu* following a vowel, e.g. *waguja-ŋgu*, 'man-ERG'; -*ŋgu* reduces to -*:ŋ* on a stem with an even number of syllables, as in *buña:ŋ* 'woman-ERG'.
>
>   -*du* following a consonant, as in *waga:l-du* 'wife-ERG'.
>
> - The -*d*- of -*du* assimilates in place of articulation to a preceding nasal or *y*, e.g. *muja:m-bu* 'mother-ERG', *ŋubirrbiñ-ju* 'leech-ERG'.
> - Between stem-final -*y* and ERG -*ju* an -*ñ*- can optionally be inserted, and the stem-final -*y* may optionally be omitted, e.g. ABS *gunduy* 'brown snake', ERG *gundu:(y)(ñ)ju*.
> - When -*du* is added to an even-syllabled stem ending in either of the two rhotics, the rhotic must drop, e.g. ABS *gugar* 'black goanna', ERG *guga:du*.

(c) PURPosive is -*gu* on all types of stem.

(d) GENitive is basically -*ni* (although when it is added to a stem ending in a nasal, one of the nasals may drop).

As described in section 14.6.5, there are some nominals with a trisyllabic root ending in a vowel which inflect in a regular manner. For example:

(5)   'broom'   'curlew'
    ROOT   gajarra   galgali
    ABSOLUTIVE   gaja:rra   galga:li
    ERGATIVE   gajarra-ŋgu   galgali-ŋgu
    PURPOSIVE   gajarra-gu   galgali-gu
    GENITIVE   gajarra-ni   galgali-ni

There are also about eighty nominals which show a trisyllabic root in oblique cases, but have disyllabic form in absolutive. For example:

(6)   'ring-tail possum' 'boy'   'flying fox' 'grey wallaby'
    ROOT   gajarrA   waŋarI   gugiñU   gangulA
    ABSOLUTIVE   gaja:rr   waŋa:r   gugi:ñ   gangu:l
    ERGATIVE   gajarra-ŋgu   waŋari-ŋgu gugiñu-ŋgu   gangula-ŋgu
    PURPOSIVE   gajarra-gu   waŋari-gu   gugiñu-gu   gangula-gu
    GENITIVE   gajarra-ni   waŋari-ni   gugiñu-ni   gangula-ni

This phenomenon can be dealt with by assigning a morphophoneme (*A*, *I*, or *U*) as the final segment of the root. The morphophoneme triggers application of Rule 2, giving absolutive *gajarrA* → *gada:rrA* (by Rule 1) → *gaja:rr* (by Rule 2), and so on. When followed by a case suffix, a morphophoneme is replaced by the corresponding vowel (*A* by *a*, etc.).

Absolutive is the unmarked, citation form for each noun. In texts, nouns occur in absolutive more often than in all oblique case forms put together. But it is not possible to infer oblique forms from the absolutive for words like *gaja:rr*. If the absolutive ends in a long vowel followed by a consonant then one knows that there must be a 'third vowel' before oblique cases, but the identity of this vowel is not inferable from the absolutive form.

It is interesting to note that cognates from nearby languages for morphophoneme-final roots in Yidiñ do show a trisyllabic root (and the third root vowel is never deleted), for example:

(7)   'ringtail possum' 'grey wallaby' 'boy'
    Yidiñ   gajarrA   gangulA   waŋarI
    Ja:bugay   gayarra   gangula   waŋari
    Warrgamay   gajarra

There is one other class of nouns that inflect on a rather special pattern. About a dozen lexemes (in my corpus of around two thousand words) inflect like:

(8)   'catfish' ABSOLUTIVE galbi:
          ERGATIVE   galbi:ñju

Now ergative is normally -*ŋgu* after a vowel but -*du* (with assimilation) after a consonant. The ergative form of 'catfish' is similar to the ergative form of *y*-final roots, mentioned above. This suggests a root *galbiy*, the final -*y* selecting ergative allomorph -*(ny)ju*. We require a phonological rule that replaces *iy* by *i:* at the end of a word, to yield absolutive form *galbi:* (there is other justification for a rule of this form—see Dixon 1977a: 77–83).

15.4 Root reassignment

For generation T, the principles for inferring the ergative from the absolutive form of a nominal were:

(a) If the absolutive ends in a consonant and there is no long vowel, add -*du* (and apply rules of assimilation, -*ñ*- insertion, rhotic deletion etc.); for example, 'flat rock' absolutive *malan*, ergative *mala:n-du*.
(b) If the absolutive ends in a vowel, add -*ŋgu*; for example, 'curlew' absolutive *galga:li*, ergative *galgali-ŋgu*.
(c) If the absolutive ends in a consonant and the preceding vowel is long, then work in terms of a trisyllabic root ending in a vowel, and add ergative -*ŋgu*.

The semi-speakers did not recognise all of the morphophoneme-final roots I had recorded from fluent speakers. And for those that were known, they only sometimes followed (c). The rest of the time semi-speakers would simply add -*du* to the absolutive form of a noun ending in a consonant, regardless of whether there was a long vowel present or not. That is, they were effectively generalising (a) to apply in circumstance (c). For example:

(9)   'ring-tail possum' 'boy'   'flying fox'
       ABSOLUTIVE for all   gaja:rr   waŋa:r   gugi:ñ
       ERGATIVE for generation T   gajarra-ŋgu   waŋari-ŋgu gugiñu-ŋgu
       ERGATIVE for generation S   gaja:rr-du   waŋa:r-du gugi:ñ-ju

Pre-Yidiñ must certainly have had trisyllabic roots *gajarra*, and so on. These were retained in oblique cases but reduced to *gaja:rr*, etc. in absolutive. A perfectly natural next step in the process of diachronic change would be for the absolutive to be generalised as a new root, for all case forms. That is:

(10)   ABSOLUTIVE ROOT   ERGATIVE
     earlier stage gaja:rra   gajarra   gajarra-ŋgu
     generation T   gaja:rr   gajarrA   gajarra-ŋgu
     generation S   gaja:rr   gaja:rr   gaja:rr-du

It could be suggested that the semi-speakers are merely representatives of the
'next stage'. This is true, in a sense. But it is a change that is a function of the language loss situation (where the language has been only partially learnt) rather
than a natural change in a living language situation. The following points are
relevant:

(I) There was a good deal of inconsistency in the forms provided. Katie Mays and Ranji
Fuller gave the ergative of 'boy' as *waŋa:r-du* on one occasion and then *waŋara-ŋgu* the
following year. The form *waŋara-ŋgu* shows a realisation that, from absolutive *waŋa:r*,
there should be a trisyllabic oblique root. But these semi-speakers did not know what
the third vowel should be (it was *i*, in fact) and so they used *a*, repeating the previous
vowels. Of course, every language situation involves some degree of variation; the
point is that the variation among semi-speakers of Yidiñ is much greater than that
for the fluent speakers, or than what would be found in any stable (i.e. non-dying-
language) context.

When talking to Katie Mays and Ranji Fuller together I asked for the Yidiñ translation of 'the grey wallaby eats grass' involving *gangulA* 'grey wallaby'. Ranji Fuller
gave the ergative form *gangu:l-du* and Katie Mays *gangula-ŋgu*. Both semi-speakers
said that either form was perfectly acceptable. Similar results were obtained for other
words.

George Davis had a slightly fuller knowledge of the language than Katie Mays and
Ranji Fuller and could be said to be on the cusp between generation T and generation
S. But he gave case forms for 'grey wallaby' on an inconsistent basis:

(11)   ABSOLUTIVE gangu:l
       DATIVE   gangu:l-gu based on a root gangu:l
       GENITIVE   gangula-ni based on a root gangula

(II) The traditional language had a minimal pair *malan* 'flat rock' and *malanU* 'right
hand'. Thus, in absolutive case and in locative (which has allomorph *-la* after a vowel
and *-da* after a consonant), fluent speakers gave:

(12)   'flat rock' 'right hand'
       ROOT   malan   malanU
       ABSOLUTIVE malan   mala:n
       LOCATIVE   mala:n-da malanu-la

But Katie Mays and Ranji Fuller consistently gave the locative of 'right hand' as *mala:nda*. When I enquired about the locative of 'flat rock', this was also given as *mala:nda*. The two locatives were accepted as identical, no concern being felt about this neutralisation.

It should be noted that the absolutive forms *malan* and *mala:n* were clearly distinguished. Semi-speakers always correctly used long vowels in absolutive forms of nominals that (for traditional speakers) show a morphophoneme-final root. And—by application of Rule 1—they always showed a long vowel in the penultimate syllable of a word with an odd number of syllables.

(III) It was noted in section 15.3 that ergative is *-du* after a stem ending in a consonant, and that, for an even-syllabled root ending in a rhotic, the rhotic drops before *-du* (as it also does before locative *-da*). If this rhotic-dropping rule were consistently retained by semi-speakers for disyllabic roots with no long vowel, there would still be a difference between the ergative form of *gugar* 'black goanna (*Varanus varius*)'—*guga:du*—and of a noun that differed from *gugar* only in having a long vowel in the second syllable of its absolutive form (like *waŋa:r* 'boy'), with the absolutive form being taken as root for oblique cases. (This is assuming that the rhotic did not drop in ergative after a long vowel.) That is, we would have:

(13)

	'black goanna' (both generations)	'boy' (generation T)	'boy' (generation S)
ROOT	gugar	waŋarI	waŋa:r
ABSOLUTIVE	gugar	waŋa:r	waŋa:r
ERGATIVE	guga:-du	waŋari-ŋgu	waŋa:r-du

But it appears that semi-speakers do not always apply the rhotic-dropping rule. Once more, there is variation. I recorded ergative *guga:rdu* and locative *dubi:rda* (from root *dubir* 'hollow log')—with the rhotic retained—but also locative *jubu:da* (from *jubur* 'stone')—with rhotic dropped—among other examples.

No minimal pairs are known ending in a rhotic, on the pattern of *malan/mala:n*. But if there were any, they might well fall together in ergative (and locative) for semi-speakers.

(IV) The semi-speakers also showed some deviation from the norms of traditional Yidiñ grammar for oblique inflections of lexemes that have absolutive ending in *-:i*, such as *galbi:* 'catfish'. One year, I recorded ergative *galbi:ŋ*; that is, *galbi:* plus the vowel-final ergative allomorph *-ŋgu*, reduced by Rules 1 and 2. But the following year Ranji Fuller gave the correct traditional Yidiñ ergative form *galbi:ñju*. For *guwiy* 'frog', Katie Mays gave the ergative form as *guwi:ŋ* while George Davis volunteered the traditional ergative form *guwi:ñju*. Note, however, that for the very common noun *gidigidiy* 'young children', absolute *gidigidi:*, all the semi-speakers gave the correct traditional Yidiñ ergative form *gidigidi:ñju*.

In summary, for nouns where traditional Yidiñ worked in terms of a root that differed from the absolutive form, there was a tendency among semi-speakers to form oblique cases directly on the absolutive as root. This was a new structural change; it was in fact the last change before the spoken language became just a memory.

But semi-speakers did not always apply the change consistently. In many cases the new form existed side-by-side with the old. It is likely that for the most common nouns the traditional inflectional forms were used, since these would be 'remembered' by semi-speakers from their youthful contact with fluent speakers. But for less common words oblique case forms have to be generated, and there is a tendency to derive them from the absolutive form, rather than from some more abstract underlying form.

The examples quoted show that the reassignment of roots was not a natural change, within a living and evolving language situation. It was, instead, an artefact of semi-speakers having learnt Yidiñ only partially, in a milieu where the major language would always have been English.

15.5 Other variations

Rule 2 shortens many odd-syllabled words. As a result of this, many inflectional affixes have variant allomorphs depending on whether they are added to stems with an odd or with an even number of syllables. Thus *waguja-ŋgu* 'man-ERGATIVE' and *bu:ña-ŋ* (reduced from *buña:-ŋgu*) 'woman-ERGATIVE'. And, with past tense inflection added to trisyllabic and disyllabic verb roots:

(14) 'walk up-PAST' majinda-ñu
      'go-PAST'   gali-ñu → gali:ñu (by Rule 1) → gali:ñ (by Rule 2)

These reduced allomorphs of nominal and verbal inflections are very common and were—in the corpus I collected—always used correctly by semi-speakers.

But Rule 2 also applies to some derivational affixes, and here there is variation in semi-speaker usage. There is an affix *-ŋa-* which can be added to nominals to derive a transitive verbal stem of the -l conjugation. Imperative inflection has zero realisation for the -l conjugation. Thus with a disyllabic vowel-final nominal we get a form that is, in traditional Yidiñ, reduced by Rule 2:

(15) underlying   bumba-ŋa-ø 'dry-MAKE-IMPERATIVE'
      rule 1 applies bumba:ŋa
      rule 2 applies bumba:ŋ

Katie Mays gave this form as *bumba:ŋa*, without the final reduction. However she did, in the same elicitation session, correctly reduce *mada-ŋa-ø* 'soft-MAKE-IMPERATIVE' to *mada:ŋ*. And on a later occasion Katie Mays did give *bumba:ŋ*. She made another deviation from fluent speaker grammar in saying *gidigidi:ŋa* 'small-MAKE-IMPERATIVE' in place of *gidigidi:ŋ* (from *gidigidi:* 'small').

Intransitive verbs also take a transitivising affix *-ŋa-* and the same reduction applies. Thus *gali-ŋa-ø* reduces to *gali:ŋ*, but with a trisyllabic root we get *majinda-ŋa-ø* and there is no reduction (since the form has four syllables). Katie Mays consistently gave *gali:ŋ* 'go with!, take!' but she also quite inappropriately reduced *-ŋa-* on the trisyllabic root *wulwuri-* 'shake' to give the imperative transitivised form *wulwuri:ŋ*. Here Rule 2 has been over-generalised to apply to a four-syllabled word, yielding one that has only three syllables.

There are a few other instances of derivational affixes appearing, within the speech of semi-speakers, in forms that are at variance with the conventions of traditional Yidiñ. The nominal comitative affix was *-ji* after a consonant and *-yi* after a vowel, reducing to *-:y* with a disyllabic root ending in *-a* or *-u* and to just vowel length with a disyllabic root ending in *-i*. Katie Mays gave the comitative form of *ñaŋgi* 'annoying noise' as *ñaŋgi:yi* (for fluent speakers it was *ñaŋgi:*).

15.6 Conclusion

Yidiñ is a language which died rather quickly. It ceased to be actively used within a hundred years of the first white invasion in the 1870s. There was a switch from people (born before about 1910) who were fluent speakers, to their present-day descendants who can speak only English. But there was an in-between generation, some people who had reduced fluency and could be regarded as 'semi-speakers'.

The semi-speakers sometimes derived oblique forms of nouns directly from the absolutive (=citation) form, rather than from a more abstract underlying root as did fluent speakers. The semi-speakers showed a good deal of variation in the oblique case forms they used.

In addition, final syllable deletion (Rule 2) was applied rather haphazardly to the derivational affix *-ŋa-*. But it was applied quite exactly, according to the norms of traditional Yidiñ grammar, to inflectional endings.

Some people have put forward the idea that a language which has died out is merely 'sleeping', and could be revived. This is day-dreaming. A language is a living organism; once its life-force has withered away, it cannot be re-ignited.

However, pride in ethnicity can be strengthened by learning *about* the language of one's forebears. Currently, David Mundraby is teaching aspects of Yidiñ in the Yarrabah Primary School, based in large part on materials in my 1991 book, *Words of our Country: Stories, place names and vocabulary in Yidiny, the Aboriginal language of the Cairns-Yarrabah region.*

The next chapter tells the rather different story of how I was able to more-or-less complete work in Dyirbal entirely with the assistance of members of generation T.

This chapter is the revision of a book chapter published in 1990, 'Reassigning underlying forms in Yidiñ: A change during language death'.

16

The gradual decline of Dyirbal

In 1963, when I began work on Dyirbal, there were several score fluent speakers, members of generation T. The language appeared to be in a reasonably healthy state. I have tried to work on all aspects of the language across as many dialects as possible—grammar, texts, songs, the kinship system, plus an extensive thesaurus/dictionary covering both everyday and Jalnguy ('mother-in-law' or avoidance) speech styles, with zoological identification of fauna and botanical identification on flora.

These tasks occupied me for thirty years. During this period, I saw the language decline from a state in which there was an abundance of speakers who could supply the information I sought to one in which there was just one good consultant left for each of several dialects, with no one to go to for a second opinion. The language had died at a slightly faster rate than I could fully record it.

This chapter tells the story of how the Dyirbal language has fared over the past 150 years, and of how I was able to record it, between 1963 and 1992.

16.1 The first hundred years after the European invasion

There must have been at least five thousand people speaking dialects of Dyirbal during the first part of the nineteenth century, when European vessels were seen sailing up and down the coast, sometimes coming ashore for water.

In the 1860s and 1870s, Europeans came to live in north-east Queensland. Many Aborigines died from catching European diseases (such as measles and influenza) to which they had no immunity. And many were shot as they tried to fight—with spears and boomerangs against guns—for their heritage. There was a 'Native Police' consisting of Aborigines brought up from southern Queensland, armed with guns and commanded by white officers to seek out local Aborigines and shoot on sight. Chinese, who came to settle on the coast, 'paid' Aborigines with used opium charcoal, which resulted in further deaths. The Aboriginal population of the Cairns rainforest region was reduced to perhaps one tenth of its original level within fifty years of the European invasion.

The most intensive settlement took place in the coastal strip, from Cairns down to Ingham, and up on the Atherton tableland; here, the forest was cleared for the cultivation of sugar cane and the raising of dairy cattle. The rugged mountain country around the upper Tully River was less attractive to white entrepreneurs; one group of Jirrbal speakers lived there, in fairly traditional style, until about 1940.

From 1910 on, the Queensland government attempted to round up those Aborigines who remained in settled areas and sequester them on the Anglican mission at Yarrabah (across the bay from Cairns) or at the semi-penal government settlement on Palm Island. But there were some Aborigines who maintained a low profile and were able to remain, as half-cowed fugitives on their own land.

In the Cairns-Atherton region, tribes had decreased in number until each was too small to continue as a viable political unit. I was told by Dick Moses—one of the last speakers of Yidiñ—that in the 1920s Aboriginal elders formed a plan. They decided that the remaining people from that area should be 'merged' into a single macro-tribe. This plan failed, partly because there were considerable language differences. Dick Moses himself had a wife who spoke the Ngajan dialect of Dyirbal, a totally different language; they communicated only in English.

A happier situation eventuated further south, around the small settlement of Murray Upper, where members of the Jirrbalngan and Girramaygan tribes gathered and to which those people who had remained in the bush eventually came. J and G are mutually comprehensible dialects of a single language; a member of the Murray Upper community would speak in their own dialect and be understood by the others.

There was a small group of white farmers who now owned all the land at Murray Upper. The Aborigines were tolerated to live among them, one family to each property, in return for a bit of cheap labour. One white settler recounted to me how, when he had arrived at Murray Upper in the 1920s, he was told: 'There are no bad Aborigines left here, they've all been shot.' There were perhaps only a couple of score Jirrbalngan and Girramaygan people at Murray Upper in the 1920s, but they had a good number of children and the community had more than doubled by 1963.

Most white settlers were only tolerant of Aboriginal culture and language as long as it was kept out of sight. Men would typically be forbidden to speak in their own language when at work within hearing of a white person. (The boss was scared a plot might be being hatched behind his back.) But the people did form a viable community and almost all of them had J or G as their first language, although they also knew English to varying degrees of proficiency. (When I arrived in 1963 there was just one old lady—a member of the group that had lived in the bush until 1940—who was monolingual in J.)

There was a small school at Murray Upper, just for white children. Then, in 1944, enrolments dropped below nine, the critical number required by the government to keep the school open. A couple of part-blood Aboriginal children were hastily admitted. Soon all Aboriginal children were allowed to attend. But if they were heard speaking their own language in the school grounds, they would be caned.

16.2 The situation in 1963

An initial survey of the Cairns rainforest region, in late 1963, revealed that northern dialects of Dyirbal were in a similar state to Yidiñ, described in the preceding chapter. There were just a few isolated speakers, but nothing resembling a speech community.

The only speech community was at Murray Upper and for the next few years I concentrated my efforts there. The community was made up of members of the Girramaygan tribe and of the lowlands local group of the Jirrbalngan, and the older people spoke G and J to one another almost all the time. Every second Thursday was pension day, and local Aborigines would trek in from every direction to the post office, draw their allowances, and then go next door to Mrs Cowan's store to buy provisions. A dozen or more old people and quite a few younger ones would squat on Mrs Cowan's concrete forecourt to exchange news and gossip. Virtually all the talk from older people, and over half of that from the younger ones, was in J or G (the remainder being in English).

Soon after I appeared there, the Murray Upper people got together to discuss this strange young white fellow from England who wanted to write down their languages. Opinion was divided as to whether this was desirable. I was later told about it all by Ernie Grant, who persuaded them that nothing was to be lost (and perhaps something was to be gained) by cooperating. Ernie's mother Chloe—with whom I had already established a warm rapport—was deputed to be the main instructor. And everyone else would be happy to help.

There were, at that time, perhaps twenty people at Murray Upper who would have been good and willing language consultants. In the 1960s, I worked with half-a-dozen. Jack Murray spoke J very fast (the text he recorded, about the origin of fire, was at an amazing speed), but he explained to me very carefully the names of trees in the forest. Jimmy Murray (no relation; they both came from the Murray River) had a rather imperious air—he had spent some years away from home as an official police tracker at Bowen—and spoke unadulterated G. He explained dialect differences: 'We say ŋayba for "me" but Jirrbal just say ŋaja.' Then I heard Jimmy use ŋaja and accused him of speaking J. He was scandalised—no, he was speaking nothing but G, 'we say ŋaja too.' It took a while for me to realise what was happening:

	Girramay	Jirrbal (and all other dialects)
intransitive subject (S)	ŋayba	ŋaja
transitive subject (A)	ŋaja	

Jimmy Murray was acknowledged to be the best singer, and two corroborees were organised (with assistance from a friendly white family, the Cowans, on whose property Jimmy lived) in October and November 1963. Six or ten Aboriginal men painted themselves with white, yellow, and red clay and performed dances mimicking the actions of emus, kangaroos, cranes, and white people, while Jimmy Murray tapped two boomerangs together and sang appropriate songs. These were the last corroborees to be held.

Paddy Biran (or Beeron) was perhaps the most knowledgeable man I worked with. Although only in his early forties, he had an unparalleled knowledge of traditional legends and songs and was an active composer. I recorded one long session of stories told by Paddy in G with interjections from Jack Murray in J (each speaking in his own dialect) and then six songs from Paddy. On another occasion, Paddy Biran spent an afternoon giving me names of flora and fauna and sentences and then recorded a text in G with his friend Mosley Digman.

The person I worked with most on my first field trip (October 1963 to August 1964) was Chloe Grant, who had been born about 1903 of a Girramaygan mother and an Irish father. She was one of the few half-bloods from that era. (I was told that others had been born but were killed, by the white father, soon after birth.) Chloe had been brought up by her grandmother; besides being fluent in both J and G, she also had a fair knowledge of the M (Dulgubarra Mamu) dialect. Unlike all the other people I worked with at Murray Upper at that time, Chloe sometimes tended to blend together G and J. She warned me that she did this, and I replied that I was aware of it. But when Chloe concentrated her mind she could clearly distinguish the dialects. We went through a vocabulary of about 2,000 items, getting an example sentence for every word, with Chloe telling me whether it was the same in J, G, and M or—if not—what forms the other dialects had. (This information correlated about 99 per cent with what I was told by mono-dialectal consultants.)

Chloe was highly intelligent, vivacious, saucy, and quick-witted. She would respond in a flash to any question I might pose, suggesting three or four alternative ways of saying something. Then, when I went to Palm Island, Chloe told me to look up George Watson, a Mamu man (born about 1899) who would also be able to help. She was right—George was every bit as intelligent as Chloe, with an unrivalled knowledge of M language and traditions. As George recorded his life story for me, twenty years later, he was the result of rape by a white man and his Mamu mother had wanted to kill him at birth but a sister dissuaded her; George was then brought up by his tribal grandfather.

Whereas Chloe was quick and impulsive, George was slower and more thoughtful. Chloe would provide an instant response and then modify it and then come back to the same point again later. George would mull over each question and provide a measured answer. George had had a Girramaygan wife and was then married to a speaker of Gambilbarra Jirrbal (A), but he used pure M in the many excellent texts we recorded.

He was also able to comment on dialect differences in N (Ngajan) and W (Waribarra Mamu), as well as in G, J, and A.

Chloe had been deputed by the Aboriginal people at Murray Upper to be my main language teacher because of her knowledge, patience, and interest. I was surprised to discover that Chloe's own children (then aged 15 to 41) had not learned the language properly, unlike almost all their contemporaries. The other Aboriginal people used J or G with children. But Chloe and her husband (who died just before I arrived) had decided that their children would have a better chance in the world if they kept English as the language of the house. When Chloe was with friends of her own generation, she spoke nothing but J, yet she always addressed her children in English.

The second week she knew me, Chloe told of a special speech style called Jalnguy or (as she put it) 'mother-in-law language', which in days gone by had been mandatory to use in the presence of a cross-cousin (mother's brother's or father's sister's child), who was a potential mother-in-law, father-in-law, daughter-in-law, or son-in-law. I discovered that Jalnguy had the same phonology and grammar as the everyday speech style but an entirely different lexicon. Every noun, verb, and adjective had a different form in Jalnguy—for instance, 'fire' is *buni* in the J everyday speech style but *yibay* in J Jalnguy.

It is really only sensible to focus on one thing at a time. Describing and explaining the intricacies of Dyirbal grammar was a demanding task. I decided to concentrate on the structural patterns of three dialects—J and G, from Chloe and others at Murray Upper, and M, from George. A good selection of texts had been recorded and transcribed, and the grammatical description was well advanced. A few score Jalnguy words were gathered from Chloe and from George on the first long field trip, but a full investigation of the 'mother-in-law style' was left until later.

I returned for a short field trip in March–April 1967, revising the grammar for a PhD thesis (submitted in December 1967), and then again in December 1970, finalising it for publication. An additional and important aim on these trips was to get the mother-in-law style equivalent for every lexeme I had recorded from the everyday style. George—who had moved from Palm Island to Innisfail, near his own tribal land—and Chloe were most helpful. For some tricky words, Chloe decided that she needed assistance, and so in 1967 we assembled a group of six old people, all of whom remembered the Jalnguy style from when it was actively used (until about 1930). A similar thing happened in 1970, and this time it was a slightly different committee. At that time, there must have been, all told, a dozen people at Murray Upper who knew Jalnguy.

I did not perceive any major changes in the language situation between 1963 and 1970. One very sad loss was that in late 1964 Paddy Biran had been thrown off the back of a truck on a slippery corner and killed. And Jimmy Murray had died, of old age, between the 1967 and 1970 visits. But there were plenty of fluent speakers from generation T remaining.

The Dyirbal grammar was published in 1972 and for the next few years I worked with the last fluent speakers of Yidiñ, Warrgamay, and Nyawaygi on grammars of those languages. Sadly, my magnificent teacher Chloe Grant died in 1974. I kept in touch with George Watson, and he promised to help with a full dictionary of the Dyirbal dialects, once I had finished the current project on Yidiñ.

In 1963, I first worked with an old lady called Mollie Raymond (born about 1890), who had a first-class knowledge of the N dialect of Dyirbal. She was not very adept at giving texts, but Mollie had a magnificent command of N vocabulary and also of the Jalnguy style. It seemed to me that Mollie might not live much longer, and on each of my field trips in the early 1970s I sought her out and recorded a few more hours of N vocabulary and mother-in-law correspondents.

16.3 Work from 1977 until 1984

After the Yidiñ grammar was published, I turned once more to Dyirbal and spent a few weeks in the field each year from 1977 through 1984, working toward as complete a dictionary as was then possible. The aim was to include information from all ten dialects, as listed in section 1.3.1.

The P (probably Jirri-barra Mamu) dialect was known only through an 1884 list of 137 words by Christy Palmerston, and L (Walmal) only from a list of 175 words gathered in 1900 by Walter E. Roth. There were rich materials gathered by Roth on U (Gulngay), spoken by the Malanbarra people. A single Gulngay man remained: Joe Kinjun (died 1983), and I worked with him a fair amount. Unfortunately, Joe mixed dialects to such a degree that it was difficult to discern what was truly U (rather than J or G), unless it could be checked against the Roth account.

For dialect Y (Jirru) there were a number of word lists, from the 1960s and early 1970s, taken down by Stephen Wurm, Estelle Aguas, and Peter Sutton. And in the 1960s I had recorded vocabulary from Joe Jamboree, at Murray Upper, and Pompey Clump-point, on Palm Island. But by 1977 there was no one remaining who knew anything of this dialect.

The Jirrbal tribe was divided into two local groups, each with its own dialect. Interestingly, the Gambil-barra ('tablelands-BELONGING.TO') group, speaking dialect A, call themselves Jirrbal-ji. (The same -*ji* ending is found in Ngajan-ji and in Yidiñ-ji; it is a suffix in Yidiñ, meaning 'with'.) In contrast, the Jabun-barra ('lowlands-BELONGING. TO') group, speaking dialect J, call themselves Jirrbal-ŋan (the suffix -*ŋan* does not occur outside this word).

I noticed that the vocabulary of dialect A was marginally more similar to M than it is to J, and asked Chloe about this. 'Why do people using A and J consider themselves to be a single tribe, speaking varieties of Jirrbal, and those who use M to be a different tribe, speaking a variety of Mamu?' I was told that the two Jirrbal-speaking groups considered themselves to be one tribe, despite slight linguistic differences, because—in

Chloe's words—they were 'all blooded'. That is, one would normally marry someone from within the tribe, either from one's own group or—preferably—from the other local group. For example, Ida Henry's mother had been born Jabunbarra and she had married a Gambilbarra man, from the tablelands. Ida had been born Gambilbarra and she had married a lowlands man, Spider Henry, from the Jabunbarra group.

During my initial survey of the region, in 1963, a fair number of fluent speakers of dialect A were encountered, and some useful vocabulary recorded. At a picnic on the banks of the Wild River (a headwater of the Herbert River) one Sunday, older people were chatting in Dyirbal, with younger ones understanding them but themselves using English. Sadly, by 1977 all the fluent speakers had passed on. However, it was possible to gather a little information from semi-speakers. I worked with Jimmie Carrick in 1977 and 1979, but the following year he was dead. In 1981, Hughie Woods gave some information, but when I returned to the field the following year he too had passed away. George Watson then introduced me to Mrs Gardner, who knew only a little.

The situation was better for the other five dialects. For the three most northerly ones, only one or two fluent speakers remained, but they were excellent (and long-lived!). Mollie Raymond was now the only member of generation T for N, but her knowledge, energy, and enthusiasm were amazing, right through her eighties and nineties. For W there was just Harry Digala (called 'Tickler' by the whites) who was more introspective, but thoughtful and reliable.

Besides working on vocabulary—and kinship and songs—I did of course pay further attention to the grammar which in the 1972 volume had dealt just with J, G, and M. As documented in chapter 11, on grammatical variation across the dialects, it was possible to cover virtually every item for N and most of them for W. Just a little grammatical information could be checked for A, and only a smattering in the case of Y. For U it was almost impossible to ascertain what was truly in that dialect (rather than in J, G, M, or Y).

For the M dialect, and for assistance with several others, George Watson was magnificent. His Gambilbarra Jirrbalji wife had died and George was now living in an old cane-cutters barracks at Boogan, just south of Innisfail. I would take him north for a few days to work with Mollie Raymond (in Malanda) on comparing N and M forms, and also N and M Jalnguy correspondents, and with Harry Digala (in Millaa Millaa) on W and M. Then we would go south to Murray Upper for a couple of days to compare M with J and G. I would also work with George alone on vocabulary and on other matters. We recorded more texts and also went through a 100-page manuscript that W. E. Roth had written in 1900 entitled, 'On the Natives of the Lower Tully River'. I would read out each paragraph and George would say whether or not it was correct and how to say it in M. We would sometimes go and see Joe Davis, who was probably the only other fluent speaker remaining of George's dialect. Joe had had one leg amputated, but still managed to drive a small tractor.

Over the next fifteen years I attempted to check every portion of the lexicon with as many speakers as I could, gradually working my way through the various semantic fields—body parts (with an anatomical atlas for identifying the various bones and muscles); nouns describing parts of the environment; verbs of motion, of rest, of affect, of talking; adjectives of dimension, of physical property, of human propensity; and so on.

All of the people I had worked with at Murray Upper in the 1960s, on the J and G dialects, were now dead, but there was still a fair number of fluent speakers, all of whom were glad to assist. Mick Murray (elder brother of Jack) became my central J consultant, but Ida Henry, Andy Denham, Daisy Denham, and Biddy Darcy also helped. When Mick died in 1982, Ida Henry took over the role of main J teacher.

When he had time, Jack Muriata helped a bit with G in 1977/78, and then in 1979 I had the good luck to start working with Bessie Jerry (born about 1930), who was most definitely in the Chloe Grant/George Watson class. Bessie was happy to spend two or three hours each morning, day after day, going over old texts and songs, recording new ones, helping to construct genealogical charts and work out the kinship system, and systematically going over each area of vocabulary. I also got useful information on G from Bessie's uncle, Paddy Bute.

When in 1972 Gough Whitlam took office as the first federal Labor government for twenty-three years, things started to improve for Aborigines. I wrote to Whitlam's Ministers for Aboriginal Affairs about the people at Murray Upper, and in 1976 a property on the Murray River was bought for them; it came to be called Jumbun, a misspelling of *jambun* which is the Dyirbal word for 'witchetty grub'. Homes were erected by the government and Aboriginal families moved in, forming a self-contained community of their own. But as the political situation improved, so the language continued to ebb away. People born in the 1940s and 1950s constituted a generation S, of semi-speakers. After that we were into generation N.

In 1967 and 1970, there were a dozen people who could help Chloe supply the mother-in-law style equivalent of almost every word in the everyday vocabulary. But by 1977, they had all died—no one at Murray Upper in 1977 remembered more than a few words of Jalnguy. (The only Jalnguy I was now able to record was in the N and M dialects, from Mollie Raymond and George Watson, who were older than anyone at Murray Upper.)

I had 150 Dyirbal names for plants but knew there must be many more; accurate botanical identification would be required. Luckily, the Tropical Forest Research Centre of the Commonwealth Scientific and Industrial Research Organisation is located in Atherton, and one of the biologists there, Tony Irvine, had an unrivalled knowledge of rainforest plants and also a keen interest in my project. We spent a day or two most years from 1979 until 1991 in the bush with Aboriginal consultants and gathered the Dyirbal names (across the N, M, J, and G dialects) and botanical identifications for over 600 plants. Because speakers of the northern dialects were so old, we began with them. Little Mollie Raymond, in her early nineties, and George Watson, a mere eighty or so, took us through their traditional country, naming all the trees and ferns and grasses in both N and M and explaining their uses. We had five days in the field with Mollie and George between 1979 and 1982. After that, Mollie became too frail for long bush walks, but in 1986 and again in 1988 Tony brought a sack of clippings and nuts to her house, and we sat around the kitchen table discussing these. Fieldwork on flora names in J and G began in 1982, and on expeditions around Murray Upper, Tony and I would be accompanied by Bessie Jerry and her brother Fred Williams, also a knowledgeable speaker of G, Ida Henry and her husband Spider, for J, and usually George Watson as well.

By 1981, I had been through the names for mammals, reptiles and amphibians, birds, fishes and other sea creatures, and insects and other small creatures. I had the scientific names for some, but expert assistance was required. This was provided, in 1982 and 1984 by Jeanette Covacevich, Senior Curator of Reptiles at the Queensland Museum in Brisbane, and other staff of the museum. Capping off many hours spent with individual speakers, one evening in July 1984 we had a slide show in the Murray Upper school with a couple of dozen Aborigines present. Jeanette described the size, habitat, habits, and cries of each rare possum, lizard, or bird and a committee of older speakers would consult together before giving us its name.

Then there was the kinship system to clarify. I had got a bit on this from Chloe in the 1960s but needed to work out the full set of rules that underlies this classificatory system. The first step was to get complete genealogies for every family (it included the names of more than 200 people, dead and alive), and then ask speakers what kin term they would use for each person on the charts. George and Mollie were unable to help on the fine details of this because their tribes had been reduced in numbers early on, and the kinship system then fell into disuse. But, down at Murray Upper, Mick Murray, Ida Henry, Bessie Jerry, Paddy Bute, Biddie Darcy, and Andy Denham patiently explained the principles underlying ordinary kinship naming and also the special Nyalal or 'polite' terms, whose use depended not only on whom you were talking about but also on whom you were talking to. It was like a kind of complicated mathematics, but by working on it year after year I was finally able to understand this complex system, in which you must marry someone from the generation above or from the generation below, never from your own generation. See chapter 4.

In the 1960s, I recorded more than a hundred Dyirbal songs from Jimmy Murray, Paddy Biran, Chloe Grant, Pompey Clump-point (a very old Jirru man on Palm Island), and three or four others. At the time, I was preoccupied with working on the grammar and did not try to get transcription, translation, and explanation for more than a handful of songs. I did realise that this would be a difficult task. Dyirbal songs have unusual grammar, special 'song words' that do not occur in normal speech, and everyday words used in metaphorical senses. They show unusual stress placement and are hard for an outsider to understand. I can transcribe and translate an unseen text in Dyirbal with perhaps 90 per cent accuracy, but I am lost when it comes to most songs.

All the singers who had recorded for me (except George Watson) had died before I began the song project in 1981. However, there were a number of people able to help. I played each song separately to at least three out of Mick Murray, Ida Henry, Andy Denham, Bessie Jerry, and George Watson, and collated the transcriptions and translations they provided, often going back another year to play a song again to Bessie or Ida for further clarification. I sent up cassettes of songs in advance, so that they could listen carefully and start on the difficult task of distinguishing words and understanding meanings.

There were five styles of Dyirbal song, each with its own metrical pattern. In Gama songs, for instance, each line contains nine or eleven syllables (and each line must end in a four-syllable word). In Marrga, each line has eight syllables; Jangala has lines of six syllables which can occur in variable order, whereas Burran alternates lines of six and three syllables in a fixed order.

Just a few more songs were recorded in the 1980s, from George Watson, Bessie Jerry, Daisy Denham, and especially from Tom Murray. Spider Henry, Ida's husband, sang a few Jangala songs, but these were very short; they seemed only half-formed by comparison with the examples of Jangala I had recorded from Paddy Biran and Jimmy Murray twenty years before.

A lot of work was involved. Eventually, in 1996 a linguistic and musical account of the 174 songs recorded was published by the University of Queensland Press, titled *Dyirbal song poetry: The oral literature of an Australian rainforest people*, co-authored with musicologist Grace Koch. There was also a CD with 94 tracks, which can be accessed at <https://research.jcu.edu.au/research/lcrc/languages-archives/australia/dyirbal-song-poetry>.

By the end of the July 1984 fieldtrip I had assiduously gone through all nouns, verbs, and adjectives, semantic type by semantic type. It was time for a new linguistic adventure. I spent six months in 1985 living in a monolingual Fijian village, and the rest of that year and all the next writing *A grammar of Boumaa Fijian*, which was published by The University of Chicago Press in 1988.

16.4 Work from 1986 until 1992, and beyond

There was still work to complete on Dyirbal, and I made short fieldtrips each year from 1986 until 1992. Obscure portions of texts recorded in earlier years required explication, and there were a considerable number of points to be checked and expanded in the thesaurus, particularly concerning adjectives.

George Watson had sunk into senility around 1984 (at the age of 85 or so) and was now in the Old Men's Home on Palm Island. When I went to visit him there, in January

1987, he seemed to have lost his English; we were able to communicate a bit in Mamu and rather better in Mamu Jalnguy. (George died there in 1991.) There were still a few points in Mamu I needed to check up on and Joe Davis—the last member of that generation T—was happy to help, until he too died, in 1989.

Mollie Raymond, though, seemed indestructible. She would think through every query I posed, explain the import of words in the everyday style, and invariably offer a Jalnguy correspondent. She became a bit deaf in the late 1980s and eventually died (as did the N dialect) in 1992, aged about 102. Molly had no patience with people who succumbed at an earlier age. Such as Harry Digala, who died (taking the W dialect with him) in 1987. 'Why did Harry have to go and die', Molly grumbled, 'he was only 87.'

Down at Murray Upper, several of my friends had also died—Biddy Darcy, Daisy Denham, and Ida Henry. If I had waited until that time to work on the kinship system and on songs, it would not have been possible to achieve anything like the detailed results which had been garnered half-a-dozen years earlier.

Bessie Jerry was a little younger, and continued in fine fettle. Tony Irvine and I were still checking the names of plants, although only Bessie was now left to come on trips into the bush with us. In July 1989, we were on the Kirrama Range and Tony pointed to the broad-leaved pepper (*Piper subpeltata*), asking Bessie what its name was in G. She replied, '*ligu*'. My mouth fell open. There are a few loan words in J and G that begin with the sound *l* (for example, *layman* 'lemon'), but in twenty-six years of fieldwork (and a dictionary of several thousand words) I had never before come across an indigenous word beginning with *l*. 'It's almost like suddenly finding a word in English that begins with the dorso-velar nasal, *ŋ*', I told Tony.

A maxim of good fieldwork is that everything should be checked with at least two people. Andy Denham had not heard of *ligu*. He would not be expected to; *Piper subpeltata* doesn't grow in his Jirrbalŋan country. The person I could have checked this with was Paddy Bute, Bessie's uncle, who I had done a little work with each year. Paddy would have been familiar with the plants of the Kirrama Range. But I discovered that he had been hit by a car and killed just a few months before. ('A black man on the dark night', one of the local whites told me, 'you couldn't blame the driver.')

It was possible to do further work on J with the last members of that generation T—Andy Denham (who died in December 1992) and Spider Henry (passed away in August 1993). And there was one other really good speaker who only came within my ken in 1983. This was Tom Murray, younger brother of Mick and Jack, who was probably born about 1920 and brought up in the bush by his father, speaking nothing but the J dialect during childhood and youth.

Tom had spent most of his working life on cattle stations in western Queensland, hundreds of miles away, although with frequent trips home, and had now retired to Mount Garnet, in what was originally Warungu territory. Tom Murray spoke J almost exactly the way he did when a boy. He criticised some of the new senses of words and new idioms that were then in use at Murray Upper as 'wrong', because 'that's not the way they spoke the language when I was growing up'.

In traditional times, anyone who composed a new song would say that it had come to them in a dream, from the spirit ancestors. No artistic creation could be attributed to human agency. Tom Murray took this one step further. He was a talented singer but all the songs he performed were taught him as a boy, compositions that he believed have been handed down from ancestral creation time. Tom was contemptuous of songs that were composed recently (people now acknowledged that they did do this) as 'not the real thing'.

There is a verbal affix in J and G meaning 'lest' with the form *-bila*. But—as mentioned in section 11.4.3—this can be shortened to *-ba* after the inchoative suffix *-bil* 'become', for example, *guli-bil-ba* 'lest (they) become angry' rather than *guli-bil-bila* (to avoid consecutive syllables beginning with *-bi-*). I had an example of this reduction in a text recorded by Jimmy Murray in 1967. In 1989, I was checking the shortened form with Tom Murray and a younger relative Bob Murray, who was visiting from Murray Upper. 'No', Tom told me, 'you can't say *gulibilba*, it must be *gulibilbila*.' But Bob Murray explained to him: 'Everyone does say *gulibilba* now, Uncle Tom.' This is a truncation that has come into use recently, but Tom, speaking still the language of his youth, had not been aware of it.

There was one noticeable change in the language situation at Murray Upper— I discovered that the dialects had effectively merged. Whereas in 1963 Jack Murray and Jimmy Murray would speak only their own dialects (J and G, respectively), keeping the small lexical and grammatical differences quite in order, by about 1980 almost everyone except the very old people effectively spoke a single dialect. This dialect had J grammar—just *ŋaja* 'I' would be used in both transitive and intransitive subject functions (the original G intransitive subject form *ŋayba* was no longer in general use). There was a single vocabulary, largely J where the two dialects had differed (for example, *jugumbil* 'woman' from J in preference to the G form, *gumbul*), although sometimes what had originally been the G form was preferred (for example, G *naŋgay* 'stone' in preference to J *diban*); just occasionally both the original J and G forms were in active circulation as synonyms. (This merged vocabulary shows up very clearly in the data collected from semi-speakers by Annette Schmidt; see the appendix.)

Ida Henry was old enough (born about 1920) to remember both dialects clearly and she always kept them apart. Ida normally spoke in J, and most of her texts were in this dialect, but she did record two texts in G, with all the original G grammar and lexicon as they had been used a generation earlier.

Bessie Jerry (ten or more years younger than Ida) was at first an enigma. She was proudly G and would carefully separate out G and J forms in our dictionary work—'to ask' is *ŋanban* in J but *barban* in G; 'black bean' (*Castanospermum australe*) is *mirrañ* in J but *gañjur* in G. But Bessie used entirely J grammar—the J reflexive verbal affix

-*yirríy*- instead of G -*rriy*-, the J negative imperative verbal inflection -*m* in place of G -*Imu* and -*mu*, and just *ŋaja* (no *ŋayba*) for the subject form of T. At first I was puzzled by this; Bessie's grammar prompted me to go back over my old materials in G and also to check with Ida Henry and Jack Muriata that G did use -*rriy*- and -*Imu* / -*mu* and *ŋayba*. When I mentioned these forms to Bessie, she recognised them as G; but a few minutes later she went back to using entirely J grammar while explaining G vocabulary items.

The explanation is simple. For Bessie Jerry—as for most people in the world—a language (or dialect) is its stock of words. If you get the words right, then you are speaking the language. Grammar is something people simply are not aware of and thus do not consider important. Bessie strove to use correct G lexemes, especially when we were explicitly discussing words. (In a running text, she would sometimes revert to forms from the new mixed dialect that did originate in J. In one text, she began by using the G word for 'head', *mugal*, and then later switched to the J/mixed dialect form *diŋgal*.) In the case of grammar, Bessie naturally used the mixed dialect forms that were now in general use among most people in the community.

Over 80 per cent of the J and G lexicons were identical. But where they differed I needed to discover which form had occurred in which dialect. Chloe Grant had given a lot of information on this but I always make a point of checking everything with at least two people; and there were lots of words that Chloe and I had not discussed. Andy Denham was always obliging. Sometimes I would mention two forms to him, 'Oh yes', he would say, 'that's two names for the same tree. One of those is Jirrbal and the other is Girramay. But I just can't remember which is which.' He undoubtedly would have been able to identify which dialect each form belonged to twenty years before, when J and G were kept separate by most of the people in the community.

Bessie was usually pretty good, but sometimes she would first give the form that was then in common use in the merged dialect and say it was G (when in fact it was originally the J term). When I then mentioned the other form, she would suggest that that was J. For *Ficus hispida*, it is clear that *wuwu* was the M name and *dagurrba* and *buwujala* were the J and G names. Andy Denham, a Jirrbalŋan, said that *dagurrba* was J and *buwujala* was G; both Bessie Jerry and Paddy Bute said that *dagurrba* was G and *buwujala* was J. Tom Murray said that *dagurrba* is J, and he didn't recognise the form *buwujala*. Tom didn't know any G and, as mentioned above, retained the J of his youth. It seems pretty certain that *dagurrba* was the J term and *buwujala* the G name. The merged dialect uses *dagurrba* and that would be the first term to come to mind for Bessie and Paddy. As they pride themselves on being Girramaygan, they then each said that *dagurrba* was the G term, so *buwujala* must be J. There are other pairs of forms where I experienced a similar inconsistency of response; such cases are, however, greatly outnumbered by instances where all consultants agreed as to which dialect a given form came from. Twenty-five years ago, before dialect boundaries became blurred in everyday use, everybody knew what was J and what was G.

In the 1980s, the merged dialect was spoken at least some of the time by most people over twenty (the semi-speakers), but it is a shadow of the language that was in use twenty years before. My final dictionary checking concentrated on unusual and esoteric words. I asked old Tom Murray some of these in the presence of Bob Murray, who was in his late forties. 'Those words you've got there', Bob said, 'I used to hear them when I was a boy but no one uses words like that today.' The language was retreating, contracting, as it gradually fell towards disuse.

There were two possessive constructions in traditional Dyirbal. A genitive marker was used for alienable possession (for example, 'John's axe') and kinship ('John's mother'), but for inalienable possession (whole–part relationship) simple apposition was used (for example, 'John ear'). In 1989, Andy Denham was using the genitive construction for inalienable possession—he said, '*riyilriyil-bin maɲa ŋaygu*' 'my ears have a ringing noise' (lit. 'ringing-noise-BECOME ear MY') in place of the traditional construction *riyilyiyilbin maɲa ŋaja* (lit. 'ringing-noise-become ear I'). The use of genitive for inalienable possession is a feature of semi-speaker talk (Schmidt 1985: 60–1).

In texts recorded in 1982, Bessie Jerry always used an appositional construction for inalienable possession. But in texts given in 1989, she sometimes used apposition and sometimes a genitive marker. A few years earlier, Andy and Bessie had spoken a lot of the time to older people who maintained the traditional grammar. Since the deaths, in the mid-1980s, of Ida Henry, Biddie Darcy, Daisy Denham, and other old people, Andy and Bessie only had younger people to talk with. A few years prior, they each spoke the traditional form of Dyirbal, but by 1989 both had in certain ways modified their grammar toward that in general use among younger members of the community, belonging to generation S.

Each time when I was in North Queensland—in 1995, 1998, and 2001—I popped in to see Bessie Jerry and Jack Muriata, both Girramaygan and the last two members of generation T. There were always a few queries about grammar and lexicon which had arisen, and they were happy to discuss these. On each visit, Bessie recorded another short text—how to make a bark blanket, traditional cures and remedies, and then how to weave a dilly-bag.

Bessie Jerry died in 2004, aged about 74. She was followed in 2011, by Jack Muriata, aged about 88. Thus did the full spoken form of this language—of such sublime character—cease to exist.

Appendix: Semi-speakers

In 1981, Bessie Jerry and I were discussing how young people spoke Dyirbal differently from the older ones. I was thoroughly documenting the traditional language, and now it was time for someone to investigate how younger people operated. An obvious person to undertake this task was Annette Schmidt, then studying at the Australian National University. She had grown up near Innisfail (in what had been Mamu country) and was conversant with the traditional language, having just taken a course in it which I taught at the ANU.

Annette Schmidt undertook six months immersion fieldwork at Murray Upper, January–June 1982, among members of generation S, aged from 15 to 39. Those below about 15 (and some older ones) knew very little, and were clearly generation N. Her work resulted in a fine MA thesis, in 1983, revised and published in 1985 as a monograph from Cambridge University Press, *Young People's Dyirbal: An example of language death from Australia.*

It appeared the semi-speakers only used their 'Young people's Dyirbal' (YD) amongst themselves. If YD were spoken to elders, the young people would be continually corrected; thus they employed just English in that situation.

Schmidt documented a scale of competence. Checking against a list of 498 common lexemes, a semi-speaker at the top of the scale knew 72 per cent and one at the bottom 34 per cent. The most adept had almost the full set of nine allomorphs for ergative case. Moving down the scale, there were five forms, then just two, then only one, with younger semi-speakers having no ergative marking at all, instead employing word order as in English.

As mentioned above, the distinction between inalienable possession, shown just by apposition, and alienable possession, marked by genitive, had been abandoned. Genitive was now used for all kinds of possession, mirroring *'s* in English.

The gender system had been simplified. First, gender III, 'edible plant food', shown by *balam*, was lost and its members included under gender IV, *bala*. As one moved down the scale of competence, more features of the traditional system became lost, such as 'fire' and 'water' being in gender II. At the bottom of the scale, gender I was just masculine, gender II just feminine, with everything else in gender IV—*bayi*, *balan*, and *bala*, very similar to English *he*, *she*, and *it*.

One male semi-speaker who still knew 'fire' as in the same gender, II, as female humans put forward a quasi-explanation: 'It [fire] is a lady, Woman is a destroyer, 'e destroys anything. A woman is a fire . . .' (Schmidt 1985: 166). This was said jokingly, probably to relieve the tedium of interrogation. It goes squarely against the tenets upon which traditional speakers had insisted—women, fire, water, harmful plants, harmful fishes, and so on just happen to be placed in the same gender; there was not believed to be association of any kind between them.

The paradigm for interrogative/indefinite forms 'where' was given at (19) in section 11.3.3. Schmidt noted (1985: 96) that only the absolutive forms were used by semi-speakers (no ergative/instrumental, dative, or genitive), with gender IV *wuñja*, gender II *wuñjan* (both as in traditional Dyirbal) but with gender I being *wuñji* in place of *wuñjiñ*. (Interestingly, *wuñji* had been the form used in dialects N, W, and A.)

More than three decades have passed, so that Schmidt's generation S are now in their fifties, sixties, and seventies. In limited circumstances, they still speak a bit of YD, in the way that she described it.

Indeed, I recently heard one elderly semi-speaker admonish her sister, in the course of being asked to record something of their language:

ŋinda   yiŋgili-ŋga/   guwal   buwa
1sg.NOMINATIVE English-LOCATIVE everyday.style tell.IMPERATIVE
you (are talking) in English, tell (it in) Guwal (Jirrbal everyday style)

Yiŋgili is here a YD loan from *English*. Fluent speakers had their own name for 'English language', *ñunarra*. And locative case onto a trisyllabic form was *-ga* (*-ŋga* being used just on a disyllabic form).

This chapter is a thorough revision and updating of a paper published in 1991, 'A changing language situation: The decline of Dyirbal, 1963–1989'.

There is a detailed account of fieldwork from 1963 to 1977 in *Searching for Aboriginal languages: Memoirs of a field worker*, published by the University of Queensland Press in 1984, reissued by the University of Chicago Press in 1989, and then by Cambridge University Press in 2010. There are also accounts in chapters 5, 6, 8, and 12 of my academic autobiography, *I am a Linguist*, published by Brill in 2011.

Acknowledgements

Gratitude is unalloyed to those guardians of Australian languages who shared their heritage with me, whether over many hundreds of hours or some shorter period.

Yidiñ language

Tablelands dialect (t): Tilly Fuller, Pompey Langdon, George Davis, Ranji Fuller, Katie Mays, Jack and Nellie Stewart, Alec Morgan
Coastal dialect (c): Dick Moses, Richard Hyde, Ida Burnett

Dyirbal language

Ngajan dialect (N): Molly Raymond, Jimmy Brown, Tommy Land, Ginnie Daniels, Jesse Callico
Waribarra Mamu dialect (W): Harry Digala, Biddy Digala, Maggie Brooks, Millie Brooks, Tom Brooks, Jimmy Moran
Dulgubarra Mamu dialect (M): George Watson, Joe Davis, Robert Major, Willie Kelly, Judy Mears, Billy Tinkum, Norma Jones, Dicky Briggs, Barney Brooks
Gambilbarra Jirrbal dialect (A): Peter Wairuna, Fred Blackman, Jackie Woods, Ginnie Watson, Jimmie Carrick, Hughie Woods, Mrs Gardner
Jabunbarra Jirrbal dialect (J): Chloe Grant, Jack Murray, Mick Murray, Tom Murray, Ida Henry, Spider Henry, Andy Denham, Daisy Denham, Tommy Warren, Biddy Darcy, Joe Chalam, Joe Garbutt, Lorna Lawrence, Lisa Murray, Rosie One-Arm, Dave Barlow, Bob Murray, Davey Lawrence
Gulngay dialect (U): Joe Kinjun
Jirru dialect (Y): Joe Jamboree, Pompey Clump-point
Girramay dialect (G): Chloe Grant, Jimmy Murray, Maryann Murray, Bessie Jerry, Paddy Biran, Mosley Digman, Jack Muriata, Tommy Springcart, Rosie Runaway, Paddy Bute, Fred Williams

Warrgamay language

Warrgamay proper dialect: John Tooth, Lambert Cocky, Alf Palmer, Arthur Wild
Biyay dialect: Nora Boyd

As always, Alexandra Aikhenvald has provided perceptive comments on every chapter. Adella Edwards drew the map with her accustomed skill. Hannah Sarvasy, Tahnee Innes, and Brigitta Flick gave invaluable assistance in checking the manuscript.

References

R. M. W. Dixon's main publications on Australian languages

[A fuller listing, up to 2011, is on pp. 359–81 of *I am a Linguist*, Leiden: Brill, 2011.]

1968a   'The Dyirbal language of North Queensland'. PhD thesis, University of London.

1968b   'Noun classes', *Lingua* 21: 104–25.

1969   'Relative clauses and possessive phrases in two Australian languages', *Language* 45: 35–44. [Dyirbal and Gumbaiŋgar.]

1970a   'Languages of the Cairns rain forest region', pp. 651–87 of *Pacific linguistics studies in honour of Arthur Capell*, edited by S. A. Wurm and D. C. Laycock. Canberra: Pacific Linguistics.

1970b   'Olgolo syllable structure and what they are doing about it', *Linguistic Inquiry* 1: 273–6.

1970c   'Proto-Australian laminals', *Oceanic Linguistics* 9: 79–103.

1971   'A method of semantic description', pp. 436–71 of *Semantics, an interdisciplinary reader in philosophy, linguistics and psychology*, edited by Danny D. Steinberg and Leon A. Jakobovits. Cambridge: Cambridge University Press.

1972   *The Dyirbal language of North Queensland*. Cambridge: Cambridge University Press. Reissued in 2009.

1973   'The semantics of giving', pp. 205–23 of *The formal analysis of natural languages*, edited by Maurice Gross, Morris Halle, and Marcel-Paul Schützenberger. The Hague: Mouton.

1977a   *A grammar of Yidiɲ*. Cambridge: Cambridge University Press. Reissued in 2010.

1977b   'Some phonological rules in Yidiny', *Linguistic Inquiry* 8: 1–34.

1977c   'The syntactic development of Australian languages', pp. 365–415 of *Mechanisms of syntactic change*, edited by Charles N. Li. Austin: University of Texas Press. [Dyirbal and Yidiñ.]

1977d   'Delocutive verbs in Dyirbal', pp. 21–38 of *Studies in descriptive and historical linguistics: Festschrift for W. P. Lehmann*, edited by Paul Hopper. Amsterdam: John Benjamins.

1979a   'A note on Dyirbal ergativity', pp. 90–1 of *Papers from the Fifteenth Regional Meeting of the Chicago Linguistic Society*.

1979b   'Comments and corrections concerning Heath's "Is Dyirbal ergative?"', *Linguistics* 17: 1003–15.

1979c   'The nature and development of Australian languages', pp. 431–43 of *Annual Review of Anthropology, 1979*.

1980   *The languages of Australia*. Cambridge: Cambridge University Press. Reissued in 2010.

1981a   'Wargamay', pp. 1–144 of *Handbook of Australian languages*, volume 2, edited by R. M. W. Dixon and Barry J. Blake. Canberra: ANU Press; and Amsterdam: John Benjamins.

1981b   'Grammatical reanalysis: an example of linguistic change from Warrgamay (North Queensland)', *Australian Journal of Linguistics* 1: 91–112.

1981c   Terry Crowley and R. M. W. Dixon. 'Tasmanian', pp. 392–421 of *Handbook of Australian languages*, volume 2, edited by R. M. W. Dixon and Barry J. Blake. Canberra: ANU Press; and Amsterdam: John Benjamins.

1982a   *Where have all the adjectives gone? and other essays in semantics and syntax.* Berlin: Mouton. [Includes revisions of 1968b, 1970b, 1971, 1973 and pp. 480–96 of 1977a.]

1982b   'Problems in Dyirbal dialectology', pp. 43–73 of *Language form and language variation: Papers dedicated to Angus McIntosh*, edited by John Anderson. Amsterdam: John Benjamins.

1983   'Nyawaygi', pp. 430–525 of *Handbook of Australian languages*, volume 3, edited by R. M. W. Dixon and Barry J. Blake. Canberra: ANU Press; and Amsterdam: John Benjamins.

1984a   *Searching for Aboriginal languages: Memoirs of a field worker.* St Lucia: University of Queensland Press. Reissued by the University of Chicago Press in 1989, and by Cambridge University Press in 2010.

1984b   'Dyirbal song types: a preliminary report', pp. 206–27 of *Problems and solutions: Occasional papers in musicology presented to Alice M. Moyle*, edited by J. C. Kassler and J. Stubington. Sydney: Hale and Iremonger.

1986   'Noun classes and noun classification in typological perspective', pp. 105–12 of *Noun classes and categorization*, edited by Colette G. Craig. Amsterdam: John Benjamins.

1987   'Words of Juluji's world', pp. 147–65 of *Australians to 1788*, edited by D. J. Mulvaney and J. Peter White (Volume 1 of *Australians: a historical library*). Sydney: Fairfax, Syme and Weldon.

1989   'The Dyirbal kinship system', *Oceania* 59: 245–68.

1990a   R. M. W. Dixon, W. S. Ramson, and Mandy Thomas. *Australian Aboriginal words in English: their origin and meaning.* Melbourne: Oxford University Press.

1990b   'Compensating phonological changes: An example from the northern dialects of Dyirbal', *Lingua* 80: 1–34.

1990c   'The origin of "mother-in-law vocabulary" in two Australian languages', *Anthropological Linguistics* 32: 1–58.

1990d   'Reassigning underlying forms in Yidiny: A change during language death', pp. 89–99 of *Language and history, essays in honour of Luise A. Hercus*, edited by Peter Austin, R. M. W. Dixon, Tom Dutton, and Isobel White. Canberra: Pacific Linguistics.

1991a   *Words of our country: Stories, place names and vocabulary in Yidiny, the Aboriginal language of the Cairns/Yarrabah region.* St Lucia: University of Queensland Press. Reissued as an e-book in 2012.

1991b   'Mbabaram', pp. 348–402 of *The handbook of Australian languages*, volume 4, *The Aboriginal language of Melbourne and other grammatical sketches*, edited by R. M. W. Dixon and Barry J. Blake. Melbourne: Oxford University Press.

1991c   'A changing language situation: the decline of Dyirbal, 1963–89', *Language in Society* 20: 183–200.

1991d   'The endangered languages of Australia, Indonesia and Oceania', pp. 229–55 of *Endangered languages*, edited by Robert H. Robins and Eugenius M. Uhlenbeck. Oxford: Berg.

1992a   'Naive linguistic explanation', *Language in Society* 21: 83–91.

1992b   'Australian languages', pp. 134–7 of *The Oxford international encyclopaedia of linguistics*, edited by William Bright. New York: Oxford University Press.

1993   'Australian Aboriginal languages', pp. 71–82 of *The languages of Australia*, edited by Gerhard Schulz. Canberra: Australian Academy of the Humanities.

1994   *Ergativity*. Cambridge: Cambridge University Press. [Includes much information on Australian languages.]

1995   'Complement clauses and complementation strategies', pp. 175–220 of *Grammar and meaning: A Festschrift for John Lyons*, edited by F. R. Palmer. Cambridge: Cambridge University Press. [Discusses complementation strategies in Dyirbal.]

1996a   R. M. W. Dixon and Grace Koch. *Dyirbal song poetry: The oral literature of an Australian rainforest people*. University of Queensland Press (with accompanying CD/cassette from Larrikin).

1996b   'Aboriginal people: Languages', pp. 76–80 of Volume 1 of *The Australian encyclopaedia*, 6th edition. Sydney: Australian Geographic.

1996c   'Origin legends and linguistic relationships', *Oceania* 67: 127–39.

1997   *The rise and fall of languages*. Cambridge: Cambridge University Press.

2001   'The Australian linguistic area', pp. 64–104 of *Areal diffusion and genetic inheritance: Problems in comparative linguistics*, edited by Alexandra Y. Aikhenvald and R. M. W. Dixon. Oxford: Oxford University Press.

2002a   *Australian languages: Their nature and development*. Cambridge: Cambridge University Press.

2002b   'Copula clauses in Australian languages: A typological perspective', *Anthropological Linguistics* 44: 1–36.

2003a   'Demonstratives: a cross-linguistic typology', *Studies in Language* 27: 61–112. [Discusses Dyirbal demonstratives.]

2003b   'Australian languages', pp. 170–6 of *International encyclopedia of linguistics*, 2nd edition, edited by William Frawley. New York: Oxford University Press. [Revised and enlarged version of 1992b.]

2006a   R. M. W Dixon, Bruce Moore, W. S. Ramson, and Mandy Thomas. *Australian Aboriginal words in English: their origin and meaning*, 2nd edition. Melbourne: Oxford University Press. [Revised and enlarged edition of 1990a.]

2006b   'Serial verb constructions: Conspectus and coda', pp. 338–50 of *Serial verb constructions: A cross-linguistic typology*, edited by Alexandra Y. Aikhenvald and

R. M. W. Dixon. Oxford: Oxford University Press. [Includes an account of asymmetrical serial verb constructions in Dyirbal.]

2006c   'Complementation strategies in Dyirbal', pp. 261–79 of *Complementation: A cross-linguistic typology*, edited by R. M. W. Dixon and Alexandra Y. Aikhenvald. Oxford: Oxford University Press.

2006d   'Grammatical diffusion in Australia: free and bound pronouns', pp. 67–93 of *Grammars in contact: A cross-linguistic typology*, edited by Alexandra Y. Aikhenvald and R. M. W. Dixon. Oxford: Oxford University Press.

2008a   'Australian Aboriginal words in dictionaries: A history', *International Journal of Lexicology* 21: 129–52.

2008b   'Language contact in the Cairns rainforest region', *Anthropological Linguistics* 50: 223–48.

2010a   *Basic linguistic theory*, Vol. 1, *Methodology*. Oxford: Oxford University Press. [Includes much information on Australian languages.]

2010b   *Basic linguistic theory*, Vol. 2, *Grammatical topics*. Oxford: Oxford University Press. [Includes much information on Australian languages.]

2011   Alexandra Y. Aikhenvald and R. M. W. Dixon. *Language at large: Essays on syntax and semantics*. Leiden: Brill. [Includes revisions of 1992a and 2008a.]

2012a   *Basic linguistic theory*, Vol. 3, *Further grammatical topics*. Oxford: Oxford University Press. [Includes much information on Australian languages.]

2012b   'Serial verb constructions in Dyirbal', *Anthropological Linguistics* 53: 185–214.

2013   'Possession and also ownership: vignettes', pp. 291–308 of *Possession and ownership: A cross-linguistic typology*, edited by Alexandra Y. Aikhenvald and R. M. W. Dixon. Oxford: Oxford University Press.

2014   'The non-visible marker in Dyirbal', pp. 171–89 of *The grammar of knowledge: A cross-linguistic typology*, edited by Alexandra Y. Aikhenvald and R. M. W. Dixon. Oxford: Oxford University Press.

2016   'The Australian linguistic area', to appear in *The Cambridge handbook of linguistic typology*, edited by Alexandra Y. Aikhenvald and R. M. W. Dixon. Cambridge: Cambridge University Press.

Other references

Aikhenvald, Alexandra Y. 2000. *Classifiers: A typology of noun categorization devices*. Oxford: Oxford University Press.

Aikhenvald, Alexandra Y. 2006. 'Serial verb constructions in comparative perspective', pp. 1–68 of *Serial verb constructions: A cross-linguistic typology*, edited by Alexandra Y. Aikhenvald and R. M. W. Dixon. Oxford: Oxford University Press.

Alpher, Barry. 1982. 'Dalabon dual-subject prefixes, kinship categories, and generation skewing', pp. 19–30 of *Languages of kinship in Aboriginal Australia* (Oceania Linguistic Monograph 24), edited by Jeffrey Heath, Francesca Merlan, and Alan Rumsey, University of Sydney.

Alpher, Barry. 1991. *Yir-Yoront lexicon: sketch and dictionary of an Australian language*. Berlin: Mouton de Gruyter.

Balmer, William T. and Grant, F. C. F. 1929. *A grammar of the Fante-Akan language*. London: Atlantis.

Bloomfield, Leonard. 1933. *Language*. New York: Holt, Rinehart, Winston.

Carlin, Eithne B. 2006. 'Feeling the need: the borrowing of Cariban functional categories into Mawayana (Arawak), pp. 313–32 of *Grammars in contact: A cross-linguistic typology*, edited by Alexandra Y. Aikhenvald and R. M. W. Dixon. Oxford: Oxford University Press.

Christaller, J. G. 1875. *A grammar of the Asante and Fante language called Tshi [Chee, Twi], based on the Akuapem dialect with references to other (Akan and Fante) dialects*, Basel: Basel Evangelical Missionary Society.

Corbett, Greville. 1991. *Gender*. Cambridge: Cambridge University Press.

Craig, Colette. 1986. 'Jacaltec noun classifiers', *Lingua* 70: 241–84.

Dench, Alan. 1991. 'Pamyjima', pp. 124–243 of *The handbook of Australian languages*, Vol. 4, edited by R. M. W. Dixon and Barry J. Blake. Melbourne: Oxford University Press.

Deutscher, Guy. 2000. *Syntactic Change in Akkadian: The evolution of sentential complementation*. Oxford: Oxford University Press.

Dorian, Nancy. 1980. 'Language shift in community and individual: The phenomenon of the laggard semi-speaker', *International Journal of the Sociology of Language* 2: 85–94.

Dorian, Nancy. 1981. *Language death: The life cycle of a Scottish Gaelic dialect*. Philadelphia: University of Pennsylvania Press.

Eather, Bronwyn. 2011. *A grammar of Nakkara (central Arnhem Land coast)*. Munich: Lincom Europa. [Facsimile publication of 1990 ANU PhD thesis.]

Elkin, A. P. 1964. *The Australian Aborigines: How to understand them*. Sydney: Angus and Robertson.

Evans, Nicholas D. 1995. *A grammar of Kayardild, with historical-comparative notes on Tangkic*. Berlin: Mouton de Gruyter.

Gaby, Alice R. 2006. 'A grammar of Kuuk Thaayorre'. PhD thesis, University of Melbourne.

Green, Rebecca. 1987. 'A sketch grammar of Burara'. BA honours sub-thesis, ANU.

Green, Rebecca. 1995. 'A grammar of Gurr-gone (north central Arnhem Land)'. PhD thesis, ANU.

Hale, Kenneth L. 1966. 'Kinship reflections in syntax: Some Australian languages', *Word* 22: 318–24.

Hale, Kenneth L. 1971. 'A note on a Warlbiri tradition of antonym', pp. 472–82 of *Semantics: An interdisciplinary reader in philosophy, linguistics and psychology*, edited by Danny D. Steinberg and Leon A. Jakobovits. Cambridge: Cambridge University Press.

Hale, Kenneth L. 1973. 'Deep-surface canonical disparities in relation to analysis and change: An Australian example', pp. 401–58 of *Current trends in linguistics*, Vol. 11 *Diachronic, areal and typological linguistics*, edited by T. A. Sebeok. The Hague: Mouton.

Hale, Ken and Nash, David. 1997. 'Damin and Lardil phonotactics', pp. 247–59 of *Boundary rider: Essays in honour of Geoffrey O'Grady*, edited by Darrell Tryon and Michael Walsh. Canberra: Pacific Linguistics.

Hall, Allen H. 1972. 'A study of the Thaayorre language of the Edward River tribe, Cape York Peninsula, Queensland, being a description of the grammar'. PhD thesis, University of Queensland.

Haviland, John B. 1979a. 'Guugu Yimidhirr', pp. 26–180 of *Handbook of Australian languages*, Vol. 1, edited by R. M. W. Dixon and Barry J. Blake. Canberra: ANU Press; and Amsterdam: John Benjamins.

Haviland, John B. 1979b. 'How to talk to your brother-in-law in Guugu Yimidhirr', pp. 161–239 of *Languages and their speakers*, edited by Timothy Shopen. Cambridge, MA: Winthrop.

Haviland, John B. 1979c. 'Guugu Yimidhirr brother-in-law language', *Language in Society* 8: 365–93.

Heath, Jeffrey, Merlan, Francesca, and Rumsey, Alan, eds. 1982. *Languages of kinship in Aboriginal Australia* (Oceania Linguistic Monograph 24). University of Sydney.

Houzé, E. and Jacques, V. 1884. 'Les Australiens du Musée du Nord', *Bulletin de la Société d'Anthropologie de Bruxelles* 3: 53–154.

Kuryłowicz, Jerzy. 1964. *The inflectional categories of Indo-European*. Heidelberg: Winter.

Lakoff, George. 1987. *Women, fire and dangerous things: What categories reveal about the mind*. Chicago: University of Chicago Press.

Lambeck, Knut and Chappell, John. 2001. 'Sea-level change through the last glacial cycle', *Science* 292.5517, p. 679.

Lehiste, Isle. 1970. *Suprasegmentals*. Cambridge, MA: MIT Press.

Lumholtz, Carl. 1889. *Among cannibals*. London: John Murray.

McConnel, Ursula H. 1950. 'Junior marriage systems: Comparative survey', *Oceania* 21: 107–43.

McGregor, William. 1989. 'Gooniyandi mother-in-law "language": dialect, register, and/or code?', pp. 630–56 of *Status and function of language and language varieties*, edited by Ulrich Ammon. Berlin: Walter de Gruyter.

McGregor, William. 1990. *A functional grammar of Gooniyandi*. Amsterdam: John Benjamins.

McKay, Graham R. 2000. 'Njebbana', pp. 154–354 of *The handbook of Australian languages*, Vol. 5, edited by R. M. W. Dixon and Barry J. Blake. Melbourne: Oxford University Press.

Mathew, John. 1926. 'Vocabulary of the Kiramai language, Herbert River, Queensland', *Report of the Australasian Association for the Advancement of Science* XVIII: 547–50.

Merlan, Francesca and Heath, Jeffery. 1982. 'Dyadic kinship terms', pp. 107–24 of *Languages of kinship in Aboriginal Australia* (Oceania Linguistic Monograph 24), edited by Jeffrey Heath, Francesca Merlan, and Alan Rumsey, University of Sydney.

Morphy, Frances. 1983. 'Djapu: a Yolngu dialect', pp. 1–188 of *Handbook of Australian languages*, Vol. 3, edited by R. M. W. Dixon and Barry J. Blake. Canberra: ANU Press; and Amsterdam: John Benjamins.

O'Grady, G. N. 1960. 'Comments on "More on Lexicostatistics"', *Current Anthropology* I: 338–9.

Palmerston, Christie. 1884. Letter to A. W. Howitt with a vocabulary of the tribes surrounding Mourilyan Harbour. Howitt Papers, Box 1, Folder 3. National Museum of Victoria.

Patz, Elisabeth. 1991. 'Djabugay', pp. 245–347 of *The handbook of Australian languages*, Vol. 4, edited by R. M. W. Dixon and Barry J. Blake. Melbourne: Oxford University Press.

Patz, Elisabeth. 2002. *A grammar of the Kuku Yalanji language of North Queensland*. Canberra: Pacific Linguistics.

Radcliffe-Brown, A. R. 1930–31. 'The social organisation of Australian tribes', *Oceania* 1: 34–63, 206–46, 322–41, 426–56.

Roth, Walter E. 1898–1900. (i) Vocabulary of Chir-pal-ji, chief camp Scrubby Creek; (ii) Vocabularies of Walmal (coast line from Tully to Murray) and Mallanparra (the scrub blacks of the Lower Tully River); (iii) Vocabularies of tribes met with around Atherton: Chirpal, Ngikoongo and Ngachan; (iv) Vocabulary of Chirpal, chief camp Herberton. Mss in the Oxley Library, Brisbane.

Roth, Walter E. 1900. 'On the natives of the Lower Tully River'. Ms in the Oxley Library, Brisbane.

Rumsey, Alan. 2000. 'Bunuba', pp. 34–152 of *The handbook of Australian languages*, Vol. 5, edited by R. M. W. Dixon and Barry J. Blake. Melbourne: Oxford University Press.

Schebeck, B., Hercus L. A., and White, I. 1973. *Papers in Australian linguistics*, No. 6. Canberra: Pacific Linguistics.

Scheffler, Harold W. 1978. *Australian kin classification*. New York: Cambridge University Press.

Schmidt, Annette. 1985. *Young people's Dyirbal: An example of language death from Australia*. Cambridge: Cambridge University Press.

Sommer, Bruce A. 1972. *Kunjen syntax: A generative view*. Canberra: Australian Institute for Aboriginal Studies.

Sutton, Peter. 1978. 'Wik: Aboriginal society, territory and language at Cape Kerwer, Cape York Peninsula, Australia'. PhD thesis, University of Queensland.

Thomson, Donald F. 1945. 'Names and naming in the Wik Moŋkan tribe', *Journal of the Royal Anthropological Society* 75: 157–68.

Thomson, Donald F. 1972. *Kinship and behaviour in North Queensland*. Canberra: Australian Institute of Aboriginal Studies.

Tindale, Norman B. 1938. Vocabularies 7, Djirubal. and 23, Keramai. Ms in South Australian Museum.

Tindale, Norman B. and Birdsell, Joseph B. 1941. 'Tasmanoid tribes in North Queensland', *Records of the South Australian Museum* 7: 1–9.

Tsunoda, Tasaku. 2003. *A provisional Warrungu dictionary*. Tokyo: Department of Asian and Pacific languages, University of Tokyo.

Tsunoda, Tasaku. 2012. *A grammar of Warrongo*. Berlin: De Gruyter Mouton.

Zubin, David and Kopcke, Klaus M. 1984. 'Affect classification in the German gender system', *Lingua* 63: 42–96.

Zubin, David and Kopcke, Klaus M. 1986. 'Gender and folk taxonomy: The indexical relation between grammatical and lexical categorization', pp. 139–80 of *Noun classes and categorization*, edited by Colette Craig. Amsterdam: John Benjamins.

Index

Books by R. M. W. Dixon

BOOKS ON LINGUISTICS

Linguistic science and logic
What is language? A new approach to linguistic description
The Dyirbal language of North Queensland
A grammar of Yidiɲ
The languages of Australia
Where have all the adjectives gone? and other essays in semantics and syntax
Searching for Aboriginal languages, memoirs of a field worker
A grammar of Boumaa Fijian
A new approach to English grammar, on semantic principles
Words of our country: Stories, place names and vocabulary in Yidiny
Ergativity
The rise and fall of languages
Australian languages: Their nature and development
The Jarawara language of southern Amazonia
A semantic approach to English grammar
Basic linguistic theory, Vol. 1, Methodology
Basic linguistic theory, Vol. 2, Grammatical topics
Basic linguistic theory, Vol. 3, Further grammatical topics
I am a linguist
Making new words: Morphological derivation in English

with Alexandra Y. Aikhenvald
Language at large: Essays on syntax and semantics

with Grace Koch
Dyirbal song poetry: The oral literature of an Australian rainforest people

with Bruce Moore, W. S. Ramson and Mandy Thomas
Australian Aboriginal words in English: Their origin and meaning

BOOKS ON MUSIC

with John Godrich
Recording the blues

with John Godrich and Howard Rye
Blues and gospel records, 1890–1943

NOVELS (under the name Hosanna Brown)

I spy, you die
Death upon a spear

EDITOR OF BOOKS ON LINGUISTICS

Grammatical categories in Australian languages
Studies in ergativity

with Barry J. Blake
Handbook of Australian languages, Vols 1–5

with Martin Duwell
The honey ant men's long song, and other Aboriginal song poems
Little Eva at Moonlight Creek: further Aboriginal song poems

with Alexandra Y. Aikhenvald
The Amazonian languages
Changing valency: Case studies in transitivity
Areal diffusion and genetic inheritance: Problems in comparative linguistics
Word: A cross-linguistic typology
Studies in evidentiality
Adjective classes: A cross-linguistic typology
Serial verb constructions: A cross-linguistic typology
Complementation: A cross-linguistic typology
Grammars in contact: A cross-linguistic typology
The semantics of clause-linking: A cross-linguistic typology
Possession and ownership: A cross-linguistic typology
The grammar of knowledge: A cross-linguistic typology
The Cambridge handbook of linguistic typology

with Alexandra Y. Aikhenvald and Masayuki Onishi
Non-canonical marking of subjects and objects